Political Ideologies and Political Philosophies

Edited by
H.B. McCullough
Okanagan College
Kelowna, British Columbia

WALL & THOMPSON
Toronto

Canadian Cataloguing in Publication Data

Main entry under title:

Political ideologies and political philosophies

ISBN 0–921332–18–1

1. Political science - History.
2. Political science - Philosophy
I. McCullough, H. B., 1944–

JA83.P64 1989   320.5   C89–093466–5

ISBN 0–921332–18–1
Printed in Canada.
1 2 3 4 5 93 92 91 90 89

Political Ideologies and Political Philosophies

This book may be ordered from:

THOMPSON Educational Publishing, Inc.

Publishing for the Social Sciences and the Humanities
11 Briarcroft Road, TORONTO, ONTARIO M6S 1H3
Telephone (416) 766-2763 / Fax: (416) 766-0398

To Photini, wife and companion

Table of Contents

Acknowledgements

It has been a pleasure working on this book. One of the reasons for this is that I have had the opportunity to benefit from the suggestions of colleagues and friends. For stylistic and substantive suggestions I owe thanks to Dr. Jay Brigham, Mr. Bill Christensen, Ms. Mary Ellen Holland, Mr. Murray Johnson, Dr. Plato Mamo, Dr. Ken Phillips, Dr. Howard Reimer, and Dr. Maury Williams. All of the foregoing individuals found time to assist me while other commitments engulfed them. And finally my gratitude is owed to my wife for her sustained support and encouragement in the preparation of the book.

Part I

General Introduction: Ideology, Ideals, and Philosophy

BERTRAND RUSSELL

Over a hundred years ago Robert Browning said that a man's reach should exceed his grasp. Browning was marking the ideals to which we individually aspire. When individual ideals become the objectives of whole communities, they become the political ideologies or political philosophies of those communities. Yet the distinction between a political ideology and a political philosophy seems elusive. It is not at all uncommon to consider the political views of our adversary as ideological and the political views of our own as philosophical. We mark our adversary's views as suspicious and our own as acceptable. To categorize something as ideological is often to speak pejoratively about that thing, because it is felt to be illusory or distortive of reality. In contrast to this, we may resist having our own political views categorized in this way because we see them as reality-preserving and therefore philosophical rather than ideological. Once political views are so understood, the elusiveness of the distinction between political ideology and political philosophy can be partially eliminated.

The foregoing distinction provides us with a semantic signpost, but not one that points in a clear direction. For example, consider the attitude of liberals toward fascists, and of fascists to liberals. Neither sees the other as reality-oriented, with the result that we are unable, except from a particular point of view, to say which perspectives are ideological and which are philosophical. Faced with this confusion, the strong temptation is to cut the perspectives into two groups and to examine them in isolation one from the other. Yet such temptation must be resisted, for it conceals the commonality of these and other political perspectives. It conceals the fact that all of them, whether they be classical liberalism, reform liberalism, conservatism, neo-conservatism, Marxism, democratic socialism, fascism, anarchism, fundamentalism, or environmentalism, offer political orientations on the world and as such offer, with varying degrees of success and in varying shades of detail, descriptions and explanations of human nature, society, government, power, justice, equality, and economic systems. Given this commonality there is merit in laying end-to-end political ideologies and political philosophies for the purpose of understanding different political perspectives.

The following writings of Bertrand Russell, Sigmund Freud, Alasdair MacIntyre, Patricia Marchak, Richard Miller, and C. Wright Mills, have as their subject-matter thematic connections between ideals, ideologies, and philosophy in the political context. Their views are refreshingly varied and informative as they work their way through minefields into which many a person has stumbled.

Political Ideals

Bertrand Russell

BERTRAND RUSSELL (1872–1970) *was a British philosopher of mathematics and metaphysics. Russell was a prolific writer on many subjects.* Principia Mathematica, *which he wrote with Alfred North Whitehead, became a classic on the philosophical foundations of mathematics. Political and social issues dominated his thinking in later years.*

In dark days, men need a clear faith and a well-grounded hope; and as the outcome of these, the calm courage which takes no account of hardships by the way. The times through which we are passing have afforded to many of us a confirmation of our faith. We see that the things we had thought evil are really evil, and we know more definitely than we ever did before the directions in which men must move if a better world is to arise on the ruins of the one which is now hurling itself into destruction. We see that men's political dealings with one another are based on wholly wrong ideals, and can only be saved by quite different ideals from continuing to be a source of suffering, devastation, and sin.

Political ideals must be based upon ideals for the individual life. The aim of politics should be to make the lives of individuals as good as possible. There is nothing for the politician to consider outside or above the various men, women, and children who compose the world. The problem of politics is to adjust the relations of human beings in such a way that each severally may have as much of good in his existence as possible. And this problem requires that we should first consider what it is that we think good in the individual life.

To begin with, we do not want all men to be alike. We do not want to lay down a pattern or type to which men of all sorts are to be made by some means or another to approximate. This is the ideal of the impatient administrator. A bad teacher will aim at imposing his opinion, and turning out a set of pupils all of whom will give the same definite answer on a doubtful point. Mr. Bernard Shaw is said to hold that *Troilus and Cressida* is the best of Shakespeare's plays. Although I disagree with this opinion, I should welcome it in a pupil as a sign of individuality; but most teachers would not tolerate such a heterodox view. Not only teachers, but all commonplace persons in authority, desire in their subordinates that kind of uniformity which makes their actions easily predictable and never inconvenient. The result is that they crush initiative and individuality when they can, and when they cannot, they quarrel with it.

It is not one ideal for all men, but a separate ideal for each separate man, that has to be realized if possible. Every man has it in his being to develop into something good or bad: there is a best possible for him, and a worst possible. His circumstances will determine whether his capacities for good are developed or crushed, and whether his bad impulses are strengthened or gradually diverted into better channels.

But although we cannot set up in any detail an ideal of character which is to be universally applicable—although we cannot say, for instance, that all men ought to be industrious, or self-sacrificing, or fond of music—there are some broad principles which can be used to guide our estimates as to what is possible or desirable.

We may distinguish two sorts of goods, and two corresponding sorts of impulses. There are goods in regard to which individual possession is possible, and there are goods in which all can share alike. The food and clothing of one man is not the food and clothing of another; if the supply is insufficient, what one man has is obtained at the expense of some other man. This applies to material goods generally, and therefore to the greater part of the present economic life of the world. On the other hand, mental and spiritual goods do not belong to one man to the exclusion of another. If one man knows a science, that does not prevent others from knowing it; on the contrary, it helps them to acquire the knowledge. If one man is a great artist or poet, that does not prevent others from painting pictures or writing poems, but helps to create the atmosphere in which such things are possible. If one man is full of good-will toward others, that does not mean that there is less good-will to be shared among the rest; the more good-will one man has, the more he is likely to create among others. In such matters there is no *possession*, because there is not a definite amount to be shared; any increase anywhere tends to produce an increase everywhere.

There are two kinds of impulses, corresponding to the two kinds of goods. There are *possessive* impulses, which aim at acquiring or retaining private goods that cannot be shared; these centre in the impulse of property. And there are *creative* or constructive impulses, which aim at bringing into the world or making available for use the kind of goods in which there is no privacy and no possession.

The best life is the one in which the creative impulses play the largest part and the possessive impulses the smallest. This is no new discovery. The Gospel says: "Take no thought, saying, What shall we eat? or What shall we drink? or, Wherewithal shall we be clothed?" The thought we give to these things is taken away from matters of more importance. And what is worse, the habit of mind engendered by thinking of these things is a bad one; it leads to competition, envy, domination, cruelty, and almost all the moral evils that infest the world. In particular, it leads to the predatory use of force. Material possessions can be taken by force and enjoyed by the robber. Spiritual possessions cannot be taken in this way. You may kill an artist or a thinker, but you cannot acquire his art or his thought. You may put a man to death because he loves his fellow-men, but you will not by so doing acquire the love which made his happiness. Force is impotent in such matters; it is only as regards material goods that it is effective. For this reason the men who believe in force are the men whose thoughts and desires are preoccupied with material goods.

The possessive impulses, when they are strong, infect activities which ought to be purely creative. A man who has made some valuable discovery may be filled with jealousy of a rival discoverer. If one man has found a cure for cancer and another has found a cure for consumption, one of them may be delighted if the others man's discovery turns out a mistake, instead of regretting the suffering of patients which would otherwise have been avoided. In such cases, instead of desiring knowledge for its own sake, or for the sake of its usefulness, a man is desiring it as a means to reputation. Every creative impulse is shadowed by a possessive impulse; even the aspirant to saintliness may be jealous of the more successful saint. Most affection is accompanied by some tinge of jealousy, which is a possessive impulse intruding into the creative region. Worst of all, in this direction, is the sheer envy of those who have missed everything worth having in life, and who are instinctively bent on preventing others from enjoying what they have not had. There is often much of this in the attitude of the old toward the young.

There is in human beings, as in plants and animals, a certain natural impulse of growth, and this is just as true of mental as of physical development. Physical development is helped by air and nourishment and exercise, and may be hindered by the sort of treatment which made Chinese women's feet small. In just the same way mental development may be helped or hindered by outside influences. The outside influences that help are those that merely provide encouragement or mental food or opportunities for exercising mental faculties. The influences that hinder are those that interfere with growth by applying any kind of force, whether discipline or authority or fear or the tyranny of public opinion or the necessity of engaging in some totally uncongenial occupation. Worst of all influences are those that thwart or twist a man's fundamental impulse, which is what shows itself as conscience in the moral sphere; such influences are likely to do a man an inward damage from which he will never recover.

Those who realize the harm that can be

done to others by any use of force against them, and the worthlessness of the goods that can be acquired by force, will be very full of respect for the liberty of others; they will not try to bind them or fetter them; they will be slow to judge and swift to sympathize; they will treat every human being with a kind of tenderness, because the principle of good in him is at once fragile and infinitely precious. They will not condemn those who are unlike themselves; they will know and feel that individuality brings differences and uniformity means death. They will wish each human being to be as much a living thing and as little a mechanical product as it is possible to be; they will cherish in each one just those things which the harsh usage of a ruthless world would destroy. In one word, all their dealings with others will be inspired by a deep impulse of *reverence*.

What we shall desire for individuals is now clear: strong creative impulses, overpowering and absorbing the instinct of possession; reverence for others; respect for the fundamental creative impulse in ourselves. A certain kind of self-respect or native pride is necessary to a good life; a man must not have a sense of utter inward defeat if he is to remain whole, but must feel the courage and the hope and the will to live by the best that is in him, whatever outward or inward obstacles it may encounter. So far as it lies in a man's own power, his life will realize its best possibilities if it has three things: creative rather than possessive impulses, reverence for others, and respect for the fundamental impulse in himself.

Political and social institutions are to be judged by the good or harm that they do to individuals. Do they encourage creativeness rather than possessiveness? Do they embody or promote a spirit of reverence between human beings? Do they preserve self-respect?

In all these ways the institutions under which we live are very far indeed from what they ought to be.

Institutions and especially economic systems, have a profound influence in moulding the characters of men and women. They may encourage adventure and hope, or timidity and the pursuit of safety. They may open men's minds to great possibilities, or close them against everything but the risk of obscure

misfortune. They may make a man's happiness depend upon what he adds to the general possessions of the world, or upon what he can secure for himself of the private goods in which others cannot share. Modern capitalism forces the wrong decision of these alternatives upon all who are not heroic or exceptionally fortunate.

Men's impulses are moulded, partly by their native disposition, partly by opportunity and environment, especially early environment. Direct preaching can do very little to change impulses, though it can lead people to restrain the direct expression of them, often with the result that the impulses go underground and come to the surface again in some contorted form. When we have discovered what kinds of impulse we desire, we must not rest content with preaching, or with trying to produce the outward manifestation without the inner spring: we must try rather to alter institutions in the way that will, of itself, modify the life of impulse in the desired direction.

At present our institutions rest upon two things: property and power. Both of these are very unjustly distributed; both, in the actual world, are of great importance to the happiness of the individual. Both are possessive goods; yet without them many of the goods in which all might share are hard to acquire as things are now.

Without property, as things are, a man has no freedom, and no security for the necessities of a tolerable life; without power, he has no opportunity for initiative. If men are to have free play for their creative impulses, they must be liberated from sordid cares by a certain measure of security, and they must have a sufficient share of power to be able to exercise initiative as regards the course and conditions of their lives...

Good political institutions would weaken the impulse toward force and domination in two ways: first, by increasing the opportunities for the creative impulses, and by shaping education so as to strengthen these impulses; secondly, by diminishing the outlets for the possessive instincts. The diffusion of power, both in the political and the economic sphere, instead of its concentration in the hands of officials and captains of industry, would greatly diminish the opportunities for acquiring the habit of command, out of which the desire for exercising tyranny is apt to spring. Autonomy, both for districts and for organizations, would leave fewer occasions when governments were called upon to make decisions as to other people's concerns. And the abolition of capitalism and the wage system would remove the chief incentive to fear and greed, those correlative passions by which all free life is choked and gagged.

Few men seem to realize how many of the evils from which we suffer are wholly unnecessary, and that they could be abolished by a united effort within a few years. If a majority in every civilized country so desired, we could, within twenty years, abolish all abject poverty, quite half the illness in the world, the whole economic slavery which binds down nine tenths of our population; we could fill the world with beauty and joy, and secure the reign of universal peace. It is only because men are apathetic that this is not achieved, only because imagination is sluggish, and what always has been is regarded as what always must be. With good-will, generosity, intelligence, these things could be brought about.

Bertrand Russell. *Political Ideals*. London: George Allen and Unwin, 1963.

Civilization and Its Discontents

Sigmund Freud

SIGMUND FREUD *(1856–1939) was the founder of psychoanalysis. His more important writings include* The Interpretation of Dreams, Introductory Lectures in Psychoanalysis, Beyond the Pleasure Principle, *and* The Ego and the Id.

The communists believe that they have found the path to deliverance from our evils. According to them, man is wholly good and is well-disposed to his neighbour; but the institution of private property has corrupted his nature. The ownership of private wealth gives the individual power, and with it the temptation to ill-treat his neighbour; while the man who is excluded from possession is bound to rebel in hostility against his oppressor. If private property were abolished, all wealth held in common, and everyone allowed to share in the enjoyment of it, ill-will and hostility would disappear among men. Since everyone's needs would be satisfied, no one would have any reason to regard another as his enemy; all would willingly undertake the work that was necessary. I have no concern with any economic criticisms of the communist system; I cannot enquire into whether the abolition of private property is expedient or advantageous.[1] But I am able to recognize that the psychological premises on which the system is based are an untenable illusion. In abolishing private property we deprive the human love of aggression of one of its instruments, certainly a strong one, though certainly not the strongest; but we have in no way altered the differences in power and influence which are misused by aggressiveness, nor have we altered anything in its nature. Aggressiveness was not created by property. It reigned almost without limit in primitive times, when property was still very scanty, and it already shows itself in the nursery almost before property has given up its primal, anal form; it forms the basis of every relation of affection and love among people (with the single exception, perhaps, of the mother's relation to her male child). If we do away with personal rights over material wealth, there still remains prerogative in the field of sexual relationships, which is bound to become the source of the strongest dislike and the most violent hostility among men who in other respects are on an equal footing. If we were to remove this factor, too, by allowing complete freedom of sexual life and thus abolishing the family, the germ-cell of civilization, we cannot, it is true, easily foresee what new paths the development of civilization could take; but one thing we can expect, and that is that this indestructible feature of human nature will follow it there.

Sigmund Freud. *Civilization and Its Discontents.* Trans. and ed. by James Strachey. New York: Norton and Co., 1961. Originally published in 1930.

---

[1] Anyone who has tasted the miseries of poverty in his own youth and has experienced the indifference and arrogance of the well-to-do, should be safe from the suspicion of having no understanding or good will towards endeavours to fight against the inequality of wealth among men and all that it leads to. To be sure, if an attempt is made to base this fight upon an abstract demand, in the name of justice, for equality for all men, there is a very obvious objection to be made—that nature, by endowing individuals with extremely unequal physical attributes and mental capacities, has introduced injustices against which there is no remedy.

Philosophy and Ideology

Alasdair MacIntyre

ALASDAIR MACINTYRE, *a contemporary philosopher, was formerly at Oxford University and is now at Brandeis University. His books include* Marxism and Christianity *and* A Short History of Ethics.

The aspiration of Marxism was to provide a perspective in which the present might be understood as a transition from the enslavement of the past to the liberation of the future. This view of the present does of course appear in vulgarized form as a commonplace of the nineteenth century, not specific to Marxism. It reappears in psychoanalysis as a doctrine about individuals: "Where id was, there ego shall be." And it plainly has a Christian ancestry. But where Christianity saw this liberation as at the end of and transcending the history of this world, Marxism placed it within history and indeed within the foreseeable future. All three doctrines therefore characterize the present in terms of its relationship to past and future: as a time of redemption from sin, as a point where neurotic entanglements with the past give way before the constructive aspirations of the ego ideal, and as the period of the revolutionary passage from exploitation and unfreedom to socialism and then to Communism.

To characterize the present in these ways, to insist indeed that the present is only adequately described when it is characterized in these ways, is to use descriptions the application of which commits the user to certain evaluations. To say of a man that he is deeply neurotic, a sinner, or either exploited or an exploiter is not only to say what he is, but also to say what he ought to be. Just what is the relationship of this "is" to this "ought?" From Kant onward at least, there have been philosophers who have insisted that judgments of fact were one thing, judgments about what is right or good quite another thing, and that the latter could never be logically derived from the former. This view of morality as an autonomous sphere was certainly a faithful rendering of a view highly influential in the society which these philosophers belonged to. For, according to a view that was often tacitly presupposed by liberal individualism, questions of fact are settled independently of what anyone wants or chooses, but questions of value are settled only by the individual's choosing and standing by some particular set of principles. The individual confronts the objective facts with a freedom to make such evaluations as he will.

But is this view of man true? Or is it a view—true to some extent at least of liberal, individualist men—made true indeed by their believing it to be true? And does the corresponding philosophical view of the autonomy of morality and of the logical gulf between "is" and "ought" express what is true only of the scheme of ideas and beliefs which informed and informs liberal individualism, or does it rather express a truth about the nature of morality as such? It was against Kant's treatment of "is" and "ought" that the young Marx reacted as early as 1837; and certainly the truth of Kant's thesis is incompatible with the truth of Marx's mature doctrine. For according to Marxism, there are not neutral, objective facts on the one hand and individuals freely choosing their values on the other. It is rather the case that an individual with a given role has norms and ends such that when he accepts a given characterization of the facts, he also evaluates them in accordance with his class role. (Class role is of course never simply a matter of having a particular kind of occupation.) Hence, for Marxism the key descriptive expressions in our vocabulary are also evaluative. Nor is this merely a matter of such expressions being composites in which a descriptive component is joined to the expression of an evaluative choice. For in a Marxist view, values are not chosen, they are given: indeed, the view that values are not given but chosen is, in a Marxist view, one of the given evaluations of a liberal, individualist society. For it itself embodies an evaluative attitude.

By contrast, the view of social science implicit or explicit in the attitudes expressed by the end-of-ideology thesis is one that accepts the separation of fact and value, usually in a version derived from Max Weber. It follows that, underlying the confrontation of these two ideologies—Marxism and that which, as I argued earlier, is embodied in the end-of-ideology thesis—there is a crucial *philosophical* disagreement. Moreover, this same issue, and a number of other closely related philosophical issues, are raised by another problem that is central to the ideological themes discussed in the first part of this book. Marx originally indicted capitalist *values* as well as capitalist methods. His belief that any appeal to the exploiters on a moral basis was bound to embody the illusion of common standards of justice governing human behaviour made him suspicious of all moralizing. But when Eduard Bernstein attempted to find a Kantian basis for socialism, the defenders of Marxist orthodoxy Karl Kautsky and Rosa Luxemburg were forced to reopen the question of the nature of the moral authority of the Marxist appeal to the working class. This question, as the experience of Luxemburg and of Lukács, of Trotsky and of Guevara shows, was never satisfactorily answered. Equally, those who broke with Marxism because of its moral failures, both under Stalin and in the post-Stalinist age, have been extremely unclear as to the kind of authority that their moral condemnation has possessed. To what were they appealing? Silone, for example, turned to so highly personal a Christian vision that it would be difficult to understand how this could provide a general and impersonal basis for the kind of moral dissidence that so many have underwritten. It does in fact seem to be the case that from the moral collapse of Marxism men can only turn back to clutch at fragments of that pre-Marxist moralizing which Marx criticized so radically and so effectively.

We therefore cannot escape asking the question: what is morality? and what is its power in the world? And this not only for the reasons I have already given. If we are to escape that "worship of the established fact" which is embodied in the end-of-ideology view of the world, if we are to criticize effectively the uncontrolled, destructive progress of advanced societies in the name of an alternative vision of human liberation—if, that is, we are to create a genuinely post-Marxist ideology of liberation, then we have to avoid the snares which Marxism did not, for all its great achievement, avoid. These snares were not only, of course, a matter of the nature of morality and the conditions under which morality can have power in the world; among the other snares was a lack of concern about philosophical truth, and such a concern is a necessary precondition of answering the questions about morality adequately and without illusion. Why is this so?

In *The German Ideology*, Marx and Engels remarked that "When reality is depicted, philosophy as an independent branch of activity loses its medium of existence"; and Marx elsewhere put this by saying that philosophy stands to a genuine understanding of reality as onanism does to real sexual activity. These aphorisms were, of course, aimed specifically at Hegelianism and Young Hegelianism, doctrines which absurdly inflated the claims of philosophy. But in discussing these pretensions, Marx and Engels proceeded to treat as unproblematic or as already resolved questions and issues which later philosophy has illuminated—but which even so have not been fully solved or resolved—but from the study of which Marxism has insulated itself.

Two groups of questions in particular are crucial, and two non-Marxist philosophical traditions have been important in contributing to the answers. The first group of questions will already be clear. It concerns the nature of moral judgment. What do the key evaluative words mean, words such as "good," "right," "virtue," "justice," "duty," "happiness," and the like? And to what kind of standards with what kind of authority are we appealing when we use them? Marxists have often shared with highly conservative philosophers the view that a concern about the theory of meaning, or about the nature of speech acts, is somehow a trivialization of philosophy, a turning away from questions of substance. But it has been precisely at the level of language that the moral inadequacies and corruptions of our age have been evident, and certainly no less so by those with ideological stances than by others. The key question for ideology—whether we (still) possess a language in which we can say what we sometimes desperately want to be able to say—cannot be answered until the philosophical problems about meaning have been resolved.

The second group of questions concerns the explanation of human action. If moral considerations are important, if socialism is to have a human face, then we shall have to understand what part reasoning and deliberation play in bringing about one sort of action rather than another. Marx and Engels at the outset rightly wished to draw a contrast between what really moved men to act in certain ways and what the same men believed to have moved them to act. This distinction is at the heart of the Marxist theory of ideology. But Marx and Engels also asserted that men could find reasons for action in the modern world which would not only enable them to act effectively, but which would be such that what they believed to be moving them to action would indeed be what was in fact moving them to action. The empirical investigation of these questions cannot proceed successfully unless it is preceded and accompanied by a philosophical account of the relationship between the kind of explanation of human action in terms of intentions, reasons, and purposes which is native to human life itself and the kind of causal explanation which is familiar in the natural sciences. Just these issues have been the focus of a good deal of discussion by philosophers influenced by Wittgenstein, Ryle, and Austin in the last two decades, and the questions in moral philosophy which I have already instanced have provided a similar focus. Since these discussions have at their best exhibited a care for rigor and for truth not always exhibited by those engaged in the ideological disputes of the age, it is all the more important that the bearing of these discussions on ideology should continuously be kept in mind.

Alasdair MacIntyre. *Against the Self-Images of the Age*. Notre Dame: University of Notre Dame Press, 1971.

Ideology and Social Organization

M. Patricia Marchak

PATRICIA MARCHAK, *a sociologist at the University of British Columbia, has written numerous papers and a book entitled* Ideological Perspectives on Canada.

There is something out there which could be called social reality. It does exist independent of our perceptions of it. Wealth and poverty are real conditions, as are power and the lack of it. There are known institutions such as corporate organizations. There are other means by which the population is organized but which are not formally recognized institutions, such as interest groups, classes, and ethnic groups. There are effects and consequences of social actions. The problem is that all of these realities exist and we know they exist, but human beings do not agree on the nature of their properties and their relationships to one another.

Social reality doesn't appear to us directly. It is revealed to our understanding through a screen of assumptions, beliefs, explanations, values, and unexamined knowledge. Together, these elements of the screen comprise an ideology, and the ideology directs our attention to some realities but not to others; interprets what our senses transmit to our brain; evaluates information not on its own merits but in terms of what is already accepted as truth. An ideology grows with us from childhood. Some parts of it are deliberately transmitted by parents, schools, the media, and the other institutions of our society. Other parts are more casually conveyed through example; the unspoken assumptions and attitudes of those around us. If a complete ideology is subjected to close scrutiny it can seldom meet the test of consistency. It provides explanations which are not logically connected to one another, permits the holding of values which are not congruent. Even so, it provides some dominant themes, some rules of thumb, some central beliefs that guide our actions and our perceptions in our habitual rounds of activity.

Some aspects of an ideology are about the political or public world of events. There is an explanation for the structure of power, for why the public world is ordered in such a fashion, whatever that fashion is perceived to be. Some elements are about a more private world, about what it is appropriate to hope for, how one ought to behave, what it is sensible to believe. These public and private worlds are connected, though many people might hold an ideology, the parts of which do not appear to them to be connected. This is in large part because much of what we think about our private motivations and hopes is perceived by us to be the result of entirely private considerations. We are not inclined to think of ourselves as socialized beings whose private ambitions are, to a large degree, conditioned by the public world in which we grow up and live out our lives.

The child asks the parent, "Why is that family poorer than us?" and receives an answer such as "Because their father is unemployed," or "Because sales clerks don't make as much money as sales managers." The accumulation of such responses provides a ready index to the organization of society in occupational terms, and with reference to age and sex roles. The child is informed by such responses that some occupations provide higher material rewards than others, that an occupation is essential, and that fathers, not mothers, earn family incomes. The child is not provided with an explanation for the differential between sales clerks and sales managers, between the employed and the unemployed, between families in one income group and families in the other, but some children think to ask. There are, then, additional responses such as, "If you work hard at school, you can go to the top," or "Managers are more important than clerks," or "Well, if people don't work, they can't expect to get along in the world."

On the surface, all of these comments are true and they are seen to be true. They do reflect the realities people experience. If one does not get an education, one clearly cannot go to the top. If one doesn't work, one will indeed have problems. Managers generally do earn more than clerks and material wealth does confer status. Ideology is not typically a systematic analysis of society. It does not generally proceed far beyond the descriptive level. For most people, at most times, this is sufficient.

This is sufficient, as well, for societies. The dominant ideology—or conventional wisdom—provides the ready references, the rules of thumb, the directives to the eyes and ears of its members. It is the glue that holds institutions together, the medium that allows members of the population to interact, predict events, understand their roles, perform adequately, and perhaps above all, strive to achieve the kinds of goals most appropriate to the maintenance of any particular social organization. That the ideology is useful, even socially necessary, does not make it true. There are members of the population who are dissatisfied with these superficial responses, and who seek explanations that better satisfy their sense of truth. They might ask, for example, why is education related to occupation? What is meant by "the top," and why should people want to go there? Why is status associated with material wealth? What does a sales manager do that makes him important, and to whom is his work important? Why would anyone not work when the penalties for unemployment are so severe?

These kinds of questions lead to three different positions. One of these is the role of the social critic who points out the inconsistencies, the lack of congruence between empirical evidence and ideological statements. Such critics often seek reforms in the social organization, not so much because they challenge the ideology, as because they find discrepan-

cies between it and their observations of social reality. Another is the role of the social analyst, who strives to understand why people believe what they believe, what relationship those beliefs have to empirical evidence, and how beliefs affect social action. These two, the critic and the analyst, strive to transcend their own ideological perspectives—an undertaking that can never be entirely successful.

There is a third position for those who ask difficult questions. It is the adoption of a counter-ideology: the placing of faith in an alternative version of society, an alternative set of beliefs, assumptions, values, and orientations.

Dominant and counter-ideologies grow out of the same social organization. They take the same economic arrangement, the same territorial boundaries, the same population as their units of analysis. But they posit different relationships between these units and different organizations within them. Although the two major ideologies of our time—which we will label liberalism and socialism—claim to explain society in historical and comparative perspective, they both originate in the period of the European Industrial Revolution, and both are unmistakably locked into industrial society as it emerged in Europe at that time.

Because they grow out of the same organization, they have much in common. They are the two sides of a single coin: one describing how the entire structure looks to one who accepts it and expects it to survive; the other, how it looks to one who rejects it and anticipates its demise. Elements of both versions are persuasive when one reviews the empirical data which they use as evidence, and neither is the whole truth.

Ideologies are explanations for the social organization, but they are, as well, evaluations of it. These evaluations tend to be circular: the social organization gives rise to certain beliefs about what is right, appropriate, and desirable, that is, to certain values. These values are then assumed, and the society judges itself by those values. The liberal democracy gave rise to positive evaluations of equality, individualism, material prosperity, and personal freedom. The society is then judged within that framework: does it allow for the realization of these values? The dominant ideology rests on an affirmative answer: yes, this society provides the necessary conditions for equality, material prosperity, and personal freedom. Where there are deficiencies, these are often not recognized. Where the deficiencies are recognized, they are explained not as symptoms of a system that fails but as aberrations or temporary problems in a system that succeeds.

Widespread acceptance of an ideology creates an incapacity for judgement of its truth. There is comfort in believing what so many others appear to believe, in accepting conventional wisdom. There is fear in doing otherwise. Sometimes there are, as well, serious social consequences. To many minds, the person who admits to a deviant perspective is out of bounds, somehow dirty and unacceptable. So successful was liberalism in Canada between the 1950s and 1970s, for example, that the labels "socialist," or "conservative," were widely viewed as repugnant, and this not because those who labelled them this way provided a systematic critique or examination of these other perspectives but because the words themselves were frightening. This occurred even within the liberal perspective which espouses the liberty of the individual to choose beliefs and express them freely.

It is only by contrast that alternative values are considered. Between 1949 and the early 1970s, China appeared to provide an alternative. Such values as community welfare, sharing and public ownership, self-reliance at the community level, and social rather than individual progress were adopted by the ruling Communist Party. These are not the values by which European and North American societies judge themselves, nor do these values grow out of the kind of social organization maintained in Europe and North America. But China, too, has become more industrialized and the values of the 1949 revolution and then of the cultural revolution in the 1960s have undergone rapid change. The "responsibility system" in China of the mid-1980s is not identical to the "free enterprise system" of North America and Europe, but it is, even so, vastly different from the "collectivist" ideology that preceded it. And with the passing of China's revolutionary communism, the world lacks a large-scale alternative social organization. The Soviet organization of Eastern Europe continues to provide an ideological justification of communism, but the social organization appears to be a variant of, rather than a radical alternative to, industrial capitalism. This lack of visible alternatives makes it very difficult for us to imagine and evaluate other ways of arranging social activity; as well, it makes it difficult to remove ourselves mentally from this historical moment and place in order to assess our own society.

Counter-ideologies involve a good deal of imagination. They provide a critique of the present society and a creative vision of an alternative. Both socialism and the "new right" provide these critiques and creative visions, and whether we agree with them or despise them, we are indebted to their proponents for enabling us to imagine other ways of doing things. Like liberalism, these ideologies have grown out of the social organization of industrial capitalism. They are concerned with apparent realities such as mass production technologies, money, wages, markets, industrial property, ownership rights, and distinctions between work and non-work.

Counter-ideologies generally begin with a critical perspective which arises from recognition of inconsistencies between what the dominant ideology portrays as truth and what the senses suggest is reality. They begin, then, as reform movements and their members are social critics. Equality, material prosperity, and personal freedom may be assumed as "right" values, but the society is judged as deficient in providing for their realization. The negative judgement leads to an analysis of social organization which diverges from that propagated by those who hold the dominant ideology and believe it to meet its own objectives. Gradually the analysis turns into a fully developed counter-ideology, an entirely different way of viewing the society.

M. Patricia Marchak. *Ideological Perspectives on Canada*. Toronto: McGraw-Hill, 1988.

Ideology

Richard W. Miller

RICHARD W. MILLER *is Associate Professor of Philosophy at Cornell University. His books include* Analyzing Marx.

Marx sometimes summarizes his rejection of morality in the statement that morality, like religion, is ideological.[1] An ideology, for Marx, is a system of beliefs and attitudes that distort reality and that result from social forces, characteristic of class societies, having no tendency to bring ideas in line with reality.

Granted that Marx analyzes the origins of moral ideas in this way, it is not clear what, if anything, the analysis adds to his criticism of morality. For one thing, the label of "ideology" presupposes the arguments already investigated, in which morality is criticized as intellectually defective. Ideology is *false* consciousness. In Marx's meta-ethics, just as much as in his economics, the case that a system of ideas is ideological must include arguments that it is invalid. So far, these arguments have been independent of historical examinations of social origins.

In defining ideology, for Marx, as a product of *truth-distorting* social forces, I have just made a very controversial claim. Its defense merits at least a short digression. That ideology distorts reality is more or less explicit in Engels' later writings.[2] But it is not explicit in Marx's discussions. Still, the conception of ideology that I have described best accounts for some pervasive features of Marx's usage. Marx often traces ideas and outlooks to their social origins. Sometimes he regards them as distortions, sometimes as valid. For example, the explanations, in the *Manifesto* and *Capital*,

of how proletarians come to perceive their common interests are in the latter category. Yet Marx only uses the term "ideology" in connection with ideas and outlooks that he takes to be distortions, and he often combines the usage with obviously pejorative language. Moreover, by making the label highly tendentious, we can explain Marx's tendency to shuttle between different emphases in his general statements about ideology. Sometimes he emphasizes its socially stabilizing role, sometimes the fact that people with ideologies do not know where their ideas come from, sometimes the specific tendency for ideologies to attribute to ideas an excessively independent role in history. Just within the first sections of *The German Ideology*, he shuttles between these emphases on pages 64f., 37 and 66f., respectively. These shifts are to be expected if, as I would propose, the concept of ideology is a theoretical device used to answer a pressing historical question, "why have so many socially important ideas distorted reality when available data, reasonable inference and the state of science dictated no corresponding mistake?" Each emphasis highlights one side of the tendency of class domination to produce such false ideas.

If the charge that morality is ideology has the force that I have described, then the question is whether it adds anything to the criticism of morality that is not contained in the more internal arguments just presented. Note that an even more pressing version of this question is raised by interpretations that make no intrinsic connection with the distortion of truth: Does the claim that morality is ideological have any connection at all with the criti-

---

[1] See, for example, *Communist Manifesto*, in Robert C. Tucker, ed. *The Marx-Engels Reader*, 1st ed. (New York, 1972), p. 351; *Critique of the Gotha Program*, in Tucker, *The Marx-Engels Reader*, p. 388.

[2] See, for example, the letters to Schmidt and to Mehring, Marx and Engels, *Selected Correspondence*, (Moscow, n.d.) pp. 400f., 434.

cism of morality as an invalid standpoint for social choice?

Apart from these issues of their relevance to his attack on morality, Marx's actual historical discussions of the social origins of moral ideas are themselves very fragmentary. The scattered remarks are intriguing. In his view, the modern ideas about equality, freedom, justice and the general welfare that he criticizes are in part a cultural inheritance from the bourgeoisie's triumph over feudal restrictions.[1] In part, they are the result of a kind of wishful thinking to which a middle-class background gives rise, a false hope that the burdens of big-business domination can be overcome within a system of individual competition.[2] In part, they result from the tendency of bourgeois media to limit and stultify discontent, say, by presenting fair treatment by employers as the only proper goal of workers' activism, or by limiting the proper role of government to the satisfaction of people's equal rights. Consider, for example, traditional conservative efforts to limit social demands by confining them to the fulfillment of rights, as in David Stockman's recent remark, "What people don't realize is that there are plenty of things they want that they don't have a right to." For Marx, such a comment simply reveals that rights are less important than many suppose. For a rights-based liberal or socialist, Stockman's remark imposes a real burden of argument.[3] These speculations about social origins are as convincing as any current hypothesis about the origins of modern moral ideas. But they are fragmentary speculations, nonetheless.

With its limited role and speculative status, does the distinctive, causal aspect of Marx's thesis that morality is ideology make any contribution to his case against morality? I think it does. By offering an alternative interpretation of our feelings of attraction toward the moral point of view in politics, the thesis of ideology undermines the use of those feelings as evidence.

Many people who are intellectually attracted to the anti-moral arguments previously sketched still feel reluctant to embrace the conclusions. I feel this way, myself. Such feelings are not irrelevant to the decision whether to accept Marx's anti-moralism. One might, after, all, find it so obvious that social choices should be made on the basis of equal concern for all that Marx's arguments merely convince one that a sufficiently abstract and flexible basis for equal concern has not yet been described. Nonetheless, one may feel, some such standard must exist. However, feelings of obviousness and implausibility, attraction and repulsion, need to be interpreted before they can be given evidential weight, and interpretation, here, includes causal explanation. Suppose crucial feelings that the interests of all must be treated equally are due to a cultural background ultimately shaped by bourgeois needs to tame discontent, and to a lack of personal exposure to hard social realities. Interpreted in this way, they should not lead one to resist the force of Marx's case against morality. And the Marxist explanation is at least as well-grounded as any claim that these feelings are based on an accurate moral sense. By analyzing their origins, Marx makes appeals to moral feelings less compelling in much the same was as Freud undermines reliance on religious feelings by offering an alternative interpretation of their origins in terms of the dependency and fears of childhood and the unity of self and world felt in early infancy.

The argument from origins to the assessment of validity is supposed to be a fallacy, so monstrous that it has a name, "the genetic fallacy." What would be fallacious is the assumption that ideas are debunked simply by tracing their origins to social interests. This assumption is especially implausible for moral ideas. For example, a strong duty to be hospitable to strangers is accepted by traditional Eskimos

---

[1] *German Ideology*, ed. C.J. Arthur (New York, 1980) p. 84; *Grundrisse*, trans. M. Nicolaus (New York, 1973) p. 245.

[2] *Communist Manifesto*, pp. 354f.; *Grundrisse*, pp. 248f.

[3] In *Wages, Price and Profit, Selected Works of Marx and Engels in Three Volumes* (Moscow, 1973), vol. II, Marx emphasizes that demands for fairness tend to presuppose basic social relations, while calling for their readjustment: "Instead of the *conservative* motto, 'A fair days' wage for a fair day's work,' they [i.e., the working class] ought to inscribe on their banner the *revolutionary* watchword, 'Abolition of the wages system'" (p.75; Marx's emphasis).

because of a common interest in such hospitality in a semi-nomadic society where any family may be struck down in the constant battle with Nature. This explanation does not debunk. If anything, it justifies. Still, some causes are so inappropriate to some beliefs that the belief should be abandoned if we find it, in the final analysis, to be due to such a cause. Historic bourgeois interests in domination, together with a protected middle-class upbringing, are not appropriate as ultimate causal bases for a belief that all should be treated equally. Similar arguments about inappropriate causes are, after all, a normal aspect of scientific criticism. If contamination from the lab-technician's hands caused the streptococcus colony in the petri dish and the consequent belief that the patient had strep throat, that is a ground for withdrawing the belief. Perhaps the patient does have a strep throat. Still it is no fallacy to deny that we are in a position to make this claim, since the causes of our belief would be inappropriate.

In all these cases, the line between appropriate and inappropriate causes of evidence is drawn in roughly the following way: the claim that a phenomenon is evidence for a hypothesis is supported by a causal explanation making it unlikely that the phenomenon would have occurred if the hypothesis had not been valid. By the same token, the evidential claim is undermined by a causal account making it likely that the phenomenon would have occurred regardless of the validity of the hypothesis. Thus, if the technician's dirty hands caused the strep colony, there would have been a strep colony regardless of whether there was a rampant strep infection in the patient's throat. Accepting that one's attraction to the moral point of view in social choice is due to bourgeois domination and a protected upbringing makes it unreasonable, for almost everyone, to give that attraction evidential weight. For almost no one believes that those causal factors have an inherent tendency to promote an accurate appreciation of how to make choices. To the extent that causal account is valid, one would have had the same feelings regardless of the validity of the moral point of view. On the other hand, the explanation in terms of Eskimo needs for hospitality is not undermining. For believers in the code of hospitality are quite prepared to assert that feelings emerging from the need for reciprocity have a tendency to reveal how one should behave.

In sum, if a feeling of commitment to the moral point of view has the ultimate sources that Marx describes, it is bad evidence for the validity of that commitment. If his is as good a causal analysis as anyone has developed, the feeling is no basis for supposing that a defensible version of the moral point of view can somehow be constructed, capable of withstanding his other criticisms. Instead, one should set about replacing morality.

Richard W. Miller. *Analyzing Marx*. Princeton: Princeton University Press, 1984.

Ideals and Ideologies

C. Wright Mills

C. WRIGHT MILLS *(1916–1962) was born in Texas and taught at the University of Maryland and Columbia University. His publications include* The Power Elite; Power, Politics, and People; *and* The Marxists.

Political philosophies are intellectual and moral creations; they contain high ideals, easy slogans, dubious facts, crude propaganda, sophisticated theories. Their adherents select some facts and ignore others, urge the acceptance of ideals, the inevitability of events, argue with this theory and debunk that one. Since in all political philosophies such a miscellany of elements is usually very much jumbled up, our task is to sort them out. To do so, each of the following four points of view may be useful:

First of all, a political philosophy is itself a social reality: it is an *ideology* in terms of which certain institutions and practices are justified and others attacked; it provides the phrases in which demands are raised, criticisms made, exhortations delivered, proclamations formulated, and, at times, policies determined.

Second, it is an ethic, an articulation of *ideals* which on various levels of generality and sophistication is used in judging men, events, and movements, and as goals and guidelines for aspirations and policies.

Third, a political philosophy designates *agencies* of action, of the means of reform, revolution, or conservation. It contains strategies and programmes that embody both ends and means. It designates, in short, the historical levers by which ideals are to be won or maintained after they have been won.

Fourth, it contains *theories* of man, society, and history, or at least assumptions about how society is made up and how it works; about what are held to be its most important elements and how these elements are typically related; its major points of conflict and how these conflicts are resolved. It suggests the methods of study appropriate to its theories. From these theories and with these methods, expectations are derived.

A political philosophy tells us how to find out where we stand and where we may be going; it gives us some answers to these questions; it prepares us for the possible futures. To examine any political philosophy, then, we must examine it as an ideology, a statement of ideals, a designation of agency or agencies, and as a set of social theories. In this chapter, I shall pay attention mainly to ideologies and ideals; the points I shall try to make are these:

As ideology, liberalism and marxism have both been made vulgar and banal; each supplies clichés for the defence of a great-power state and for the abuse of the other bloc and all its works.

As statements of ideals, both carry the secular humanism of Western civilization. These ideals are the only ideals available that are at once part of a comprehensive political philosophy and proclaimed by both the leaders and the led of the most powerful nation-states of the world.

In their classic versions, liberalism and marxism embody the assurances and hopes, the ambiguities and fears of the modern age. Taken in all their varieties, they now constitute our major, even our only, political alternatives. Yet they are more than political philosophies: they are political realities of the first order, the proclaimed creeds of the two most powerful states in world history. Looking upon the U.S.A. and the U.S.S.R. (and the blocs of nations around each), the rest of the world sees them in terms of these creeds; in these terms, the underdeveloped world thinks of them as alternative models for their own development.

From the standpoint of modern times, the

differences between the classic versions of these political philosophies are often less important than what they have in common. Above all they are animated by common ideals: the major secular ideals that have been developed during the course of Western civilization. Both marxism and liberalism embody the ideals of Greece and Rome and Jerusalem: the humanism of the Renaissance, the rationalism of the eighteenth-century enlightenment. That is why to examine liberalism or marxism is to examine the politics of this humanist tradition; to find either or both ambiguous is to find this tradition ambiguous.

Liberalism and marxism have also each provided grand views of the nature of the social world, designated the agencies of historic change, and suggested programmes for achieving these goals. For many decades now, within each advanced nation, they have confronted each other, differing about what their experts consider to be facts, and differing about the means they think necessary to reach their proclaimed goals. But these goals have not changed very much. First they were the goals of the English, the American, the French Revolutions; then they were the goals, reformulated to be sure, of the Russian Revolution; quickly they were again reformulated—in reaction, both liberal and marxist, to the consolidation of this revolution.[1]

The moral and political dilemmas of the marxists, and especially of the communists among them, overlap heavily the dilemmas of any liberal. Both share in the ideals of the big tradition; neither realizes them fully. And these ideals, as well as certain theoretical assumptions, are carried further and more consistently, are taken more seriously by several of the best marxists than by any liberal I know of. It is the crisis of this humanist tradition itself, I believe, that is at the bottom of our crisis in political orientation. One of the most direct ways to confront that crisis in all its aspects is to examine the ideas of Karl Marx— and the fate of these ideas.

What is most valuable in classic liberalism is most cogently and most fruitfully incorporated in classic marxism. Much of the failure to confront marxism in all its variety is in fact a way of *not* taking seriously the ideals of liberalism itself, for despite the distortions and vulgarizations of Marx's ideas, and despite his own errors, ambiguities, and inadequacies, Karl Marx remains the thinker who has articulated most clearly—and most perilously—the basic ideals which liberalism shares. Hence, to confront Marx and marxism is to confront this moral tradition...

Both liberalism and marxism have been insurgent creeds: in their several varieties they have been the rhetoric of movements, parties, and classes on the road to power. And in due course each has become a conservative creed: the ideology and the rhetoric of consolidated political and economic systems.

With their insurgent creed, liberals have denounced feudalism and its remnants as a social system; they have denounced all forms of political absolutism. Marxists too have denounced feudalism and pre-industrial absolutism; but they have gone further, coming down hard against liberal capitalism, as a type of economy which they have held to be the keystone of capitalist societies as a whole.

As an ideology, and on a world-wide scale, liberalism now becomes conservative. In its terms, liberals justify capitalist democracy, seated primarily in the richer nations of Western Europe and North America, and in Japan and Australia. In their stalinist variety, marxists have officially justified the Soviet Union and the states in various ways affiliated with it.

As a political "utopia" liberalism has been historically specific to the rising middle classes of advancing capitalist societies; marxism, the proclaimed creed of working-class movements and parties. But in each case, as power is achieved, these political philosophies become official ideologies, become—in differing ways—engulfed by nationalism. In terms of each, the world encounter of the superstates is defined and, from either side, fought out. In the Soviet Union marxism has become ideologically consolidated and subject to official control; in the United States liberalism has

---

[1] For a scholarly, relevant, and exciting account of the eighteenth-century revolutions, see R.R. Palmer, *The Age of the Democratic Revolution* (Princeton, 1959).

become less an ideology than an empty rhetoric.

As a rhetoric, liberalism is commonly used by everyone who talks in public for every divergent and contradictory purpose. One spokesman can remain liberal and be *for*, another can remain liberal and be *against* a vast range of contradictory political propositions. The business man and the labour leader, the Democrat and the Republican, the general and the foot soldier, the subsidized farmer and the subsidized watch-maker—all speak in the terms of the liberal rhetoric, defending their interests and making their demands. This means that liberalism as publicly used is without coherent content, that its goals have been made so formal and abstract as to provide no clear moral standards, that in its terms genuine conflicts of interest and ideal can no longer be stated clearly. Used by virtually all interests, classes, parties, it lacks political, moral, and intellectual clarity; this very lack of clarity is exploited by all interests. In this situation, as has often been noted, professional liberals, politicians, and intellectuals make a fetish of indecision, which they call open-mindedness; of the absence of moral criteria, which they call tolerance; and of the formality—and hence political irrelevance—of the criteria, which they call speaking broadly.

This crisis of liberalism—and in turn, of political reflection in the United States—is due to liberalism's very success in becoming the official language for all public statement and debate, the political language of all mass communication. To this fact must be added the use of liberalism since the New Deal period, as an administrative rationale: in close contact with power, liberalism has become more administrative and less political. It has become practical, flexible, realistic, pragmatic—as liberals assert—and not at all utopian. All of which means, I think, that as an ideology, as a rhetoric, liberalism has often become irrelevant to political positions having moral content.

In the Soviet bloc, elements from marxism have become essential ingredients of an official creed subject to official interpretation, and the official guide line for all cultural and political life. In this form, marxism-as-ideology is *the* coin of all public transactions, the basic premise of an elaborate cultural and political apparatus which is oriented to the presumed interests of the one-party state. Since marxism enjoys an ideological monopoly, intellectual freedom is limited by official interpretations of it. From an image of the future, elaborated in nineteenth-century capitalist society, marxism has been transformed into the ideology of the Soviet bloc.

Ideological uniformity and doctrinaire realignment have accompanied every phase and every turn of Soviet political and economic development, domestic and foreign. There have been many such twists and turns, each of them duly proclaimed in the name of marxism. Politics and doctrine are closely linked; political directions often shift: it is not surprising that the doctrine itself has become banalized and in the process emptied of much of its moral force and intellectual cogency. It has often become a morally curious and intellectually empty ideology in which the communist-on-the-make must be expert—truly a red tape of an ideology, which he must tie and untie and tie again if he would act at all.

Moreover, such use of Soviet marxism has been accompanied by its use as the one basic doctrine of the entire Soviet cultural apparatus, which has had to swing into line with each shift in policy. In the course of such zigzags, cultural workmen have been brutally eliminated. The political and status purge of intellectuals, artists, and scientists—as during Stalin's era—has thus accompanied the tight joining of culture and politics, both controlled by officials of party and of state.

Now these two folklores—the ideology of vulgar marxism and the rhetoric of abstracted liberalism—confront each other, each offering the publics of the world various images of the Soviet Union and of the United States, each providing the contrasting vocabularies, often in the same words, with which leaders and led talk about their own societies and about those of The Enemy.

Inside each country and around the world as well, a vast and elaborate machinery of propaganda is kept busy night and day grinding out these folklores, adapting them to every turn of events and to events imagined; to threat and counter-threat, to policies and to lack of policies.

In the folklore of liberalism, America is a free country in which men at large truly govern their own affairs; Soviet Russia is an absolute tyranny, monolithic and totalitarian, in which men are forcibly held down and there is neither freedom nor joy—and it is aggressive, too, out to conquer the world for its unchristian creed.

In the folklore of communism, the U.S.S.R. is The Great Step Forward of Humanity in the twentieth century; the U.S.A. is a reactionary laggard in which the injustices of capitalism are matched only by the hypocrisies of formal democracy. It is run by warmongers, out to use military and any other means available ruthlessly to expand and consolidate their imperialistic domination.

In this realm of folklore, the ideas of Karl Marx and of his intellectual followers are indeed in a sorry condition.

In Soviet societies, the work of Marx—joined with that of Lenin—is always celebrated and often vulgarized. Indeed marxism-leninism has become an official rhetoric with which the authority of a one-party state has been defended, its expedient brutalities obscured, its achievements proclaimed.

In capitalist societies, the ideas of Marx are ignored or worse, ignorantly *identified* with "mere communist ideology." Thus, here too, the work of Marx, and of his followers, has become "marxism-leninism"—an official target of confused and ignorant abuse, rather than an object of serious study.

C. Wright Mills. *The Marxists.* Harmondsworth: Penguin Books, 1962.

Part II

Classical Democratic Liberalism

JOHN STUART MILL

The pivotal point of classical democratic liberalism is the minimal state. This is probably most clearly seen first in the case of John Locke who believes the responsibility of government only extended to the protection of life, liberty, and property. Of course the state could extract its tolls from one, but the areas in which it could properly act were limited to taxation and military service. Clearly the state was hedged in by the natural rights of man. In the case of Jean-Jacques Rousseau, the story is somewhat different. For him, between the state of nature and the political state lies the political society within which each man gives himself to everyone and thus, paradoxically, gives himself to nobody. In other words his freedom and power remain unchanged, the only difference being that now he lives in a society that is both legitimate and the foundation of his rights. The political state, so far as it exists, does so in the form of a god-like legislator who discerns the general will and thereby acts more like a servant of the people than a master. The equality of the law as guaranteed by the legislator preserves man's freedom. For Rousseau there is to be found in political societies a reconciliation of both man's freedom as an individual and man's need for security through social organization. What results is something more obscure than Locke's government and state.

Adam Smith provides a refreshing contrast with the sometimes obscure notions and paradoxical style of Rousseau. The former introduces in bold print the doctrine of laissez-faire economics as the counterpart to Locke's political doctrines of the minimal state. Here for the first time is an elegant presentation of the notion of the market theory of value and the notion of division of labour. Such was the fruitfulness of these ideas that from Smith onwards, they played a large role in political theory in every succeeding century down to the present. For Smith, the lifting of the economic shackles of the state from the backs of individuals would promote the interests of society, as if they were directed by an invisible hand. In the event, the state is displaced from the centre of economic activity and by that from the centre of political activity.

Next we come to Thomas Paine, who shares some of the ideas of Rousseau and of the anarchist William Godwin. In particular he shares with them the idea of a distinction between society and government. But he also shares at least with Locke and possibly Rousseau the belief that the power produced by the aggregate, i.e. the state and government, cannot be allowed to invade the natural rights of the individual. Consistent with this belief, Paine goes on to say that a constitution is antecedent to government and is an act of the people. Undoubtedly his emphasis upon the constitution reflects his experience in the United States, in its preparation for revolution and constitutional change, which left him with a recognition of the limits of state interference in the lives of its subjects.

Finally we come to John Stuart Mill who outlines the classical liberal view of liberty, asserting that the sole end for which man may individually or collectively interfere with another is to prevent harm to himself or another. Initially in his *On Liberty*, Mill applies his principle narrowly, and only belatedly raises issues of rights and justice. However he is not so restrained about connecting his principle of liberty to human happiness and individuality, for which it functions as a necessary condition. Certainly in the early part of his book Mill leaves the impression of adopting an almost libertarian position.

The present readings represent one political tradition that established itself in Anglo and European environs. Briefly, we might say that in this tradition the state is marginalized and the individual and his natural rights emphasized.

Of Property

John Locke

JOHN LOCKE *(1632–1704) was one of the three great British empiricists along with Bishop George Berkeley and David Hume. His two major works were, in epistemology,* An Essay Concerning Human Understanding, *and, in politics,* Two Treatises on Government.

27. Though the earth and all inferior creatures be common to all men, yet every man has a property in his own person; this nobody has any right to but himself. The labour of his body and the work of his hands we may say are properly his. Whatsoever, then, he removes out of the state that nature hath provided and left it in, he hath mixed his labour with, and joined to it something that is his own, and thereby makes it his property. It being by him removed from the common state nature placed it in, it hath by this labour something annexed to it that excludes the common right of other men. For this labour being the unquestionable property of the labourer, no man but he can have a right to what that is once joined to, at least where there is enough, and as good left in common for others.

28. He that is nourished by the acorns he picked up under an oak, or the apples he gathered from the trees in the wood, has certainly appropriated them to himself. Nobody can deny but the nourishment is his. I ask, then, When did they begin to be his—when he digested, or when he ate, or when he boiled, or when he brought them home, or when he picked them up? And 'tis plain if the first gathering made them not his, nothing else could. That labour put a distinction between them and common; that added something to them more than Nature, the common mother of all, had done, and so they became his private right. And will any one say he had no right to those acorns or apples he thus appropriated, because he had not the consent of all mankind to make them his? Was it a robbery thus to assume to himself what belonged to all in common? If such a consent as that was necessary, man had starved, notwithstanding the plenty God had given him. We see in commons which remain so by compact that 'tis the taking any part of what is common and removing it out of the state nature leaves it in, which begins the property; without which the common is of no use. And the taking of this or that part does not depend on the express consent of all the commoners. Thus the grass my horse has bit, the turfs my servant has cut, and the ore I have dug in any place where I have a right to them in common with others, become my property without the assignation or consent of anybody. The labour that was mine removing them out of that common state they were in, hath fixed my property in them.

29. By making an explicit consent of every commoner necessary to any one's appropriating to himself any part of what is given in common, children or servants could not cut the meat which their father or master had provided for them in common without assigning to every one his peculiar part. Though the water running in the fountain be every one's, yet who can doubt but that in the pitcher is his only who drew it out? His labour hath taken it out of the hands of Nature, where it was common, and belonged equally to all her children, and hath thereby appropriated it to himself.

30. Thus this law of reason makes the deer that Indian's who hath killed it; 'tis allowed to be his goods who hath bestowed his labour upon it, though before it was the common right of every one. And amongst those who are counted the civilised part of mankind, who have made and multiplied positive laws to determine property, this original law of nature, for the beginning of property in what was before common, still takes place; and by

virtue thereof, what fish any one catches in the ocean, that great and still remaining common of mankind, or what ambergris any one takes up here, is, by the labour that removes it out of that common state nature left it in, made his property who takes that pains about it. And even amongst us, the hare that any one is hunting is thought his who pursues her during the chase. For being a beast that is still looked upon as common, and no man's private possession, whoever has employed so much labour about any of that kind as to find and pursue her has thereby removed her from the state of nature wherein she was common, and hath begun a property.

31. It will perhaps be objected to this, that if gathering the acorns, or other fruits of the earth, &c., makes a right to them, then any one may engross as much as he will. To which I answer, Not so. The same law of nature that does by this means give us property, does also bound that property too. "God has given us all things richly" (I Tim. vi. 17), is the voice of reason confirmed by inspiration. But how far has He given it to us? To enjoy. As much as any one can make use of to any advantage of life before it spoils, so much he may by his labour fix a property in; whatever is beyond this, is more than his share, and belongs to others. Nothing was made by God for man to spoil or destroy. And thus considering the plenty of natural provisions there was a long time in the world, and the few spenders, and to how small a part of that provision the industry of one man could extend itself, and engross it to the prejudice of others—especially keeping within the bounds, set by reason, of what might serve for his use—there could be then little room for quarrels or contentions about property so established.

32. But the chief matter of property being now not the fruits of the earth, and the beasts that subsist on it, but the earth itself, as that which takes in and carries with it all the rest, I think it is plain that property in that, too, is acquired as the former. As much land as a man tills, plants, improves, cultivates, and can use the product of, so much is his property. He by his labour does as it were enclose it from the common. Nor will it invalidate his right to say, everybody else has an equal title to it; and therefore he cannot appropriate, he cannot enclose, without the consent of all his fellow-commoners, all mankind. God, when He gave the world in common to all mankind, commanded man also to labour, and the penury of his condition required it of him. God and his reason commanded him to subdue the earth, *i.e.*, improve it for the benefit of life, and therein lay out something upon it that was his own, his labour. He that, in obedience to this command of God, subdued, tilled, and sowed any part of it, thereby annexed to it something that was his property, which another had no title to, nor could without injury take from him.

33. Nor was this appropriation of any parcel of land, by improving it, any prejudice to any other man, since there was still enough and as good left; and more than the yet unprovided could use. So that in effect there was never the less left for others because of his enclosure for himself. For he that leaves as much as another can make use of, does as good as take nothing at all. Nobody could think himself injured by the drinking of another man, though he took a good draught, who had a whole river of the same water left him to quench his thirst; and the case of land and water, where there is enough of both, is perfectly the same.

34. God gave the world to men in common; but since He gave it them for their benefit, and the greatest conveniences of life they were capable to draw from it, it cannot be supposed He meant it should always remain common and uncultivated. He gave it to the use of the industrious and rational (and labour was to be his title to it), not to the fancy or covetousness of the quarrelsome and contentious. He that had as good left for his improvement as was already taken up, needed not complain, ought not to meddle with what was already improved by another's labour; if he did, it is plain he desired the benefit of another's pains, which he had no right to, and not the ground which God had given him in common with others to labour on, and whereof there was as good left as that already possessed, and more than he knew what to do with, or his industry could reach to.

35. It is true, in land that is common in England, or any other country where there is plenty of people under Government, who

have money and commerce, no one can enclose or appropriate any part without the consent of all his fellow-commoners: because this is left common by compact, *i.e.*, by the law of the land, which is not to be violated. And though it be common in respect of some men, it is not so to all mankind; but is the joint property of this country, or this parish. Besides, the remainder, after such enclosure, would not be as good to the rest of the commoners as the whole was, when they could all make use of the whole; whereas in the beginning and first peopling of the great common of the world it was quite otherwise. The law man was under was rather for appropriating. God commanded, and his wants forced him, to labour. That was his property, which could not be taken from him wherever he had fixed it. And hence subduing or cultivating the earth, and having dominion, we see are joined together. The one gave title to the other. So that God, by commanding to subdue, gave authority so far to appropriate. And the condition of human life, which requires labour and materials to work on, necessarily introduces private possessions.

36. The measure of property nature has well set by the extent of men's labour and the convenience of life. No man's labour could subdue or appropriate all; nor could his enjoyment consume more than a small part; so that it was impossible for any man this way, to intrench upon the right of another, or acquire to himself a property to the prejudice of his neighbour, who would still have room for as good and as large a possession (after the other had taken out his) as before it was appropriated. Which measure did confine every man's possession to a very moderate proportion, and such as he might appropriate to himself without injury to anybody, in the first ages of the world, when men were more in danger to be lost by wandering from their company in the then vast wilderness of the earth than to be straitened for want of room to plant in. And the same measure may be allowed still without prejudice to anybody, as full as the world seems. For supposing a man or family in the state they were at first peopling of the world by the children of Adam or Noah; let him plant in some inland vacant places of America, we shall find that the possessions he could

make himself, upon the measures we have given, would not be very large, nor, even to this day, prejudice the rest of mankind, or give them reason to complain or think themselves injured by this man's encroachment, though the race of men have now spread themselves to all the corners of the world, and do infinitely exceed the small number that was at the beginning. Nay, the extent of ground is of so little value without labour, that I have heard it affirmed that in Spain itself a man may be permitted to plough, sow, and reap, without being disturbed, upon land he has no other title to but only his making use of it. But, on the contrary, the inhabitants think themselves beholden to him who by his industry on neglected and consequently waste land has increased the stock of corn which they wanted. But be this as it will, which I lay no stress on, this I dare boldly affirm—that the same rule of propriety, viz., that every man should have as much as he could make use of, would hold still in the world without straitening anybody, since there is land enough in the world to suffice double the inhabitants, had not the invention of money, and the tacit agreement of men to put a value on it, introduced (by consent) larger possessions and a right to them; which how it has done I shall by-and-bye show more at large.

37. That is certain, that in the beginning, before the desire of having more than man needed had altered the intrinsic value of things, which depends only on their usefulness to the life of man; or had agreed that a little piece of yellow metal which would keep without wasting or decay should be worth a great piece of flesh or a whole heap of corn, though men had a right to appropriate by their labour, each one to himself, as much of the things of nature as he could use, yet this could not be much, nor to the prejudice of others, where the same plenty was still left to those who would use the same industry.

Before the appropriation of land, he who gathered as much of the wild fruits, killed, caught, or tamed as many of the beasts as he could; he that so employed his pains about any of the spontaneous products of nature as any way to alter them from the state which nature put them in, by placing any of his labour on them, did thereby acquire a propriety in them. But if they perished in his possession without their due use; if the fruits rotted, or the venison putrefied before he could spend it, he offended against the common law of nature, and was liable to be punished; he invaded his neighbour's share, for he had no right further than his use called for any of them and they might serve to afford him conveniences of life...

46. The greatest part of things really useful to the life of man, and such as the necessity of subsisting made the first commoners of the world look after, as it doth the Americans now, are generally things of short duration, such as, if they are not consumed by use, will decay and perish of themselves: gold, silver, and diamonds are things that fancy or agreement have put the value on more than real use and the necessary support of life. Now, of those good things which nature hath provided in common, every one hath a right, as hath been said, to as much as he could use, and had a property in all he could effect with his labour—all that his industry could extend to, to alter from the state nature had put it in, was his. He that gathered a hundred bushels of acorns or apples had thereby a property in them; they were his goods as soon as gathered. He was only to look that he used them before they spoiled, else he took more than his share, and robbed others; and, indeed, it was a foolish thing, as well as dishonest, to hoard up more than he could make use of. If he gave away a part to anybody else, so that it perished not uselessly in his possession, these he also made use of; and if he also bartered away plums that would have rotted in a week, for nuts that would last good for his eating a whole year, he did no injury; he wasted not the common stock, destroyed no part of the portion of goods that belonged to others, so long as nothing perished uselessly in his hands. Again, if he would give his nuts for a piece of metal, pleased with its colour, or exchange his sheep for shells, or wool for a sparkling pebble or a diamond, and keep those by him all his life, he invaded not the right of others; he might heap up as much of these durable things as he pleased, the exceeding of the bounds of his just property not lying in the largeness of his possessions, but the perishing of anything uselessly in it.

47. And thus came in the use of money—some lasting thing that men might keep without spoiling, and that, by mutual consent, men would take in exchange for the truly useful but perishable supports of life.

48. And as different degrees of industry were apt to give men possessions in different proportions, so this invention of money gave them the opportunity to continue and enlarge them; for supposing an island, separate from all possible commerce with the rest of the world, wherein there were but a hundred families—but there were sheep, horses, and cows, with other useful animals, wholesome fruits, and land enough for corn for a hundred thousand times as many, but nothing in the island, either because of its commonness or perishableness, fit to supply the place of money—what reason could any one have there to enlarge his possessions beyond the use of his family and a plentiful supply to its consumption, either in what their own industry produced, or they could barter for like perishable useful commodities with others? Where there is not something both lasting and scarce, and so valuable to be hoarded up, there men will not be apt to enlarge their possessions of land, were it never so rich, never so free for them to take; for I ask, what would a man value ten thousand or a hundred thousand acres of excellent land, ready cultivated, and well stocked too with cattle, in the middle of the inland parts of America, where he had no hopes of commerce with other parts of the world, to draw money to him by the sale of the product? It would not be worth the enclosing, and we should see him give up again to the wild common of nature whatever was more than would supply the conveniences of life to be had there for him and his family.

49. Thus in the beginning all the world was America, and more so than that is now, for no such thing as money was anywhere known. Find out something that hath the use and value of money amongst his neighbours, you shall see the same man will begin presently to enlarge his possessions.

50. But since gold and silver, being little useful to the life of man in proportion to food, raiment, and carriage, has its value only from the consent of men, whereof labour yet makes, in great part, the measure, it is plain that the

consent of men have agreed to a dispropor-
tionate and unequal possession of the earth—I
mean out of the bounds of society and compact; for in governments the laws regulate it;
they having, by consent, found out and agreed
in a way how a man may rightfully and without injury possess more than he himself can
make use of by receiving gold and silver,
which may continue long in a man's possession, without decaying for the overplus, and
agreeing those metals should have a value.

John Locke. *Of Civil Government Second Treatise.*
Originally published in 1689.

The Social Pact

Jean-Jacques Rousseau

JEAN-JACQUES ROUSSEAU (1712–1778) was a Swiss thinker who wrote philosophy, novels, essays, and music. The Social Contract, Discourse on the Origin and Bases of Inequality among Men, *and* Confessions *were his most famous writings; the first, from which the present selection is taken, is his major work on society and politics.*

I assume that men have reached a point at which the obstacles that endanger their preservation in the state of nature overcome by their resistance the forces which each individual can exert with a view to maintaining himself in that state. Then this primitive condition can no longer subsist, and the human race would perish unless it changed its mode of existence.

Now, as men cannot create any new forces, but only combine and direct those that exist, they have no other means of self-preservation than to form by aggregation a sum of forces which may overcome the resistance, to put them in action by a single motive power, and to make them work in concert.

This sum of forces can be produced only by the combination of many; but the strength and freedom of each man being the chief instruments of his preservation, how can he pledge them without injuring himself, and without neglecting the cares which he owes to himself? This difficulty, applied to my subject, may be expressed in these terms:—

"To find a form of association which may defend and protect with the whole force of the community the person and property of every associate, and by means of which each, coalescing with all, may nevertheless obey only himself, and remain as free as before." Such is the fundamental problem of which the social contract furnishes the solution.

The clauses of this contract are so determined by the nature of the act that the slightest modification would render them vain and ineffectual; so that, although they have never perhaps been formally enunciated, they are everywhere the same, everywhere tacitly admitted and recognized, until, the social pact being violated, each man regains his original rights and recovers his natural liberty, while losing the conventional liberty for which he renounced it.

These clauses, rightly understood, are reducible to one only, viz., the total alienation to the whole community of each associate with all his rights; for, in the first place, since each gives himself up entirely, the conditions are equal for all; and, the conditions being equal for all, no one has any interest in making them burdensome to others.

Further, the alienation being made without reserve, the union is as perfect as it can be, and an individual associate can no longer claim anything; for, if any rights were left to individuals, since there would be no common superior who could judge between them and the public, each, being on some point his own judge, would soon claim to be so on all; the state of nature would still subsist, and the association would necessarily become tyrannical or useless.

In short, each giving himself to all, gives himself to nobody; and as there is not one associate over whom we do not acquire the same rights which we concede to him over ourselves, we gain the equivalent of all that we lose, and more power to preserve what we have.

If, then, we set aside what is not of the essence of the social contract, we shall find that it is reducible to the following terms: "Each of us puts in common his person and his whole power under the supreme direction of the general will; and in return we receive every member as an indivisible part of the whole."

Jean-Jacques Rousseau. *The Social Contract*. Originally published in 1762.

The Wealth of Nations

Adam Smith

ADAM SMITH (1723–1790) was the father of
economics. He was born in Scotland and educated
at Glasgow and Oxford University. He served as
professor of logic and then professor of moral
philosophy at the University of Glasgow. In
retirement he wrote his now famous Wealth of
Nations, from which the present selection is taken.

Of Restraints Upon the Importation From Foreign Countries of Such Goods as Can Be Produced at Home

By restraining, either by high duties or by absolute prohibitions, the importation of such goods from foreign countries as can be produced at home, the monopoly of the home market is more or less secured to the domestic industry employed in producing them. Thus the prohibition of importing either live cattle or salt provisions from foreign countries secures to the graziers of Great Britain the monopoly of the home market for butcher's meat. The high duties upon the importation of corn, which in times of moderate plenty amount to a prohibition, give a like advantage to the growers of that commodity. The prohibition of the importation of foreign woollens is equally favourable to the woollen manufacturers. The silk manufacture, though altogether employed upon foreign materials, has lately obtained the same advantage. The linen manufacture has not yet obtained it, but is making great strides towards it. Many other sorts of manufacturers have, in the same manner, obtained in Great Britain, either altogether or very nearly, a monopoly against their countrymen. The variety of goods of which the importation into Great Britain is prohibited, either absolutely, or under certain circumstances, greatly exceeds what can easily be suspected by those who are not well acquainted with the laws of the customs.

That this monopoly of the home market frequently gives great encouragement to that particular species of industry which enjoys it, and frequently turns towards that employment a greater share of both the labour and stock of the society than would otherwise have gone to it, cannot be doubted. But whether it tends either to increase the general industry of the society, or to give it the most advantageous direction, is not, perhaps, altogether so evident.

The general industry of the society never can exceed what the capital of the society can employ. As the number of workmen that can be kept in employment by any particular person must bear a certain proportion to his capital, so the number of those that can be continually employed by all the members of a great society must bear a certain proportion to the whole capital of that society, and never can exceed that proportion. No regulation of commerce can increase the quantity of industry in any society beyond what its capital can maintain. It can only divert a part of it into a direction into which it might not otherwise have gone; and it is by no means certain that this artificial direction is likely to be more advantageous to the society than that into which it would have gone of its own accord.

Every individual is continually exerting himself to find out the most advantageous employment for whatever capital he can command. It is his own advantage, indeed, and not that of the society, which he has in view. But the study of his own advantage naturally, or rather necessarily, leads him to prefer that employment which is most advantageous to the society.

First, every individual endeavours to employ his capital as near home as he can, and consequently as much as he can in the support of domestic industry; provided always that he can thereby obtain the ordinary, or not a great deal less than the ordinary profits of stock.

Thus, upon equal or nearly equal profits, every wholesale merchant naturally prefers the home trade to the foreign trade of consumption, and the foreign trade of consumption to the carrying trade. In the home trade his capital is never so long out of his sight as it frequently is in the foreign trade of consumption. He can know better the character and the situation of the persons whom he trusts, and if he should happen to be deceived, he knows better the laws of the country from which he must seek redress. In the carrying trade, the capital of the merchant is, as it were, divided between two foreign countries, and no part of it is ever necessarily brought home, or placed under his own immediate view and command. The capital which an Amsterdam merchant employs in carrying corn from Konnigsberg to Lisbon, and fruit and wine from Lisbon to Konnigsberg, must generally be the one-half of it at Konnigsberg and the other half at Lisbon. No part of it need ever come to Amsterdam. The natural residence of such a merchant should either be at Konnigsberg or Lisbon, and it can only be some very particular circumstances which can make him prefer the residence of Amsterdam. The uneasiness, however, which he feels at being separated so far from his capital generally determines him to bring part both of the Konnigsberg goods which he destines for the market of Lisbon, and of the Lisbon goods which he destines for that of Konnigsberg, to Amsterdam: and though this necessarily subjects him to a double charge of loading and unloading, as well as to the payment of some duties and customs, yet for the sake of having some part of his capital always under his own view and command, he willingly submits to this extraordinary charge; and it is in this manner that every country which has any considerable share of the carrying trade becomes always the emporium, or general market, for the goods of all the different countries whose trade it carries on. The merchant, in order to save a second loading and unloading, endeavours always to sell in the home market as much of the goods of all those different countries as he can, and thus, so far as he can, to convert his carrying trade into a foreign trade of consumption. A merchant, in the same manner, who is engaged in the foreign trade of consumption, when he collects goods for foreign markets, will always be glad, upon equal or nearly equal profits, to sell as great a part of them at home as he can. He saves himself the risk and trouble of exportation, when, so far as he can, he thus converts his foreign trade of consumption into a home trade. Home is in this manner the centre, if I may say so, round which the capitals of the inhabitants of every country are continually circulating, and towards which they are always tending, though by particular causes they may sometimes be driven off and repelled from it towards more distant employments. But a capital employed in the home trade, it has already been shown, necessarily puts into motion a greater quantity of domestic industry, and gives revenue and employment to a greater number of the inhabitants of the country, than an equal capital employed in the foreign trade of consumption: and one employed in the foreign trade of consumption has the same advantage over an equal capital employed in the carrying trade. Upon equal, or only nearly equal profits, therefore, every individual naturally inclines to employ his capital in the manner in which it is likely to afford the greatest support to domestic industry, and to give revenue and employment to the greatest number of people of his own country.

Secondly, every individual who employs his capital in the support of domestic industry, necessarily endeavours so to direct that industry that its produce may be of the greatest possible value.

The produce of industry is what it adds to the subject or materials upon which it is employed. In proportion as the value of this produce is great or small, so will likewise be the profits of the employer. But it is only for the sake of profit that any man employs a capital in the support of industry; and he will always, therefore, endeavour to employ it in the support of that industry of which the produce is likely to be of the greatest value, or to exchange for the greatest quantity either of money or of other goods.

But the annual revenue of every society is always precisely equal to the exchangeable value of the whole annual produce of its industry, or rather is precisely the same thing with that exchangeable value. As every individual, therefore, endeavours as much as he can both to employ his capital in the support of domestic industry, and so to direct that industry that its produce may be of the greatest value; every individual necessarily labours to render the annual revenue of the society as great as he can. He generally, indeed, neither intends to promote the public interest, nor knows how much he is promoting it. By preferring the support of domestic to that of foreign industry, he intends only his own security; and by directing that industry in such a manner as its produce may be of the greatest value, he intends only his own gain, and he is in this, as in many other cases, led by an invisible hand to promote an end which was no part of his intention. Nor is it always the worse for the society that it was no part of it. By pursuing his own interest he frequently promotes that of the society more effectually than when he really intends to promote it. I have never known much good done by those who affected to trade for the public good. It is an affectation, indeed, not very common among merchants, and very few words need be employed in dissuading them from it.

What is the species of domestic industry which his capital can employ, and of which the produce is likely to be of the greatest value, every individual, it is evident, can, in his local situation, judge much better than any statesman or lawgiver can do for him. The statesman who should attempt to direct private people in what manner they ought to employ their capitals would not only load himself with a most unnecessary attention, but assume an authority which could safely be trusted, not only to no single person, but to no council or senate whatever, and which would nowhere be so dangerous as in the hands of a man who had folly and presumption enough to fancy himself fit to exercise it.

To give the monopoly of the home market to the produce of domestic industry, in any particular art or manufacture, is in some measure to direct private people in what manner they ought to employ their capitals, and must, in almost all cases, be either a useless or a hurtful regulation. If the produce of domestic can be brought there as cheap as that of foreign industry, the regulation is evidently useless. If it cannot, it must generally be hurtful.

It is the maxim of every prudent master of a family never to attempt to make at home what it will cost him more to make than to buy. The tailor does not attempt to make his own shoes, but buys them of the shoemaker. The shoemaker does not attempt to make his own clothes, but employs a tailor. The farmer attempts to make neither the one nor the other, but employs those different artificers. All of them find it for their interest to employ their whole industry in a way in which they have some advantage over their neighbours, and to purchase with a part of its produce, or what is the same thing, with the price of a part of it, whatever else they have occasion for.

What is prudence in the conduct of every private family can scarce be folly in that of a great kingdom. If a foreign country can supply us with a commodity cheaper than we ourselves can make it, better buy it of them with some part of the produce of our own industry employed in a way in which we have some advantage. The general industry of the country, being always in proportion to the capital which employs it, will not thereby be diminished, no more than that of the above-mentioned artificers; but only left to find out the way in which it can be employed with the greatest advantage. It is certainly not employed to the greatest advantage when it is thus directed towards an object which it can buy cheaper than it can make. The value of its annual produce is certainly more or less diminished when it is thus turned away from producing commodities evidently of more value than the commodity which it is directed to produce. According to the supposition, that commodity could be purchased from foreign countries cheaper than it can be made at home. It could, therefore, have been purchased with a part only of the commodities, or, what is the same thing, with a part only of the price of the commodities, which the industry employed by an equal capital would have produced at home, had it been left to follow its natural course. The industry of the country, therefore, is thus turned away from a more to a less advantageous employment, and the exchangeable value of its annual produce, instead of being increased, according to the intention of the lawgiver, must necessarily be diminished by every such regulation.

By means of such regulations, indeed, a particular manufacture may sometimes be acquired sooner than it could have been otherwise, and after a certain time may be made at home as cheap or cheaper than in the foreign country. But though the industry of the society may be thus carried with advantage into a particular channel sooner than it could have been otherwise, it will by no means follow that the sum total, either of its industry, or of its revenue, can ever be augmented by any such regulation. The industry of the society can augment only in proportion as its capital augments, and its capital can augment only in proportion to what can be gradually saved out of its revenue. But the immediate effect of every such regulation is to diminish its revenue, and what diminishes its revenue is certainly not very likely to augment its capital faster than it would have augmented of its own accord had both capital and industry been left to find out their natural employments.

Though for want of such regulations the society should never acquire the proposed manufacture, it would not, upon that account, necessarily be the poorer in any one period of its duration. In every period of its duration its whole capital and industry might still have been employed, though upon different objects, in the manner that was most advantageous at the time. In every period its revenue might have been the greatest which its capital could afford, and both capital and revenue might have been augmented with the greatest possible rapidity.

The natural advantages which one country has over another in producing particular commodities are sometimes so great that it is acknowledged by all the world to be in vain to struggle with them. By means of glasses, hotbeds, and hot walls, very good grapes can be raised in Scotland, and very good wine too can be made of them at about thirty times the expense for which at least equally good can be brought from foreign countries. Would it be a reasonable law to prohibit the importation of all foreign wines merely to encourage the making of claret and burgundy in Scotland? But if there would be a manifest absurdity in turning towards any employment thirty times more of the capital and industry of the country than would be necessary to purchase from foreign countries an equal quantity of the commodities wanted, there must be an absurdity, though not altogether so glaring, yet exactly of the same kind, in turning towards any such employment a thirtieth, or even a three-hundredth part more of either. Whether the advantages which one country has over another be natural or acquired is in this respect of no consequence. As long as the one country has those advantages, and the other wants them, it will always be more advantageous for the latter rather to buy of the former than to make. It is an acquired advantage only, which one artificer has over his neighbour, who exercises another trade; and yet they both find it more advantageous to buy of one another than to make what does not belong to their particular trades.

Adam Smith. *The Wealth of Nations.* Originally published in 1776.

Rights of Man

Thomas Paine

THOMAS PAINE *(1737–1809), an Englishman, travelled to America at the age of 37, where he soon became familiar with the instability of the pre-revolutionary years. Later in 1790, while in France, he began writing a defence of the fundamental ideas of revolution. This culminated in an attack upon Edmund Burke's* Reflections on the French Revolution, *in his own* The Rights of Man.

The error of those who reason by precedents drawn from antiquity, respecting the rights of man, is, that they do not go far enough into antiquity. They do not go the whole way. They stop in some of the intermediate stages of an hundred or a thousand years, and produce what was then done, as a rule for the present day. This is no authority at all. If we travel still farther into antiquity, we shall find a direct contrary opinion and practice prevailing; and if antiquity is to be authority, a thousand such authorities may be produced, successively contradicting each other: But if we proceed on, we shall at last come out right; we shall come to the time when man came from the hand of his Maker. What was he then? Man. Man was his high and only title, and a higher cannot be given him.—But of titles I shall speak hereafter.

We are now got at the origin of man, and at the origin of his rights. As to the manner in which the world has been governed from that day to this, it is no further any concern of ours than to make a proper use of the errors or the improvements which the history of it presents. Those who lived a hundred or a thousand years ago, were then moderns, as we are now. They had *their* ancients, and those ancients had others, and we also shall be ancients in our turn. If the mere name of antiquity is to govern in the affairs of life, the people who are to live an hundred or a thousand years hence, may as well take us for a precedent, as we make a precedent of those who lived an hundred or a thousand years ago. The fact is, that portions of antiquity, by proving everything, establish nothing. It is authority against authority all the way, till we come to the divine origin of the rights of man at the creation. Here our inquiries find a resting-place, and our reason finds a home. If a dispute about the rights of man had arisen at the distance of an hundred years from the creation, it is to this source of authority they must have referred, and it is to the same source of authority that we must now refer.

Though I mean not to touch upon any sectarian principle of religion, yet it may be worth observing, that the genealogy of Christ is traced to Adam. Why then not trace the rights of man to the creation of man? I will answer the question. Because there have been upstart governments, thrusting themselves between, and presumptuously working to *unmake* man.

If any generation of men ever possessed the right of dictating the mode by which the world should be governed for ever, it was the first generation that existed; and if that generation did it not, no succeeding generation can show any authority for doing it, nor can set any up. The illuminating and divine principle of the equal rights of man, (for it has its origin from the Maker of man) relates, not only to the living individuals, but to generations of men succeeding each other. Every generation is equal in rights to the generation which preceded it, by the same rule that every individual is born equal in rights with his contemporary.

Every history of the creation, and every traditionary account, whether from the lettered or unlettered world, however they may vary in their opinion or belief of certain particulars, all agree in establishing one point, *the unity of man*; by which I mean, that men are all of *one degree*, and consequently that all men are born equal, and with equal natural right, in the same manner as if posterity had been continued by *creation* instead of *generation*, the latter being only the mode by which the former is carried forward; and consequently, every child born into the world must be considered as deriving its existence from God. The world is as new to him as it was to the first man that existed, and his natural right in it is of the same kind.

The Mosaic account of the creation, whether taken as divine authority, or merely historical, is full to this point, *the unity or equality of man*. The expressions admit of no controversy. "And God said, Let us make man in our own image. In the image of God created he him; male and female created he them." The distinction of sexes is pointed out, but no other distinction is even implied. If this be not divine authority, it is at least historical authority, and shows that the equality of man, so far from being a modern doctrine, is the oldest upon record.

It is also to be observed, that all the religions known in the world are founded, so far as they relate to man, on the *unity of man*, as being all of one degree. Whether in heaven or in hell, or in whatever state man may be supposed to exist hereafter, the good and the bad are the only distinctions. Nay, even the laws of governments are obliged to slide into this principle, by making degrees to consist in crimes, and not in persons.

It is one of the greatest of all truths, and of the highest advantage to cultivate. By considering man in this light, and by instructing him to consider himself in this light, it places him in a close connexion with all his duties, whether to his Creator, or to the creation, of which he is a part; and it is only when he forgets his origin, or, to use a more fashionable phrase, his *birth and family*, that he becomes dissolute. It is not among the least of the evils of the present existing governments in all parts of Europe, that man, considered as man, is thrown back to a vast distance from his Maker, and the artificial chasm filled up by a succession of barriers, or sort of turnpike gates, through which he has to pass. I will quote Mr Burke's catalogue of barriers that he

has set up between man and his Maker. Putting himself in the character of a herald, he says—"We fear God—we look with *awe* to kings—with affection to parliaments—with duty to magistrates—with reverence to priests, and with respect to nobility." Mr Burke has forgotten to put in "*chivalry*." He has also forgotten to put in Peter.

The duty of man is not a wilderness of turnpike gates, through which he is to pass by tickets from one to the other. It is plain and simple, and consists but of two points. His duty to God, which every man must feel; and with respect to his neighbour, to do as he would be done by. If those to whom power is delegated do well, they will be respected; if not, they will be despised: and with regard to those to whom no power is delegated, but who assume it, the rational world can know nothing of them.

Hitherto we have spoken only (and that but in part) of the natural rights of man. We have now to consider the civil rights of man, and to show how the one originates from the other. Man did not enter into society to become *worse* than he was before, nor to have fewer rights than he had before, but to have those rights better secured. His natural rights are the foundation of all his civil rights. But in order to pursue this distinction with more precision, it will be necessary to mark the different qualities of natural and civil rights.

A few words will explain this. Natural rights are those which appertain to man in right of his existence. Of this kind are all the intellectual rights, or rights of the mind, and also all those rights of acting as an individual for his own comfort and happiness, which are not injurious to the natural rights of others. Civil rights are those which appertain to man in right of his being a member of society. Every civil right has for its foundation, some natural right pre-existing in the individual, but to the enjoyment of which his individual power is not, in all cases, sufficiently competent. Of this kind are all those which relate to security and protection.

From this short review, it will be easy to distinguish between that class of natural rights which man retains after entering into society, and those which he throws into the common stock as a member of society.

The natural rights which he retains, are all those in which the *power* to execute is as perfect in the individual as the right itself. Among this class, as is before mentioned, are all the intellectual rights, or rights of the mind: consequently, religion is one of those rights. The natural rights which are not retained, are all those in which, though the right is perfect in the individual, the power to execute them is defective. They answer not his purpose. A man, by natural right, has a right to judge in his own cause; and so far as the right of mind is concerned, he never surrenders it: But what availeth it him to judge, if he has not power to redress? He therefore deposits this right in the common stock of society, and takes the arm of society, of which he is a part, in preference and in addition to his own. Society *grants* him nothing. Every man is a proprietor in society, and draws on the capital as a matter of right.

From these premises, two or three certain conclusions will follow.

First, That every civil right grows out of a natural right; or, in other words, is a natural right exchanged.

Secondly, That civil power, properly considered as such, is made up of the aggregate of that class of the natural rights of man, which becomes defective in the individual in point of power, and answers not his purpose; but when collected to a focus, becomes competent to the purpose of every one.

Thirdly, That the power produced from the aggregate of natural rights, imperfect in power in the individual, cannot be applied to invade the natural rights which are retained in the individual, and in which the power to execute is as perfect as the right itself.

We have now, in a few words, traced man from a natural individual to a member of society, and shown, or endeavoured to show, the quality of the natural rights retained, and of those which are exchanged for civil rights.

Thomas Paine. *The Rights of Man.* Originally published in 1791/2.

Of Individuality, As One of the Elements of Well-Being

John Stuart Mill

JOHN STUART MILL *(1806–1873), a British utilitarian philosopher, wrote several important philosophical works, notably* On Liberty, Utilitarianism, *and* System of Logic. *The first of these has had a lasting impression upon western political thought and proved to be one of the original analytical treatments of the subject of social freedom.*

Such being the reasons which make it imperative that human beings should be free to form opinions and to express their opinions without reserve; and such the baneful consequences to the intellectual, and through that to the moral nature of man, unless this liberty is either conceded or asserted in spite of prohibition; let us next examine whether the same reasons do not require that men should be free to act upon their opinions—to carry these out in their lives without hindrance, either physical or moral, from their fellow men, so long as it is at their own risk and peril. This last proviso is of course indispensable. No one pretends that actions should be as free as opinions. On the contrary, even opinions lose their immunity when the circumstances in which they are expressed are such as to constitute their expression a positive instigation to some mischievous act. An opinion that corn dealers are starvers of the poor, or that private property is robbery, ought to be unmolested when simply circulated through the press, but may justly incur punishment when delivered orally to an excited mob assembled before the house of a corn dealer, or when handed about among the same mob in the form of a placard. Acts, of whatever kind, which without justifiable cause do harm to others may be, and in the more important cases absolutely require to be, controlled by the unfavorable sentiments, and, when needful, by the active interference of mankind. The liberty of the individual must be thus far limited; he must not make himself a nuisance to other people. But if he refrains from molesting others in what concerns them, and merely acts according to his own inclination and judgment in things which concern himself, the same reasons which show that opinion should be free prove also that he should be allowed, without molestation, to carry his opinions into practice at his own cost. That mankind are not infallible; that their truths, for the most part, are only half-truths; that unity of opinion, unless resulting from the fullest and freest comparison of opposite opinions, is not desirable, and diversity not an evil, but a good, until mankind are much more capable than at present of recognizing all sides of the truth, are principles applicable to men's modes of action not less than to their opinions. As it is useful that while mankind are imperfect there should be different opinions, so it is that there should be different experiments of living; that free scope should be given to varieties of character, short of injury to others; and that the worth of different modes of life should be proved practically, when anyone thinks fit to try them. It is desirable, in short, that in things which do not primarily concern others individuality should assert itself. Where not the person's own character but the traditions or customs of other people are the rule of conduct, there is wanting one of the principal ingredients of human happiness, and quite the chief ingredient of individual and social progress.

In maintaining this principle, the greatest difficulty to be encountered does not lie in the appreciation of means toward an acknowledged end, but in the indifference of persons in general to the end itself. If it were felt that the free development of individuality is one of the leading essentials of well-being; that it is not only a co-ordinate element with all that is designated by the terms civilization, instruction, education, culture, but is itself a necessary part and condition of all those things, there would be no danger that liberty should be undervalued, and the adjustment of the boundaries between it and social control would present no extraordinary difficulty. But the evil is that individual spontaneity is hardly recognized by the common modes of thinking as having any intrinsic worth, or deserving any regard on its own account. The majority, being satisfied with the ways of mankind as they now are (for it is they who make them what they are), cannot comprehend why those ways should not be good enough for everybody; and what is more, spontaneity forms no part of the ideal of the majority of moral and social reformers, but is rather looked on with jealousy, as a troublesome and perhaps rebellious obstruction to the general acceptance of what these reformers, in their own judgement, think would be best for mankind. Few persons, out of Germany, even comprehend the meaning of the doctrine which Wilhelm van Humboldt,[1] so eminent both as a *savant* and as a politician, made the text of a treatise—that "the end of man, or that which is prescribed by the eternal or immutable dictates of reason, and not suggested by vague and transient desires, is the highest and most harmonious development of his powers to a complete and consistent whole"; that, therefore, the object "toward which every human being must ceaselessly direct his efforts, and on which especially those who design to influence their fellow men must ever keep their eyes, is the individuality of power and development"; that for this there are two requisites, "freedom, and variety of situations"; and that from the union of these arise "individual vigor and manifold diversity," which combine themselves in "originality."[2]

Little, however, as people are accustomed to a doctrine like that of von Humboldt, and surprising as it may be to them to find so high a value attached to individuality, the question, one must nevertheless think, can only be one of degree. No one's idea of excellence in conduct is that people should do absolutely nothing but copy one another. No one would assert that people ought not to put into their mode of life, and into the conduct of their concerns, any impress whatever of their own judgment or of their own individual character. On the other hand, it would be absurd to pretend that people ought to live as if nothing whatever had been known in the world before they came into it; as if experience had as yet done nothing toward showing that one mode of existence, or of conduct, is preferable to another. Nobody denies that people should be so taught and trained in youth as to know and benefit by the ascertained results of human experience. But it is the privilege and proper condition of a human being, arrived at the maturity of his faculties, to use and interpret experience in his own way. It is for him to find out what part of recorded experience is properly applicable to his own circumstances and characters. The traditions and customs of other people are, to a certain extent, evidence of what their experience has taught *them*—presumptive evidence, and as such, have a claim to his deference: but, in the first place, their experience may be too narrow, or they may have not interpreted it rightly. Secondly, their interpretation of experience may be correct, but unsuitable to him. Customs are made for customary circumstances and customary characters; and his circumstances or his character may be uncustomary. Thirdly, though the customs be both good as customs and suitable to him, yet to conform to custom merely *as* custom does not educate or develop in him any of the qualities which are the distinctive endowment of a human being. The human faculties of perception, judgment, discriminative feeling, mental activity, and even moral preference are exercised only in making a choice. He who does anything because it is the

<hr>

[1] Wilhelm von Humboldt (1767–1835) was a Prussian humanist and linguist who influenced Mill.
[2] These notions come from von Humboldt's *Sphere and Duties of Government*.

custom makes no choice. He gains no practice either in discerning or in desiring what is best. The mental and moral, like the muscular, powers are improved only by being used. The faculties are called into no exercise by doing a thing merely because others do it, no more than by believing a thing only because others believe it. If the grounds of an opinion are not conclusive to the person's own reason, his reason cannot be strengthened, but is likely to be weakened, by his adopting it: and if the inducements to an act are not such as are consentaneous to his own feelings and character (where affection, or the rights of others, are not concerned), it is so much done toward rendering his feelings and character inert and torpid instead of active and energetic.

He who lets the world, or his own portion of it, choose his plan of life for him has no need of any other faculty than the ape-like one of imitation. He who chooses his plan for himself employs all his faculties. He must use observation to see, reasoning and judgment to foresee, activity to gather materials for decision, discrimination to decide, and when he has decided, firmness and self-control to hold to his deliberate decision. And these qualities he requires and exercises exactly in proportion as the part of his conduct which he determines according to his own judgment and feelings is a large one. It is possible that he might be guided in some good path, and kept out of harm's way, without any of these things. But what will be his comparative worth as a human being? It really is of importance, not only what men do, but also what manner of men they are that do it. Among the works of man which human life is rightly employed in perfecting and beautifying, the first in importance surely is man himself. Supposing it were possible to get houses built, corn grown, battles fought, causes tried, and even churches erected and prayers said by machinery—by automatons in human form—it would be a considerable loss to exchange for these automatons even the men and women who at present inhabit the more civilized parts of the world, and who assuredly are but starved specimens of what nature can and will produce. Human nature is not a machine to be built after a model, and set to do exactly the work prescribed for it, but a tree, which requires to grow and develop itself on all sides, according to the tendency of the inward forces which make it a living thing.

John Stuart Mill. *On Liberty*. Originally published in 1859.

Part III
Reform Liberalism

JOHN MAYNARD KEYNES

The nineteenth century saw much of the optimism that characterised classical liberalism crushed by the jaws of the industrial revolution. Further, the competitive labour market and free trade that had come to be linked with classical liberalism proved not to be as beneficent as expected. There is an inkling of some of these difficulties in Mill's writings and more in T.H. Green's, but it is in John Dewey's work that we see the emergence of a new form of liberalism, chastened from the experiences of the nineteenth century. Dewey's pragmatism leads him to be skeptical of panaceas and grand solutions for eliminating injustices, but it also leads him to believe that scientific knowledge of social conditions when aided by a fertile imagination could improve the human condition. With Dewey there began to emerge the recognition, not only of negative liberty, but also of positive liberty wherein government facilitated the creation of institutions which helped man cultivate himself. Such was the social component of reform liberalism.

The economic component of reform liberalism was left for John Maynard Keynes to complete. Rather early in his career, he began to express serious doubts about the convergence of self-interest and public-interest. He grew less and less patient with laissez-faire economics and its invisible-hand explanation. Government, he thought, had to assume in society a role larger than that advocated by liberals in the past. In more recent times, this position of Keynes has been given fresh reinterpretation by John Kenneth Galbraith who claims the liberal's respect for the market is based on function not faith, requiring constant attention and choice. He draws attention to some areas in which

the market is categorically defective: in its failure to supply good housing to people of moderate income or below and in its failure to provide proper medical services to these same people. In saying this he parts company with classical liberals and with modern day conservatives.

Pursuing themes familiar to Dewey and Galbraith, C.B. Macpherson wrestles with the question: Can liberal-democracies retain the values of freedom and individuality? Referring to communist revolutions and revolutions in underdeveloped countries, Macpherson says these revolutions may teach us how to strengthen and retain our liberal values. They may do this by helping us see that the view of scarcity in relation to unlimited desire is a creation of the capitalist market. Once liberals recognize this, says Macpherson, they can move beyond dilemmas based on scarcity and unlimited desires, and thereby retain and strengthen their values.

William Sullivan casts doubt upon the ability of liberalism to construct a civic philosophy. Within liberalism he finds three parts: a theory of politics and society, a theory of human nature, and a conception of science and the nature of reason. Through the writings of Fred Hirsch, Daniel Bell, and Robert Heilbroner, Sullivan sees evidence of the liberal world coming unstuck.

In his seminal work, *A Theory of Justice*, John Rawls thinks of justice as fairness and proceeds to lay down two principles which he thinks would guide agents forced to choose behind a veil of ignorance: the equal liberty principle and the difference principle. The fact that these principles are meant to apply to institutions does much to drive Rawls's account in a liberal direction, even if the liberal direction is one rooted in a constititutional framework that seems remarkably American.

Finally John Lucas takes Rawls to task on his interpretation of justice, at least as given by his two principles. Lucas's accusation is directed not at Rawls's introduction of egalitarian measures of social democracy, but at his advocacy of a maximum strategy (a strategy which would make an adherent of it least badly off) which is a strategy of prudence rather than of justice. In short, he contends that the liberal constitution which Rawls argues for via egalitarianism may have little or nothing to do with justice.

The following writings are suggestive of fruitful lines of research in political philosophy. However, serious questions remain as to whether liberalism in its reformed variety can be restructured and altered to make it a viable and living ideology in a technological world.

Renascent Liberalism

John Dewey

JOHN DEWEY (1859–1952) was an influential American philosopher who wrote widely in the field of education and social philosophy. Studying at Johns Hopkins University, he went on to positions at the University of Michigan and University of Chicago where he established a reputation for his educational ideas. His most important writings are Experience and Nature, Logic: the Theory of Inquiry, and Liberalism and Social Action.

When, then, I say that the first object of a renascent liberalism is education, I mean that its task is to aid in producing the habits of mind and character, the intellectual and moral patterns, that are somewhere near even with the actual movements of events. It is, I repeat, the split between the latter as they have externally occurred and the ways of desiring, thinking, and of putting emotion and purpose into execution that is the basic cause of present confusion in mind and paralysis in action. The educational task cannot be accomplished merely by working upon men's minds, without action that effects actual change in institutions. The idea that dispositions and attitudes can be altered by merely "moral" means conceived of as something that goes on wholly inside of persons is itself one of the old patterns that has to be changed. Thought, desire and purpose exist in a constant give and take of interaction with environing conditions. But resolute thought is the first step in that change of action that will itself carry further the needed change in patterns of mind and character.

In short, liberalism must now become radical, meaning by "radical" perception of the necessity of thorough-going changes in the set-up of institutions and corresponding activity to bring the changes to pass. For the gulf between what the actual situation makes possible and the actual state itself is so great that it cannot be bridged by piecemeal policies undertaken *ad hoc*. The process of producing the changes will be, in any case, a gradual one. But "reforms" that deal now with this abuse and now with that without having a social goal based upon an inclusive plan, differ entirely from effort at re-forming, in its literal sense, the institutional scheme of things. The liberals of more than a century ago were denounced in their time as subversive radicals, and only when the new economic order was established did they become apologists for the *status quo* or else content with social patchwork. If radicalism be defined as perception of need for radical change, then today any liberalism which is not also radicalism is irrelevant and doomed.

But radicalism also means, in the minds of many, both supporters and opponents, dependence upon use of violence as the main method of effecting drastic changes. Here the liberal parts company. For he is committed to the organization of intelligent action as the chief method. Any frank discussion of the issue must recognize the extent to which those who decry the use of any violence are themselves willing to resort to violence and are ready to put their will into operation. Their fundamental objection is to change in the economic institution that now exists, and for its maintenance they resort to the use of the force that is placed in their hands by this very institution. They do not need to advocate the use of force; their only need is to employ it. Force, rather than intelligence, is built into the procedures of the existing social system, regularly as coercion, in times of crisis as overt violence. The legal system, conspicuously in its penal aspect, more subtly in civil practice, rests upon coercion. Wars are the methods recurrently used in settlement of disputes between nations. One school of radicals dwells upon the fact that in the past the transfer of power in one society has either been accomplished by or attended with violence. But what we need to realize is that physical force is used, at least in the form of coercion, in the very set-up of our society. That the competitive system, which was thought of by early liberals as the means by which the latent abilities of individuals were to be evoked and directed into socially useful channels, is now in fact a state of scarcely disguised battle hardly needs to be dwelt upon. That the control of the means of production by the few in legal possession operates as a standing agency of coercion of the many, may need emphasis in statement, but is surely evident to one who is willing to observe and honestly report the existing scene. It is foolish to regard the political state as the only agency now endowed with coercive power. Its exercise of this power is pale in contrast with that exercised by concentrated and organized property interests.

It is not surprising in view of our standing dependence upon the use of coercive force that at every time of crisis coercion breaks out into open violence. In this country, with its tradition of violence fostered by frontier conditions and by the conditions under which immigration went on during the greater part of our history, resort to violence is especially recurrent on the part of those who are in power. In times of imminent change, our verbal and sentimental worship of the Constitution, with its guarantees of civil liberties of expression, publication and assemblage, readily goes overboard. Often the officials of the law are the worst offenders, acting as agents of some power that rules the economic life of a community. What is said about the value of free speech as a safety valve is then forgotten with the utmost of ease: a comment, perhaps, upon the weakness of the defense of freedom of expression that values it simply as a means of blowing-off steam.

It is not pleasant to face the extent to which, as matter of fact, coercive and violent force is relied upon in the present social system as a means of social control. It is much more agreeable to evade the fact. But unless the fact is acknowledged as a fact in its full depth and breadth, the meaning of dependence upon intelligence as the alternative method of social direction will not be grasped. Failure in acknowledgment signifies, among other things, failure to realize that those who propagate the dogma of dependence upon force have the sanction of much that is already entrenched in the existing system. They would but turn the use of it to opposite ends. The assumption that the method of intelligence already rules and that those who urge the use of violence are introducing a new element into the social picture may not be hypocritical but it is unintelligently unaware of what is actually involved in intelligence as an alternative method of social action.

I begin with an example of what is really involved in the issue. Why is it, apart from our tradition of violence, that liberty of expression is tolerated and even lauded when social affairs seem to be going in a quiet fashion, and yet is so readily destroyed whenever matters grow critical? The general answer, of course, is that at bottom social institutions have habituated us to the use of force in some veiled form. But a part of the answer is found in our ingrained habit of regarding intelligence as an individual possession and its exercise as an individual right. It is false that freedom of inquiry and of expression are not modes of action. They are exceedingly potent modes of action. The reactionary grasps this fact, in practice if not in express idea, more quickly than the liberal, who is too much given to holding that this freedom is innocent of consequences, as well as being a merely individual right. The result is that this liberty is tolerated as long as it does not seem to menace in any way the *status quo* of society. When it does, every effort is put forth to identify the established order with the public good. When this identification is established, it follows that any merely individual right must yield to the general welfare. As long as freedom of thought and speech is claimed as a merely individual right, it will give way, as do other merely personal claims, when it is, or is successfully represented to be, in opposition to the general welfare.

I would not in the least disparage the noble fight waged by early liberals in behalf of individual freedom of thought and expression. We owe more to them than it is possible to record in words. No more eloquent words have ever come from any one than those of Justice Brandeis in the case of a legislative act that in fact restrained freedom of political expression. He said: "Those who won our independence believed that the final end of the State was to make men free to develop their faculties, and that in its government the deliberative faculties should prevail over the arbitrary. They valued liberty both as an end and as a means. They believed liberty to be the secret of happiness and courage to be the secret of liberty. They believed that freedom to think as you will and to speak as you think are means indispensable to the discovery and spread of political truth; that without free speech and assembly discussion would be futile; that with them, discussion affords ordinarily adequate protection against the dissemination of noxious doctrines; that the greatest menace to freedom is an inert people; that public discussion is a political duty; and that this should be a fundamental principle of the American government." This is the creed of a fighting liberalism. But the issue I am raising is connected with the fact that these words are found in a dissenting, a minority opinion of the Supreme Court of the United States. The public function of free individual thought and speech is clearly recognized in the words quoted. But the reception of the truth of the words is met by an obstacle: the old habit of defending liberty of thought and expression as something inhering in individuals apart from and even in opposition to social claims.

John Dewey. *Liberalism and Social Action*. New York: Capricorn Books, G.P. Putnam's Sons, 1963.

Laissez-Faire and Communism

John Maynard Keynes

JOHN MAYNARD KEYNES *(1883–1946) was one of the most influential economists of the twentieth century. His best known works are* A Treatise on Money; The General Theory of Employment, Interest and Money; *and* A Treatise on Probability.

The Assumptions of Economic Individualism

The principles of *laissez-faire* have had other allies besides economic text-books. They have been reinforced by the poor quality of the opponent proposals—Protectionism on one hand, and Marxian Socialism on the other. Yet these doctrines are both characterised, not only or chiefly by their infringing the general presumption in favour of *laissez-faire*, but by mere logical fallacy. Both are examples of poor thinking, of inability to analyse a process and follow it out to its conclusion. The arguments against them, though reinforced by the principle of *laissez-faire*, do not strictly require it. Of the two, Protectionism is at least plausible, and the forces making for its popularity are nothing to wonder at. But Marxian Socialism must always remain a portent to the historians of Opinion—how a doctrine so illogical and so dull can have exercised so powerful and enduring an influence over the minds of men, and, through them, the events of history. At any rate, the obvious scientific deficiencies of these two schools greatly contributed to the prestige and authority of nineteenth-century *laissez-faire*.

Nor has the most notable divergence into centralised social action on a great scale—the conduct of the late war—encouraged reformers or dispelled old-fashioned prejudices. There is much to be said on both sides. War experience in the organisation of socialised production has left some observers anxious to repeat it in peace conditions. War socialism unquestionably achieved a production of wealth on a scale far greater than we ever knew in Peace, for though the goods and services delivered were destined for immediate and fruitless extinction, none the less they were wealth. Nevertheless the dissipation of effort was also prodigious, and the atmosphere of waste and not counting the cost was disgusting to any thrifty or provident spirit.

Finally, Individualism and *laissez-faire* could not, in spite of their deep roots in the political and moral philosophies of the late eighteenth and early nineteenth centuries, have secured their lasting hold over the conduct of public affairs, if it had not been for their conformity with the needs and wishes of the business world of the day. They gave full scope to our erstwhile heroes, the great business men. "At least one-half of the best ability in the Western world," Marshall used to say, "is engaged in business." A great part of "the higher imagination" of the age was thus employed. It was on the activities of these men that our hopes of Progress were centred. "Men of this class," Marshall wrote,[1] "live in constantly shifting visions, fashioned in their own brains, of various routes to their desired end; of the difficulties which Nature will oppose to them on each route, and of the contrivances by which they hope to get the better of her opposition. This imagination gains little credit with the people, because it is not allowed to run riot; its strength is disciplined by a stronger will; and

---

[1] "The Social Possibilities of Economic Chivalry," *Economic Journal* (1907), xvii, p. 9.

its highest glory is to have attained great ends by means so simple that no one will know, and none but experts will even guess, how a dozen other expedients, each suggesting as much brilliancy to the hasty observer, were set aside in favour of it. The imagination of such a man is employed, like that of the master chess-player, in forecasting the obstacles which may be opposed to the successful issue of his far-reaching projects, and constantly rejecting brilliant suggestions because he has pictured to himself the counter-strokes to them. His strong nervous force is at the opposite extreme of human nature from that nervous irresponsibility which conceives hasty Utopian schemes, and which is rather to be compared to the bold facility of a weak player, who will speedily solve the most difficult chess problem by taking on himself to move the black men as well as the white."

This is a fine picture of the great Captain of Industry, the Master-Individualist, who serves us in serving himself, just as any other artist does. Yet this one, in his turn, is becoming a tarnished idol. We grow more doubtful whether it is he who will lead us into Paradise by the hand.

These many elements have contributed to the current intellectual bias, the mental make-up, the orthodoxy of the day. The compelling force of many of the original reasons has disappeared, but, as usual, the vitality of the conclusions outlasts them. To suggest social action for the public good to the City of London is like discussing the *Origin of Species* with a Bishop sixty years ago. The first reaction is not intellectual, but moral. An orthodoxy is in question, and the more persuasive the arguments the graver the offence. Nevertheless, venturing into the den of the lethargic monster, at any rate I have traced his claims and pedigree so as to show that he has ruled over us rather by hereditary right than by personal merit.

The Future Organisation of Society

Let us clear from the ground the metaphysical or general principles upon which, from time to time, *laissez-faire* has been founded. It is *not* true that individuals possess a prescriptive "natural liberty" in their economic activities. There is *no* "compact" conferring perpetual rights on those who Have or on those who Acquire. The world is *not* so governed from above that private and social interest always coincide. It is *not* so managed here below that in practice they coincide. It is *not* a correct deduction from the Principles of Economics that enlightened self-interest always operates in the public interest. Nor is it true that self-interest generally *is* enlightened; more often individuals acting separately to promote their own ends are too ignorant or too weak to attain even these. Experience does *not* show that individuals, when they make up a social unit, are always less clear-sighted than when they act separately.

We cannot therefore settle on abstract grounds, but must handle on its merits in detail what Burke termed "one of the finest problems in legislation, namely, to determine what the State ought to take upon itself to direct by the public wisdom, and what it ought to leave, with as little interference as possible, to individual exertion."[1] We have to discriminate between what Bentham, in his forgotten but useful nomenclature, used to term *Agenda* and *Non-Agenda*, and to do this without Bentham's prior presumption that interference is, at the same time, "generally needless" and "generally pernicious."[2] Perhaps the chief task of Economists at this hour is to distinguish afresh the *Agenda* of Government from the *Non-Agenda*; and the companion task of Politics is to devise forms of Government within a Democracy which shall be capable of accomplishing the *Agenda*. I will illustrate what I have in mind by two examples.

(1) I believe that in many cases the ideal size for the unit of control and organisation lies somewhere between the individual and the modern State. I suggest, therefore, that progress lies in the growth and the recognition of semi-autonomous bodies within the State— bodies whose criterion of action within their own fields is solely the public good as they

---

[1] Quoted by M'Culloch in his *Principles of Political Economy*.

[2] Bentham's *Manual of Political Economy*, published posthumously, in Bowring's edition (1843).

understand it, and from whose deliberations motives of private advantage are excluded, though some place it may still be necessary to leave, until the ambit of men's altruism grows wider, to the separate advantage of particular groups, classes, or faculties—bodies which in the ordinary course of affairs are mainly autonomous within their prescribed limitations, but are subject in the last resort to the sovereignty of the democracy expressed through Parliament.

I propose a return, it may be said, towards mediæval conceptions of separate autonomies. But, in England at any rate, corporations are a mode of government which has never ceased to be important and is sympathetic to our institutions. It is easy to give examples, from what already exists, of separate autonomies which have attained or are approaching the mode I designate—the Universities, the Bank of England, the Port of London Authority, even perhaps the Railway Companies. In the United States there are doubtless analogous instances.

But more interesting than these is the trend of Joint Stock Institutions, when they have reached a certain age and size, to approximate to the status of public corporations rather than that of individualistic private enterprise. One of the most interesting and unnoticed developments of recent decades has been the tendency of big enterprise to socialise itself. A point arrives in the growth of a big institution—particularly a big railway or big public utility enterprise, but also a big bank or a big insurance company—at which the owners of the capital, *i.e.* the shareholders, are almost entirely dissociated from the management, with the result that the direct personal interest of the latter in the making of great profit becomes quite secondary. When this stage is reached, the general stability and reputation of the institution are more considered by the management than the maximum of profit for the shareholders. The shareholders must be satisfied by conventionally adequate dividends; but once this is secured, the direct interest of the management often consists in avoiding criticism from the public and from the customers of the concern. This is particularly the case if their great size or semi-monopolistic position renders them conspicuous

in the public eye and vulnerable to public attack. The extreme instance, perhaps, of this tendency in the case of an institution, theoretically the unrestricted property of private persons, is the Bank of England. It is almost true to say that there is no class of persons in the Kingdom of whom the Governor of the Bank of England thinks less when he decides on his policy than of his shareholders. Their rights, in excess of their conventional dividend, have already sunk to the neighborhood of zero. But the same thing is partly true of many other big institutions. They are, as time goes on, socialising themselves.

Not that this is unmixed gain. The same causes promote conservatism and a waning of enterprise. In fact, we already have in these cases many of the faults as well as the advantages of State Socialism. Nevertheless we see here, I think, a natural line of evolution. The battle of Socialism against unlimited private profit is being won in detail hour by hour. In these particular fields—it remains acute elsewhere—this is no longer the pressing problem. There is, for instance, no so-called important political question so really unimportant, so irrelevant to the re-organisation of the economic life of Great Britain, as the Nationalisation of the Railways.

It is true that many big undertakings, particularly Public Utility enterprises and other business requiring a large fixed capital, still need to be semi-socialised. But we must keep our minds flexible regarding the forms of this semi-socialism. We must take full advantage of the natural tendencies of the day, and we must probably prefer semi-autonomous corporations to organs of the Central Government for which Ministers of State are directly responsible.

I criticise doctrinaire State Socialism, not because it seeks to engage men's altruistic impulses in the service of Society, or because it departs from *laissez-faire*, or because it takes away from man's natural liberty to make a million, or because it has courage for bold experiments. All these things I applaud. I criticise it because it misses the significance of what is actually happening; because it is, in fact, little better than a dusty survival of a plan to meet the problems of fifty years ago, based on a misunderstanding of what someone said a hundred years ago. Nineteenth-century State Socialism sprang from Bentham, free competition, etc., and is in some respects a clearer, in some respects a more muddled version of just the same philosophy as underlies nineteenth-century individualism. Both equally laid all their stress on freedom, the one negatively to avoid limitations on existing freedom, the other positively to destroy natural or acquired monopolies. They are different reactions to the same intellectual atmosphere.

John Maynard Keynes. *Laissez-Faire and Communism*. New York: New Republic, 1926.

What It Means to be a Liberal Today

John Kenneth Galbraith

JOHN KENNETH GALBRAITH (1908–),
*Canadian-born economist and writer, is Professor
of Economics at Harvard University. He has
written widely including the well-known books*
The New Industrial State *and* The Affluent
Society. *During the Kennedy administration he
served as economic advisor to the President and as
the American ambassador to India.*

The liberal views the market in practical terms. Our respect for the market derives from function, not faith. As the conservative righteously avoids the insufferable pain of thought by saying, "we must not interfere with the free market," we recognize that this is a matter requiring clear and careful and constantly changing choice.

There are certain things the market does not do, products and services it does not provide. And from the free operation of the market there is injustice, pain and hardship, which no society, either from compassion or wisdom, can tolerate. This we accept; from this acceptance comes the complementary role of the state. This role we support not with reluctance or apology but with fully avowed belief in its necessity and advantage.

There are some matters on which the market is in inescapable default. In no industrial country does it supply good housing to people of moderate income or below. Nor does it supply medical and health services to the least advantaged people. Or good mass transportation in the cities. Or, needless to say, education of the required universality and quality. These things the market does not do.

The market in its pristine form also administers hardship that no civilized community can tolerate, hardships that are in conflict with the social tranquility that even conservatives should value. The experience here is wholly evident.

In the market economy of the last century, which numerous conservatives now seek romantically to recover, the old were discarded without income. So also were workers when no longer needed. Children were ruthlessly exploited, as also their mothers.

It was one of the great civilizing steps of modern society when these (and other) oppressions were corrected. Without this action—old-age pensions, unemployment compensation, aid to the otherwise financially distressed, public housing, medical care—capitalism would not have survived.

There was other needed remedial action, some still acutely controversial. The free market was never tolerable for agriculture except in the more vacuous rhetoric of the free market supplicants and the writings of the more ideologically disciplined economists.

In industry generally there is a measure of implicit control over production with resulting protection of prices; that is the nature of modern large-scale industry. In agriculture no individual producer has any influence on aggregate production. This and the high rate of productivity gains in modern times have committed agriculture to an insouciant over-production. In consequence, no advanced industrial country—none—leaves its farmers to the market. The oratory to the contrary, none ever will.

There is a further matter on which liberals take an adverse view of current ideological fashion. As always, we seek an economic world in which all can participate and from which all have a decent return. We want progress toward greater equality of return; we see this as a broadly civilizing tendency in modern society. In support of this goal we stand firmly for the principle of effectively progressive taxation and for income and other welfare support to the disadvantaged and the poor.

Here we encounter another ideological aberration of our time. That is the effort to make increasing inequality socially respectable. It is not permissible in the modern democratic polity ever to legislate explicitly for the rich. Accordingly, there must be a cover story, however implausible; what is wanted cannot be admitted. I speak of the recent experience of the U.S. We have had, in recent years, large reductions in the effective rates of the income tax on the very rich. And also a powerful crusade against the welfare services to the poor.

The rich, it is held, need incentive to greater economic effort; the poor need release from the debilitating effect of welfare; they must, in the words of one exceptionally convenient contemporary philosopher, have "the spur of their own poverty." The rich have not been working because they have too little money; the poor have not been working because they have too much.

As liberals, we accord the rich and privileged the full right to urge economic policy and legislative action that are in their own interest. We accept that this will be disguised as a profound service to the public interest. Accordingly, we are relentless in our efforts to expose such effort and in subjecting it to well-articulated ridicule. Never should we deny ourselves the pleasure of making clear the truth. We relish free speech not least when it is inconvenient to comfortable privilege.

In keeping with the now fully recognized need, liberals are committed to effective macroeconomic management of the economy—to the prevention of inflation and mass unemployment. Unlike conservatives, we see no magic in monetary policy that will accomplish this task through the genius of the central bank and my friend Prof. Milton Friedman.

This is economic escapism.

And since the instrument of monetarism against inflation is high interest rates, it is also a policy that rewards the affluent. People with money to lend, it will be broadly agreed, have more money than those who do not have money to lend.

The liberal reliance must be on fiscal policy—budget restraint when demand presses on industrial capacity, budget support to the economy when this is needed. This is politically the more difficult course. It is far easier to reduce taxes to support economic activity than to raise them as an act of restraint.

We do not retreat from this difficulty as, I regret to say, conservatives and some liberals now do in the U.S. and perhaps also here in Canada. Modern conservative policy in the U.S., as all will have observed, combines large budget deficits with relatively high real interest rates and places its faith in the somewhat questionable proposition that God is a good Republican.

With a sensible macroeconomic policy must go a system of negotiated restraints in wage and price policy in the organized sector of the economy as a primary weapon in the defence against inflation. This—a wage policy that is consistent as to result with stable prices—is now commonplace in Austria, Switzerland, Scandinavia, broadly in Germany and, needless to say, in Japan. It is the English-speaking countries that, in the main, have been reluctant to come to such a policy. We evidently see ourselves as the last refuge of the class struggle.

John Kenneth Galbraith. "What It Means to be a Liberal Today." *The Financial Post*. September 21, 1987: 10. The substance of this was given in an address to the Liberal International Congress in Ottawa.

The Near Future of Democracy and Human Rights

C. B. Macpherson

C.B. MACPHERSON *(1911–1987) was a distinguished Canadian political philosopher whose best known works are* The Political Theory of Possessive Individualism: Hobbes to Locke, The Real World of Democracy, *and* The Life and Times of Liberal Democracy.

In the first lecture of this series I raised certain questions about the future of democracy. And in the five lectures so far I have drawn attention to some facts about the present world position of democracy which are often neglected or under-rated, and have pointed to some of the implications of these facts. We might pause now to take stock to see whether the results of our factual analysis so far can help us with our original questions or with any reformulation of the questions which might now seem to be in order.

The original questions themselves arose from the recognition of one new fact about democracy, or rather, from the conjunction of this new fact with an older-established one. The new fact was that the Western democracies no longer have or expect to have a monopoly of civilization or world leadership, but that two other concepts of democracy now share the world with us. These are the Soviet concept and the one that prevails in most of the newly-independent underdeveloped countries; both are embodied in actually operating political systems, and both are non-liberal.

This new fact impinges on the somewhat older fact that the great majority of people in the Western liberal-democracies place a high value on the unique characteristics of the liberal-democratic state. What is valued most highly is the civil liberties which it generally affords: freedom of speech, freedom of association, and freedom from arbitrary arrest and detention. Beyond that, we value the way our governments can be held somewhat responsible to the majority will through the competition of political parties, parties which can be freely formed and between which individuals are free to choose at the periodical general elections which authorize governments. These civil and political liberties, though far from perfectly realized in liberal-democracies, are their unique achievement, and we put a high value on them.

So there are two facts. The one is that we put a high value on these liberties. The other is that liberal-democracy now has to live in a world two-thirds of which is practising some other political system, and practising or aspiring to some other kind of society. It is the conjunction of these two facts that raises the important questions for democracy today. The questions I proposed arose directly or indirectly out of this new situation. Can we keep our unique system? Or can we keep what we most value in it?

These were our questions. What material have we for dealing with them? We might summarize the propositions that have come out of our analysis.

First, the liberal-democratic state was liberal and market-oriented first and democratic later. That is to say, the democratic franchise was a later addition to a well-established liberal state, the mechanism of which was competitive non-democratic parties, and the purpose of which was to provide the conditions for a competitive, capitalist, market society. By the time the liberal state was democratized, the demand of the democratic forces was to get into the competition, not to discard it for any other kind of social order.

Second, the democratic franchise was used to turn the old liberal *laissez-faire* state into a welfare and regulatory state. The change would have taken place anyway, since the politicians of the day were aware that this was necessary to buy off politically dangerous discontent. But the welfare and regulatory state has not altered the essential nature of the capitalist market society. The proof of this depends on our third proposition.

Third, the capitalist market society necessarily contains a continuous transfer of part of the powers of some men to others. It does so because it requires concentrated ownership and control, in relatively few hands, of the capital and resources which are the only means of labour for the rest. Since the rest must have access to the means of labour, they must pay for that access by a transfer of part of their powers (or part of the product of their powers) to the owners of the means of labour. The welfare state may enforce transfers in the other direction, but these can never be as large as the original and continuing transfer. For that would kill capitalist enterprise, whereas the welfare state relies on capitalist enterprise to carry on the main productive work of the society. The welfare state is only a variation on the theme of capitalist market society.

Fourth, on any non-slavish definition of the powers of a man, or of the human essence as the rational pursuit of conscious purposes, the transfer of part of the powers of a man that is inherent in the capitalist market society is a diminution of the human essence.

Fifth, while the justifying theory of the liberal-democratic market society has leaned heavily on the theory that the fully competitive market maximizes utilities over the whole society, the maximizing theory is demonstrably inadequate to justify the system, for it assumes what it is supposed to prove. You can only demonstrate that the market maximizes utilities if you take for granted a given distribution of incomes: the market only maximizes the satisfactions people can afford to buy. And in a capitalist market society, however fully competitive, incomes cannot be proportional to people's expenditure of energy and skill, because the market has to reward ownership as well as exertion. Moreover, we have moved a long way from the fully competitive market: to the extent that corporations can control output and prices, their decisions no longer contribute to the maximizing of utilities over the whole society.

Sixth, in the justifying theories of all three kinds of democracy the ultimate ethical principle, at the highest level of generality, is the same. In each case the aim is to provide the conditions for the free development of human capacities, and to do this equally for all members of the society. In each case the essence of man is taken to be activity in pursuit of a rational conscious purpose. And in each case the realization of this essence is seen to require both freedom and equality: freedom of each individual from subservience to the wills of others, and equality in this freedom.

It is when we move down from the highest level of generality that the serious differences between the three kinds become apparent. It will be sufficient here, in summary, to concentrate on the distinction between the liberal and the non-liberal types, which we may try to state in the next two propositions.

Seventh, the non-liberal concepts of democracy, that is, the Marxian concept which prevails in the Soviet countries, and what we may call the Rousseauan concept which is more typical of the newly-independent underdeveloped countries, have one thing in common. They both hold that the requisite equality of human rights or human freedom cannot be provided in a market society, and therefore they put first on their agenda the move away from the market society. They are not interested in the freedom of individual acquisition of property, for they find this to be not only not necessary to but inconsistent with their vision of real human freedom and equal human rights. Nor do they give a high priority in their scale of values to the political freedoms. Believing as they do that the most important thing is the reformation of society, and realizing that this requires political power, they are not prepared to encourage or even allow such political freedoms as might hinder their power to reform the society. Thus political freedoms come a poor second to the drive for the new kind of society they believe to be necessary for the realization of equal human rights. Freedom is sacrificed to equality; or, more accurately, present freedoms are sacrificed to a vision of fuller and more equal freedom in the future. Freedom, in this view, contradicts itself: to get it in the future is to deny it in the present.

Eighth, the liberal concept of democracy, emphasizing the present freedoms of the market society and the political freedoms of a competitive party system, is caught up in a different contradiction. The freedom of the market society necessarily includes the freedom to acquire material possessions. Freedom of acquisition is absolutely essential, for the market society relies on the motive of acquisition to get the work of the society done. Freedom of acquisition is so necessary to the market society that it tends to take first place in the scale of values. But this freedom contradicts itself. For given the natural inequalities of strength and skill, freedom of acquisition leads to some men getting possession of the capital and resources that are the means of labour for all the others. This makes it impossible for the others to have freedom of acquisition: they have to pay for access to the means of labour with the loss of some of their powers.

Ninth, the technological advances made by capitalism have enormously increased our material productivity, with different effects on freedom and the human essence in different parts of the world. In the West, the sheer increase in the volume of material satisfactions has overshadowed the shortcomings of capitalist society in respect of freedom and of equality of individual opportunity to realize the human essence. At the same time, in the non-capitalist countries, the need for increasing productivity is largely responsible for their greater lack of freedom. The effort to catch up with the high productivity of capitalism, starting from a low base, requires a compulsive accumulation of social capital by the use of state power. It requires, that is to say, more, and more obvious, compulsions than are required in an advanced capitalist society with an already accumulated stock of capital.

Tenth, we have to expect, as a result of automation and the discovery and control of new sources of non-human energy, increases in productivity in the next few decades far exceeding the increases of the past, both in amount and in speed. But since these increases can now be expected not only in the most advanced capitalist countries but also in the most advanced socialist countries, the increases will not be attributable to capitalism and so will not automatically be taken to offset the shortcomings of capitalist society. On the contrary, such future increases in productivity will heighten two effects that are already apparent as a result of recent increases. First, the liberal, capitalist ethos will have to meet increasingly stiff ideological competition from the Soviet, socialist ethos. And second, the level of expectation of the underdeveloped peoples will increase, thus increasing their present sense of injustice at the unequal distribution of human opportunity between the rich countries (which are mostly capitalist) and the poor countries. This sense of injustice is already pressing somewhat on the conscience of the West, and the moral feedback is likely to get stronger.

With these ten propositions before us we may return to our central question. Can we in the liberal-democracies retain the values of freedom and individuality that we most cherish?

I shall suggest that the communist revolutions, and the revolutions in the underdeveloped countries, which together seem to threaten our way of life, may be the saving of it. If we read the lessons of these revolutions properly, they may lead us to a recognition of what we have to do to retain and strengthen our liberal values. Liberal values have now to compete, as they never had to do before, with non-liberal democratic values. But the very thing that has brought competitors to the liberal society into the field can release us from the dilemma which has plagued the liberal capitalist society up to now. What has brought competitors into the field is the fact, and the prospect, that the present and future productive techniques of capitalism can be transferred to non-capitalist societies, and can in those societies be used to enlarge the freedom and humanity of man. This same prospective increase in productive powers can, if we will it and if we see what we are about, release us from the dilemma of the liberal capitalist market society. For the dilemma exists only when it is assumed, as the Western market societies have up to now assumed, that the permanent condition of mankind is a condition of scarcity in relation to unlimited desires. The dilemma has been that if we allow freedom to naturally unequal individuals, we are in fact denying equal freedom and humanity to all but the stronger and more skilful. For to allow freedom of enterprise and of acquisition has been to deny equal access to the means of labour, that is, to deny equal access to the means of a fully human life. The choice had to be made between freedom along with denial of full humanity to all but the stronger and more skilful, or denial of freedom in the interest of more equal chances of humanity. The liberal capitalist society chose freedom and denial of full humanity. The choice no longer has to be made. It had to be made only while scarcity was king, and while, therefore, the incentive of unlimited freedom of acquisition was needed to get the increased production that was desired.

The implacable force in the drama of liberal society was scarcity in relation to unlimited desire. It was scarcity and unlimited desire that made the drama, and while it lasted it was tragedy. But now we can see it for what it has become, melodrama. Scarcity in relation to unlimited desire can now be seen for what it

is, merely the villain in a melodrama, who can be disposed of before the play is finished. We can begin to recognize now that the vision of scarcity in relation to unlimited desire was a creation of the capitalist market society. Certainly, before the advent of that society, nobody assumed that unlimited desire was the natural and proper attribute of the human being. You do not find it in Aristotle or in St. Thomas Aquinas. You begin to find it only with the rise of the capitalist market society in the seventeenth century, in Hobbes and in Locke, and it is carried to its logical conclusion by James Mill, at the beginning of the nineteenth century, for whom the "grand governing law of human nature" was the insatiable desire of every man for power to render the person and properties of others subservient to his pleasures.

The dilemma was still a real one when James Mill grappled with it. But it is no longer so. We have been, or rather we can be, liberated from the dilemma of scarcity by the new productivity of which we dispose in prospect. We can see now that men are not by nature infinitely desirous creatures, but were only made so by the market society, which compelled men to seek ever greater power in order to maintain even a modest level of satisfactions.

C.B. Macpherson. *The Real World of Democracy*. Toronto: CBC Enterprises, 1965.

The Contemporary Crisis of Liberal Society

William M. Sullivan

WILLIAM M. SULLIVAN *is Associate Professor of Philosophy at LaSalle College. He is the co-editor of* Interpretive Social Science: a Reader.

The present crisis of government is a general crisis of the liberal capitalist form of society. The word *liberal* here refers in particular to the philosophy of government that has dominated political discourse in modern America, but it also suggests a general cast of mind found throughout the society and typical of much of American culture. Liberalism is thus both a philosophical teaching usually identified with the European Enlightenment thinkers of the seventeenth and eighteenth centuries and also a popular set of attitudes at work in day-to-day life. As a philosophy, liberalism includes three parts: a theory of politics and society, a theory of human nature, and a conception of science and the nature of reason. Liberalism views politics as a structure of institutions designed to protect civil society, which it sees as a realm of contracts among individuals. These contractual relationships are entered into because they are necessary or useful for individuals as means to pursue their private ends. Both the compulsory realm of government and the voluntary, contractual realm of social institutions including the family, church, and business are instruments to be utilized by individuals to advance their own needs and desires.

Thus the moral and political outlook of liberalism is instrumental in its view of political and social life. It identifies value with what is useful to the individual. Human beings are conceived of as self-interested individuals driven by their passions to fulfill their needs by means of rational calculation and planning. This view of human nature is in turn sup-ported by the notion that reason is a tool for analysis, taking apart the elements of a situation or entity so as to reorganize it for greater usefulness. The logical goal of liberal rationality is a scientific social engineering that will be able to bring about a perfect adjustment of needs and wants. Economics has thus represented the nearest approximation to the liberal ideal of a social science with applications for social engineering.

In practical life, liberalism has been embodied in a public philosophy that has conceived of government as a balancing of private interests, the social basis for which is the operation of the market economy. The great mission of government, and in particular the law, has been understood as the defense of individual security of person and possessions, a liberty to be extended with equal care to all citizens. It was this public philosophy that after World War II ruled American political discussion virtually without challenge. But today, as this utilitarian and instrumental spirit weakens in the face of apparently intractable obstacles, philosophic liberalism is forced to play a role it is ill-suited to play. It must answer not simply problems of management but root questions about the moral justification of the whole economic and social order.

As a public philosophy liberalism has from its early formulations in the seventeenth century deliberately restricted its aim and aspirations toward promoting the human good to a manageable, calculative level. Promoting freedom, that is, security and prosperity through economic calculation, promised to provide a safer basis for public peace and order than the dangerous passions of aristocratic honor, religious enthusiasm, or civic virtue. Yet the pursuit of prosperity, the augmentation of what is one's own, not only dampens the dangerous ardor for glory; it also threatens to slacken the sinews of self-restraint and moral virtue. As Alexis de Tocqueville noted, liberal societies need restraints upon self-interest precisely as they succeed in becoming prosperous, if they are to maintain the public concern and respect for fellow citizens upon which their cohesion depends.[1] Yet modern American society, persuaded by corporate advertising and politicians alike, has come increasingly to empty the domain of public morality of traditional imperatives of loyalty and obligation, and has come to see social life only in terms of the self-interest of the isolated individual. And now the end of the era of cheap resources is putting tremendous strain on the American system of government-guided capitalism by throttling the engine of economic growth.

The crisis of legitimacy or, as it is sometimes called, the crisis of authority is straining to their limits the cultural and intellectual resources of the liberal tradition.[2] The questioning of the basic assumptions of liberal society is of necessity a piecemeal process. Our ways of thought, like our day-to-day lives, have been formed through an historical experience of which liberalism is a major part. Yet, the sense of malaise is pervasive and the search for an understanding of our problems is opening up questions about the whole liberal conception of life. Such fundamental questioning of the premises of philosophic liberalism is necessary to gain an understanding of our possibilities as a people.

If our crisis is as severe as much current social analysis suggests, then a renewed sense of public commitment cannot be generated by a return to the earlier policy of economic growth or by appeals to self-interest alone. The larger problems dogging government require a confrontation with the hard questions of moral and political experience: what changes will have to take place in the Unites States if there is to develop a consensus about the general welfare that will arouse citizen initiative? Over the long run, the only alternative

to a public process of struggling with these difficulties is an imposed social discipline. Social changes are inevitable.

Several contemporary social analysts are particularly helpful in grasping the dimensions of our contemporary situation. Fred Hirsch was until his death in 1979 an eminent British economist of world stature. Daniel Bell is a major American social theorist whose career has involved him for many years in trying to gain an overview of the changes our society is undergoing. Robert Heilbroner is also an American and an economist of extraordinary historical and theoretical breadth. All three thinkers have been deeply engaged in studying the workings of liberal society. They have likewise given prolonged reflection to liberal theories of government and culture, and yet display no unanimity in ideology or political stance. Thus it is particularly noteworthy that they all portray the liberal world as coming unstuck as the workings of its basic institutions generate effects destructive of the natural and social environment they depend upon for their survival. The whole liberal construction of an analytic science, an individualistic motivation, and an instrumental, utilitarian politics, which had seemed a complete and objectively secured—almost self-evident— view of human affairs, is now at sea.

It is as though a long-familiar background were suddenly being removed, a background so familiar it had become largely invisible, yet one which, it can now be seen, had been indispensable if the clearly etched foreground was to maintain its shape. The foreground is the world of liberal thought and practice, so long the focus of public discussion and interest. The rediscovered background is a dimension of moral and social life that liberalism has ignored or denied, yet one that is crucial if the values of liberal morality, particularly liberty and equal justice for all, are to be maintained and extended. Hirsch, Bell, and Heilbroner reveal in persuasive ways that the world of liberal individualism has depended for its

---

[1] See Alexis de Tocqueville, *Democracy in America*, translated by George Lawrence (Garden City, New York: Doubleday, 1969). pp. 534, 540.

[2] From the Left, the issue has been explored trenchantly by Jürgen Habermas, *Legitimation Crisis* (Boston: Beacon Press, 1975). Sociologist Robert Nisbet has addressed a similar problem from a neo-conservative perspective in *The Twilight of Authority* (New York: Basic Books, 1975).

viability upon moral and social relations of a quite different texture. The paradoxical effect of the growth of liberal capitalist society has been to undermine those social relations which have historically restrained and modified self-interested competition. Discussion of these relationships against this wider background will provide a perspective on the efforts of contemporary liberal thinkers to address the problems of political legitimacy and social cohesion. Since the difficulties these liberal theorists encounter are bound up with the suppressed social and moral background, a critical examination of their work will provide a basis for attempting to recover a public philosophy more adequate than liberalism, a civic philosophy that has been with us all along, though it has often been eclipsed. Articulation of a renewed civic philosophy is vital if the American promises of liberty and genuine equality are to be extended—as they must be if the nation is to survive as a free society. It is now time that civic philosophy again find its voice.

William M. Sullivan. *Reconstructing Public Philosophy*. Berkeley: University of California Press, 1982.

The Principles of Justice

John Rawls

JOHN RAWLS *(1921–) is Professor of Philosophy at Harvard University. He has made numerous contributions to journals and written* A Theory of Justice, *one of the most widely read books in political philosophy.*

Two Principles of Justice

I shall now state in a provisional form the two principles of justice that I believe would be chosen in the original position. In this section I wish to make only the most general comments, and therefore the first formulation of these principles is tentative. As we go on I shall run through several formulations and approximate step by step the final statement to be given much later. I believe that doing this allows the exposition to proceed in a natural way.

The first statement of the two principles reads as follows.

First: each person is to have an equal right to the most extensive basic liberty compatible with a similar liberty for others.

Second: social and economic inequalities are to be arranged so that they are both (a) reasonably expected to be to everyone's advantage, and (b) attached to positions and offices open to all. There are two ambiguous phrases in the second principle, namely "everyone's advantage" and "equally open to all." ...

By way of general comment, these principles primarily apply, as I have said, to the basic structure of society. They are to govern the assignment of rights and duties and to regulate the distribution of social and economic advantages. As their formulation suggests, these principles presuppose that the social structure can be divided into two more or less distinct parts, the first principle applying to the one, the second to the other. They distinguish between those aspects of the social system that define and secure the equal liberties of citizenship and those that specify and establish social and economic inequalities. The basic liberties of citizens are, roughly speaking, political liberty (the right to vote and to be eligible for public office) together with freedom of speech and assembly; liberty of conscience and freedom of thought; freedom of the person along with the right to hold (personal) property; and freedom from arbitrary arrest and seizure as defined by the concept of the rule of law. These liberties are all required to be equal by the first principle, since citizens of a just society are to have the same basic rights.

The second principle applies, in the first approximation, to the distribution of income and wealth and to the design of organizations that make use of differences in authority and responsibility, or chains of command. While the distribution of wealth and income need not be equal, it must be to everyone's advantage, and at the same time, positions of authority and offices of command must be accessible to all. One applies the second principle by holding positions open, and then, subject to this constraint, arranges social and economic inequalities so that everyone benefits.

These principles are to be arranged in a serial order with the first principle prior to the second. This ordering means that a departure from the institutions of equal liberty required by the first principle cannot be justified by, or compensated for, by greater social and economic advantages. The distribution of wealth and income, and the hierarchies of authority, must be consistent with both the liberties of equal citizenship and equality of opportunity.

It is clear that these principles are rather specific in their content, and their acceptance rests on certain assumptions that I must eventually try to explain and justify. A theory of justice depends upon a theory of society in ways that will become evident as we proceed. For the present, it should be observed that the two principles (and this holds for all formulations) are a special case of a more general conception of justice that can be expressed as follows.

All social values—liberty and opportunity, income and wealth, and the bases of self-respect—are to be distributed equally unless an unequal distribution of any, or all, of these values is to everyone's advantage.

Injustice, then, is simply inequalities that are not to the benefit of all. Of course, this conception is extremely vague and requires interpretation.

As a first step, suppose that the basic structure of society distributes certain primary goods, that is, things that every rational man is presumed to want. These goods normally have a use whatever a person's rational plan of life. For simplicity, assume that the chief primary goods at the disposition of society are rights and liberties, powers and opportunities, income and wealth... These are the social primary goods. Other primary goods such as health and vigor, intelligence and imagination, are natural goods; although their possession is influenced by the basic structure, they are not so directly under its control. Imagine, then, a hypothetical initial arrangement in which all the social primary goods are equally distributed: everyone has similar rights and duties, and income and wealth are evenly shared. This state of affairs provides a benchmark for judging improvements. If certain inequalities of wealth and organizational powers would make everyone better off than in this hypothetical starting situation, then they accord with the general conception.

Now it is possible, at least theoretically, that by giving up some of their fundamental liberties men are sufficiently compensated by the resulting social and economic gains. The general conception of justice imposes no restrictions on what sort of inequalities are permissible; it only requires that everyone's position be improved. We need not suppose anything so drastic as consenting to a condition of slavery. Imagine instead that men forego certain political rights when the economic returns are significant and their capacity to influence the course of policy by the exercise of these rights would be marginal in any case. It is this kind of exchange which the two principles as stated rule out; being arranged in serial order they do not permit exchanges between basic liberties and economic and social gains. The serial ordering of principles expresses an underlying preference among primary social goods. When this preference is rational so likewise is the choice of these principles in this order.

In developing justice as fairness I shall, for the most part, leave aside the general conception of justice and examine instead the special case of the two principles in serial order. The advantage of this procedure is that from the first the matter of priorities is recognized and an effort made to find principles to deal with it. One is led to attend throughout to the conditions under which the acknowledgment of the absolute weight of liberty with respect to social and economic advantages, as defined by the lexical order of the two principles, would be reasonable. Offhand, this ranking appears extreme and too special a case to be of much interest; but there is more justification for it than would appear at first sight... Furthermore, the distinction between fundamental rights and liberties and economic and social benefits marks a difference among primary social goods that one should try to exploit. It suggest an important division in the social system. Of course, the distinctions drawn and the ordering proposed are bound to be at best only approximations. There are surely circumstances in which they fail. But it is essential to depict clearly the main lines of a reasonable conception of justice; and under many conditions anyway, the two principles in serial order may serve well enough. When necessary we can fall back on the more general conception.

The fact that the two principles apply to institutions has certain consequences. Several points illustrate this. First of all, the rights and liberties referred to by these principles are those which are defined by the public rules of the basic structure. Whether men are free is determined by the rights and duties established by the major institutions of society. Liberty is a certain pattern of social forms. The first principle simply requires that certain sorts of rules, those defining basic liberties, apply to everyone equally and that they allow the most extensive liberty compatible with a like liberty for all. The only reason for circumscribing the rights defining liberty and making men's freedom less extensive than it might otherwise be is that these equal rights as institutionally defined would interfere with one another.

Another thing to bear in mind is that when principles mention persons, or require that everyone gain from an inequality, the reference is to representative persons holding the various social positions, or offices, or whatever, established by the basic structure. Thus in applying the second principle I assume that it is possible to assign an expectation of well-being to representative individuals holding these positions. This expectation indicates their life prospects as viewed from their social station. In general, the expectations of representative persons depend upon the distribution of rights and duties throughout the basic structure. When this changes, expectations change. I assume, then, that expectations are connected: by raising the prospects of the representative man in one position we presumably increase or decrease the prospects of representative men in other positions. Since it applies to institutional forms, the second principle (or rather the first part of it) refers to the expectations of representative individuals... [N]either principle applies to distributions of particular goods to particular individuals who may be identified by their proper names. The situation where someone is considering how to allocate certain commodities to needy persons who are known to him is not within the scope of the principles. They are meant to regulate basic institutional arrangements. We must not assume that there is much similarity from the standpoint of justice between an administrative allotment of goods to specific persons and the appropriate design of society. Our common sense intuitions for the former may be a poor guide to the latter.

Now the second principle insists that each person benefit from permissible inequalities in the basic structure. This means that it must be reasonable for each relevant representative man defined by this structure, when he views it as a going concern, to prefer his prospects with the inequality to his prospects without it. One is not allowed to justify differences in income or organizational powers on the ground that the disadvantages of those in one position are outweighed by the greater advantages of those in another. Much less can infringements of liberty be counterbalanced in this way. Applied to the basic structure, the principle of utility would have us maximize the sum of expectations of representative men (weighted by the number of persons they represent, on the classical view); and this would permit us to compensate for the losses of some by the gains of others. Instead, the two principles require that everyone benefit from economic and social inequalities. It is obvious, however, that there are indefinitely many ways in which all may be advantaged when the initial arrangement of equality is taken as a benchmark. How then are we to choose among these possibilities? The principles must be specified so that they yield a determinate conclusion.

John Rawls. *A Theory of Justice*. Cambridge: Harvard University Press, 1971.

The Theory of Rawls

J. R. Lucas

J.R. LUCAS *is a Fellow of Merton College at Oxford University. He is the author of several books in recent years including* The Principle of Politics, The Concept of Probability, The Freedom of the Will, *and* On Justice.

Much interest has been aroused by John Rawls's volume *A Theory of Justice*,[1] and it is appropriate to consider it from the standpoint adopted in our present work, the more so because Rawls denies any connection between justice and desert, and seeks to elucidate justice in a wholly different, egalitarian way.

Rawls's theory is a variant on utilitarianism. He shares the same conceptual scheme as the utilitarians, but seeks to mitigate the most obnoxious conclusions which they are forced to draw. Like the utilitarians, he believes that goods can be compared and aggregated, that states of affairs are to be evaluated in terms of goods, and the prime concern of politics is to bring it about that desirable states of affairs obtain. Unlike the utilitarians, however, Rawls does not seek simply to maximise the total goods produced. He shrinks from the callous unconcern manifested by utilitarians towards particular individuals, whose interests they are prepared to trample on without scruple, so long as the sum of good is thereby increased. Instead, he focusses attention on those who are likely to come off worst, and to alleviate their lot. In the terminology of the Theory of Games, Rawls would have us pursue, subject to certain constraints about individual rights and liberties, a maximin policy.[2]

Rawls claims that his policy is the rational one for anybody to adopt if he were to make his choice without knowing how he was going to fare. If we were setting up a society from scratch, a prudent man, knowing that he could not know how he was going to fare, would opt for that constitution under which, if things went ill with him, he would be least badly off. Any other choice could work out to his greater disadvantage, and therefore, according to Rawls, would be a less sensible one to make. Hence, if we are wise, we shall all agree on the maximin strategy which Rawls commends. Not only is this the rational policy for us all to adopt, but it is the only basis of a social contract which could include everyone; and therefore an acceptance of it can be imputed to everyone, and everyone can be held to it. The arguments of Locke are thus adduced to defend, not the rights of property, but the egalitarian measures of social democracy.

Rawls's recommendation of a maximin strategy carries some weight: but it seems to be a rational reconstruction not of justice but of prudence. If I found myself deliberating what constitution to set up, it would be wise to ensure that, if the next turn of the wheel of fortune went against me, I should none the less fare not too ill. But this counsel, thus presented, has little to do with justice. It is prospective, not retrospective: it is based on ignorance, not knowledge: and it is concerned with my own advantage, not others' rights. Prudence may suggest, but justice has not been shown to demand, a maximin strategy. Indeed, although a maximin strategy may be prudent, Rawls has not shown either that it is the pre-eminently rational one or that it is in fact widely adopted. It could be argued, with some show of reason, that it was better to run risks. Although a prudent man may seek to minimise possible losses, a man might equally

[1] Cambridge, Mass., 1971; Oxford, 1972.
[2] Ch. 3, p. 66.

wisely risk some losses for great gains. Rather than minimise losses, a rational man should, according to one course of reckoning, seek to maximise the expectation, in the technical sense elucidated in probability theory, of gain. Or he might chance his arm even further. He might be guided by Pascal instead of Rawls, and pursue a maximax strategy, reckoning that all the ordinary goods he could reasonably be sure of getting were of so little value that it was worth staking everything on some slim chance of achieving a break-through, and really making good. Certainly this is how many people reason, and although we can deem them imprudent, we cannot dub them irrational, and must admit that in the event they may prove wiser than we. Even if no pearl of great price comes their way, it is good to be able to hope. Hopes are as important as fears, and if it is good to know nothing very bad can happen, it is also good not to know that nothing very good can happen. We should not seek security at the cost of frustrating all our fondest dreams and highest hopes. And therefore men, who are rational rather than merely prudent, are ready to take risks, and sometimes trade in security for the possibility of great achievement. We cannot say that they are wrong, and even more surely we cannot say that they do not exist. Rawls cannot argue convincingly for social democracy on the basis that nobody ever spends money on the pools.

Non-Americans find contract theories unconvincing. There never was a constitutional convention in Britain: to suppose oneself a Founding Father is not only a counterfactual hypothetical, but an idle and totally unhistorical fancy. Nevertheless, contract theories are not to be dismissed simply on that score. Historically false, they still may be vehicles for conveying philosophical truth. And much of Rawls's argument can be separated from his account of what it would be prudent to choose in the original position behind the veil of ignorance. In particular, Rawls often seems to be engaged in a dialogue with the least favoured members of modern industrial society, seeking to reconcile them to their lot. The janitor in the university building, the driver in the streetcar, the attendant in the gasoline station, the unemployed in Harlem or Bronx, may feel deprived and believe that they are being ill done by, and ought, by rights, to have as much as a college professor. Rawls concedes their main, egalitarian point, and agrees that there is no *a priori* reason why they ought to have less than anyone else: but then goes on with an *ad hominem* argument that poorer though they are than many members of modern society, they would be worse off still if those other members of society were brought down to their level. The poor benefit from the crumbs that fall from the rich man's table. Business men, if they are allowed to get rich, will do so by meeting public wants as efficiently as possible, and we all benefit by their self-interested labours. And therefore we should not be jealous of the rich. They may be richer than we are, but we are richer than we otherwise would be, and if we tried to cut them down to size, we should only be cutting off our noses to spite our faces. As Abraham Lincoln said, you can't make the poor rich by making the rich poor.

It is a familiar argument in modern times, and, within its limits, a cogent one. It is a powerful dissuasive to extreme egalitarian measures, and should go some way to reconciling the victims of modern industrial society to their lot. Although they have come off worst, they have done better than they would have done in a pre-industrial society. They may have lost out, but the consolation prizes are quite large. But, once again, we protest that this is barely an argument of justice. Justice is more exact. It is concerned with particular individuals and their particular wrongs, and seeks to remedy these. Sometimes we may be willing to set off against admitted wrongs other uncovenanted benefits, and allow our complaints to be assuaged by a consideration of our credit account in blessings; but any such reckoning is only a rough justice, and it is noteworthy how unavailing such arguments have been in modern Britain. Time and again grievances have been pursued without any regard to countervailing advantages, and often entirely contrary to all counsels of expediency. Strikers, convinced of the justice of their cause, have continued their strikes, even to their long-term disadvantage: and public policy has often been governed by egalitarian considerations rather than those of economic efficiency or general prosperity. Rawls's argument with the worst off is only a partial answer to the politics of envy, more effective in America than in Britain, and is much more an argument of expediency than of justice.

J.R. Lucas. *On Justice*. Oxford: Oxford University Press, 1980.

Part IV
Conservatism

FRIEDRICH A. HAYEK

In his *Reflections*, Edmund Burke says, "the nature of man is intricate; the objects of society are of the greatest possible complexity." These remarks compress into a single thread a whole web of ideas that Burke uses to advance his vision of what came to be known as conservatism. Institutions, thinks Burke, are a manifestation of the wisdom of the species and ought to be respectfully treated as such. The result is that Burke advances a philosophy which aims to conserve rather than to erode or destroy.

T.S. Eliot advances something similar to Burke in his idea of a Christian society. Eliot recognizes that liberalism can mean chaos and conservatism petrification, but in the end he cautiously sides with some version of the latter in the belief that the only hopeful course for a society which is to continue its creative activity is to become Christian. Like Eliot, Eric Voegelin takes aim at liberalism. Voegelin sees liberalism as a species of gnosticism, a school of thought which seeks salvation in knowledge. Voegelin sees liberalism and communism as being connected inasmuch as the latter is the most radical expression of the former, both being versions of gnosticism. He thinks the spirit of gnosticism, with all its dangers, will continue to haunt the West until its clichés are abandoned and it returns to the values of a more classical and Christian tradition.

While the main line of thought pursued by conservatives is the preservation of tradition (a thought that is particularly visible in Burke's writings), nonetheless we should not lose sight of one key element, namely the state, in the traditions which conservatives have sought to preserve. Therefore it is useful to look at Robert Nozick's contemporary libertarian-cum-conservative interpretation of John

Locke's political state. Nozick very effectively explores the possibility of modelling this institution on a dominant protective association. In drawing our attention to the state in this way, Nozick spells out in more detail one of Burke's hidden assumptions: the legitimacy of the political state. But Nozick brings out more clearly than Burke the fine textures of the state, by illuminating in Lockean protectionist terms the limited role it plays.

Robert Wolff disagrees with Nozick's attempt to justify the state as a dominant protective association. Wolff claims Nozick's account suffers from a persistent failure to recognize the nature of social reality. In confronting Nozick in this way, Wolff virtually meets head on the conservative vision of society.

Following Wolff's paper is one by Friedrich Hayek, who does indeed represent a genuine conservative position. He adamantly opposes socialism which, he thinks, has displaced liberalism as the doctrine adhered to by progressives. Liberals have mistakenly followed the calls of socialists to more freedom and have in the process walked relentlessly down the road to servitude rather than the road to freedom. For Hayek, the systems of socialism and fascism are closely connected: both lead to the loss of freedom. And the pity for Hayek is that the old liberal simply cannot see this fact.

The freedom which Hayek fears is lost through socialism is not just political, but also economic. This is the same freedom which T. Boone Pickins discusses in the final article. He quite openly endorses the invisible-hand approach to economics advocated by Adam Smith and in this sense shares in the classical liberal philosophy. However he begins his discussion by registering concern about the loss of the

American spirit of capitalism. With his eyes focussed upon the past he clearly shares with other conservatives (only on this occasion for economic reasons) the view that traditions have a value worth preserving. In this case the tradition is that of American capitalism, a tradition which he sees being stifled by bureaucratic administrative corporations. In this article Pickins's concern is less with governmental than with internal corporate stifling.

The following articles are diverse yet they have a common focus on tradition. While conservatives do share capitalistic inclinations with Adam Smith and other classical liberals, the articles make clear that conservatives go further than liberals in preferring the familiar to the untried and untested. For conservatives, there is, to be sure, in the established institutions, some wisdom of the species.

Reflections on the Revolution in France

Edmund Burke

EDMUND BURKE *(1729–1797) was an Irish political philosopher perhaps most famous for* Reflections on the Revolution in France (1790). *He placed considerable faith in the wisdom of the species as personified in the major institutions in society.*

Far am I from denying in theory, full as far is my heart from withholding in practice (if I were of power to give or to withhold), the *real* rights of men. In denying their false claims of right, I do not mean to injure those which are real, and are such as their pretended rights would totally destroy. If civil society be made for the advantage of man, all the advantages for which it is made become his right. It is an institution of beneficence; and law itself is only beneficence acting by a rule. Men have a right to live by that rule; they have a right to do justice, as between their fellows, whether their fellows are in public function or in ordinary occupation. They have a right to the fruits of their industry; and to the means of making their industry fruitful. They have a right to the acquisitions of their parents; to the nourishment and improvement of their offspring; to instruction in life, and to consolation in death. Whatever each man can separately do, without trespassing upon others, he has a right to do for himself; and he has a right to a fair portion of all which society, with all its combinations of skill and force, can do in his favour. In this partnership all men have equal rights; but not to equal things. He that has but five shillings in the partnership, has as good a right to it, as he that has five hundred pounds has to his larger proportion. But he has not a right to an equal dividend in the product of the joint stock; and as to the share of power, authority, and direction which each individual ought to have in the management of the state, that I must deny to be amongst the direct original rights of man in civil society; for I have in my contemplation the civil social man, and no other. It is a thing to be settled by convention.

If civil society be the offspring of convention, that convention must be its law. That convention must limit and modify all the descriptions of constitution which are formed under it. Every sort of legislative, judicial, or executory power are its creatures. They can have no being in any other state of things; and how can any man claim under the conventions of civil society, rights which do not so much as suppose its existence? rights which are absolutely repugnant to it? One of the first motives to civil society, and which becomes one of its fundamental rules, is, *that no man should be judge in his own cause.* By this each person has at once divested himself of the first fundamental right of uncovenanted man, that is, to judge for himself, and to assert his own cause. He abdicates all right to be his own governor. He inclusively, in a great measure, abandons the right of self-defence, the first law of nature. Men cannot enjoy the rights of an uncivil and of a civil state together. That he may obtain justice, he gives up his right of determining what it is in points the most essential to him. That he may secure some liberty, he makes a surrender in trust of the whole of it.

Government is not made in virtue of natural rights, which may and do exist in total independence of it; and exist in much greater clearness, and in a much greater degree of abstract perfection: but their abstract perfection is their practical defect. By having a right to everything they want everything. Government is a contrivance of human wisdom to provide for human *wants*. Men have a right that these wants should be provided for by this wisdom. Among these wants is to be reckoned the want, out of civil society, of a sufficient restraint upon their passions. Society requires not only that the passions of individuals should be subjected, but that even in the mass and body, as well as in the individuals, the inclinations of men should frequently be thwarted, their will controlled, and their passions brought into subjection. This can only be done *by a power out of themselves*; and not, in the exercise of its function, subject to that will and to those passions which it is its office to bridle and subdue. In this sense the restraints on men, as well as their liberties, are to be reckoned among their rights. But as the liberties and the restrictions vary with times and circumstances, and admit of infinite modifications, they cannot be settled upon any abstract rule; and nothing is so foolish as to discuss them upon that principle.

The moment you abate anything from the full rights of men, each to govern himself, and suffer any artificial, positive limitation upon those rights, from that moment the whole organization of government becomes a consideration of convenience. This it is which makes the constitution of a state, and the due distribution of its powers, a matter of the most delicate and complicated skill. It requires a deep knowledge of human nature and human necessities, and of the things which facilitate or obstruct the various ends, which are to be pursued by the mechanism of civil institutions. The state is to have recruits to its strength, and remedies to its distempers. What is the use of discussing a man's abstract right to food or medicine? The question is upon the method of procuring and administering them. In that deliberation I shall always advise to call in the aid of the farmer and the physician, rather than the professor of metaphysics.

The science of constructing a commonwealth, or renovating it, or reforming it, is, like every other experimental science, not to be taught *à priori*. Nor is it a short experience that can instruct us in that practical science; because the real effects of moral causes are not always immediate; but that which in the first instance is prejudicial may be excellent in its remoter operation; and its excellence may arise even from the ill effects it produces in the beginning. The reverse also happens: and very plausible schemes, with very pleasing commencements, have often shameful and lamentable conclusions. In states there are often some obscure and almost latent causes, things which appear at first view of little moment, on which a very great part of its prosperity or adversity may most essentially depend. The science of government being therefore so practical in itself, and intended for such practical purposes, a matter which requires experience, and even more experience than any person can gain in his whole life, however sagacious and observing he may be, it is with infinite caution that any man ought to venture upon pulling down an edifice, which has answered in any tolerable degree for ages the common purposes of society, or on building it up again, without having models and patterns of approved utility before his eyes.

These metaphysic rights entering into common life, like rays of light which pierce into a dense medium, are, by the laws of nature, refracted from their straight line. Indeed in the gross and complicated mass of human passions and concerns, the primitive rights of men undergo such a variety of refractions and reflections, that it becomes absurd to talk of them as if they continued in the simplicity of their original direction. The nature of man is intricate; the objects of society are of the greatest possible complexity: and therefore no simple disposition or direction of power can be suitable either to man's nature, or to the quality of his affairs. When I hear the simplicity of contrivance aimed at and boasted of in any new political constitutions, I am at no loss to decide that the artificers are grossly ignorant of their trade, or totally negligent of their duty. The simple governments are fundamentally defective, to say no worse of them. If you were to contemplate society in but one point of view, all these simple modes of polity are infinitely captivating. In effect each would answer its single end much more perfectly than the more complex is able to attain all its complex purposes. But it is better that the whole should be imperfectly and anomalously answered, than that, while some parts are provided for with great exactness, others might be totally neglected, or perhaps materially injured, by the overcare of a favourite member.

The pretended rights of these theorists are all extremes: and in proportion as they are metaphysically true, they are morally and politically false. The rights of men are in a sort of *middle*, incapable of definition, but not impossible to be discerned. The rights of men in governments are their advantages; and these are often in balances between differences of good; in compromises sometimes between good and evil, and sometimes between evil and evil. Political reason is a computing principle; adding, subtracting, multiplying, and dividing, morally and not metaphysically, or mathematically, true moral denominations.

Edmund Burke. *Reflections on the Revolution in France*. Originally published in 1790.

The Idea of a Christian Society

T. S. Eliot

T.S. ELIOT *(1888–1965) was born in St. Louis, Missouri, and educated at Harvard University, the Sorbonne, and Oxford University. He became famous as a poet for "The Love Song of J. Alfred Prufrock" and* The Waste Land. *The major work of his later period is the* Four Quartets.

What the Western world has stood for— and by that I mean the terms to which it has attributed sanctity—is "Liberalism" and "Democracy." The two terms are not identical or inseparable. The term "Liberalism" is the more obviously ambiguous, and is now less in favour; but the term "Democracy" is at the height of its popularity. When a term has become so universally sanctified as "democracy" now is, I begin to wonder whether it means anything, in meaning too many things: it has arrived perhaps at the position of a Meroving- ian Emperor, and wherever it is invoked, one begins to look for the Major of the Palace. Some persons have gone so far as to affirm, as something self-evident, that democracy is the only régime compatible with Christianity; on the other hand, the word is not abandoned by sympathisers with the government of Ger- many. If anybody ever attacked democracy, I might discover what the word meant. Cer- tainly there is a sense in which Britain and America are more democratic than Germany; but on the other hand, defenders of the totali- tarian system can make out a plausible case for maintaining that what we have is not de- mocracy, but financial oligarchy.

Mr. Christopher Dawson considers that "what the nondictatorial States stand for today is not Liberalism but Democracy," and goes on to foretell the advent in these States of a kind of totalitarian democracy. I agree with his prediction, but if one is considering, not merely the non-dictatorial States, but the soci- eties to which they belong, his statement does less than justice to the extent to which Liberal- ism still permeates our minds and affects our attitude towards much of life. That Liberalism may be a tendency towards something very different from itself, is a possibility in its na- ture. For it is something which tends to release energy rather than accumulate it, to relax, rather than to fortify. It is a movement not so much defined by its end, as by its starting point; away from, rather than towards, some- thing definite. Our point of departure is more real to us than our destination; and the desti- nation is likely to present a very different pic- ture when arrived at, from the vaguer image formed in imagination. By destroying tradi- tional social habits of the people, by dissolv- ing their natural collective consciousness into individual constituents, by licensing the opin- ions of the most foolish, by substituting in- struction for education, by encouraging cleverness rather than wisdom, the upstart rather than the qualified, by fostering a notion of *getting on* to which the alternative is a hope- less apathy, Liberalism can prepare the way for that which is its own negation: the artifi- cial, mechanised or brutalised control which is a desperate remedy for its chaos.

It must be evident that I am speaking of Liberalism in a sense much wider than any which can be fully exemplified by the history of any political party, and equally in a wider sense than any in which it has been used in ecclesiastical controversy. True, the tendency of Liberalism can be more clearly illustrated in religious history than in politics, where princi- ple is more diluted by necessity, where obser- vation is more confused by detail and distracted by reforms each valid within its own limited reference. In religion, Liberalism may be characterised as a progressive discarding of elements in historical Christianity which appear superfluous or obsolete, confounded with practices and abuses which are legitimate objects of attack. But as its movement is controlled rather by its origin than by any goal, it loses force after a series of rejections, and with nothing to destroy is left with nothing to uphold and with nowhere to go. With religious Liberalism, however, I am no more specifically concerned than with political Liberalism: I am concerned with a state of mind which, in certain circumstances, can become universal and infect opponents as well as defenders. And I shall have expressed myself very ill if I give the impression that I think of Liberalism as something simply to be rejected and extirpated, as an evil for which there is a simple alternative. It is a necessary negative element; when I have said the worst of it, that worst comes only to this, that a negative element made to serve the purpose of a positive is objectionable. In the sense in which Liberalism is contrasted with Conservatism, both can be equally repellant: if the former can mean chaos, the latter can mean petrifaction. We are always faced both with the question "what must be destroyed?" and with the question "what must be preserved?" and neither Liberalism nor Conservatism, which are not philosophies and may be merely habits, is enough to guide us.

In the nineteenth century the Liberal Party had its own conservatism, and the Conservative Party had its own liberalism; neither had a political philosophy. To hold a political philosophy is in fact not the function of a political, that is, a Parliamentary party: a party with a political philosophy is a revolutionary party. The politics of political parties is not my concern. Nor am I concerned with the politics of a revolutionary party. If a revolutionary party attains its true end, its political philosophy will, by a process of growth, become that of a whole culture; if it attains its more facile end, its political philosophy will be that of a dominant class or group, in a society in which the majority will be passive, and the minority oppressed. But a political philosophy is not merely a formalised system set forth by a theorist. The permanent value of such treaties as Aristotle's *Politics* and *Poetics* is found at the

opposite extreme to anything that we can call *doctrinaire*. Just as his views on dramatic poetry were derived from a study of the existing works of Attic drama, so his political theory was founded on a perception of the unconscious aims implicit in Athenian democracy at its best. His limitations are the condition of his universality; and instead of ingenious theories spun out of his head, he wrote studies full of universal wisdom. Thus, what I mean by a political philosophy is not merely even the conscious formulation of the ideal aims of a people, but the substratum of collective temperament, ways of behaviour and unconscious values which provides the material for the formulation. What we are seeking is not a programme for a party, but a way of life for a people: it is this which totalitarianism has sought partly to revive, and partly to impose by force upon its peoples. Our choice now is not between one abstract form and another, but between a pagan, and necessarily stunted culture, and a religious, and necessarily imperfect culture.

The attitudes and beliefs of Liberalism are destined to disappear, are already disappearing. They belong to an age of free exploitation which has passed; and our danger now is, that the term may come to signify for us only the disorder the fruits of which we inherit, and not the permanent value of the negative element. Out of Liberalism itself come philosophies which deny it. We do not proceed, from Liberalism to its apparent end of authoritarian democracy, at a uniform pace in every respect. There are so many centres of it—Britain, France, America and the Dominions—that the development of Western society must proceed more slowly than that of a compact body like Germany, and its tendencies are less apparent. Furthermore, those who are the most convinced of the necessity of *étatisme* as a control of some activities of life, can be the loudest professors of libertarianism in others, and insist upon the preserves of "private life" in which each man may obey his own convictions or follow his own whim: while imperceptibly this domain of "private life" becomes smaller and smaller, and may eventually disappear altogether. It is possible that a wave of terror of the consequences of depopulation might lead to legislation having the effect of compulsory breeding.

If, then, Liberalism disappears from the philosophy of life of a people, what positive is left? We are left only with the term "democracy," a term which, for the present generation, still has a Liberal connotation of "freedom." But totalitarianism can retain the terms "freedom" and "democracy" and give them its own meaning: and its right to them is not so easily disproved as minds inflamed by passion suppose. We are in danger of finding ourselves with nothing to stand for except a *dislike* of everything maintained by Germany and/or Russia: a dislike which, being a compost of newspaper sensations and prejudice, can have two results, at the same time, which appear at first incompatible. It may lead us to reject possible improvements, because we should owe them to the example of one or both of these countries; and it may equally well lead us to be mere imitators *à rebours*, in making us adopt uncritically almost any attitude which a foreign nation rejects.

We are living at present in a kind of doldrums between opposing winds of doctrine, in a period in which one political philosophy has lost its cogency for behaviour, though it is still the only one in which public speech can be framed. This is very bad for the English language: it is this disorder (for which we are all to blame) and not individual insincerity, which is responsible for the hollowness of many political and ecclesiastical utterances. You have only to examine the mass of newspaper leading articles, the mass of political exhortation, to appreciate the fact that good prose cannot be written by a people without convictions. The fundamental objection to fascist doctrine, the one which we conceal from ourselves because it might condemn ourselves as well, is that it is pagan. There are other objections too, in the political and economic sphere, but they are not objections that we can make with dignity until we set our own affairs in order. There are still other objections, to oppression and violence and cruelty, but however strongly we feel, these are objections to means and not to ends. It is true that we sometimes use the word "pagan," and in the same context refer to ourselves as "Christian." But we always dodge the real issue. Our newspapers have done all they could with the red

herring of the "German national religion," an eccentricity which is after all no odder than some cults held in Anglo-Saxon countries: this "German national religion" is comforting in that it persuades us that *we* have a Christian civilisation; it helps to disguise the fact that our aims, like Germany's, are materialistic. And the last thing we should like to do would be to examine the "Christianity" which, in such contexts as this, we say we keep.

If we have got so far as accepting the belief that the only alternative to a progressive and insidious adaptation to totalitarian worldliness for which the pace is already set, is to aim at a Christian society, we need to consider both what kind of a society we have at this time, and what a Christian society would be like. We should also be quite sure of what we want: if your real ideals are those of materialistic efficiency, then the sooner you know your own mind, and face the consequences, the better. Those who, either complacently or despairingly, suppose that the aim of Christianisation is chimerical, I am not here attempting to convert. To those who realise what a well-organised pagan society would mean for us, there is nothing to say. But it is as well to remember that the imposition of a pagan theory of the State does not necessarily mean a wholly pagan society. A compromise between the theory of the State and the tradition of society exists in Italy, a country which is still mainly agricultural and Catholic. The more highly industrialised the country, the more easily a materialistic philosophy will flourish in it, and the more deadly that philosophy will be. Britain has been highly industrialised longer than any other country. And the tendency of unlimited industrialism is to create bodies of men and women—of all classes—detached from tradition, alienated from religion and susceptible to mass suggestion: in other words, a mob. And a mob will be no less a mob if it is well fed, well clothed, well housed, and well disciplined.

The Liberal notion that religion was a matter of private belief and of conduct in private life, and that there is no reason why Christians should not be able to accommodate themselves to any world which treats them good-naturedly, is becoming less and less tenable. This notion would seem to have become accepted gradually, as a false inference from the subdivision of English Christianity into sects, and the happy results of universal toleration. The reason why members of different communions have been able to rub along together, is that in the greater part of the ordinary business of life they have shared the same assumptions about behaviour. When they have been wrong, they have been wrong together. We have less excuse than our ancestors for un-Christian conduct, because the growth of an un-Christian society about us, its more obvious intrusion upon our lives, has been breaking down the comfortable distinction between public and private morality. The problem of leading a Christian life in a non-Christian society is now very present to us, and it is a very different problem from that of the accommodation between an Established Church and dissenters. It is not merely the problem of a minority in a society of *individuals* holding an alien belief. It is the problem constituted by our implication in a network of institutions from which we cannot dissociate ourselves: institutions the operation of which appears no longer neutral, but non-Christian. And as for the Christian who is not conscious of his dilemma—and he is in the majority—he is becoming more and more de-Christianised by all sorts of unconscious pressure: paganism holds all the most valuable advertising space. Anything like Christian traditions transmitted from generation to generation within the family must disappear, and the small body of Christians will consist entirely of adult recruits. I am saying nothing at this point that has not been said before by others, but it is relevant. I am not concerned with the problem of Christians as a persecuted minority. When the Christian is treated as an enemy of the State, his course is very much harder, but it is simpler. I am concerned with the dangers to the tolerated minority; and in the modern world, it may turn out that the most tolerable thing for Christians is to be tolerated.

To attempt to make the prospect of a Christian society immediately attractive to those who see no prospect of deriving direct personal benefit from it, would be idle; even the majority of professing Christians may shrink from it. No scheme for a change of society can be made to appear immediately palatable, except by falsehood, until society has become so desperate that it will accept any change. A Christian society only becomes acceptable after you have fairly examined the alternatives. We might, of course, merely sink into an apathetic decline: without faith, and therefore without faith in ourselves; without a philosophy of life, either Christian or pagan; and without art. Or we might get a "totalitarian democracy," different but having much in common with other pagan societies, because we shall have changed step by step in order to keep pace with them: a state of affairs in which we shall have regimentation and conformity, without respect for the needs of the individual soul; the puritanism of a hygienic morality in the interest of efficiency; uniformity of opinion through propaganda, and art only encouraged when it flatters the official doctrines of the time. To those who can imagine, and are therefore repelled by, such a prospect, one can assert that the only possibility of control and balance is a religious control and balance; that the only hopeful course for a society which would thrive and continue its creative activity in the arts of civilisation, is to become Christian. That prospect involves, at least, discipline, inconvenience and discomfort: but here as hereafter the alternative to hell is purgatory.

T.S. Eliot. *Christianity and Culture*. New York: Harcourt, Brace, and World, 1949.

The Dangers of Gnosticism

Eric Voegelin

ERIC VOEGELIN *(1901–1985) was born in Cologne and taught law at the University of Vienna, government at Louisiana State University, and most recently political science at the University of Munich. He is famous as an interpreter of the conservative streams of European thought. His writings include* Order and History *and* The New Science of Politics.

This exposition of the dangers of gnosticism as a civil theology of Western society will probably have aroused some misgivings. The analysis did fully pertain only to the progressive and idealistic varieties which prevail in Western democracies; it would not equally well apply to the activist varieties which prevail in totalitarian empires. Whatever share of responsibility for the present plight may be laid on the doorsteps of progressivists and idealists, the most formidable source of imminent danger seems to be the activists. The intimate connection between the two dangers, therefore, requires clarification—all the more so because the representatives of the two Gnostic varieties are antagonists in battle on the world scene. The analysis of this further question can appropriately use as a preface the pronouncements of a famous liberal intellectual on the problem of communism:

> Lenin was surely right when the end he sought for was to build his heaven on earth and write the precepts of his faith into the inner fabric of a universal humanity. He was surely right, too, when he recognized that the prelude to peace is a war, and that it is futile to suppose that the tradition of countless generations can be changed, as it were, overnight.[1]

The power of any supernatural religion to build that tradition has gone; the deposit of scientific inquiry since Descartes has been fatal to its authority. It is therefore difficult to see upon what basis the civilized tradition can be rebuilt save that upon which the idea of the Russian Revolution is founded. It corresponds, its supernatural basis apart, pretty exactly to the mental climate in which Christianity became the official religion of the West.[2]

> It is, indeed, true in a sense to argue that the Russian principle cuts deeper than the Christian since it seeks salvation for the masses by fulfilment in this life, and, thereby, orders anew the actual world we know.[3]

Few passages could be more revealing for the plight of the liberal intellectual in our time. Philosophy and Christianity are beyond his range of experience. Science, besides being an instrument for power over nature, is something that makes you sophisticated enough not to believe in God. Heaven will be built on earth. Self-salvation, the tragedy of gnosticism which Nietzsche experienced to the full until it broke his soul, is a fulfilment of life that will come to every man with the feeling that he is making his contribution to society according to his ability, compensated by a weekly paycheck. There are no problems of human existence in society except the immanent satisfaction of the masses. Political analysis tells you who will be the winner, so that the intellectual can advance in proper time to the position of a court theologian of the Communist empire. And, if you are bright, you will follow him in his expert surf-riding on the wave of the future. The case is too well known today to need further comment. It is the case of the petty paracletes in whom the spirit is stirring, who feel the duty to play a public role

---

[1] Harold J Laski, *Faith, Reason and Civilization: An Essay in Historical Analysis* (New York: Viking Press, 1944), p. 184.

[2] *Ibid.*, p. 51.

[3] *Ibid.*, p. 143.

and be teachers of mankind, who with good faith substitute their convictions for critical knowledge, and with a perfectly good conscience express their opinions on problems beyond their reach. Moreover, one should not deny the immanent consistency and honesty of this transition from liberalism to communism; if liberalism is understood as the immanent salvation of man and society, communism certainly is its most radical expression; it is an evolution that was already anticipated by John Stuart Mill's faith in the ultimate advent of communism for mankind.

In more technical language one can formulate the problem in the following manner. The three possible varieties of immanentization— teleological, axiological, and activist—are not merely three co-ordinated types but are related to one another dynamically. In every wave of the Gnostic movement the progressivist and utopian varieties will tend to form a political right wing, leaving a good deal of the ultimate perfection to gradual evolution and compromising on a tension between achievement and ideal, while the activist variety will tend to form a political left wing, taking violent action toward the complete realization of the perfect realm. The distribution of the faithful from right to left will in part be determined by such personal equations as enthusiasm, temperament, and consistency; to another, and perhaps the more important part, however, it will be determined by their relation to the civilizational environment in which the Gnostic revolution takes place. For it must never be forgotten that Western society is not all modern but that modernity is a growth within it, in opposition to the classic and Christian tradition. If there were nothing in Western society but gnosticism, the movement toward the left would be irresistible because it lies in the logic of immanentization, and it would have been consummated long ago. In fact, however, the great Western revolutions of the past, after their logical swing to the left, settled down to a public order which reflected the balance of the social forces of the moment, together with their economic interests and civilizational traditions. The apprehension or hope, as the case

may be, that the "partial" revolutions of the past will be followed by the "radical" revolution and the establishment of the final realm rests on the assumption that the traditions of Western society are now sufficiently ruined and that the famous masses are ready for the kill.[1]

The dynamics of gnosticism, thus, moves along two lines. In the dimension of historical depth, gnosticism moves from the partial immanentization of the high Middle Ages to the radical immanentization of the present. And with every wave and revolutionary outburst it moves in the amplitude of right and left. The thesis, however, that these two lines of dynamics must now meet according to their inner logic, that Western society is ripe to fall for communism, that the course of Western history is determined by the logic of its modernity and nothing else, is an impertinent piece of Gnostic propaganda at both its silliest and most vicious and certainly has nothing to do with a critical study of politics. Against this thesis must be held a number of facts which today are obscured because the public debate is dominated by the liberal clichés. In the first place, the Communist movement in Western society itself, wherever it had to rely on its own mass appeal without aid from the Soviet government, has got exactly nowhere at all. The only Gnostic activist movement that achieved a noteworthy measure of success was the National Socialist movement on a limited national basis; and the suicidal nature of such an activist success is amply testified by the atrocious internal corruption of the regime while it lasted as well as by the ruins of the German cities. Second, the present Western plight in the face of the Soviet danger, in so far as it is due to the creation of the previously described power vacuum, is not of Communist making. The power vacuum was created by the Western democratic governments freely, on the height of a military victory, without pressure from anybody. Third, that the Soviet Union is an expanding great power on the Continent has nothing to do with communism. The present extension of the Soviet empire over the satellite nations corresponds

---

[1] The concepts of "partial" and "radical" revolution were developed by Karl Marx in *Kritik der Hegelschen Rechtsphilosophie, Einleitung(1843), Vol. I: Gesamtausgabe, p. 617.*

substantially to the program of a Slavic empire under Russian hegemony as it was submitted, for instance, by Bakunin to Nicolai I. It is quite conceivable that a non-Communist Russian hegemonic empire would today have the same expanse as the Soviet empire and be a greater danger because it might be better consolidated. Fourth, the Soviet empire, while it is a formidable power, is no danger to Western Europe on the level of material force. Elementary statistics shows that Western manpower, natural resources, and industrial potential are a match to any strength the Soviet empire can muster—not counting our own power in the background. The danger strictly arises from national particularism and the paralyzing intellectual and moral confusion.

The problem of Communist danger, thus, is thrown back on the problem of Western paralysis and self-destructive politics through the Gnostic dream. The previously quoted passages show the source of the trouble. The danger of a sliding from right to left is inherent in the nature of the dream; in so far as communism is a more radical and consistent type of immanentization than progressivism or social utopianism, it has the *logique du coeur* on its side. The Western Gnostic societies are in a state of intellectual and emotional paralysis because no fundamental critique of left-wing gnosticism is possible without blowing up right-wing gnosticism in its course. Such major experiential and intellectual revolutions, however, take their time and the change of at least one generation. One can do no more than formulate the conditions of the problem. There will be a latent Communist danger under the most favorable external circumstances as long as the public debate in Western societies is dominated by the Gnostic clichés. That is to say: as long as the recognition of the structure of reality, the cultivation of the virtues of *sophia* and *prudentia*, the discipline of the intellect, and the development of theoretical culture and the life of the spirit are stigmatized in public as "reactionary," while disregard for the structure of reality, ignorance of facts, fallacious misconstruction and falsification of history, irresponsible opining on the basis of sincere conviction, philosophical illiteracy, spiritual dulness, and agnostic sophistication are considered the virtues of man and their possession opens the road to public success. In brief: as long as civilization is reaction, and moral insanity is progress.

Eric Voegelin. *The New Science of Politics*. Chicago: University of Chicago Press, 1966.

The State of Nature

Robert Nozick

ROBERT NOZICK *(1938–) is currently a professor of philosophy at Harvard University. His* Anarchy, State, and Utopia *made him one of the most influential figures in recent years in political philosophy in the English-speaking philosophical world. Another of his works is* Philosophical Explanations.

The Dominant Protective Association

Out of anarchy, pressed by spontaneous groupings, mutual-protection associations, division of labor, market pressures, economies of scale, and rational self-interest, there arises something very much resembling a minimal state or a group of geographically distinct minimal states. Why is this market different from all other markets? Why would a virtual monopoly arise in this market without the government intervention that elsewhere creates and maintains it?[1] The worth of the product purchased, protection against others, is *relative*: it depends upon how strong the others are. Yet unlike other goods that are comparatively evaluated, maximal competing protective services cannot coexist; the nature of the service brings different agencies not only into competition for customers' patronage, but also into violent conflict with each other. Also, since the worth of the less than maximal product declines disproportionately with the number who purchase the maximal product, customers will not stably settle for the lesser

good, and competing companies are caught in a declining spiral. Hence the three possibilities we have listed.

Our story above assumes that each of the agencies attempts in good faith to act within the limits of Locke's law of nature.[2] But one "protective association" might aggress against other persons. Relative to Locke's law of nature, it would be an outlaw agency. What actual counterweights would there be to its power? (What actual counterweights are there to the power of a state?) Other agencies might unite to act against it. People might refuse to deal with the outlaw agency's clients, boycotting them to reduce the probability of the agency's intervening in their own affairs. This might make it more difficult for the outlaw agency to get clients: but this boycott will seem an effective tool only on very optimistic assumptions about what cannot be kept secret, and about the costs to an individual of partial boycott as compared to the benefits of receiving the more extensive coverage offered by an "outlaw" agency. If the "outlaw" agency simply is an *open* aggressor, pillaging, plundering, and extorting under no plausible claim of justice, it will have a harder time than states. For the state's claim to legitimacy induces its citizens to believe they have some duty to obey its edicts, pay its taxes, fight its battles, and so on: and so some persons cooperate with it voluntarily. An openly aggressive agency could not depend upon, and would not receive, any

---

[1] See Yale Brozen, "Is Government the Source of Monopoly?" *The Intercollegiate Review*, 5, no. 2 (1968–69), 67–78; Fritz Machlup, *The Political Economy of Monopoly* (Baltimore: Johns Hopkins Press, 1952).

[2] Locke assumed that the preponderant majority, though not all, of the persons living in the state of nature would accept the law of nature. See Richard Ashcroft, "Locke's State of Nature," *American Political Science Review*, September 1968, pp. 898–915, especially pt. I.

such voluntary cooperation, since persons would view themselves simply as its victims rather than as its citizens[1]...

Is the Dominant Protective Association a State?

Have we provided an invisible-hand explanation of the state? There are at least two ways in which the scheme of private protective associations might be thought to differ from a minimal state, might fail to satisfy a minimal conception of a state: (1) it appears to allow some people to enforce their own rights, and (2) it appears not to protect all individuals within its domain. Writers in the tradition of Max Weber[2] treat having a monopoly on the use of force in a geographical area, a monopoly incompatible with private enforcement of rights, as crucial to the existence of a state. As Marshall Cohen points out in an unpublished essay, a state may exist without *actually* monopolizing the use of force it has not authorized others to use; within the boundaries of a state there may exist groups such as the Mafia, the KKK, White Citizens Councils, striking unionists, and Weathermen that also use force. *Claiming* such a monopoly is not sufficient (if *you* claimed it you would not become the state), nor is being its sole claimant a necessary condition. Nor need everyone grant the legitimacy of the state's claim to such monopoly, either because as pacifists they think no one has the right to use force, or because as revolutionaries they believe that a given state lacks this right, or because they believe they are entitled to join in and help out no matter what the state says. Formulating sufficient conditions for the existence of the state thus turns out to be a difficult and messy task.[3]

For our purposes here we need focus only upon a necessary condition that the system of private protective agencies (or any component agency within it) apparently does not satisfy.

A state claims a monopoly on deciding who may use force when; it says that only it may decide who may use force and under what conditions; it reserves to itself the sole right to pass on the legitimacy and permissibility of any use of force within its boundaries; furthermore it claims the right to punish all those who violate its claimed monopoly. The monopoly may be violated in two ways: (1) a person may use force though unauthorized by the state to do so, or (2) though not themselves using force a group or person may set themselves up as an alternative authority (and perhaps even claim to be the sole legitimate one) to decide when and by whom the use of force is proper and legitimate. It is unclear whether a state must claim the right to punish the second sort of violator, and doubtful whether any state actually would refrain from punishing a significant group of them within its boundaries. I glide over the issue of what sort of "may," "legitimacy," and "permissibility" is in question. Moral permissibility isn't a matter of decision, and the state need not be so egomaniacal as to claim the sole right to decide moral questions. To speak of legal permissibility would require, to avoid circularity, that an account of a legal system be offered that doesn't use the notion of the state.

We may proceed, for our purposes, by saying that a necessary condition for the existence of a state is that it (some person or organization) announce that, to the best of its ability (taking into account costs of doing so, the feasibility, the more important alternative things it should be doing, and so forth), it will punish everyone whom it discovers to have used force without its express permission. (This permission may be a particular permission or may be granted via some general regulation or authorization.) This still won't quite do: the state may reserve the right to forgive someone, *ex post facto*; in order to punish they may have not only to discover the "unauthorized"

---

[1] See Morris and Linda Tannehill, *The Market for Liberty*. On the importance of voluntary cooperation to the functioning of governments see, for example, Adam Roberts, ed., *Civilian Resistance as National Defense* (Baltimore: Penguin Books, 1969) and Gene Sharp, *The Politics of Non-Violent Action* (Boston: Porter Sargent, 1973).

[2] See Max Weber, *Theory of Social and Economic Organization* (New York: Free Press, 1947), p. 156; and Max Rheinstein, ed., *Max Weber on Law in Economy and Society* (Cambridge, Mass.: Harvard University Press, 1954), Ch.13.

[3] Compare H.L.A. Hart's treatment of the parallel problem for the existence of a legal system in *The Concept of Law* (Oxford: The Clarendon Press, 1961), pp. 113–120.

use of force but also prove via a certain specified procedure of proof that it occurred, and
so forth. But it enables us to proceed. The protective agencies, it seems, do not make such an
announcement, either individually or collectively. *Nor does it seem morally legitimate for
them to do so.* So the system of private protective associations, if they perform no morally
illegitimate action, appears to lack any monopoly element and so appears not to constitute or contain a state. To examine the
question of the monopoly element, we shall
have to consider the situation of some group
of persons (or some one person) living within
a system of private protective agencies who
refuse to join any protective society; who insist on judging for themselves whether their
rights have been violated, and (if they so
judge) on personally enforcing their rights by
punishing and/or exacting compensation
from those who infringed them.

The second reason for thinking the system
described is not a state is that, under it (apart
from spillover effects) only those paying for
protection get protected; furthermore, differing degrees of protection may be purchased.
External economies again to the side, no one
pays for the protection of others except as they
choose to; no one is required to purchase or
contribute to the purchasing of protection for
others. Protection and enforcement of people's
rights is treated as an economic good to be
provided by the market, as are other important goods such as food and clothing. However, under the usual conception of a state,
each person living within (or even sometimes
traveling outside) its geographical boundaries
gets (or at least, is entitled to get) its protection. Unless some private party donated sufficient funds to cover the costs of such
protection (to pay for detectives, police to
bring criminals into custody, courts, and prisons), or unless the state found some service it
could charge for that would cover these costs,[1]
one would expect that a state which offered
protection so broadly would be redistributive.
It would be a state in which some persons
paid more so that others could be protected.
And indeed the most minimal state seriously
discussed by the mainstream of political theorists, the night-watchman state of classical liberal theory, appears to be redistributive in this
fashion. Yet how can a protection agency, a
business, charge some to provide its product
to others?[2] (We ignore things like some partially paying for others because it is too costly
for the agency to refine its classification of,
and charges to, customers to mirror the costs
of the services to them.)

Thus it appears that the dominant protective agency in a territory not only lacks the
requisite monopoly over the use of force, but
also fails to provide protection for all in its
territory; and so the dominant agency appears
to fall short of being a state. But these appearances are deceptive.

Robert Nozick. *Anarchy, State, and Utopia.* New
York: Basic Books, 1974.

---

[1] I have heard it suggested that the state could finance itself by running a lottery. But since it would have no right to
forbid private entrepreneurs from doing the same, why think the state will have any more success in attracting
customers in this than in any other competitive business.

[2] On the claim that physicians do this, see Reuben Kessell, "Price Discrimination in Medicine," *Journal of Law and
Economics,* I, no. I (October 1958), 20–53.

Robert Nozick's Derivation of the Minimal State

Robert Paul Wolff

ROBERT PAUL WOLFF *is Professor of Philosophy at the University of Massachusetts and has taught also at Brandeis University.*

An External Critique of the Argument

Perhaps the most irritating weakness of Nozick's book is its complete failure to take account of the most obvious and well-known facts of human motivation and social experience. For example, much of his discussion of the workings of a protective association seems to presuppose that the serious rights-violations against which one needs protection, are committed, by and large, by the sorts of solid citizens who will have joined a competing association, will be paid up on their premiums, and will have known addresses where they can be found. This may indeed be so in a small, rural society—one in which everyone knows everyone else, and in which an act of barn-burning or cattle-rustling can pretty certainly be laid at the door of those no-account Finkelstein brothers. But in the context of big-city street crime, Nozick's model is simply irrelevant. To put the point more generally, Nozick presupposes a society so settled, so orderly, that one might never feel the need for a protective association at all, let alone a state!

Nozick seems to me equally insensitive to the psychological, social, and institutional problems involved in creating and staffing a responsible, controllable police force, whether "public" or "private." The problem begins as soon as one introduces the notion of an *agent*. An agent is a private individual who adopts a social role. As an occupant of that role, he has rights, powers, responsibilities, and duties which he would not have were he not occupy-

ing the role, and which he puts aside when he steps out of the role. Thence—given the limits of the power of reason—comes the function of uniforms, titles, oaths of office, and similar accoutrement. They serve both to inform others of the role one is playing and to strengthen one's identification with the role. From this follows also the importance of internalizing the norms associated with a role, as opposed merely to making the appropriate adjustments in one's expected utility calculations. Nozick knows all of this, of course. He simply ignores it in the construction of his model of the rational individual and his analysis of the moral relationship between individuals.

Perhaps we can develop the philosophical underpinnings of these observations more systematically by examining the protective association on which Nozick erects his justification of the state. Following the standard libertarian account, Nozick represents such associations as companies that offer a service in the market, advertise for customers, promote sales by such devices as 13 weeks free protection with a 2–year subscription, money-back guarantees, and so forth. As he repeatedly insists, these companies are *groups of individuals*, and they have only individual rights and aggregates of individual rights which they, as individuals, exercise either directly or through their agents. There are no emergent rights, attaching only to corporate bodies and incapable of being decomposed into component individual rights.

The possibility of a protective association (that is to say, of a morally legitimate protective association) rests on four supposed moral facts, asserted (but not shown) to be facts by Nozick:

1. Each person in the state of nature has the right to enforce his (other) rights in a morally proper manner, and to exact suitable compensation in an appropriate manner from those who have violated his rights.

2. Each person has the right—suitably hedged around—to punish rights violations against third parties.

3. Several persons may, through free and mutual agreement, do collectively in the way of rights enforcement and infraction punishment whatever they may do severally and singly.

4. An individual, and hence a group of individuals, may assign the tasks of enforcement, punishment, and so forth, to other persons *as their agents* (perhaps, but not necessarily, as their employees). These agents will act *not* in their own right as persons, but in their role as the authorized representatives of others. Rights are transferable in such manner that one person might, through a number of such transfers, come to be the bearer of many rights, just as one representative might bear many proxies in a committee election, or one lawyer represent the property interest of many clients in a suit.[1]

The operative assumption is clearly assumption 4, which underlies the moral legitimacy of protective associations as opposed to mere mutual aid societies. Let us assume that I can assign my rights to an agent, hire him to represent me, to do in my name what I have a right to do but what he, merely as an individual, might not have the right to do. Even granting all that, it must be obvious that I would stand under an obligation to monitor the actions of my representative, to ascertain that he has done only what I have authorized him to do, and *that* only in permissible ways. This obligation follows from the fact that I have the same obligation when I act as my own agent. If my agent violates the rights of others, I as well as he can be held responsible.[2]

Although it may be a relatively simple matter to monitor the behavior of my personal bodyguard, my personal lawyer, or the holder of my personal proxy, it very quickly becomes impossible in practice for me to exercise effective oversight as the protective association grows. Bureaucratic rationalization and institutionalization take over. It is not I who hire the association's enforcers (or private policemen); bureaucrats in the association's employment office do. I merely write out a monthly check to pay the premium on my comprehensive insurance policy. Since the protective association is, we may suppose, a mutual benefit insurance company, I receive in the mail each year a notice of the annual shareholders' meeting, together with a request from the management for my proxy. I have roughly the same sort of control over the actions taken by the protective association in my name as I do now over the actions of the telephone company—*with one exception*: Now, if I get mad enough at the telephone company, I can write to my Congressman and ask that the government pass a law regulating the telephone company. In Nozick's model, however, the dominant protective association *is* the government! As a device for guaranteeing individual liberties and enforcing absolute side constraints, this is, to put it gently, a trifle feckless.

Nozick, we must recall, is not an anarchist. His purpose is to prove that the just state is possible, not that it is impossible. Perhaps it is not de facto tyranny to which he objects, only income redistribution. Therefore, we cannot defeat his argument merely by observing that it is an ideological rationalization for AT&T. Let us therefore take a closer look at assumption 4, with which we began this line of analysis, and at the argument that depends upon it.

The key to the assumption is the claim that person *A* can transfer a right in toto to person

---

[1] To see the force of this assumption, we need only observe that even though *A*, in a state of nature, has a right to punish *B*'s violation of *C*'s rights, he may *not* have the same right that *C* does to punish *B*. *C* may have the right to use riskier methods of defense or of compensation; he may have a right, that *A* does not have, to forgive *B* for the infraction, or to offer *B* alternative modes of compensation. Should *A* become the agent of a protective association to which *C* has transferred his rights of retaliation and enforcement, however, he would then acquire in his role as *C*'s agent the rights that *C*, but not he, possessed in the state of nature.

[2] This is a point on which Nozick's mentor, Locke, lays heavy emphasis. See J. Locke, *Two Treatises of Government* (Laslett ed. 1963) (Second Treatise), at 365–66.

B. In Nozick's view, the full right passes, by means of a contractual agreement. (His theory of justice in transfers, which is part of his theory of entitlement, is merely a special case of this general claim.) Hence the entrepreneurs who own the protective association accumulate a stack of rights from their clients. They can in turn transfer those rights, in aggregation, to employees of the firm who walk the streets, staff the jails, run the courts, and collect the fines, all of them living bearers of those aggregated rights.

If total transfers of that sort are in fact permissible and possible, then Nozick might be able to carry his argument through (leaving to one side such objections as have already been raised earlier in this Article). However, Nozick is guilty here of an error that we might label "the fallacy of the transitivity of rights transfers." It bears a resemblance to the notion that indifference is transitive, although not too much weight can be placed on that comparison. When an individual is called upon to order a set of elements by means of the relation "preferred or indifferent to," he may judge himself to be indifferent between x and y, and indifferent between y and z, and indifferent between z and w, and yet *not* indifferent between x and w. This would be explained by the fact that the differences between the members of each pair were too small to affect his preference judgments, too small to be noticed, whereas the aggregated differences, as revealed in the comparison of x with w, might exceed his threshold of indifference.

By analogy, in a simple rights transfer, as when I hire a lawyer to close a real estate sale for me, there is a minute slippage or blockage in the rights transfer, due to the fact that my agent is also an independent human being. Because he is a person as well as an agent, there is a small but nonzero probability that he will exceed his authority, or get his instructions confused, or interpret a situation in a manner that I would not approve. There is also a nonzero probability that I will be unaware of the breakdown of agency, or will be unable to rectify it. Because Nozick focuses his attention on simple rights-transfers, where the

probability of slippage falls below the minimal threshold of moral awareness, he fails to see that as the protective association grows, as the rights collected are transferred and retransferred, as my relationship to my so-called agent grows ever more attenuated, I will become less and less able to see my own will, my own moral agency, in the actions of the association's owners and employees. As the imperfection of the transfer magnifies, my right to consider the transfer as having taken place diminishes. Eventually, I must recognize that for all practical moral purposes, I cannot exercise the oversight that is a necessary component of any permissible rights-transfer. I must therefore withdraw my authorization from the association. The net result is an unstable fluctuation in the size of the clienteles of the protective associations, with the mean size oscillating between limits the higher of which is no where near large enough to permit even a momentary pretense of dominance.

Obviously, this point could be expanded upon at great length, but inasmuch as others have done so,[1] there is no need to elaborate on the subject here. Suffice it to say that Nozick appears to have no appreciation of the staggering problems of controlling a protective association, of monitoring those actually entrusted with the tasks of enforcement. Since he must assume some level of rights violation, and hence some tendency of individuals to commit such violations, in order to get his argument going (otherwise, who needs a state?), he cannot pass this off as a practical detail from which his model abstracts.

The real problem—indeed, the underlying problem with all of *Anarchy, State, and Utopia*—is Nozick's persistent failure to take account of the nature of social reality. Nozick's models, methods, and arguments all treat social relationships as *transparent* rather than as *opaque*. He portrays social interactions as marginal to the existence, integrity, and coherent identity of the individuals who participate in them, rather than as central and constitutive. It follows that he can have no usable notions of false consciousness, of self-deception, of alienation, and of the objectification of subjec-

---

[1] For a brilliant exposition of this point, see Rousseau, *The Social Contract* 88–96 (Cranston ed. 1970).

tive categories. The demystification of social reality, which ought to be set as a major task for social theory and social practice, is simply assumed by Nozick as a given presupposition of his analysis.[1]

Robert Paul Wolff. "Robert Nozick's Derivation of the Minimal State." *Arizona Law Review* 19, No. 7 (1977): 20–25.

---

[1] If I had been trained on the continent, in the dialectical mode, rather than in America by analytic philosophers, I might be tempted to suggest that there is, in the history of modern social theory, a dialectical progression: FROM the classical liberal assumption that social relationships are transparent, so that rational individuals already possess an adequate understanding of the true nature of society; which is the *first thesis:* TO the conservative, irrationalist view that society is mysterious, nonrational, incomprehensible, so that human reason cannot fathom it; which is the *first antithesis:* TO the higher claim that society is now opaque, mysterious, incomprehensible, but that reason can, by developing or perfecting itself, arrive finally at the realization that society is truly rational, and hence that social relationships can be grasped by reason; which is the *first, or Hegelian, synthesis:* FROM the Hegelian synthesis, which becomes the *new, or second thesis:* TO the utopian socialist doctrine that society is now irrational, and must be changed immediately by action to make it conform to reason's dictates; which is the *second antithesis:* TO the recognition that the achievement of collective, or social, rationality is a collective human project, requiring the union of thought and action, and requiring both a transformation of social institutions and a transformation of our thought about social institutions, each transformation both assisting and drawing assistance from the other; which is the *final, or Marxian, synthesis.*

The Great Utopia

Friedrich A. Hayek

FRIEDRICH A. HAYEK *(1899–) was born in Austria but subsequently became a British citizen. He taught economic theory at the University of London and the University of Chicago. His books include* The Pure Theory of Capital, Individualism and Economic Order, *and* The Road to Serfdom.

What has always made the state a hell on earth has been precisely that man has tried to make it his heaven.—*F. Hoelderlin.*

That socialism has displaced liberalism as the doctrine held by the great majority of progressives does not simply mean that people had forgotten the warnings of the great liberal thinkers of the past about the consequences of collectivism. It has happened because they were persuaded of the very opposite of what these men had predicted. The extraordinary thing is that the same socialism that was not only early recognized as the gravest threat to freedom, but quite openly began as a reaction against the liberalism of the French Revolution, gained general acceptance under the flag of liberty. It is rarely remembered now that socialism in its beginnings was frankly authoritarian. The French writers who laid the foundations of modern socialism had no doubt that their ideas could be put into practice only by a strong dictatorial government. To them socialism meant an attempt to "terminate the revolution" by a deliberate reorganization of society on hierarchical lines and by the imposition of a coercive "spiritual power." Where freedom was concerned, the founders of socialism made no bones about their intentions. Freedom of thought they regarded as the root-evil of nineteenth-century society, and the first

of modern planners, Saint-Simon, even predicted that those who did not obey his proposed planning boards would be "treated as cattle."

Only under the influence of the strong democratic currents preceding the revolution of 1848 did socialism begin to ally itself with the forces of freedom. But it took the new "democratic socialism" a long time to live down the suspicions aroused by its antecedents. Nobody saw more clearly than De Tocqueville that democracy as an essentially individualist institution stood in an irreconcilable conflict with socialism:

"Democracy extends the sphere of individual freedom," he said in 1848; "socialism restricts it. Democracy attaches all possible value to each man; socialism makes each man a mere agent, a mere number. Democracy and socialism have nothing in common but one word: equality. But notice the difference: while democracy seeks equality in liberty, socialism seeks equality in restraint and servitude."[1]

To allay these suspicions and to harness to its cart the strongest of all political motives—the craving for freedom—socialism began increasingly to make use of the promise of a "new freedom." The coming of socialism was to be the leap from the realm of necessity to the realm of freedom. It was to bring "economic freedom," without which the political freedom already gained was "not worth having." Only socialism was capable of effecting the consummation of the age-long struggle for freedom, in which the attainment of political freedom was but a first step.

The subtle change in meaning to which the word "freedom" was subjected in order that this argument should sound plausible is important. To the great apostles of political free-

[1] "Discours prononcé à l'assemblée constituante le 12 septembre 1848 sur la question du droit au travail," (Envres complètes d'Alexis de Tocqueville (1866), IX, 546.

dom the word had meant freedom from coercion, freedom from the arbitrary power of other men, release from the ties which left the individual no choice but obedience to the orders of a superior to whom he was attached. The new freedom promised, however, was to be freedom from necessity, release from the compulsion of the circumstances which inevitably limit the range of choice of all of us, although for some very much more than for others. Before man could be truly free, the "despotism of physical want" had to be broken, the "restraint of the economic system" relaxed.

Freedom in this sense is, of course, merely another name for power[1] or wealth. Yet, although the promises of this new freedom were often coupled with irresponsible promises of a great increase in material wealth in a socialist society, it was not from such an absolute conquest of the niggardliness of nature that economic freedom was expected. What the promise really amounted to was that the great existing disparities in the range of choice of different people were to disappear. The demand for the new freedom was thus only another name for the old demand for an equal distribution of wealth. But the new name gave the socialists another word in common with the liberals, and they exploited it to the full. And, although the word was used in a different sense by the two groups, few people noticed this and still fewer asked themselves whether the two kinds of freedom promised could really be combined.

There can be no doubt that the promise of greater freedom has become one of the most effective weapons of socialist propaganda and that the belief that socialism would bring freedom is genuine and sincere. But this would only heighten the tragedy if it should prove that what was promised to us as the Road to Freedom was in fact the High Road to Servitude. Unquestionably, the promise of more freedom was responsible for luring more and more liberals along the socialist road, for blinding them to the conflict which exists between the basic principles of socialism and liberalism and for often enabling socialist to usurp the very name of the old party of freedom. Socialism was embraced by the greater part of the intelligentsia as the apparent heir of the liberal tradition: therefore it is not surprising that to them the idea of socialism's leading to the opposite of liberty should appear inconceivable.

In recent years, however, the old apprehensions of the unforeseen consequences of socialism have once more been strongly voiced from the most unexpected quarters. Observer after observer, in spite of the contrary expectation with which he approached his subject, has been impressed with the extraordinary similarity in many respects of the conditions under "fascism" and "communism." While "progressives" in England and elsewhere were still deluding themselves that communism and fascism represented opposite poles, more and more people began to ask themselves whether these new tyrannies were not the outcome of the same tendencies. Even communists must have been somewhat shaken by such testimonies as that of Max Eastman, Lenin's old friend, who found himself compelled to admit that "instead of being better, Stalinism is worse than fascism, more ruthless, barbarous, unjust, immoral, antidemocratic, unredeemed by any hope or scruple," and that it is "better described as superfascist"; and when we find the same author recognizing that "Stalinism *is* socialism, in the sense of being an inevitable although unforeseen political accompaniment of the nationalization and collectivization which he had relied upon as part of his plan for erecting a classless society,"[2] his conclusion clearly

---

[1] The characteristic confusion of freedom with power, which we shall meet again and again throughout this discussion, is too big a subject to be thoroughly examined here. As old as socialism itself, it is so closely allied with it that almost seventy years ago a French scholar, discussing its Saint-Simonian origins, was led to say that this theory of liberty "est à elle seule tout le socialisme" (Paul Janet, *Saint-Simon et le Saint-Simonisme* [1878]. p. 26 n.). The most explicit defender of this confusion is, significantly, the leading philosopher of American left-wingism, John Dewey, according to whom "liberty is the effective power to do specific things" so that "the demand for liberty is demand for power" ("Liberty and Social Control," *Social Frontier*, November, 1935, p. 41).
[2] *Stalin's Russia and the Crisis of Socialism* (1940), p. 82.

achieves wider significance.

Mr. Eastman's case is perhaps the most remarkable, yet he is by no means the first or the only sympathetic observer of the Russian experiment to form similar conclusions. Several years earlier W.H. Chamberlin, who in twelve years in Russia as an American correspondent had seen all his ideals shattered, summed up the conclusions of his studies there and in Germany and Italy in the statement that "socialism is certain to prove, in the beginning at least, the road NOT to freedom, but to dictatorship and counter-dictatorships, to civil war of the fiercest kind. Socialism achieved and maintained by democratic means seems definitely to belong to the world of utopias."[1] Similarly a British writer, F.A. Voigt, after many years of close observation of developments in Europe as a foreign correspondent, concludes that "Marxism has led to Fascism and National Socialism, because, in all essentials, it is Fascism and National Socialism."[2] And Walter Lippmann has arrived at the conviction that "the generation to which we belong is now learning from experience what happens when men retreat from freedom to a coercive organization of their affairs. Though they promise themselves a more abundant life, they must in practice renounce it; as the organized direction increases, the variety of ends must give way to uniformity. That is the nemesis of the planned society and the authoritarian principle in human affairs."[3]

Many more similar statements from people in a position to judge might be selected from publications of recent years, particularly from those by men who as citizens of the now totalitarian countries have lived through the transformation and have been forced by their experience to revise many cherished beliefs. We shall quote as one more example a German writer who expresses the same conclusion perhaps more justly than those already quoted.

"The complete collapse of the belief in the attainability of freedom and equality through Marxism," writes Peter Drucker, "has forced Russia to travel the same road toward a totalitarian, purely negative, non-economic society of unfreedom and inequality which Germany has been following. Not that communism and fascism are essentially the same. Fascism is the stage reached after communism has proved an illusion, and it has proved as much an illusion in Stalinist Russia as in pre-Hitler Germany."[4]

No less significant is the intellectual history of many of the Nazi and Fascist leaders. Everyone who has watched the growth of these movements in Italy[5] or in Germany has been struck by the number of leading men, from Mussolini downward (and not excluding Laval and Quisling), who began as socialists and ended as Fascists or Nazis. And what is true of the leaders is even more true of the rank and file of the movement. The relative ease with which a young communist could be converted into a Nazi or vice versa was generally known in Germany, best of all to the propagandists of the two parties. Many a university teacher during the 1930's has seen English and American students return from the Continent uncertain whether they were communists or Nazis and certain only that they hated Western liberal civilization.

It is true, of course, that in Germany before 1933, and in Italy before 1922, communists and Nazis or Fascists clashed more frequently with each other than with other parties. They competed for the support of the same type of mind and reserved for each other the hatred of the heretic. But their practice showed how closely they are related. To both, the real enemy, the man with whom they had nothing in common and whom they could not hope to convince, is the liberal of the old type. While to the Nazi the communist, and to the communist the Nazi, and to both the socialist, are potential recruits who are made of the right

---

[1] *A False Utopia* (1937), pp. 202–3.

[2] *Unto Caesar* (1939), p. 95.

[3] *Atlantic Monthly*, November, 1936, p. 552.

[4] *The End of Economic Man* (1939), p. 230.

[5] An illuminating account of the intellectual history of many of the Fascist leaders will be found in Robert Michels (himself a former Marxist Fascist), *Sozialismus and Faszismus* (Munich, 1925), II, 264–66, 311–12.

timber, although they have listened to false prophets, they both know that there can be no compromise between them and those who really believe in individual freedom.

Lest this be doubted by people misled by official propaganda from either side, let me quote one more statement from an authority that ought not to be suspect. In an article under the significant title of "The Rediscovery of Liberalism," Professor Eduard Heimann, one of the leaders of German religious socialism, writes: "Hitlerism proclaims itself as both true democracy and true socialism, and the terrible truth is that there is a grain of truth for such claims—an infinitesimal grain, to be sure, but at any rate enough to serve as a basis for such fantastic distortions. Hitlerism even goes so far as to claim the role of protector of Christianity, and the terrible truth is that even this gross misinterpretation is able to make some impression. But one fact stands out with perfect clarity in all the fog: Hitler has never claimed to represent true liberalism. Liberalism then has the distinction of being the doctrine most hated by Hitler."[1] It should be added that this hatred had little occasion to show itself in practice merely because, by the time Hitler came to power, liberalism was to all intents and purposes dead in Germany. And it was socialism that had killed it.

While to many who have watched the transition from socialism to fascism at close quarters the connection between the two systems has become increasingly obvious, in the democracies the majority of people still believe that socialism and freedom can be combined. There can be no doubt that most socialists here still believe profoundly in the liberal ideal of freedom and that they would recoil if they became convinced that the realization of their program would mean the destruction of freedom. So little is the problem yet seen, so easily do the most irreconcilable ideals still live together, that we can still hear such contradictions in terms as "individualist socialism" seriously discussed. If this is the state of mind which makes us drift into a new world, nothing can be more urgent than that we should seriously examine the real significance of the evolution that has taken place elsewhere. Although our conclusion will only confirm the apprehensions which others have already expressed, the reasons why this development cannot be regarded as accidental will not appear without a rather full examination of the main aspects of this transformation of social life. That democratic socialism, the great utopia of the last few generations, is not only unachievable, but that to strive for it produces something so utterly different that few of those who now wish it would be prepared to accept the consequences, many will not believe until the connection has been laid bare in all its aspects.

Friedrich Hayek. *The Road to Serfdom*. Chicago: University of Chicago Press, 1944.

---

[1] *Social Research*, Vol. VIII, No. 4 (November, 1941). It deserves to be recalled in this connection that, whatever may have been his reasons, Hitler thought it expedient to declare in one of his public speeches as late as February, 1941, that "basically National Socialism and Marxism are the same" (cf. the *Bulletin of International News* [published by the Royal Institute of International Affairs], XVIII, No. 5, 269).

Free Enterprise Without the Entrepreneur?

T. Boone Pickens, Jr.

T. BOONE PICKENS, JR., *an American, is President and Chairman of the Board of Mesa Petroleum Company.*

The American spirit of capitalism—American ingenuity and drive—built this country, but I am concerned today that we're losing part of that spirit in the corporate framework. Corporate America has become an administrative institution, bent on perpetuating itself rather than invigorating and stimulating the free enterprise system. The entrepreneurial instinct has been stifled by a bureaucratic structure that encourages an administrative rather than entrepreneurial system. In some ways, we really have forgotten our roots.

Some people today would even try to debase the innovative spirit by trying to create a bad name for those people who, I believe, are true risk-takers and who are forcing necessary changes in corporate America. The recent buzzword is "corporate raider," a label meant to reflect something sinister in the business world. In reality, these risk-takers epitomize the spirit of people like Henry Ford and others who built great companies in this country.

Several months ago, when Mesa was attempting to acquire Phillips Petroleum Company, some in the media tried to make a distinction between Frank Phillips, the founder, and me. "We need more builders like Frank Phillips," they said. My response was that Frank Phillips probably had more characteristics in common with me than with current Phillips management. Frank was a risk-taker, an entrepreneur. And if he were alive today, I'd bet we would be making some deals together. Entrepreneurs are the same throughout history. It's the opportunities available to them that change.

Unfortunately, much of corporate America today has lost that risk-taking spirit. Instead of continuing the legacies of such leaders as Frank Phillips and encouraging more innovation and competition, today many members of corporate America are asking the government to protect them from these very things.

I recently testified before the House Ways and Means Committee in Washington. Two CEOs of major oil companies followed my presentation, and, during his remarks, one CEO asked for help three times from Washington. He wanted import tariffs on products, he wanted legislation to stop takeovers, and he wanted additional shale oil subsidies. But he concluded his address by asking Washington to get out of his business. There is an executive who has forgotten the rules of capitalism and free enterprise.

He's not alone. Many executives have forgotten the traditional goal of business: to make money for stockholders. Let me give you a classic example: Andy Siegler, the CEO of Champion International and self-proclaimed spokesman for the Business Roundtable, an organization composed of the 200 largest corporations in America. Mr. Siegler says that the overriding concern of business is whether the public interest is served. So the framework for business decisions, Mr. Siegler believes, is not the shareholders' interest, but that of society. Does this guy understand the free enterprise system? I don't think so.

It is very straightforward. Shareholders own the company. If shareholders do well, the employees of the company do well, as does the community in which the company operates and, in turn, the general economy. But the shareholders are at the top of the list. Otherwise, the foundation of our economy weakens, the system falls apart and the public interest is not served.

Shareholders are the most important link in the chain of capital formation and of a soundly functioning economy. But that important connection has been weakened in recent years by the ever-growing pressure of administrative management more interested in corporate amenities than in looking out for shareholders' concerns. Much of the problem stems from managements who have lost their entrepreneurial instincts because they do not own significant amounts of stock in their own companies.

For instance, the CEOs of the Business Roundtable own less than 1/300th of 1 percent of the outstanding shares in the companies they manage. It is also interesting that the salaries of those CEOs are just slightly over $1 million a year. It would appear they're not spending their money on company stock.

Let me illustrate that. On December 23, after Mesa Partners had made an agreement with Phillips Petroleum Company, I had a conversation with Bill Douce, the chairman of Phillips. He told me that he didn't appreciate the comments I had made about his ownership in Phillips. I had said previously that Mr. Douce only owned 37,000 shares of stock in Phillips, he had been reporting for years that his annual salary was over $1 million and that he had received a bonus of a million dollars a year, as well. I told him that I felt if he was not spending his money on company stock, he was spending it elsewhere. So Mr. Douce said, "There was one thing left out of those remarks." I asked what it was. He replied, "You should have told them we didn't have a stock option plan." I followed up with, "Why don't you have a stock option plan?" He said, "Well, Boone, we could never make any money off of it." Incredible. He couldn't make any money on a stock option plan at no risk. Yet, he expected investors to own stock in his company.

Do you think these executives consider themselves employees of the company? No. Do you think they consider themselves to be the owners of the company? I think that they do.

The shareholder-management relationship is the ultimate form of a supervisor-employee relationship. Each of us has been in the employee's position. We know that each day we are not "safe." We know that if we don't do our job to the satisfaction of our supervisor, he can criticize us and tell us to do a better job, and if we don't get it done, he can run us off. That is the same role corporate managements fill. As employees of the shareholders, managements are to do the job their shareholders require or they will find themselves looking for a new job.

But all too often management's attitude has placed it above the shareholders' interest. These managements don't consider themselves to be employees. During Phillips' shareholders meeting in February, an employee asked Chairman Douce, "Why not put an employee on the board of directors if you are going to load up our ESOP plan (with debt)?" He replied, "We'll have to consider that." Why wasn't Douce's response, "We have four employees on the board right now. We may consider expanding that to more employees?" Because he didn't consider himself to be an employee.

This attitude has grown beyond the executive suite. An article on takeovers in the March 14, 1985 issue of the *Detroit News* said: "Whatever the circumstances of the stockholders, they seldom have any control over the outcome of a takeover fight. They have voting rights, but except in unusual cases, the only players who really count are the company's managers, large financial institutions and wealthy deal makers." That's not true. The stockholders' rights are paramount.

Last week before the House Judiciary Committee Hearings, Mr. Douce of Phillips and Robert Eckman of Rorer Group were on the panel just ahead of me. Douce was expressing that hostile takeovers are bad, but friendly takeovers are good. And when asked who determined whether a bid was friendly or hostile, Mr. Douce said the decision rested with the outside board members. You and I both know how most outside directors are chosen. Often times, it's the "Good Old Boys Club." So the more realistic answer to the question would be that if the chairman says it's hostile, then it's hostile.

As the testimony proceeded, Mr. Eckman said he was disturbed about all the money being made on takeovers. He had some sinister thought as to where the money went. The

Congressman looked at him and said, "Where do you think it's going Mr. Eckman?" Mr. Eckman replied, "I think these funds are going into the underground economy and then to Morocco." There was a pause and no laughter in the room, and I know everybody was thinking, "Did I hear that right?" The Congressman said, "I beg your pardon." And Mr. Eckman repeated his answer. Then everybody laughed.

That's just one example of the length to which executives will go to discourage the competitive market confronting them. They want protection—especially from their own shareholders, who they relegate to nothing more than a nuisance. In this country, at one time, many people—including blacks—didn't think the black vote counted. Everyone knows that it does count today. And in the same way, the shareholders' vote counts, also. Shareholders own companies, and they are people just like you and me. That's why they must be protected from management abuse.

Forty-two million Americans own stock in publicly held companies. Detroit is the fifth-largest shareholder city in the United States—930,000 people in Detroit own stock directly in publicly owned companies. In addition, hundreds of thousands of others participate in share ownership through such organizations as the retirement and pension fund plans of the United Auto Workers and Chrysler, the Stroh's Brewery Thrift Plan and the City of Detroit Retirement System.

Everyone involved in our securities markets—either directly or indirectly—has a stake in the way corporate management views its job. We must bring back management accountability by encouraging management to take a risk in the company just as the shareholders have. Ownership puts everything in perspective—day-to-day operating results or takeover bids. Sharing the risk stimulates the entrepreneurial drive.

Mesa is a case in point. Our staff is innovative and hard working, due primarily to the fact that 96 percent of Mesa's employees are stockholders in the company. I continually put my money in Mesa. In fact, 90 percent of my net worth is in Mesa.

We aren't asking corporate America's management to do anything more than return to the tradition on which this country was founded. We owe it to the future to put corporate America back on track—to put the entrepreneurial spirit back into the free enterprise system.

T. Boone Pickens, Jr. *Vital Speeches of the Day*. 51, No. 18 (1985): 565–567. This speech was delivered to the Economic Club of Detroit, Detroit, Michigan, April 15, 1985.

Part V

Neo-Conservatism

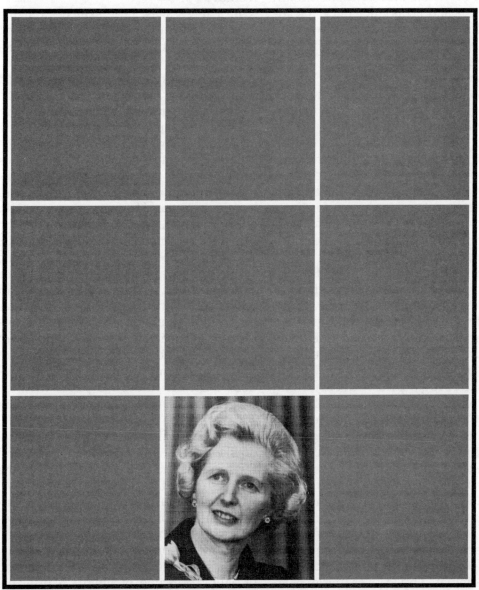

MARGARET THATCHER

One of the most important figures in neo-conservative thought is Milton Friedman. He has campaigned indefatigably defending a strict monetarist policy as a means of combatting some of the worst economic evils of capitalism. In "Economists and Economic Policy" he addresses the difficult question of how economists can influence public policy. Of course he answers this question within the parameters of a certain view of human nature, namely one predicated on the idea that persons aim to satisfy their own interests. Within these parameters Friedman argues in support of free trade, institutional changes that would prohibit restrictions on free trade, institutional changes that would necessitate a balanced budget, and keeping one's options open for times of crisis. Economists can, thinks Friedman, influence public policy by supporting these objectives.

In a very candid essay, Philip Resnick speaks of three different derivations of neo-conservatism: one associated with the Trilateral Commission, a second growing out of the work of Hayek and Friedman, and a third rooted in time-honoured conceptions of morality and religion. The resulting ideology pits individualism against collectivism, rejects redistributionism, evokes populism, and adheres strongly to allegedly democratic principles. And, says Resnick, this ideology has had effective appeal—an appeal which the left can reverse only by mounting vigorous moral and practical arguments to the contrary.

In discussing neo-conservatism, Resnick refers in passing to the frontal attack on government spending and social priorities initiated by Prime Minister Margaret Thatcher in Great Britain. What he neglects to say anything about is the individual, namely Madsen Pirie, who stands behind most of Thatcher's initiatives. For this reason, we may fittingly look at this individual, the head of the Adam Smith Institute.

In a few pages, Pirie sketches out the direction which the Thatcher government has followed at his beckoning. This direction comprises the policy of privatization. Pirie canvasses hastily the areas affected by this policy and they include ports, docks, telecommunications, shipping lines, Jaguar cars, Leyland buses, the state airline, the aerospace industry and airports. Alongside this action he places some raw facts including Britain's low inflation rate, low incidence of strikes, and low income tax. He proceeds to explain why privatization was undertaken by the British government and how it was done. The former he gives in terms of public sector under-capitalization, public sector expense, public sector inefficiency, and public sector unresponsiveness. The latter he gives in terms of what he calls a systematic approach: first, make friends of enemies; second, privatize the process of privatization; and third, disarm the objections. Pirie concludes his paper with the prognosis that the whole public sector in Britain must be privatized.

Ayn Rand shares with Pirie a strong dislike for the state. According to Rand the result of the power of the state is the persecution of a minority in the USA, namely big business. Liberals she castigates for supporting a state which violates the rights of others rather than supporting a state which protects the rights of others. In this sense she subscribes to one version of Mill's principle of liberty, a principle which she sees allied with laissez-faire capitalism and the marketplace.

In the final paper, Desmond King confirms some of the findings already cited in connection with Pirie, namely the detailed moves toward privatization introduced by the Thatcher government. However King points out that in some cases the public monopolies dismantled by Thatcher have in fact been replaced by private monopolies thereby contradicting the free market principle of competition. Whilst not identifying Thatcher's program as neo-conservative, King nonetheless sees fit to identify it as New Right and echoing some of the harsher aspects of classical liberalism. Finally he makes note of other often unmentioned aspects of privatization, including reduced subsidies and increased charges for welfare services, the extension of private-sector practices into urban aid projects, and the paradox at the heart of this policy: the major role played by government in dismantling government.

Running through all of the foregoing papers is an implicit or explicit recognition that in neo-conservatism, sometimes called the New Right, is a fundamental recognition of the importance of market forces as the touchstone of social truth. In a peculiar way, neo-conservatism represents a dramatic return to the classical liberalism of Smith and Mill with their emphasis on the individual and his place in the economic order. Yet there is at least one difference between the old and the new perspectives and that is the clarity with which the recent ideas have been presented. Perhaps therein lies some of the appeal of neo-conservatism.

Economists and Economic Policy

Milton Friedman

MILTON FRIEDMAN *(1912–) was Professor of Economics at the University of Chicago and currently is Senior Research Fellow at The Hoover Institution. He is noted for adopting a strong monetarist position, a position which he sees as the logical extension of laissez-faire capitalism.*

The founder of our discipline as we view it today was Adam Smith. His book *The Wealth of Nations*, published in 1776, is both the first scientific treatise in economics and one of the most effective tracts intended to influence public policy that has ever been published. Nonetheless, it took seventy years before the doctrines of *The Wealth of Nations* were adopted in Great Britain, before his arguments for free trade and against mercantilist policies were put into practice.

From that time to this, economists have followed the same dual goal: to improve our understanding of how the economy works and to influence public policy. In trying to influence policy, economists have typically adopted a public interest view of government. They have written as if governmental officials, whether elected or appointed, were selflessly dedicated to achieving the public's welfare and as if the role of economists were simply to figure out how to do so—to decide what is the right thing to do and to persuade people dedicated to the public interest that it is the right thing to do.

The most distinguished representative of that point of view is doubtless John Maynard Keynes. He made his attitude crystal clear in a letter to Friedrich Hayek commenting on the *Road to Serfdom*. The excerpt from his letter that is most often quoted is: "[I]t is a grand book...[M]orally and philosophically I find myself in agreement with virtually the whole of it; and not only in agreement with it, but in a deeply moved agreement." It comes as a surprise to most people that Keynes gave such an unqualified endorsement to the *Road to Serfdom*. However, when you read the rest of the letter you come to the inevitable "but." (Incidentally, "but" is the most important single word in most letters, like the one I got the other day from a gentleman who said he was 98 percent in agreement with my views in favor of free markets, *but* we must continue to protect honey from foreign competition in order to have bees around to pollinate the crops.) And so Keynes came to his "but"; "What we need...is not a change in our economic programmes...but perhaps even...an enlargement of them...[W]hat we need is a restoration of right moral thinking—a return to proper moral values in our social philosophy....Dangerous acts can be done safely in a community which thinks and feels rightly, which would be the way to hell if they were executed by those who think and feel wrongly."[1]

That approach to public policy was Keynes's political legacy to economists. I believe that it may well be both a more important and a more dangerous legacy than his economic legacy.

I'm no exception to my generalization about the typical approach of the economist in dealing with public policy. Most of my own work dealing with public policy has had the same character of proceeding as if I were addressing governmental officials selflessly ded-

---

[1] John Maynard Keynes [1980, 385, 387, 388]. [Ed. note: See end of article for details of citations.]

icated to the public interest. As you know, for many years I have studied and analyzed monetary policy. On the basis of that work, I have attempted to persuade the Federal Reserve System that it was doing the wrong thing and that it ought to adopt a different policy. That was time ill-spent. It has had no appreciable results on the behavior of the Federal Reserve System and there is a good reason why it did not: because the public-interest characterization of government is basically flawed. That way of viewing government is very different from the way we view business. We do not regard a businessman as selflessly devoted to the public interest. We think of a businessman as in business to improve his own welfare, to serve his own interest. Adam Smith taught us that "It is not from the benevolence of the butcher, the brewer, or the baker, that we expect our dinner, but from their regard to their own interest. We address ourselves not to their humanity but to their self-love, and never talk to them of our own necessities but of their advantages."[1] In his famous phrase, though "every individual intends only his own gain, he is...led by an invisible hand to promote an end which was no part of his intention."[2]

Why should we regard government officials differently? They too aim to serve their own interest, and in government as in business we must try to set up institutions under which individuals who intend only their own gain are led by an invisible hand to serve the public interest, instead of, as so often happens, by an "invisible foot" to serve private interests that it was no part of their intention to serve. The inconsistency between our treatment of government and our treatment of business has long been recognized, but generally only in asides.[3] The great contribution of what has become known as the theory of public choice, developed by such writers as Anthony Downs in *The Economic Theory of Democracy*, and James Buchanan and Gordon Tullock in *The Calculus of Consent*, has been to make this inconsistency explicit, and to force all of us to recognize that we should analyze governmen-

tal officials in the same way that we analyze businessmen, as promoting their own self-interest.

I can illustrate the importance of this change of viewpoint by using it to show why it was a waste of my time to try to convert the Fed to my point of view. Suppose that ten or twenty years ago the Federal Reserve had adopted the policies that I and other monetarists were proposing. Suppose that it had then embarked on a policy of increasing the quantity of money at about 3 percent a year, year after year, and doing nothing else—at least in respect of aggregate monetary policy. I believe that there would be wide agreement among economists in general and monetary economists in particular that such a policy would have avoided the major inflation of the 1970s and the resulting turmoil in the financial structure. It would also have avoided the ups and downs in interest rates and the economy of the early 1980s. Today, the economic situation of the U.S. and of the world would be very different and, I believe, far preferable.

Indeed, even an institution that I disapprove of very much, the International Monetary Fund, might still be serving its original purpose. Its purpose disappeared in 1971 when the Bretton Woods agreement was ended and floating exchange rates were introduced, but it's not only old soldiers who don't die. From 1971 on, the IMF was an institution in search of a purpose instead of a purpose in search of an institution.

But now look at another set of consequences of the hypothetical adoption by the Fed of a policy of steady monetary growth at 3 percent a year. Is there any possibility whatsoever that polls of public opinion would, on that hypothesis, now be recording that the second most important person in the U.S. is the Chairman of the Federal Reserve? If the Federal Reserve had followed that policy, the readers of this talk, let alone members of the public at large, would not even know the names of the members of the Federal Reserve Board any more than they know the names of

---

[1] Smith [1930, 16].

[2] Smith [1930, 42].

[3] An exceptionally explicit statement is made by Joseph Schumpeter [1949, 208–209].

the officials who run the Bureau of Engraving and Printing. The Federal Reserve would have become a bureaucratic agency carrying on a simple mechanical task. It would be performing a useful function, as the Bureau of Engraving and Printing does. Clearly, it was not in the self-interest of the Federal Reserve hierarchy to follow the hypothetical policy. It was therefore a waste of time to try to persuade them to do so.

To avoid misunderstanding, let me stress that I'm not criticizing the people in the Federal Reserve System just as I'm not criticizing businessmen when I say that they pursue their self-interest. On the contrary, as already emphasized, I and most of us as economists have learned from Adam Smith that the world will run best if there is a fundamental framework under which people who pursue their self-interest are led by an invisible hand also to serve the public interest. I'm not criticizing anybody except those who were responsible for setting up institutions that are not consistent with such a framework. The Federal Reserve System puts a great deal of power in the hands of a few people and it is so constructed that it has been in their self-interest to pursue a policy which, I believe, has been very harmful for the public rather than helpful. Let me make explicit also that I am not accusing the persons in control of monetary policy of *knowingly* doing harm. On the contrary, I have no doubt that they are sincerely persuaded that they acted in the public interest and that economic conditions would have developed in an even more undesirable way if they had acted differently. Everyone of us knows that what is in his interest is in the public interest—and as Charles Wilson said about General Motors, "and conversely."

From the public choice perspective, the interesting question is, how can economists influence public policy as well as simply describe it? Simply describing it is not an unimportant task. Indeed, the major task of scholars is to understand the way the world works rather than to influence it. However, insofar as we want not only to understand the way the world works, but also would like to influence it, how can economists exercise influence while at the same time recognizing that they are dealing with human beings who pursue their own interest whether they be politicians whose self-interest is to get re-elected, or members of bureaucracies whose self-interest is to have that bureaucracy bigger and more powerful, or idealists whose self-interest is to promote a special version of the public interest? After all, the notion of self-interest is not restricted, as we economists long ago learned, to narrow pecuniary self-interest. It includes many nonpecuniary motives. The saints of this world are pursuing their self-interest no less than the devils.

In my opinion, economists can nonetheless have an influence on public policy in three ways. The oldest, the way that we have practiced the most, is simply to try to inform the public, to give the public a better idea of what is in the public's own interest. The most obvious example is the near-unanimity among economists on the advantages of free trade. We do not have tariffs because they are in the self-interest of the public at large. We have tariffs because most members of the public are uninformed about the effect of the tariffs on them. A particular tariff tends to be promoted by a small concentrated group—producers of a product, including both employers and employees. It pays them to devote a lot of effort and to spend a lot of money to get a tariff or other barrier to foreign competition adopted. Consider the case I mentioned earlier—honey. Few if any of us know the names of the producers of honey, but they do and they are in touch with one another. It is worth their while to lobby for restraint on the importation of honey. The costs of the restraint are spread thinly among the rest of us. It costs each of us a few cents or a few dollars a year. It is not rational for us even to spend the effort required to learn how much harm the honey tariff does to us. As a result, legislators, considering each item separately, can identify the support at the polls that they would gain by favoring the restraint; they cannot identify any support that they would lose; hence they tend to vote for it.

To take into account the insights of the public choice school, it's hopeless for economists to try to persuade the public that its interests are harmed by a particular tariff. We can't possibly hope to educate the public at large sufficiently about honey to make it politically profitable for politicians to vote against restraining imports of honey—let alone, to make it personally profitable for economists to make the attempt. We weren't even able—or sufficiently motivated—to do that about import quotas on automobiles from Japan, even though that restraint on foreign trade probably cost the public more than any other single interference with foreign trade. Quotas on the import of sugar are another striking example. Because of them, we all pay five times the world price for every pound of sugar we use.

In order to be successful in promoting free trade, we must educate the public about tariffs in general, about the virtues of free trade as a general policy, and not dissipate our energies by attacking each tariff separately. They can provide illustrations, and nothing more. Clearly, that is not an easy task. We have been trying it for two centuries without notable success, so obviously we have not been tackling it the right way.

That leads me to the second way in which economists can hope to influence public policy. That way is by analyzing the changes in institutional arrangements that would bring about the desired results and trying to persuade the public to introduce those institutional changes rather than trying to influence policy makers directly. For example, in the case of the tariff, I believe that rather than attacking each individual restraint as it is proposed in Congress, we might have a greater chance of success if we promoted a constitutional amendment saying "Congress shall make no laws imposing tariffs or trade restrictions," or an even broader constitutional amendment saying "Congress shall make no laws prohibiting voluntary contracts between consenting adults." Such an amendment would eliminate tariffs, as well as many restrictions on internal trade, because a seller in a foreign country and a buyer here constitute two consenting adults. I don't mean here to give the precise wording of an amendment; my point is simply to set forth the principle that what we need to do to be effective in promoting free trade is to direct our efforts at changing institutional arrangements through a constitutional provision or in some other way. Such a procedure has two advantages. First, the cost of foreign restraints as a whole

on an individual consumer is substantial, sufficiently large to make it worth his while to be informed about them—provided, there is a chance of putting that information to effective use. Second, it takes only one sustained "crusade" to enact a constitutional amendment, and once enacted it has a continuing effect, whereas it takes a continuous campaign to defeat individual tariff proposals.

A public-choice perspective will sometimes suggest proceeding in ways that seem wrong economically. Let me illustrate with the current Congressional action on the budget. There is wide agreement that the Federal government budget should be cut. How should the budget be cut? Straightforward economic reasoning recommends operating on the margin, namely, cutting a little bit here, a little bit there, and a little bit somewhere else. Economists are well acquainted with that implication of equating marginal costs and returns. We all are amused when consumer researchers ask people what they would do if they had, say, $200 extra to spend, and report that people answer that they would spend it on a single large item—a refrigerator or a calculator or the like. We all know what consumers would actually do. They would spend 5 cents extra on toothpaste, 3 cents extra on something else, and so on.

The marginal principle similarly implies that the optimal way to cut the government budget is to cut it evenly all down the line. However, in terms of political effects, that is precisely the wrong way to do it. The right way to do it is to eliminate agencies, to eliminate functions. Why? If Amtrak's budget is cut by 15 percent, next year the Amtrak bureaucracy will still be there pleading for a higher budget. If you eliminate Amtrak, there will be no bureaucracy in existence to lobby for Amtrak. Eliminate agencies, and the gain will be permanent; make marginal cuts, and the gain will almost invariably be temporary. Both the President, who wants to cut spending, and his Congressional opponents, who clearly do not, have recognized this principle. The President, in the budget he submitted to Congress, proposed to terminate more than a dozen programs, including Revenue Sharing, Job Corps, Amtrak, the Small Business Administration, etc. The Senate cut that down to about five or six, the House has now reduced it to two and proposed instead to make little cuts all over. The final resolution passed by both Houses terminates no major programs and gets its advertised budget cuts by a combination of small cuts and mirrors. The result: the bureaucracy lobbying for larger appropriations will remain intact. That, I believe, is a nice illustration of how the economic analysis of politics makes it necessary to modify correct economic principles when they are applied to political issues.

The campaign underway to enact a constitutional amendment to require a balanced budget and limit spending is another example of attempting to influence policy by changing institutional arrangements so as to make it in the self-interest of legislators to behave in a way that is in the public interest. Currently, if a lobbyist asks a legislator to vote for a program to do something—it's always to do something good, of course—and the legislator says to him: "I can't do that because that would mean higher taxes," the lobbyist says, "What are you talking about? You are a mean nasty fellow. You want to grind those poor people (or whatever group would benefit from the legislation) under your heels." The legislator has no effective answer. He knows as well as the lobbyist that any increase in taxes to finance the specific program would be small and widespread, and so invisible, while the specific spending action would be concentrated and highly visible. That is why the process of considering each spending action separately produces a total budget that is larger than the public desires. That defect in our institutional structure explains the paradox that every public opinion poll shows a majority of the public in favor of a smaller budget and opposed to higher taxes, yet at the same time, Congress consistently votes for more spending and prefers higher taxes to spending restraints.

If a constitutional amendment required total spending to be limited, the legislator's self-interest would change. He could now tell the lobbyist, "You're right. Your project is excellent. However, the Constitution limits the total amount we can spend. I can only vote for your project if I vote less for something else. What else shall I vote less for?" That would pit one special interest against another and change the rules of the game in such a way that the legislator would now find it in his self-interest to operate in the public interest. Similar considerations underlie the attempt by some of us to promote a constitutional amendment enacting a monetary rule.

A third, and perhaps the most effective, way that economists can and do influence public policy is by keeping options open for times of crisis. Major changes in institutional arrangements seldom if ever occur except at a time of crisis. The only reason we have a ghost of a show now of enacting a constitutional amendment to require a balanced budget and to limit spending is because there exists a budgetary crisis. Most commentators bemoan the large budget deficit. I welcome it. The deficit is the only thing that is forcing us to think seriously about how to control Federal spending. The economic effect of the deficit is unquestionably bad; but the political effect of the deficit is good.

The best recent example of this third kind of influence is the introduction of floating exchange rates. From the end of World War II to 1971, the Bretton Woods fixed exchange rate system was in effect. Some economists like myself, Gottfried Haberler, and others had for decades been writing and talking about the advantages of floating exchange rates compared with the existing system of administratively pegged exchange rates. The reaction of policy makers was always that we were unrealistic theorists who simply didn't understand how the "real" world worked. I remember participating in a prestigious gathering of international bankers in Copenhagen at which I shared a platform with the then Managing Director of the IMF. He dismissed out-of-hand my support for floating exchange rates, calling it utterly unworkable and unrealistic. Fixed exchange rates, he proclaimed, was the only feasible system. Two years later, after Bretton Woods had been abandoned, the same group met in Montreal. I again shared a platform with the Managing Director of the IMF—a new one—but this time his line was, "Of course, floating exchange rates are the only feasible possibility in today's world."

As this example demonstrates, floating exchange rates were not adopted because we persuaded anybody that floating exchange rates were the right policy. Floating exchange rates were adopted because a crisis emerged—the drain of gold from the United States—that required drastic action. That option was open because economists had been writing and talking about floating exchange rates. If that option hadn't been open, if it hadn't been a well thought through scheme with respectable academic backing—indeed backed by most economists specializing in money and international trade—something would still have had to be done. However, it would almost certainly have been something other than floating exchange rates.

I want to talk about another example because I do not quite know how to fit it into my tripartite classification of ways economists can influence policy. In his talk at the 1985 annual meeting of the WEA, Walter Oi referred to the influence of economists in abolishing the draft and establishing a volunteer army. He is right, and yet his example doesn't easily fit into my tripartite schema. In December 1966, a large-scale conference on the draft was convened at the University of Chicago under the leadership of Sol Tax. It was unusual because the conferees included not only academics from many fields but also political activists and politicians: economists like Walter Oi and myself, anthropologists like Margaret Mead, politicians like Senator Ted Kennedy, and so on. It was unusual in a more important way: it was one of the few conferences that I've ever attended in which opinions were changed. A vote taken at the outset of the conference recorded about two-thirds of the participants in favor of a draft, only about one-third in favor of a volunteer army. A similar vote taken at the end of the conference recorded the reverse: about two-thirds in favor of a volunteer army and only about one-third in favor of a draft.

In my opinion, the one episode in that four-day conference that did more than anything else to change opinions was a talk that Walter Oi gave on the economics of the draft. It was an extraordinarily effective performance. Walter is always a very good speaker, but on this particular occasion he was particularly effective, if I may be pardoned for referring to his virtual blindness, because it meant that he was obviously not speaking from personal interest.

There he was, with a seeing-eye dog, in front of a large audience talking in his calm, unemotional, highly rational way about the inequity of the draft, about how it was a highly selective and discriminatory implicit tax on the people who were drafted. He presented the case effectively, but I have no doubt that the emotional aura he unwittingly created had much to do with changing the minds of many participants.

Subsequently, when President Nixon appointed a President's Commission on an All Volunteer Armed Force—partly, I may say, under the influence of another economist, Martin Anderson—it consisted of twelve people of whom at the outset six were in favor of a volunteer army and six in favor of the draft. Three of the six in favor of a volunteer army were economists (Alan Greenspan, W. Allen Wallis, and myself), and there were no other economists on the commission. We ended up with a unanimous report in favor of a volunteer army. I must admit that this is one case in which I believe economists did influence public policy through their arguments, and not in the ways I have been talking about, so I don't quite know where to fit it into my pattern.

This leaves me, and this is my closing comment, with a paradox about economists. We too are pursuing our own interests. We cannot in good conscience interpret ourselves as behaving differently from those we analyze. We cannot treat ourselves as an exception. The question then arises: Is it in our self-interest to promote public policy in the ways I have described? That is by no means clear. After all, the New Deal was the greatest employment program for economists that ever existed. I can speak with feeling about it: that's where I got my first job. Most of the readers of this talk are too young to remember how important the New Deal was in opening jobs up for economists. More generally, government is a major source of employment for economists, both directly and through the effect of government intervention on private enterprises. One of the oldest government interventions, antitrust, for example, creates a large and highly remunerative demand for economists as expert witnesses on both sides of many antitrust cases. Similarly, other government interventions create jobs for us in private enterprises to figure out the effects of the interventions and to provide arguments for changes favorable to particular enterprises. They also create jobs for us in government to analyze the effects of the interventions and provide arguments for their retention or modification. I've often wondered whether I was being cynical in interpreting along these lines the tendency for economists to favor free markets in general but, at the same time, to be extremely ingenious in figuring out exceptions that could be justified by externalities, imperfect markets, distributive effects, and so on.

To give another example, one reason for the prompt acceptance by the profession at large of John Maynard Keynes's *General Theory* was because it opened up such wonderful opportunities for employment and influence by economists. After all, if an economy could be controlled by altering taxes and spending, who was going to do the altering of the taxes and spending? Who was going to be occupying those positions of power? I believe that one reason our monetarist rule has had such unenthusiastic acceptance in many quarters is because it would sharply reduce the number of jobs available for economists. So I don't believe we're any exception.

Let me repeat what I said earlier about the businessmen and the government officials. I'm not saying that economists, any more than the rest of the population, deliberately and explicitly put their self-interest above the public interest. I referred earlier to the famous statement during World War II by "Engine" Charlie Wilson, then head of General Motors, that "What's good for General Motors is good for the country, and conversely." Similarly, everyone of us knows that what's good for us is good for the country, and conversely. Every member of the Federal Reserve Board knows that he's an important person and is in an important position. It would be psychologically impossible for him to believe that his actions are harmful. Similarly, the economists who find external effects in every corner of the economy are in the same position. So I'm not saying that anybody explicitly uses his position to do harm; I'm saying something very different. I'm saying that as analysts we should recognize that all of us, ourselves included, are human beings who know our own

self-interest better than we know anything else and who will pursue our self-interest. As Armen Alchian once said, "One thing you can depend on absolutely everybody to do is to put his interest above yours." Again, let me emphasize that self-interest is not restricted to narrow material interest. It includes the desire to serve the public interest, to help other people.

To conclude, how economists have in the past and can in the future influence public policy is an important topic for scientific research. The public choice school has made an important contribution to that topic, but so have the rest of the economics profession— monetary and price theorists, and applied economists alike. Despite my reservations and qualifications, my own self-interest leads me to believe that on the whole economists have exercised a good influence. Maybe tariffs are 10 percent lower than they otherwise would be because of our long-term advocacy of free trade: if so, that 10 percent would pay the salaries of the members of the economics profession many times over.

References

Buchanan, James M. and Gordon Tullock. *The Calculus of Consent: Logical Foundation of Constitution.* Ann Arbor: University of Michigan Press, 1962.

Downs, Anthony. *An Economic Theory of Democracy.* New York: Harper, 1957.

Hayek, Friedrich A. Von. *Road to Serfdom.* London: Routledge, 1945.

Keynes, John Maynard. *The General Theory of Employment, Interest, and Money.* New York: Harcourt, Brace, 1935.

Keynes, John Maynard. *Activities 1940–1946,* Vol. XXVII of *Collected Writings.* Cambridge: Cambridge University Press, 1980.

Schumpeter, Joseph. "The *Communist Manifesto* in Sociology and Economics." *Journal of Political Economy,* June 1949, 208–209.

Smith, Adam. *The Wealth of Nations,* 5th Cannan ed. London: Macmillan and Co., 1930.

Milton Friedman. "Economists and Economic Policy." *Economic Inquiry* 24 (1986): 1–10. This paper was presented as the Presidential Address, Western Economic Association International Conference, July 2, 1985.

The Ideology of Neo-Conservatism

Philip Resnick

PHILIP RESNICK *is Associate Professor of Political Science at the University of British Columbia. He has written on the political economy of Canada and is the author of* The Land of Cain: Class and Nationalism in English Canada 1945–1975 *and* Parliament vs. People.

The Election of Margaret Thatcher in Great Britain and Ronald Reagan in the United States symbolized more than a passing moment in the evolution of western societies. It unleashed a frontal attack on government spending and social priorities. It placed some of the familiar values of western society, such as equality and social justice, into jeopardy. It entailed a re-definition of the relationship between private and public goods. And it forced the left—in both its social democratic and socialist versions—onto the defensive.

For almost 30 years after 1945 the western world experienced a long wave of prosperity and economic growth, coinciding with the adoption by governments of Keynesian-type economic policies and vastly expanded social programmes. Large-scale unemployment became a distant memory, associated with the Depression of the 1930s. Steadily increasing productivity had resulted in higher real per capita incomes and provided the means to increase government services, from health and hospital insurance to public housing. Such measures alleviated the old class differences and gave a reformed capitalist system a new lease on life.

Liberals, social democrats and moderate conservatives all seemed to agree on the basic premises of the new order. The role of the state—as entrepreneur and regulator of the economy—was significantly enlarged. Trade unions were recognized as legitimate economic actors with whom governments and corporations had to deal. The large (and sometimes smaller) corporations continued to dominate the process of production and distribution, but with a greater acceptance of their social responsibilities in a modern economy. Taxation was used, not to *radically* redistribute wealth, but to allow for a modest reallocation of the fruits of increased prosperity. In other words, an expanding economic pie helped pay for the welfare state.

The economic crisis of the 1970s—the balance of payments problems experienced by the United States largely as a result of the Vietnam War, the quadrupling in the price of oil, increased industrial competition from south European and third world countries—led to a profound change in the equation which had formed the foundation of economic policy-making until then. The rates of growth of western economies were severely pruned, to half or less of what they had been a decade or two earlier. Western economies began to experience high rates of inflation while unemployment rates edged stubbornly upward. Governments incurred ever-larger deficits, having failed to accumulate surpluses during the long years of post-war prosperity with which to balance these out. The increase in government spending exceeded the increase in economic growth.

While some on the left talked about a "fiscal crisis of the state" and a potential "legitimacy crisis" in the capitalist system, a quite different attack was about to be mounted from the right. For spokesmen from this camp, it was the legitimacy of Keynesianism and of the welfare state that was in question, and the post-war consensus that needed to be rejected.

There are different versions of this onslaught from the right. One, associated with the Trilateral Commission,[1] says the "excessive" expectations and demands of people posed a threat to representative governments. The language of participation and of rights, so typical of the 1960s, had drowned out reverence for more traditional values such as authority and obedience. In this view, what is needed is a return to the old pattern of relations between governors and governed, coupled with reduced expectations of what economic and other goods governments should provide.

A second version of the neo-conservative view is derived from the writings of old-fashioned "liberal" economists like Hayek and Friedman, who for decades have defended market principles against state intervention. These men oppose the Keynesian policies practiced by Western governments as inherently inflationary. They reject the "redistributionist" logic of social democracy and the more progressive versions of liberalism, calling for a roll-back in the functions of the state to those specified by 18th or 19th century laissez-faire doctrine (i.e., defence, the administration of justice, certain public works). Not all go quite so far in their proclaimed intentions, but the adherents of Friedmanite or "public choice" economics agree strongly on the need to deregulate large sectors of economic life, privatize public corporations and activities, and impose strict limitations on government spending. For them, "the Keynesian paradigm is afloat without a rudder, and its own internal forces, if left to themselves, are likely to ground the system on the rocks of deep depression."[2] The pursuit of balanced budgets becomes an overriding obsession, at the expense of all other ends.

The third element to enter into neo-conservative thinking is a throwback to time-honoured conservative conceptions of morality, religion, etc. The "Moral Majority" in the United States, for example, talks of permissiveness in the schools, promiscuous sexual behaviour, and the decline in religious observance as the supposed consequences of excessively liberal attitudes. It associates the latter with "dissident" elements in American society—middle class intellectuals, unpatriotic film stars, male-hating feminists, environmentalists, gays. Neo-conservatives of this stripe support school prayers, the sacredness of pregnancy, law and order, and anti-communism in their invocation of the good society. This argument often has a strongly populist underpinning, attacking the liberal members of the "new class" who supposedly dominate big government, the media and the bureaucracy, for having instigated undesirable change....

Neo-conservatism thus encompasses a number of elements. It invokes individualism against collectivism, and repudiates the principle of equality (both of opportunity and condition). It rejects the redistributionist ethic of the welfare state and the interventionist role of government. It evokes populism and traditional morality in defending the social order of capitalism. It claims to be more democratic than its liberal or social democratic rivals. In various combinations, these ideas have contributed to the electoral victories of the New Right in the U.S., Britain and Canada.

It is tempting to think of the New Right as a passing aberration, or to convince ourselves that the welfare state is really the best of all possible worlds. If we can somehow survive these few years of low economic growth, the argument goes, we will be able to return to the expansionist policies of the Keynesian past. If the left could only remind the electorate of all the good things that had come its way from the state, public opinion would pay less heed to the barrage of New Right propaganda; if we could only reiterate the virtues of crown corporations such as the CNR, the CBC and Petro-Canada, all would be well. It would be nice to think that if we could stick to the prescribed agenda of large-scale expenditures for health or education or social services, the electorate would once again come to see where its

---

[1] Michael Crozier, Samuel P. Huntington and J. Watanuki, *The Crisis of Democracy: Report on the Governability of Democracies to the Trilateral Commission* (New York: New York University Press, 1975.)

[2] James M. Buchanan and Richard E. Wagner, *Democracy in Deficit: The Political Legacy of Lord Keynes* (New York: Academic Press, 1977), p. 28.

true interests lie.

But we need a different model of socialism for the 1980s. As David Held and John Keane recently remarked:

Socialists who call for less bureaucracy have failed, with few exceptions, to recognize that some positive things can be learned by engaging the new right, which has taken the lead in populariz- ing the demand for less state action.[1]

This does not accept the agenda of neo-conser- vatism, but recognizes that the theme of anti- statism is important. It is the left that should be putting forth an anti-statist position. The crisis of capitalism and the corresponding cri- sis in both Keynesianism and social democ- racy should be an occasion for rethinking our position on major questions—parliamentary vs. participatory democracy, community con- trol vs. state control, industrial democracy vs. state ownership, social security as we know it today vs. a new social contract for an increas- ingly automated society.

This does not mean that we must jettison the welfare state or follow the New Right into an orgy of privatization and slashing neces- sary services, but we must recognize that the welfare state has come to be associated with the bureaucratic state. Here the New Right (in- cluding its nasty, local variant) has been able to make much hay. What is required is "a long-term socialist public philosophy which emphasizes decentralization, less bureaucracy and more democracy."[2] More concretely, we must start developing the basis for a non-stat- ist (or at least less-statist) version of socialism, which does not simply equate collective own- ership with a more powerful state machine. One derives no particular joy from knowing that B.C. Hydro is a publicly-owned enter- prise, for example; in their disregard for com- munity concerns, or environmental factors, or the long-term public interests, crown corpora- tions such as B.C. Hydro are hardly distin- guishable from MacMillan-Bloedel.

Back in the 19th century the left, in both its anarchist and Marxist variants, was a commit- ted critic of the state. The state was seen as an instrument of class domination, of aristocratic privilege and capitalist power. "The emanci- pation of the working class will be carried out by the working class itself," proclaimed the Statutes of the First International in 1864. The alternatives they envisaged lay beyond the pa- rameters of the existing state machinery, in a world where the state would "wither away."

In practice, the state has done anything but wither. As an institution, it has emerged enor- mously strengthened out of economic depres- sion and two world wars. It has been strengthened even more through Marxist-Le- ninist revolutions. Much of the dissatisfaction in the West with socialism comes from the negative features of the Soviet Union and other self-professedly socialist states. But it also arises from a perception that social de- mocracy has only a somewhat more chastened version of state bureaucracy to offer in its place.

When Kafka in the early 1900s wrote, "The chains of the world are made of office paper," he could not anticipate the microfiche and the computer, but he was not wrong. We need something better than a model of undiluted state and bureaucratic power to propose to the electorate today. The neo-conservatives have their version on the agenda—the left will not become relevant again until it develops its own.

The key components would include:

1. a clear distinction between civil society and the state, and an attempt to maximize the role of autonomous citizen-controlled institu- tions;

2. some form of base-level democracy, to allow direct and ongoing citizen participation between elections in political affairs;

3. an economy based on worker-controlled industries and community-controlled activi- ties rather than on the large corporation or the bureaucratically administered state;

4. a fairer sharing of work, a general reduc- tion in working hours, and better protection for the environment;

5. a recognition of our place in a larger in- ternational order that imposes obligations as

[1] David Held and John Keane, "In a Fit State," *New Socialist*, March-April 1984.
[2] Bernard Crick, cited in Held and Keane, op. cit.

well as opportunities.

The *economics* of this model can be called market socialism. It entails the continued existence of private property and small-scale private ownership (shops, land). But it also entails a form of workers' control in all larger enterprises as an alternative to both the large corporation and the centrally planned (and coercive) system of the socialist states.[1]

The *politics* of such a model would be distinctly participatory. We would not have to galvanize a Solidarity Coalition into existence every time we want to react against unpopular measures taken by governments. If a mechanism for fostering ongoing citizen involvement—at the base level—existed, the nature of politics would be radically transformed.

The *social arrangements* of such a model would address more closely the problems of the two-class society we are entering. This is a society divided between those who have jobs and those who do not, in which work-sharing and similar schemes constitute the only fair response, in which we may finally begin to move away from the work ethic of the capitalist system to a different definition of socially valuable activities.

I do not hold out much prospect for any immediate move toward a market socialist economy, toward a more participatory type of political structure, or toward a reorientation in our international relations with the third world. These, however, are the sorts of ideas the left should be putting on the agenda.

We fool ourselves if we underestimate the ideological appeal of neo-conservatism and the intellectual activity that has gone into it. The failures of Keynesianism and the deficiencies of the welfare state are the starting points for the selfish market and free enterprise solutions now being proposed. Not all of this political and economic thinking is trite or silly— some is as sophisticated as anything proposed on the centre or on the left. If we are to win back ground from the New Right, it will have to be through the vigour of our arguments in making socialism once more a *morally* and *practically* attractive proposition, one whose economics and politics differ significantly from the heavy-handed politics that, rightly or wrongly, many have come to associate with both Marxism-Leninism *and* social democracy. In trying to win back the 20– and 30–year-olds in our society, the organized and unorganized working class, white collar workers and professionals, to a collectivist—as opposed to individualist—solution to our problems, we will need generosity, imagination, honesty, a willingness to think through *radically*, and to drop those elements of earlier arguments that stand in the way of rejuvenation.

In this period of structural change and high unemployment, there is a very important place for a left alternative. But it can no longer espouse the political philosophy of the classical welfare state, the Regina Manifesto, or the Communist Manifesto. It will have to be a philosophy that combines the best movement groups—environmental, women's and other citizen groups—with the egalitarianism of the socialist tradition and the emancipatory objectives of democratic theory. It is only such a perspective that can attempt with any conviction to slay the dragon of neo-conservatism.

Philip Resnick. "The Ideology of Neo-Conservativism." In *The New Reality*. Ed. by W. Magnusson, W.K. Carroll, C. Doyle, M. Langer, and R. Walker. Vancouver: New Star Books, 1984.

---

[1] For a good discussion of such a system, see the recent study by Alec Nove, *The Economics of Feasible Socialism* (London: George Allen and Unwin, 1983).

The Principles and Practice of Privatization: The British Experience

Madsen Pirie

MADSEN PIRIE *is a British economist and advocate of privatization, as well as the head of the Adam Smith Institute. He has been one of Prime Minister Margaret Thatcher's close advisers on economic reform inside the UK.*

Let me start by sharing with you a report from last month's *Financial Times*. Very significant—it described a story in which Britain's largest union of public sector workers had employed a public opinion poll agency to guide them in spending $2 million in a campaign against privatization. And they had asked the independent polling agency how they could spend it most effectively. And the story in the *Financial Times* was that the agency had told them not to waste their money, for there was nothing on earth that they could do to change the British public's opinion on privatization and, furthermore, there was a deeply ingrained attitude in British public opinion which thought of public sector workers as "People who sat on their backsides all day and did nothing." The report said that the union had decided not to make public the results of their survey. But they are going to spend the $2 million anyway so...it'll be interesting to see if that was correct.

What an astonishing change—that that should happen in 1987. Consider, if you will, Britain as she was in the Stone Age. By that I mean 1979! The economy was dominated entirely by the public sector. The government ran the airplanes, it ran the ships and the buses. It actually made the airplanes, the ships and the buses. It ran the telephone service, it ran the gas system, it extracted oil from the North Sea and sold it, it ran hotels and the Hovercraft service, it made radio-chemicals and microchips, it made trucks and motorcars, it ran the freight services, it cleared the garbage, it swept the streets and it even rented out the deck chairs at Margate.

What was Britain like in the Stone Age? Very difficult to remember now. It was characterized by extremely poor services, which were grossly overpriced, which required massive public subsidies, which took high taxation. It was a nation characterized by astronomical inflation, it was strike-ridden, it was uncompetitive and it was on the skids. It was referred to as the Sick Man of Europe, and had a living standard which was heading pretty close to that of Bulgaria. People spoke of the British Disease, and tourists, if they came at all, attempted to leave in a hurry in case they caught it.

Emerging from the Stone Age

And it was into that Stone Age climate in 1979 that the New Breed appeared. Homothaturius or Thatcherite Man will be readily identified by future archaeologists because of the subtle physical differences—the slightly domed skull to accommodate visions of a prosperous and a free society. The creature walks a little more upright with its eyes fixed firmly on the future, one of choice and enterprise, and takes longer and longer strides as it gains confidence in its ability to set loose the forces of innovation and productivity.

I might add that the most remarkable characteristic of the New Breed, is that it's led by a woman. Archaeologists will be amazed that the New Breed under such leadership accomplished so much in so short a time. I'm amazed, I was there to see it.

In eight years, for that is all it has been, we have privatized the ports and the docks. We have privatized the tele-communications industry, the radionics industry, the petroleum industry and North Sea oil extraction. We've privatized the state bus companies and the state shipping lines. We've privatized ship-building in Britain, Jaguar cars, Leyland buses, Leyland trucks, freight haulage, the telephone service, the state airline, the aerospace industry, the state gas service, to name but a few.

We have sold over one million state houses to the people who live in them, and we are well on our way to the next million. In July, this year, we will be privatizing the airports and later in the summer we'll be privatizing Rolls Royce.

And what has been the effect of all this in eight years? When I was in Toronto, in the Fall, I said then that Britain had acquired the lowest inflation rate for twenty years. It's now lower, it is 3.5 percent. I said then that Britain had the lowest level of strikes in forty years, it's now lower. I said then, that Britain had achieved the lowest income tax it has had in fifty years, it is now two points lower still. Mrs. Thatcher, at the time I spoke, was down in the opinion polls but I said not to worry it will all work out. British people like to keep her humble so they keep her low in the polls between elections. She only surges ahead very briefly when we take the real poll. She's now well ahead in the opinion polls which probably means that the election is not far away. All is set for a third term of the Thatcher Administration.

What is going to happen in that third term? Well, last October our Finance Minister said, "We have privatized 20 percent of public sector, in the next year we will privatize another 20 percent, and then in our next term of office we'll privatize whatever is left."

Privatization: Two Key Questions

There are two questions I want to ask before I turn the subject over to Canada. And the first question is "Why was this done in Britain" and the second is "How was it done?"

Why? is the first question. We did it because the public sector is no good. Now there

are 114 reasons why it is no good. I shall deal with the first four and then give the remainder in answers to questions, if anyone expresses interest.

The first reason we found is that the public sector is always under-capitalized. The Crown corporations need money to modernize, to update their equipment, to expand their services but alas, because they are in the public sector they are facing competing claims for hospitals, for education, for the care of the sick. The money they do get goes overwhelmingly to the payment of wages because the unions in the public sector have this extraordinary power that they know that no matter how big their demands, the firm they work for, that is the government, is not going to go bankrupt. And so there is no limit to the claims they make, or the measures they take to pursue them. They are restrained in the private sector by the knowledge that their firm might go bankrupt and they'd lose their jobs. There is no such threat in the public sector so they can always command more of the resources. The result is that the public sector is chronically under-capitalized, and you look at its equipment in Britain and you find it's out of date, it's shoddy, it needed replacing long ago, but the money hasn't been available for it. There were always too many competing claims.

Secondly, the public sector is always too expensive. It doesn't have to compete. It's normally protected by a monopoly. It always has the bottom-less purse of taxpayers waiting to support it, it's always got customers, it doesn't need to streamline its act and always you pay more for your public services than you would for the private equivalent. We reckon it's always somewhere between 20 and 40 percent more expensive in the public sector than for the equivalent private service.

Thirdly, don't forget I'm not doing the 114, I'm only doing the four. So, thirdly, the public sector is always inefficient, there's absolutely no incentive to keep it lean and streamlined, there are no gains to be had by doing so. In the private sector you would gain extra profits, you'd become more competitive, you'd gain a wider share of the market. All of those incentives are absent in the public sector, there are no pressures on it to be efficient so it is characterized by a chronic inefficiency.

And fourthly, the public sector is unresponsive. It doesn't need to provide what consumers want. It is fundamentally dominated by these two words. Producer capture. They don't have to attract consumers. Since you've got a guarantee of money from taxpayers, why should the service be responsive to the needs of consumers? It might just as well serve the needs of the producers, because they are, in fact, more powerful. And so you have state railways whose function is not to carry passengers, it's to provide jobs for railway workers. You have state mines, whose function is not to dig coal out of the ground. It's to give a comfortable living to those employed in the industry. You actually examine, one by one, your public sector operations and you find out that overwhelmingly they serve the needs of the producers. And look at something like, for example, the post office. Over the years the quality of its service to the public has declined almost as rapidly as the price of that service has gone up. The second deliveries on Saturday are gone as is the Sunday collection. It's increasingly orienting its activities towards what the producers want to do rather than what the consumers want to buy.

I gave you four reasons why we had to begin to privatize the public sector in Britain. Now it's quite possible that it is totally different here. It is quite possible that in Canada your public sector is cheap, efficient, streamlined, anxious to please. But then again it's possible that it isn't.

The effect of all this in Britain was to give us an inflated and over extensive public sector. It was producing inadequate goods and services and we paid too much for their product. And what that meant for British industry was that it was paying more than it should for its freight, for its transport, for its telecommunications, for its mail services. In other words, all of the costs of British industry were put up and on top of all those increased costs and the extra costs which delays and inefficiencies brought, was the added injury that all of this had to be paid for by a monstrous rate of taxation.

This was Britain in the Stone Age, in 1979. The nation was uncompetitive, it took so much money to sustain all of these public sector activities, that there was not enough left for private enterprise, for private investment, and the wealth creating private sector.

Right, so much for why we did it. The second question—how did we do it? And the answer is—systematically. There are two approaches you can take here, you take your choice.

The first, we call the hair-shirt politics method. This operates in the belief that you must do this stuff as fast as possible and as soon as you get into office. It is so terribly unpleasant that you must do it now so that the inevitable chaos and unpopularity which follows will have time to recede by the time the election comes. It will all work out in the long run so you'd better do it in your first year to allow as long as possible to recover from it. Well that's approach number one, the notion that you should strike while your mandate's hot. We rejected that because it had been tried before and it always takes much longer to do unpopular things than you suppose possible, and there are always more groups coming along to slow the process down and you end up four and a half years later having done half of one thing, incurred vast odium of unpopularity without sufficient time to recover before the next election.

So, we opted for the systematic method. Its basis is, do it a little at a time and follow three golden rules.

The first is you must do it in such a way as to make friends out of enemies. What this means is that you identify all of the people who could oppose you, whose interests, whose livelihood, whose benefits and advantages are tied up in the public sector and you make sure they have more advantage from your privatized version.

So, for example, when we sold British Gas, (this was last December) the management of British Gas became the new Board of Directors of the private company, and they liked that. They liked it particularly because they thought they'd have more independence once they were free from government. And it's possible they also saw that private sector salaries for top management tended to be twice as high as those limited by civil service guidelines. So, that was the management.

The work-force were given two hundred shares each and allowed to buy special allocation of shares for which they didn't have to compete in the general draw. And the 98 percent of the work-force of British Gas chose to invest in their own company and pool their savings into buying British Gas shares. So that was the workers gaining more benefit.

The general public and gas consumers were given reductions on their gas bills if they bought shares in British Gas. The shares were priced in such a way that you only had to pay one-third of the cost at the time of purchase and you could pay the balance over a period of a year, sort of a credit sale, designed to encourage as many people as possible to buy the shares. They were so attractively priced that everyone who did buy them was pretty confident of making money on the deal, so that was the public taken care of.

Of course, that left the fourth significant group—the legislators. Well, it turned out that what helped them most was the success of the operation. Once British Gas was privatized successfully everyone applauded the legislators who did it. Instead of gaining the unpopularity that needs four years to recover from, they found themselves with a political success coming right on the verge of a general election.

In February, we privatized British Airways. This summer we're privatizing British Airports and Rolls Royce. You see we're continuing the program right into the election itself, because it doesn't bring unpopularity which has to be recovered from. It makes the government very popular if it's done right so that all the different groups gain the advantages.

Look at some of the other things we did in Britain. When we privatized National Freight Corporation, for example, we faced a report (in 1979) from the Secretary of the company who said, "I see no prospect of National Freight Corporation being privatized until there are substantial and long-term changes in the attitude of the work-force." Two years later it was a profitable, private company owned by its work-force.

That was the magic formula for National Freight. The workers pooled their savings, some of them mortgaged their houses. They bought shares in their own company, and the company immediately became profitable. So profitable has it been since that for every dol-

lar they put in then, they are now worth $41 today. Forty-one times increased in value, and how is that brought about? Because when they are working for their own firm, they work a lot harder, a lot more efficiently. They are a lot less bothered about who does what and more concerned about how much trade they can bring their way to increase the profits of their company. That's the performance of a management-work-force collective set up.

Look at the way this was done in British Airways, which we sold in February. Five years ago that company was losing a lot of money. By the time we sold it, it was making a lot of money. The work-force was trimmed down from 60,000 to 39,000, and not one of them was fired. Very generous terms were offered to encourage voluntary retirement and enough people took it to bring the work-force down to efficient operating levels. The index-linked public sector pensions were brought out by cash funds and turned into conventional pensions and what had been an airline requiring horrendous subsidies became a very profitable, private company which got a good price when it was sold.

The unsung story in some ways is the state houses in Britain. Up until last September, the government had taken more money from the sale of its state houses than from all other privatizations added together—including big firms like Telecom. It was only the sale of British Gas in December that changed the relative balance.

People enjoyed living in subsidized council housing owned by the state. They like having subsidized rents. They liked even more the substantial cash discounts which were offered starting at 20 percent off going up to 50 percent off. It's now by the way, under the latest act, 70 percent off market value to those who buy their own houses. It depends on how long you've lived in them. But it is very much more effective to many people to get that substantial capital asset. More attractive, indeed, than the subsidized rents which they were enjoying before. Trade one benefit for a better one.

We learned three rules, I said. The first was make friends of enemies. The second was privatize the process of privatization. Government doesn't have to learn how to sell companies, how to float them on the stock exchange, how to sell them to their management and work-force. There are firms which know how to do that already. There are firms in the City of London Financial Sector that buy and sell companies every day. Since they have that expertise it's folly for government to try to acquire it. So we learned early on, that you must buy in the expertise and government began hiring merchant banks and stockbrokers to handle its privatization. This keeps government at quite an attractive distance. It doesn't get as much criticism over the technical details if this is contracted out to experts who are assumed to know how it's done. And we learned very rapidly that privatizing the process is a very efficient message of getting the thing done properly.

We learned the third rule which is disarm the objections. Anticipate in advance every single objection which will be raised against you when you privatize, and deal with it. We're going to privatize British Telecom, we said. What are people going to say? They are going to say, "Will a private company push up prices to gain exploitation profits?" So we wrote in a clause that says for ten years they cannot increase their prices. They have to keep them 3 percent below increases in the cost of living. Three percent below the increases in the cost of living...that is written into the act. And lo and behold that dealt with that objection.

People said, "When we privatize our aerospace industry are we not open to foreign takeover?" Would not a foreign company perhaps buy it out and then we would be without this vital strategic industry in British hands. So we built in a Golden Share, and if foreign ownership ever amounts to over half the company, that Golden Share is activated giving the British government voting control. So that one was dealt with.

When we privatized Telecom—"Would they still maintain the remote services to rural areas, very scattered, where it can't pay very much?" We wrote it into the act that they have to do so. You see one by one we identify every possible source of objection and write it into the bill. We deal with it in advance. And, when you then introduce the bill to privatize Telecom, as the objectors stand up one by one they discover to their horror that you've already dealt with every single conceivable possible objection. So British Telecom was privatized, a great political success. So, point three was disarm the objectors.

A few more case histories. Again, the figures for privatization that make the news over here tend to be the ones involving the big public flotations like Telecom and British Gas. But there are unsung stories in the use of local contractors throughout Britain's cities now. Privatization of the garbage collection, the street sweeping, the deck chairs at Margate, and various other activities saves us money. The Institute of Fiscal Studies calculated the average savings so far as 26 percent, but significantly you don't only get the savings, you get better service. When you are controlling and monitoring work done by a private contractor you can have more control over it than over your own rather recalcitrant work-force which has a long history of getting its own way and resents attempts to make it do things in the way you want. You have actually, paradoxically, more control over an outside firm than you used to have over your own force-work.

How do you deal with the objections of the trade unions? The answer is again, remorselessly. First of all, we found the golden formula is to outflank them, go over their heads directly to their members. The union activists told their workers to go on strike to oppose the privatization of Telecom. What does the management do? It offers shares, and it offers shares at very attractive rates. And, given a straight choice between loyalty to the union leadership or enrichment via the shares well, you can guess the outcome. You know, the average take up in Britain has exceeded 90 percent whenever we have made that offer to a work-force. On average, 90 percent of them have taken the government line rather than that of the union leadership.

Reiterating the other points, if there has to be job reductions make sure nobody is fired against their will. If benefits have to be altered make sure it's done voluntarily. Once those are done you find that you've basically dealt with the unions by dealing with their members.

We now look at Canada briefly. We see Crown corporations waiting to be privatized.

Some small ones have gone and the world is waiting to see the big ones. Wherever else this has been done in the world, it's been successful. The moral of the story is don't be timid. Look at the example of the rest of the world, learn from any mistakes they've made and then do something which is uniquely suited to your own situation here. You've got to produce a Canadian policy to achieve a Canadian success. But there's no reason why you have to learn from scratch. The rest of the world has been doing this for eight years and there is plenty of experience to be learned from.

We look here at transport services, these are privatized all over the world. We look at city services which are being contracted out. We wonder why private sector disciplines aren't introduced into some of the big public services like education, because this is being done elsewhere in the world. So basically Canada does not stand alone. There are one hundred countries in the world privatizing. I can do a quick sort of two minute world tour. Starting as I'm sure they would like, with the French whose five-year campaign aims to privatize $130 billion worth of the public sector. The French might have come to privatization a bit late but they certainly make up in passion what they lack in punctuality—as they do in other fields too, I am told. Spain has just privatized its car manufacturer. There we had the spectacle of Phillippe Gonzales, a so-called socialist, talking about the public sector as a "white elephant graveyard" and expressing his determination to privatize.

We have privatization taking place across Europe. Really the cases are coming thick and fast: Germany, Denmark, nominally socialist Sweden, Italy. Astonishingly the big success story outside Britain is to be found probably in Asia. In countries like Bangladesh, really a very poor country, which has gained huge success in privatizing its shoes and textile mills. You've got the Pacific Rim countries Singapore, Malayisa, privatizing their telephone services and their state airlines. You have your banana farms being privatized in Belize, you have sugar refineries in Jamaica. They just privatized their national bank in Jamaica. It amounted to 5 percent of the total available capital in Jamaica and yet it was done. We have the Bosphorous bridge in Turkey that

was privatized. Japan is privatizing its telephone system and its railway—by the way the single biggest piece of privatization in the world. In India, it's textile cooperatives.

Then we look and find with astonishment that privatization is overtaking the communist world. Cuba is selling their houses to their tenants on the Thatcher model. In China, private businesses are starting up restaurants and shops at four times the rate of the state ones. In the Soviet Union they're allowing private firms of taxi drivers in Riga to compete with the state sector and what do they find everywhere? When they do it, it's more efficient, the service goes up, the prices go down. There is less subsidy and less taxation to support.

So Britain, to sum up, was indeed an example to avoid in 1979. Don't be naughty or you'll end up like Britain was what mothers used to frighten their children with in other countries. Well, Britain, is now the example, but the example to follow. So my advice in Canada is step in, the water is warm. The rest of the world is already bathing and you'll find once you've been into that little dip in privatization you'll come out a lot cleaner, your economy will come out fitter, and you'll feel a lot healthier too.

So, let me close by, of course giving you the stock market tip. I always like to do this, it's great fun. Buy British Airport Society when it comes on sale in July. The last time I did that I was telling people to buy British Gas, and those who took my advice would have done very well, and the time before that it was Telecom. But now my current hot tip is British Airport Society. I take no liability, by the way, I simply give it as a recommendation. Do it for three reasons. One, of course, you'll make money which is always very nice. The other is so that you'll get a piece of Britain to put up on your wall and you can show your grandchildren—see, when they dismantled Britain I got a piece. The third reason, though, is fundamentally because the writing is on the wall for the public sector in Britain and that writing comes to three words: Everything Must Go.

Madsen Pirie. *Vital Speeches of the Day* 53, No. 21 (August 15, 1987): 655–658. This speech was delivered to the Fraser Institute, Vancouver, British Columbia, Canada, March 30, 1987.

America's Persecuted Minority: Big Business

Ayn Rand

AYN RAND (1905–1982) was born in St. Petersburg, Russia, and moved to the USA in 1926. She wrote several best-selling novels including The Fountainhead and Atlas Shrugged. The virtue of rational self-interest and its connection with laissez-faire economics is a frequent theme in her writings.

If a small group of men were always regarded as guilty, in any clash with any other group, regardless of the issues or circumstances involved, would you call it persecution? If this group were always made to pay for the sins, errors, or failures of any other group, would you call *that* persecution? If this group had to live under a silent reign of terror, under special laws, from which all other people were immune, laws which the accused could not grasp or define in advance and which the accuser could interpret in any way he pleased—would you call *that* persecution? If this group were penalized, not for its faults, but for its virtues, not for its incompetence,but for its ability, not for its failures, but for its achievements, and the greater the achievement, the greater the penalty—would you call *that* persecution?

If your answer is "yes"—then ask yourself what sort of monstrous injustice you are condoning, supporting, or perpetrating. That group is the American businessmen.

The defense of minority rights is acclaimed today, virtually by everyone, as a moral principle of a high order. But this principle, which forbids discrimination, is applied by most of the "liberal" intellectuals in a *discriminatory* manner: it is applied only to racial or religious minorities. It is not applied to that small, exploited, denounced, defenseless minority which consists of businessmen.

Yet every ugly, brutal aspect of injustice toward racial or religious minorities is being practiced toward businessmen. For instance, consider the evil of condemning some men and absolving others, without a hearing, regardless of the facts. Today's "liberals" consider a businessman guilty in any conflict with a labor union, regardless of the facts or issues involved, and boast that they will not cross a picket line "right or wrong." Consider the evil of judging people by a double standard and of denying to some the rights granted to others. Today's "liberals" recognize the workers' (the majority's) right to their livelihood (their wages), but deny the businessmen's (the minority's) right to *their* livelihood (their profits). If workers struggle for higher wages, this is hailed as "social gains"; if businessmen struggle for higher profits, this is damned as "selfish greed." If the workers' standard of living is low, the "liberals" blame it on the businessmen; but if the businessmen attempt to improve their economic efficacy, to expand their markets, and to enlarge the financial returns of their enterprises, thus making higher wages and lower prices possible, the same "liberals" denounce it as "commercialism." If a non-commercial foundation—*i.e.*, a group which did not have to *earn* its funds—sponsors a television show, advocating its particular views, the "liberals" hail it as "enlightenment," "education," "art," and "public service"; if a businessman sponsors a television show and wants it to reflect *his* views, the "liberals" scream, calling it "censorship," "pressure," and "dictatorial rule." When three locals of the International Brotherhood of Teamsters deprived New York City of its milk supply for fifteen days—no moral indignation or condemnation was heard from the "liberal" quarters; but just imagine what would happen if businessmen stopped that milk supply for one hour—and how swiftly they would be struck down by that legalized lynching or pogrom known as "trust-busting."

Whenever, in any era, culture, or society, you encounter the phenomenon of prejudice, injustice, persecution, and blind, unreasoning hatred directed at some minority group—look for the gang that has something to gain from that persecution, look for those who have a vested interest in the destruction of these particular sacrificial victims. Invariably, you will find that the persecuted minority serves as a scapegoat for some movement that does not want the nature of its own goals to be known. Every movement that seeks to enslave a country, every dictatorship or potential dictatorship, needs some minority group as a scapegoat which it can blame for the nation's troubles and use as a justification of its own demands for dictatorial powers. In Soviet Russia, the scapegoat was the bourgeoisie; in Nazi Germany, it was the Jewish people; in America, it is the businessmen.

America has not yet reached the stage of a dictatorship. But, paving the way to it, for many decades past, the businessmen have served as the scapegoat for *statist* movements of all kinds: communist, fascist, or welfare. For whose sins and evils did the businessmen take the blame? For the sins and evils of the bureaucrats.

A disastrous intellectual package-deal, put over on us by the theoreticians of statism, is the equation of *economic* power with *political* power. You have heard it expressed in such bromides as : "A hungry man is not free," or "It makes no difference to a worker whether he takes orders from a businessman or from a bureaucrat." Most people accept these equivocations—and yet they know that the poorest laborer in America is freer and more secure than the richest commissar in Soviet Russia. What is the basic, the essential, the crucial principle that differentiates freedom from slavery? It is the principle of voluntary action *versus* physical coercion or compulsion.

The difference between political power and any other kind of social "power," between a government and any private organization, is the fact that a *government holds a legal monopoly on the use of physical force*. This distinction is so

important and so seldom recognized today that I must urge you to keep it in mind. Let me repeat it: *a government holds a legal monopoly on the use of physical force.*

No individual or private group or private organization has the legal power to initiate the use of physical force against other individuals or groups and to compel them to act against their own voluntary choice. Only a government holds that power. The nature of governmental action is: *coercive* action. The nature of political power is: the power to force obedience under threat of physical injury—the threat of property expropriation, imprisonment, or death.

Foggy metaphors, sloppy images, unfocused poetry, and equivocations—such as "A hungry man is not free"—do not alter the fact that *only* political power is the power of physical coercion and that freedom, in a political context, has only one meaning: *the absence of physical coercion.*

The only proper function of the government of a free country is to act as an agency which protects the individual's rights, *i.e.,* which protects the individual from physical violence. Such a government does not have the right to *initiate* the use of physical force against anyone—a right which the individual does not possess and, therefore, cannot delegate to any agency. But the individual does possess the right of self-defense and *that* is the right which he delegates to the government, for the purpose of an orderly, legally defined enforcement. A proper government has the right to use physical force *only* in retaliation and *only* against those who initiate its use. The proper functions of a government are: the police, to protect men from criminals; the military forces, to protect men from foreign invaders; and the law courts, to protect men's property and contracts from breach by force or fraud, and to settle disputes among men according to objectively defined laws.

These, implicitly, were the political principles on which the Constitution of the United States was based; implicitly, but not explicitly. There were contradictions in the Constitution, which allowed the statists to gain an entering wedge, to enlarge the breach, and, gradually, to wreck the structure.

A statist is a man who believes that some

men have the right to force, coerce, enslave, rob, and murder others. To be put into practice, this belief has to be implemented by the political doctrine that the government—the state—has the right to *initiate* the use of physical force against its citizens. How often force is to be used, against whom, to what extent, for what purpose and for whose benefit, are irrelevant questions. The basic principle and the ultimate results of all statist doctrines are the same: dictatorship and destruction. The rest is only a matter of time.

Now let us consider the question of economic power.

What is economic power? It is the power to produce and to trade what one has produced. In a free economy, where no man or group of men can use physical coercion against anyone, economic power can be achieved only by *voluntary* means: by the voluntary choice and agreement of all those who participate in the process of production and trade. In a free market, all prices, wages, and profits are determined—not by the arbitrary whim of the rich or of the poor, not by anyone's "greed" or by anyone's need—but by the law of supply and demand. The mechanism of a free market reflects and sums up all the economic choices and decisions made by all the participants. Men trade their goods or services by mutual consent to mutual advantage, according to their own independent, uncoerced judgment. A man can grow rich only if he is able to offer better *values*—better products or services, at a lower price—than others are able to offer.

Wealth, in a free market, is achieved by a free, general, "democratic" vote—by the sales and the purchases of every individual who takes part in the economic life of the country. Whenever you buy one product rather than another, you are voting for the success of some manufacturer. And, in this type of voting, every man votes only on those matters which he is qualified to judge: on his own preferences, interests, and needs. No one has the power to decide for others or to substitute *his* judgment for theirs; no one has the power to appoint himself "the voice of the public" and to leave the public voiceless and disfranchised.

Now let me define the difference between economic power and political power: eco-

nomic power is exercised by means of a *positive*, by offering men a reward, an incentive, a payment, a value; political power is exercised by means of a *negative*, by the threat of punishment, injury, imprisonment, destruction. The businessman's tool is *values*; the bureaucrat's tool is *fear*.

America's industrial progress, in the short span of a century and a half, has acquired the character of a legend: it has never been equaled anywhere on earth, in any period of history. The American businessmen, as a class, have demonstrated the greatest productive genius and the most spectacular achievements ever recorded in the economic history of mankind. What reward did they receive from our culture and its intellectuals? The position of a hated, persecuted minority. The position of a scapegoat for the evils of the bureaucrats.

A system of pure, unregulated laissez-faire capitalism has never yet existed anywhere. What did exist were only so-called mixed economies, which means: a mixture, in varying degrees, of freedom and controls, of voluntary choice and government coercion, of capitalism and statism. America was the freest country on earth, but elements of statism were present in her economy from the start. These elements kept growing, under the influence of her intellectuals who were predominantly committed to the philosophy of statism. The intellectuals—the ideologists, the interpreters, the assessors of public events—were tempted by the opportunity to seize political power, relinquished by all other social groups, and to establish their own versions of a "good" society at the point of a gun, *i.e.*, by means of legalized physical coercion. They denounced the free businessmen as exponents of "selfish greed" and glorified the bureaucrats as "public servants." In evaluating social problems, they kept damning "economic power" and exonerating political power, thus switching the burden of guilt from the politicians to the businessmen.

All the evils, abuses, and iniquities, popularly ascribed to businessmen and to capitalism, were not caused by an unregulated economy or by a free market, but by government intervention into the economy. The giants of American industry—such as James Jerome Hill or Commodore Vanderbilt or Andrew Carnegie or J.P. Morgan—were self-made men who earned their fortunes by personal ability, by free trade on a free market. But there existed another kind of businessmen, the products of a mixed economy, the men with political pull, who make fortunes by means of special privileges granted to them by the government, such men as the Big Four of the Central Pacific Railroad. It was the political power behind their activities—the power of forced, unearned, economically unjustified privileges—that caused dislocations in the country's economy, hardships, depressions, and mounting public protests. But it was the free market and the free businessmen that took the blame. Every calamitous consequence of government controls was used as a justification for the extension of the controls and of the government's power over the economy.

Ayn Rand. *Capitalism: The Unknown Ideal.* New York: Signet, Signet Classics, Mentor and Plume, 1967. The extract is part of a lecture given at The Ford Hall Forum, Boston, on December 17, 1961, and at Columbia University on February 15, 1962.

The New Right

Desmond S. King

DESMOND S. KING *is Professor in the Department of Economics at the University of Edinburgh in Scotland. His most recent publication is* The New Right.

Privatisation: state revenues and market solutions

Privatisation was a relatively late discovery by the Conservative Party under Margaret Thatcher's leadership. The objective of privatisation is to alter the balance between the public and the private sectors in the British political economy in favour of the latter; and to subject the public sector to market pressures and practices to as great an extent as possible. Ideologically, privatisation follows logically from liberalism. New Right liberals stress the superiority of market mechanisms over public sector provision of services. In policy terms, privatisation covers the sale of state enterprises, the allocation of public sector services amongst private competitors, eliminating or loosening state monopolies, and the introduction of private companies into public-based or initiated investment projects. Privatisation allows the state under the Thatcher Government to dispose of previously acquired state commitments. Financially, the privatisation programme has also been useful for the Government; the funds accruing to the Treasury from these measures increases the Government's policy flexibility in other areas.

Selling off council housing was a 1979 electoral pledge but the success of this programme made privatisation a very attractive policy for the Government. The 1980 Housing Act set out provisions for the sale of council houses and provisions to overcome the resistance of Labour-controlled local authorities. By September 1986 a million dwellings had been sold to their occupants. The success of this policy transformed privatisation from a fairly low-key item in the 1979 manifesto into a major policy initiative. After council housing the most publicised privatisation measure has been the sale of British Telecom, where the Government engaged in considerable pre-sales promotion. In addition, the Thatcher Government has privatised British Aerospace, Britoil, Cable and Wireless, National Freight, Associated British Ports, Enterprise Oil and Jaguar. There are plans to privatise British Airways, British Gas, British water authorities (postponed indefinitely in July 1986), British Shipbuilders' warship yards, National Bus Company, British Steel, British Leyland, Rolls Royce, Short Bros., and some of Britain's airports (see Table). Many of the companies initially privatised (and some of those designated for privatisation in the future) were both relatively prosperous and/or had only recently been nationalised because of economic difficulties; in contrast, most of the "traditional, immediate post-Secondary World War nationalised industries" have not yet been privatised (Thompson, 1984, p. 290; Webster, 1985).[1]

Curiously, the Thatcher Government chose to replace public monopolies with private ones in implementing privatisation, which contradicts liberal free market principles. According to these principles, the way to increase efficiency in services (and in the economy) is by maximising competition. But, in fact, the Thatcher Government has not ended monopolistic practices: most glaringly in the case of British Telecom which has been transferred into the private sector as one large corporation rather than broken into separate

---

[1] [Ed. note: These citations are located at the end of the article.]

TABLE: Privatisation under the Thatcher Government

Major asset shares	Date	Percentage	£m raised
British Petroleum	June 1977	17	548
	Oct 1979	5	276
	Sept 1983	7	543
British Aerospace	Feb 1981	52	43
	May 1985	48	346
National Freight Corporation (now Consortium)	Feb 1982	100	5
Cable and Wireless	Oct 1981	49	182
	Dec 1983	28	263
	Dec 1985	23	600
Britoil	Nov 1982	51	627
	Aug 1985	49	425
Associated British Ports	Feb 1983	52	46
	Apr 1984	48	51
Enterprise Oil	June 1984	100	380
Jaguar	July 1984	100	297
British Telecom	Nov 1984	50	3,916

To be privatised (100 per cent in each case):
British Airways [early 1987]
British Gas [November 1986]
British Airports Authority
National Bus Company
Royal Ordinance Factories
Water authorities (England and Wales) [postponed indefinitely]

SOURCES: *The Economist*, 21 December 1985; *The Sunday Times*, 10 November 1985.

units (the course followed by the Reagan Administration with the American Telephone and Telegraph Corporation); alternatively, licences could have been granted to competitors in the different areas of telecommunications. Similar practices characterise other areas of this Government's privatisation policy.

Overall, this is a very substantial programme and constitutes an important legacy of the Government. The Government has also ended monopolies in some industries to allow the entry of new competitors (for example, on bus routes), and it has reduced public subsidies to some nationalised industries. In the non-industrial public sector—such as hospital laundry and refuse collection—the Thatcher Government has introduced contracting-out to private firms (Shackleton, 1985, p. 8).

Between 1981 and the middle of 1986, fifty-six public tenders for refuse and street-cleaning services had been issued by district councils, twenty-nine of which were won by private contractors over the councils' direct-labour organisations. Most recently, in August 1986, Lincolnshire County Council awarded a £3.3m cleaning contract for its buildings to a private company—one of the biggest service contracts to be awarded by the public sector. By cutting hourly wages from £2.24 to £1.70 the private cleaning company will save the company £400,000 a year: such is the nature of private competitive servicing over public sector provision (*Financial Times*, 22 August 1986). Such contracting-out, and the introduction of competition in the state sector, concurs with the policies advocated by public choice critics of the public sector reviewed in Chapter 6[1] (see Dunleavy, 1985 and 1986). Young (1986) identifies additional privatisation measures instituted by the Thatcher Government: reduced subsidies and increased charges for welfare services (for example, in April 1985 the National Health Service stopped providing spectacles except to children, students and social security claimants); the extension of private-sector practices into the public-sector, as in urban aid projects; private provision of services (for example, getting private companies to provide school meals); and private sector responsibility for investment projects.

To reverse the drift toward privatisation will be a sizeable task for any subsequent administration not sharing the Thatcher Government's anti-nationalisation aims. In terms of the general mix of public (state) and private (market)-based activities in the British political economy, the Thatcher Government's policy of privatisation represents a strong prod towards more of the second. But to implement privatisation, the Government has had to play a major role, as Young (1986) notes: "at the heart of privatisation there appears to be a paradox. Its promotion depends on government playing an active and interventionist role on a continuing basis" (p. 248). To achieve the liberal objective of a minimal government and an expanded market through privatisation measures requires considerable Government activity not just initially but on a sustained basis. This is the paradox which Young correctly identifies.

References

Dunleavy, Patrick (1985 "Bureaucrats, Budgets and the Growth of the State: Reconstructing an Instrumental Model," *British Journal of Political Science* vol. 15, pp. 299–328.

Dunleavy, Patrick (1986a) "Explaining the Privitization Boom: Public Choice Versus Radical Approaches," *Public Administration*, vol. 64 pp. 13–34.

Dunleavy, Patrick (1986b) "Theories of the State in British Politics," in Henry Drucker, Patrick Dunleavy, Andrew Gamble and Gillian Peele (eds) *Developments in British Politics 2* (London: Macmillan).

Shackleton, J.R. (1985) "UK Privatisation—US Deregulation," *Politics*, no. 5, pp. 8–16.

Thompson, Grahame (1984) "'Rolling back' the state? Economic Intervention 1975–82," in Gregor McLennan, David Held and Stuart Hall (eds) *State and Society in Contemporary Britain* (Cambridge: Polity Press).

Young, Stephen (1986) "The Nature of Privatisation in Britain, 1979–85," *West European Politics*, vol. 9, no. 2, pp. 235–52.

Desmond S. King. *The New Right*. Chicago: Dorsey Press, 1987.

---

[1] [Ed. note: Here King discusses Public Choice Theory of Liberal Economics.]

Part VI
Marxism

KARL MARX

Karl Marx and Friedrich Engels begin *The Communist Manifesto* with the famous words "the history of all hitherto existing society is the history of class struggles." These words set the stage for Marx and Engel's declaration of the ingredients of communism— ingredients which include an analysis of the nineteenth century in Europe as a century of conflict between the bourgeoisie and the proletariat, a description of expanding world markets, an assessment of the revolutionary nature of the bourgeoisie, and an argument linking capital to wage labour and then to competition. The purpose of the foregoing is to show the inevitable demise of the bourgeoisie and the equally inevitable rise to power of the proletariat.

Vladimir Ulyanov, otherwise known as Lenin, carries the message of Marx and Engels further. As a strategist with a remarkably analytic and incisive mind, he writes to educate, to revolutionize, and to bring about change in the working class. He insists that "class political consciousness" of the working people can only be brought to it from outside, i.e. from outside the economic struggle between employers and employees. The social-democratic (read "Bolshevik") ideal, which he seeks, aims to go beyond trade unionism and to have contact with all classes of the population. Lenin believes that, in working on behalf of the emancipation of the working class, social-democrats must go among all classes as theoreticians, propagandists, agitators, and organizers. At least so he contends in *What Is To Be Done?* In *Imperialism, The Highest Stage of Capitalism*, Lenin concentrates on giving a definition and an account of imperialism as it relates to capitalism. In the excerpt contained herein

he undertakes only the first of these tasks but his intent is ultimately to show that the role played by imperialism is to forestall the demise of capitalism.

In his article, Mao Tse-Tung carries on the tradition laid down by Marx, Engels, Lenin, and Stalin. In fact one might say that he eulogizes them and their place in this tradition. He reaffirms the Leninist idea that a revolutionary party is indispensable for revolution, and he takes pride in the fact that the Chinese Communist Party is modelled on the Communist Party of the Soviet Union. US imperialism he sees as having taken the place of fascism as the menace of the whole world, but he sees this new menace as reflecting the decay of capitalism. Mao believes that the Chinese Communist Party has achieved victories against the US as well as against the Kuomintang government of Chiang Kai-shek, and is capable of achieving liberation with the support of both the communist parties and the working class of the world.

Writing from within a Marxist framework, Herbert Marcuse provides thoughtful suggestions and occasional argument concerning the titanic struggle currently being waged between capitalism and communism throughout the world. His suggestions and argument turn on an acknowledgement of a linkage in a technological society between containment of change, technological rationality, and the Welfare State. The last of these he alleges is a historical freak standing as it does between organized capitalism and organized socialism; moreover he alleges it is in fact a state of unfreedom largely owing to its systematic restriction on self-determination. In adopting this stand, Marcuse comes closer to Marx the humanist than Marx the economist, for what concerns

Marcuse is human well-being and fulfilment.

Marcuse's comments are followed by
D.F. Tucker's careful exegesis of Marx's
idea of alienation—an exegesis which he
accomplishes by placing Marx squarely in
the context of the writings of Rousseau
and Hegel. Tucker plausibly suggests that
Marx tries to give an improved understanding of alienation by combining
Rousseau's insight into the alienating effects of property claims and Hegel's sense
of historical progress. In summation,
Tucker asserts that Marx claims to have
located the primary cause of the alienation of humanity in the fact that individual choices are dictated by the needs of
market competition. Here we see once
again, much in the spirit of Marcuse, an
attempt to draw to our attention the hu-
manistic side of Marx's thought.

The final essay is written by Harold
Berman, a legal scholar and non-Marxist.
He argues, rather persuasively, that
Marx's historical analysis of class conflict
relies rather heavily upon his notion of
feudalism but that this notion itself is—as
given by Marx—inadequately developed.
Berman considers the possibility that the
integration of law and economy in the
feudal society might threaten the Marxian
analysis, but admits that perhaps the analysis can be saved by limiting its application. Limited or not, he argues that in the
end the monistic formula which Marx
uses to explain historical events is oversimplified and in need of replacement by
the pluralistic formula as advanced by
Max Weber.

The thought of Marx alone and as developed by Lenin and Mao represents a
bold new departure for political thinking:
nothing quite like this existed before the
middle of the nineteenth century. Marcuse
helps to show that there is there is still
plenty of scope for the application and development of Marxist ideas, and Tucker
helps to illuminate the historical context
of some of these ideas. Finally Berman
raises very interesting questions about the
theoretical adequacy of Marxism. Together these essays help confirm the seminal importance of Karl Marx and his
successors.

Bourgeois and Proletarians

Karl Marx and Friedrich Engels

KARL MARX *(1818–1883) was born in Tiers, Germany, and became a renowned economic and social thinker. His most famous early work, written in collaboration with Fredrich Engels, was the pamphlet and classic statement of communist theory,* The Communist Manifesto. *Much of his life was spent in London where he wrote* Das Kapital.

FRIEDRICH ENGELS *(1820–1895) was born in Germany and was both a socialist intellectual and a textile manufacturer. He is best known as the collaborator and intellectual companion of Karl Marx. He was the co-author with Marx of* The Communist Manifesto, *and he edited and completed the manuscript for Volumes II and III of Marx's* Das Kapital.

A spectre is haunting Europe—the spectre of Communism. All the Powers of old Europe have entered into a holy alliance to exorcize this spectre: Pope and Czar, Metternich and Guizot, French Radicals and German police spies.

Where is the party in opposition that has not been decried as Communistic by its opponents in power? Where the Opposition that has not hurled back the branding reproach of Communism, against the more advanced opposition parties, as well as against its reactionary adversaries?

Two things result from this fact:

I. Communism is already acknowledged by all European Powers to be itself a Power.

II. It is high time that Communists should openly, in the face of the whole world, publish their views, their aims, their tendencies, and meet this nursery tale of the Spectre of Communism with a Manifesto of the party itself.

To this end, Communists of various nationalities have assembled in London, and sketched the following Manifesto, to be published in the English, French, German, Italian, Flemish and Danish languages.

Bourgeois and Proletarians[1]

The history of all hitherto existing society[2] is the history of class struggles.

Freeman and slave, patrician and plebeian, lord and serf, guild-master[3] and journeyman, in a word, oppressor and oppressed, stood in constant opposition to one another, carried on an uninterrupted, now hidden, now open fight, a fight that each time ended, either in a revolutionary reconstitution of society at large, or in the common ruin of the contending classes.

---

[1] By bourgeoisie is meant the class of modern Capitalists, owners of the means of social production and employers of wage labour. By proletariat, the class of modern wage-labourers who, having no means of production of their own, are reduced to selling their labour power in order to live. [*Added by Engels to the English edition, 1888.*]

[2] That is, all *written* history. In 1847, the pre-history of society, the social organization existing previous to recoded history, was all but unknown. Since then, Haxthausen discovered common ownership of land in Russia, Maurer proved it to be the social foundation from which all Teutonic races started in history, and by and by village communities were found to be, or to have been the primitive form of society everywhere from India to Ireland. The inner organization of this primitive Communistic society was laid bare, in its typical form, by Morgan's crowning discovery of the true nature of the *gens* and its relation to the *tribe*. With the dissolution of these primeval communities society begins to be differentiated into separate and finally antagonistic classes. I have attempted to retrace this process of dissolution in: *Der Ursprung der Familie, des Privateigenthums und des Staats (The Origin of the Family, Private Property and the State)*, 2nd edition, Stuttgart 1886. [*Added by Engels to the English edition, 1888.*]

[3] Guild-master, that is, a full member of a guild, a master within, not a head of a guild. [*Added by Engels to the English edition, 1888.*]

In the earlier epochs of history, we find almost everywhere a complicated arrangement of society into various orders, a manifold gradation of social rank. In ancient Rome we have patricians, knights, plebeians, slaves; in the Middle Ages, feudal lords, vassals, guildmasters, journeymen, apprentices, serfs; in almost all of these classes, again, subordinate gradations.

The modern bourgeois society that has sprouted from the ruins of feudal society has not done away with class antagonisms. It has but established new classes, new conditions of oppression, new forms of struggle in place of the old ones.

Our epoch, the epoch of the bourgeoisie, possesses, however, this distinctive feature: it has simplified the class antagonisms. Society as a whole is more and more splitting up into two great hostile camps, into two great classes directly facing each other: Bourgeoisie and Proletariat.

From the serfs of the Middle Ages sprang the chartered burghers of the earliest towns. From these burgesses the first elements of the bourgeoisie were developed.

The discovery of America, the rounding of the Cape, opened up fresh ground for the rising bourgeoisie. The East-Indian and Chinese markets, the colonization of America, trade with the colonies, the increase in the means of exchange and in commodities generally, gave to commerce, to navigation, to industry, an impulse never before known, and thereby, to the revolutionary element in the tottering feudal society, a rapid development.

The feudal system of industry, under which industrial production was monopolized by closed guilds, now no longer sufficed for the growing wants of the new markets. The manufacturing system took its place. The guildmasters were pushed on one side by the manufacturing middle class; division of labour between the different corporate guilds vanished in the face of division of labour in each single workshop.

Meantime the markets kept ever growing, the demand ever rising. Even manufacture no longer sufficed. Thereupon, steam and machinery revolutionized industrial production. The place of manufacture was taken by the giant, Modern Industry, the place of the industrial middle class, by industrial millionaires, the leaders of whole industrial armies, the modern bourgeois.

Modern industry has established the world market, for which the discovery of America paved the way. This market has given an immense development to commerce, to navigation, to communication by land. This development has, in its turn, reacted on the extension of industry; and in proportion as industry, commerce, navigation, railways extended, in the same proportion the bourgeoisie developed, increased its capital, and pushed into the background every class handed down from the Middle Ages.

We see, therefore, how the modern bourgeoisie is itself the product of a long course of development, of a series of revolutions in the modes of production and of exchange.

Each step in the development of the bourgeoisie was accompanied by a corresponding political advance of that class. An oppressed class under the sway of the feudal nobility, an armed and self-governing association in the medieval commune;[1] here independent urban republic (as in Italy and Germany), there taxable "third estate" of the Monarchy (as in France), afterwards, in the period of manufacture proper, serving either the semi-feudal or the absolute monarchy as a counterpoise against the nobility, and, in fact, corner-stone of the great monarchies in general, the bourgeoisie has at last, since the establishment of Modern Industry and of the world market, conquered for itself, in the modern representative State, exclusive political sway. The executive of the modern State is but a committee for managing the common affairs of the whole bourgeoisie.

---

[1] "Commune" was the name taken, in France, by the nascent towns even before they had conquered from their feudal lords and masters local self-government and political rights as the "Third Estate." Generally speaking, for the economical development of the bourgeoisie, England is here taken as the typical country; for its political development, France. [*Added by Engels to the English edition, 1888.*]

This was the name given their urban communities by the townsmen of Italy and France, after they had purchased or wrested their initial rights of self-government from their feudal lords. [*Added by Engels to the German edition, 1890.*]

The bourgeoisie, historically, has played a most revolutionary part.

The bourgeoisie, wherever it has got the upper hand, has put an end to all feudal, patriarchal, idyllic relations. It has pitilessly torn asunder the motley feudal ties that bound man to his "natural superiors," and has left remaining no other nexus between man and man than naked self-interest, than callous "cash payment." It has drowned the most heavenly ecstasies of religious fervour, of chivalrous enthusiasm, of philistine sentimentalism, in the icy water of egotistical calculation. It has resolved personal worth into exchange value, and in place of the numberless indefeasible chartered freedoms, has set up that single, unconscionable freedom—Free Trade. In one word, for exploitation, veiled by religious and political illusions, it has substituted naked, shameless, direct, brutal exploitation.

The bourgeoisie has stripped of its halo every occupation hitherto honoured and looked up to with reverent awe. It has converted the physician, the lawyer, the priest, the poet, the man of science, into its paid wage-labourers.

The bourgeoisie has torn away from the family its sentimental veil, and has reduced the family relation to a mere money relation.

The bourgeoisie has disclosed how it came to pass that the brutal display of vigour in the Middle Ages, which Reactionists so much admire, found its fitting complement in the most slothful indolence. It has been the first to show what man's activity can bring about. It has accomplished wonders far surpassing Egyptian pyramids, Roman aqueducts, and Gothic cathedrals; it has conducted expeditions that put in the shade all former Exoduses of nations and crusades.

The bourgeoisie cannot exist without constantly revolutionizing the instruments of production, and thereby the relations of production, and with them the whole relations of society. Conservation of the old modes of production in unaltered form, was, on the contrary, the first condition of existence for all earlier industrial classes. Constant revolutionizing of production, uninterrupted disturbance of all social conditions, everlasting uncertainty and agitation distinguish the bourgeois epoch from all earlier ones. All fixed, fast-frozen relations, with their train of ancient and venerable prejudices and opinions are swept away, all new-formed ones become antiquated before they can ossify. All that is solid melts into air, all that is holy is profaned, and man is at last compelled to face with sober senses, his real conditions of life, and his relations with his kind.

The need of a constantly expanding market for its products chases the bourgeoisie over the whole surface of the globe. It must nestle everywhere, settle everywhere, establish connexions everywhere...

Hitherto, every form of society has been based, as we have already seen, on the antagonism of oppressing and oppressed classes. But in order to oppress a class, certain conditions must be assured to it under which it can, at least, continue its slavish existence. The serf, in the period of serfdom, raised himself to membership in the commune, just as the petty bourgeois, under the yoke of feudal absolutism managed to develop into a bourgeois. The modern labourer, on the contrary, instead of rising with the progress of industry, sinks deeper and deeper below the conditions of existence of his own class. He becomes a pauper, and pauperism develops more rapidly than population and wealth. And here it becomes evident, that the bourgeoisie is unfit any longer to be the ruling class in society, and to impose its conditions of existence upon society as an overriding law. It is unfit to rule because it is incompetent to assure an existence to its slave within his slavery, because it cannot help letting him sink into such a state, that it has to feed him, instead of being fed by him. Society can no longer live under this bourgeoisie, in other words, its existence is no longer compatible with society.

The essential condition for the existence, and for the sway of the bourgeois class, is the formation and augmentation of capital; the condition for capital is wage labour. Wage labour rests exclusively on competition between the labourers. The advance of industry, whose involuntary promoter is the bourgeoisie, replaces the isolation of the labourers, due to competition, by their revolutionary combination, due to association. The development of Modern Industry, therefore, cuts from under its feet the very foundation on which the bourgeoisie produces and appropriates products. What the bourgeoisie, therefore, produces, above all, is its own grave-diggers. Its fall and the victory of the proletariat are equally inevitable.

Karl Marx and Friedrich Engels. *The Communist Manifesto*. Originally published in 1849.

The Working Class As Vanguard Fighter for Democracy

V. I. Lenin

V. I. LENIN *(1870–1924) was born in Simbirsk, Russia. At an early age and following the hanging of his brother, Lenin became a revolutionary. He soon became the driving force behind the Bolshevik movement in its struggle with the Mensheviks and ultimately with the Tsarist authorities. Two of his famous works were* What Is to Be Done? *(1905) and* Imperialism, the Highest Stage of Capitalism *(1917).*

We have seen that the conduct of the broadest political agitation, and consequently the organization of comprehensive political exposures, is an absolutely necessary, and the *most urgently* necessary, task of activity, that is, if that activity is to be truly Social-Democratic. However, we arrived at this conclusion *solely* on the grounds of the pressing needs of the working class for political knowledge and political training. But presenting the question in this way alone is too narrow, for it ignores the general democratic tasks of Social-Democracy in general, and of present-day Russian Social-Democracy in particular. In order to explain the point more concretely we shall approach the subject from an aspect that is "nearest" to the Economist, namely, from the practical aspect. "Everyone agrees" that it is necessary to develop the political consciousness of the working class. The question is, *how* is that to be done, what is required to do it? The economic struggle merely "brings home" to the workers questions concerning the attitude of the government towards the working class. Consequently, *however much we may try* to "lend the economic struggle itself a political

character" *we shall never be able* to develop the political consciousness of the workers (to the level of Social-Democratic political consciousness) by keeping within the framework of the economic struggle, for *that framework is too narrow.* The Martynov formula has some value for us, and not because it illustrates Martynov's ability to confuse things, but because it strikingly expresses the fundamental error that all the Economists commit, namely, their conviction that it is possible to develop the class political consciousness of the workers *from within,* so to speak, their economic struggle, i.e., making this struggle the exclusive (or, at least, the main) starting point, making it the exclusive, or, at least, the main basis. Such a view is fundamentally wrong. Just because the Economists are piqued by our polemics against them, they refuse to ponder deeply over the origins of these disagreements, with the result that we absolutely fail to understand each other. It is as if we spoke in different tongues.

Class political consciousness can be brought to the workers *only from without,* that is, only from outside of the economic struggle, from outside of the sphere of relations between workers and employers. The sphere from which alone it is possible to obtain this knowledge is the sphere of relationships between *all* the classes and strata and the state and the government, the sphere of the interrelations between *all* the classes. For that reason, the reply to the question as to what must be done to bring political knowledge to the workers cannot be merely the answer with which, in the majority of cases, the practical workers, especially those inclined towards

Economism, mostly content themselves, namely: "To go among the workers." To bring political knowledge to the *workers* the Social-Democrats must *go among all classes of the population*, must dispatch units of their army *in all directions*.

We deliberately select this awkward formula, we deliberately express ourselves in a simplified, blunt way—not because we desire to indulge in paradoxes, but in order to "bring home" to the Economists those tasks which they unpardonably ignore, to make them understand the difference between trade-unionist and Social-Democratic politics, which they refuse to understand. We therefore beg the reader not to get excited, but to listen patiently to the end.

Take the type of Social-Democratic circle that has become most widespread in the past few years, and examine its work. It has "contacts with the workers," and rests content with this, issuing leaflets in which abuses in the factories, the government's partiality towards the capitalists and the tyranny of the police are strongly condemned. At meetings of workers the discussions never, or rarely, go beyond the limits of these subjects. Lectures and discussions on the history of the revolutionary movement, on questions of the home and foreign policy of our government, on questions of the economic evolution of Russia and of Europe, and the position of the various classes in modern society, etc., are extremely rare. As to systematically acquiring and extending contact with other classes of society, no one even dreams of that. In fact the ideal leader, as the majority of the members of such circles picture him, is something far more in the nature of a trade union secretary than a socialist political leader. For the trade union secretary of any, say British trade union, always helps the workers to conduct the economic struggle, helps to expose factory abuses, explains the injustice of the laws and of measures which hamper the freedom to strike and the freedom to picket (i.e., to warn all and sundry that a strike is proceeding at a certain factory), explains the partiality of arbitration court judges who belong to the bourgeois classes, etc., etc. In a word, every trade union secretary conducts and helps to conduct "the economic struggle against the employers and the gov-

ernment." It cannot be too strongly insisted that *this is not yet* Social-Democracy. The Social-Democrat's ideal should not be a trade union secretary, but *a tribune of the people*, able to react to every manifestation of tyranny and oppression, no matter where it takes place, no matter what stratum or class of the people it affects; he must be able to generalize all these manifestations to produce a single picture of police violence and capitalist exploitation; he must be able to take advantage of every event, however small, in order to explain his Socialistic convictions and his democratic demands to *all*, in order to explain to *all* and everyone the work-historic significance of the proletariat's struggle for emancipation...

Let us return, however, to our thesis. We said that a Social-Democrat, if he really believes it is necessary to develop comprehensively the political consciousness of the proletariat, must "go among all classes of the population." This gives rise to the questions: How is this to be done? Have we enough forces to do this? Is there a basis for such work among all the other classes? Will this not mean a retreat, or lead to a retreat, from the class point of view? Let us deal with these questions.

We must "go among all classes of the population" as theoreticians, as propagandists, as agitators and as organizers. No one doubts that the theoretical work of Social-Democrats should aim at studying all the features of the social and political position of the various classes. But extremely little, little beyond proportion, is done in this direction as compared with the work that is done in studying the features of factory life. In the committees and circles, you will meet people who are immersed even in the study of, say, some special branch of the metal industry, but you will hardly ever find members of organizations (obliged, as often happens, for some reason or other to give up practical work) especially engaged in the collection of material concerning some pressing question of social and political life in our country which could serve as a means for conducting Social-Democratic work among other strata of the population. In speaking of the lack of training of the majority of present-day leaders of the working-class movement, we cannot refrain from mentioning the point about training in this connection also, for it too is bound up with the "economic" conception of "close organic contact with the proletarian struggle." The principal thing, of course, is *propaganda* and *agitation* among all strata of the people. The work of the West-European Social-Democrat is in this respect facilitated by the public meetings and rallies, to which *all* are free to go, and by the fact that in parliament he addresses the representatives of *all* classes. We have neither a parliament nor freedom of assembly, nevertheless we are able to arrange meetings of workers who desire to listen to a *Social-Democrat*. We must also find ways and means of calling meetings of representatives of all classes of the population that desire to listen to *a democrat*; for he is no Social-Democrat who forgets that "the Communists support every revolutionary movement," that we are obliged for that reason to expound and emphasize *general democratic tasks before the whole people,* without for a moment concealing our socialist convictions. He is no Social-Democrat who forgets his obligation to be *ahead of everybody* in advancing, accentuating and solving *every* general democratic problem...

To proceed: Have we sufficient forces to direct our propaganda and agitation among *all* classes of the population? Of course we have. Our Economists, frequently inclined as they are to deny this, lose sight of the gigantic progress our movement has made from 1894 (approximately) to 1901. Like real "tail-enders," they frequently live in the distant past, in the period when the movement was just beginning. At that time, indeed, we had astonishingly few forces, and it was perfectly natural and legitimate then to devote ourselves exclusively to activities among the workers, and severely condemn any deviation from this. The whole task then was to consolidate our position in the working class. At the present time, however, gigantic forces have been attracted to the movement; the best representatives of the young generation of the educated classes are coming over to us; all over the country there are people, compelled to live in the provinces, who have taken part in the movement in the past or who desire to do so now, who are gravitating towards Social-Democracy (whereas in 1894 you could count the Social-Democrats on your fingers). One of the principal political and organizational shortcomings of our movement is that we *do not know how* to utilize all these forces and give them appropriate work (we shall deal with this in greater detail in the next chapter). The overwhelming majority of these forces entirely lack the opportunity of "going among the workers," so there are no grounds for fearing that we shall deflect forces from our main work. And in order to be able to provide the workers with real, comprehensive and live political knowledge, we must have "our own people," Social-Democrats, everywhere, among all social strata, and in all positions from which we can learn the inner springs of our state mechanism. Such people are required not only for propaganda and agitation, but in a still larger measure for organization.

V.I. Lenin. *What Is To Be Done?* Originally published in 1902.

Imperialism, as a Special Stage of Capitalism

V. I. Lenin

We must now try to sum up, put together what has been said above on the subject of imperialism. Imperialism emerged as the development and direct continuation of the fundamental characteristics of capitalism in general. But capitalism only became capitalist imperialism at a definite and very high stage of its development, when certain of its fundamental characteristics began to change into their opposites, when the features of the epoch of transition from capitalism to a higher social and economic system had taken shape and revealed themselves all along the line. Economically, the main thing in this process is the displacement of capitalist free competition by capitalist monopoly. Free competition is the fundamental characteristic of capitalism, and of commodity production generally; monopoly is the exact opposite of free competition, but we have seen the latter being transformed into monopoly before our eyes, creating large-scale by still larger-scale industry, and carrying concentration of production and capital to the point where out of it has grown and is growing monopoly: cartels, syndicates and trusts, and merging with them, the capital of a dozen or so banks, which manipulate thousands of millions. At the same time the monopolies, which have grown out of free competition, do not eliminate the latter, but exist over it and alongside of it, and thereby give rise to a number of very acute, intense antagonisms, frictions and conflicts. Monopoly is the transition from capitalism to a higher system.

If it were necessary to give the briefest possible definition of imperialism we should have to say that imperialism is the monopoly stage of capitalism. Such a definition would include what is most important, for, on the one hand, finance capital is the bank capital of a few very big monopolist banks, merged with the capital of the monopolist combines of industrialists; and, on the other hand, the division of the world is the transition from a colonial policy which has extended without hindrance to territories unseized by any capitalist power, to a colonial policy of monopolistic possession of the territory of the world which has been completely divided up.

But very brief definitions, although convenient, for they sum up the main points, are nevertheless inadequate, since very important features of the phenomenon that has to be defined have to be especially deduced. And so, without forgetting the conditional and relative value of all definitions in general, which can never embrace all the concatenations of a phenomenon in its complete development, we must give a definition of imperialism that will include the following five of its basic features: 1) the concentration of production and capital has developed to such a high stage that it has created monopolies which play a decisive role in economic life; 2) the merging of bank capital with industrial capital, and the creation, on the basis of this "finance capital," of a financial oligarchy; 3) the export of capital as distinguished from the export of commodities acquires exceptional importance; 4) the formation of international monopolist capitalist combines which share the world among themselves, and 5) the territorial division of the whole world among the biggest capitalist powers is completed. Imperialism is capitalism in that stage of development in which the dominance of monopolies and finance capital has established itself; in which the export of capital had acquired pronounced importance; in which the division of the world among the international trusts has begun; in which the division of all territories of the globe among the biggest capitalist powers has been completed.

We shall see later that imperialism can and must be defined differently if we bear in mind, not only the basic, purely economic concepts—to which the above definition is limited—but also the historical place of this stage of capitalism in relation to capitalism in general, or the relation between imperialism and the two main trends in the working-class movement. The point to be noted just now is that imperialism as interpreted above, undoubtedly represents a special stage in the development of capitalism. To enable the reader to obtain the most well-grounded idea of imperialism possible, we deliberately tried to quote as largely as possible *bourgeois* economists who are obliged to admit the particularly incontrovertible facts concerning the latest stage of capitalist economy. With the same object in view, we have quoted detailed statistics which enable one to see to what degree bank capital, etc., has grown, in what precisely the transformation of quantity into quality, of developed capitalism into imperialism, was expressed. Needless to say, of course, all boundaries in nature and in society are conditional and changeable, that it would be absurd to argue, for example, about the particular year or decade in which imperialism "definitely" became established.

V.I. Lenin. *Imperialism, the Highest State of Capitalism.* Originally published in 1912.

Revolutionary Forces of the World Unite, Fight Against Imperialist Aggression!

Mao Tse-Tung

MAO TSE-TUNG *(1893–1976) was born in Hunan Province in China. He became converted to Marxism and by 1927 led a revolutionary force into hiding in the Ching-kang Mountains. For about twenty-two years he directed his attack upon his adversaries, first Chiang Kai-shek and later the Japanese. During the years 1936–1940 he wrote most of his essays including "On Practice" and "On Contradiction."*

At this time, when the awakened working class and all genuine revolutionaries of the world are jubilantly celebrating the thirty-first anniversary of the Great October Socialist Revolution of the Soviet Union, I recall a well-known article by Stalin, written in 1918 on the first anniversary of that revolution. In that article Stalin said:

The great world-wide significance of the October Revolution chiefly consists in the fact that:

1) It has widened the scope of the national question and converted it from the particular question of combating national oppression in Europe into the general question of emancipating the oppressed peoples, colonies and semi-colonies from imperialism;

2) It has opened up wide possibilities for their emancipation and the right paths towards it, has thereby greatly facilitated the cause of the emancipation of the oppressed peoples of the West and the East, and has drawn them into the common current of the victorious struggle against imperialism;

3) *It has thereby erected a bridge between the socialist West and the enslaved East*, having created a new front of revolutions *against* world imperialism, extending from the proletarians of the West, through the Russian revolution, to the oppressed peoples of the East.[1]

History has developed in the direction pointed out by Stalin. The October Revolution has opened up wide possibilities for the emancipation of the peoples of the world and opened up the realistic paths towards it; it has created a new front of revolutions against world imperialism, extending from the proletarians of the West, through the Russian revolution, to the oppressed peoples of the East. This front of revolutions has been created and developed under the brilliant guidance of Lenin and, after Lenin's death, of Stalin.

If there is to be revolution, there must be a revolutionary party. Without a revolutionary party, without a party built on the Marxist-Leninist revolutionary theory and in the Marxist-Leninist revolutionary style, it is impossible to lead the working class and the broad masses of the people to defeat imperialism and its running dogs. In the more than one hundred years since the birth of Marxism, it was only through the example of the Russian Bolsheviks in leading the October Revolution, in leading socialist construction and in defeating fascist aggression that revolutionary parties of a new type were formed and developed in the world. With the birth of revolutionary parties of this type, the face of the world revolution has changed. The change has been so great that transformations utterly inconceivable to people of the older generation have come into being amid fire and thunder. The Communist Party of China is a party built and developed on the model of the Communist Party of the Soviet Union. With the birth of the Commu-

---

[1] From "The October Revolution and the National Question," Section III, "The World-wide Significance of the October Revolution," J.V. Stalin, *Works*, Eng. ed., Moscow, 1953, Vol. IV, pp. 169–70.

nist Part of China, the face of the Chinese revolution took on an altogether new aspect. Is
this fact not clear enough?

The world revolutionary united front, with
the Soviet Union at its head, defeated fascist
Germany, Italy and Japan. This was a result of
the October Revolution. If there had been no
October Revolution, if there had been no
Communist Party of the Soviet Union, no Soviet Union and no anti-imperialist revolutionary united front in the West and in the East led
by the Soviet Union, could one conceive of
victory over fascist Germany, Italy, Japan and
their running dogs? If the October Revolution
opened up wide possibilities for the emancipation of the working class and the oppressed
peoples of the world and opened up realistic
paths towards it, then the victory of the anti-
fascist Second World War has opened up still
wider possibilities for the emancipation of the
working class and the oppressed peoples of
the world and has opened up still more realistic paths towards it. It will be a very great mistake to underestimate the significance of the
victory of World War II.

Since the victory of World War II, U.S. imperialism and its running dogs in various
countries have taken the place of fascist Germany, Italy and Japan and are frantically pre-
paring a new world war and menacing the
whole world; this reflects the utter decay of
the capitalist world and its fear of imminent
doom. This enemy still has strength; therefore,
all the revolutionary forces of each country
must unite, and the revolutionary forces of all
countries must likewise unite, must form an
anti-imperialist united front headed by the Soviet Union and follow correct policies; otherwise, victory will be impossible. This enemy
has a weak and fragile foundation, he is disin-
tegrating internally, he is alienated from the
people, he is confronted with inextricable economic crises; therefore, he can be defeated. It
will be a very great mistake to overestimate
the enemy's strength and underestimate the
strength of the revolutionary forces.

Under the leadership of the Communist
Party of China, tremendous victories have now
been won in the great Chinese people's democratic revolution directed against the frenzied
aggression of U.S. imperialism in China and
against the traitorous, dictatorial and reaction-

ary Kuomintang government that has been
slaughtering the Chinese people by civil war.
During the two years from July 1946 to June
1948, the People's Liberation Army led by the
Communist Party of China beat back the attacks of 4,300,000 troops of the reactionary
Kuomintang government and went over from
the defensive to the offensive. During those
two years of fighting (not including developments since July 1948), the People's Liberation
Army captured and wiped out 2,640,000
Kuomintang troops. China's Liberated Areas
now cover 2,350,000 square kilometres, or 24.5
per cent of the country's 9,597,000 square
kilometres; they have a population of 168 million, or 35.3 per cent of the country's 475 million; and they contain 586 cities and towns, or
29 per cent of the 2,009 in the whole country.
Because our Party has resolutely led the peasants to carry out the reform of the land system,
the land problem has been thoroughly solved
in areas with a population of about 100 million,
and the land of the landlords and old-type rich
peasants has been more or less equally distributed among the peasants, primarily among the
poor peasants and farm labourers. The membership of the Communist Party of China has
grown from 1,210,000 in 1945 to 3,000,000
today. The task of the Communist Party of
China is to unite the revolutionary forces of the
whole country to drive out the aggressive
forces of U.S. imperialism, overthrow the reactionary rule of the Kuomintang and establish a
united, democratic people's republic. We know
that there are still many difficulties ahead. But
we are not afraid of them. We believe that difficulties must be and can be overcome.

The radiance of the October Revolution
shines upon us. The long-suffering Chinese
people must win their liberation, and they
firmly believe they can. Always isolated in the
past, China's revolutionary struggle no longer
feels isolated since the victory of the October
Revolution. We enjoy the support of the Communist Parties and the working class of the
world. This point was understood by Dr. Sun
Yat-sen, forerunner of the Chinese revolution,
who established the policy of alliance with the
Soviet Union against imperialism. On his
death-bed he wrote a letter to the Soviet
Union as part of his testament. It is the Chiang
Kai-shek bandit gang of the Kuomintang that

is betraying Sun Yat-sen's policy, standing on the side of the imperialist counter-revolutionary front and opposing the people of their own country. But before long, people will witness the complete destruction of the whole reactionary regime of the Kuomintang by the Chinese people. The Chinese people are brave, so is the Communist Party of China, and they are determined to liberate all China.

This article was written in commemoration of the thirty-first anniversary of the October Revolution in Russia for the organ of the Information Bureau of the Communist and Workers' Parties of Europe, *For a Lasting Peace, For a People's Democracy*. It appeared in the 21st issue of the publication in 1948.

One Dimensional Man

Herbert Marcuse

HERBERT MARCUSE *(1898–1979) was born in Berlin but fled to the USA in 1936 with the rise of Nazism. He taught at Columbia, Harvard, and Brandeis Universities, and later at the University of California in San Diego.* Eros and Civilization *and* One Dimensional Man *are among his better known works.*

The Welfare and Warfare State

By way of summary: the prospects of containment of change, offered by the politics of technological rationality, depend on the prospects of the Welfare State. Such a state seems capable of raising the standard of *administered* living, a capability inherent in all advanced industrial societies where the streamlined technical apparatus—set up as a separate power over and above the individuals—depends for its functioning on the intensified development and expansion of productivity. Under such conditions, decline of freedom and opposition is not a matter of moral or intellectual deterioration or corruption. It is rather an objective societal process insofar as the production and distribution of an increasing quantity of goods and services make compliance a rational technological attitude.

However, with all its rationality, the Welfare State is a state of unfreedom because its total administration is a systematic restriction of (a) "technically" available free time;[1] (b) the quantity and quality of goods and services "technically" available for vital individual needs; (c) the intelligence (conscious and unconscious) capable of comprehending and realizing the possibilities of self-determination.

Late industrial society has increased rather than reduced the need for parasitical and alienated functions (for society as a whole, if not for the individual). Advertising, public relations, indoctrination, planned obsolescence are no longer unproductive overhead costs but rather elements of basic production costs. In order to be effective, such production of socially necessary waste requires continuous rationalization—the relentless utilization of advanced techniques and science. Consequently, a rising standard of living is the almost unavoidable by-product of the politically manipulated industrial society, once a certain level of backwardness has been overcome. The growing productivity of labour creates an increasing surplus-product which, whether privately or centrally appropriated and distributed, allows an increased consumption—notwithstanding the increased diversion of productivity. As long as this constellation prevails, it reduces the use-value of freedom; there is no reason to insist on self-determination if the administered life is the comfortable and even the "good" life. This is the rational and material ground for the unification of opposites, for one-dimensional political behaviour. On this ground, the transcending political forces *within* society are arrested, and qualitative change appears possible only as a change from *without*.

Rejection of the Welfare State on behalf of abstract ideas of freedom is hardly convincing. The loss of the economic and political liberties which were the real achievement of the preceding two centuries may seem slight damage in a state capable of making the administered life secure and comfortable. If the individuals are satisfied to the point of happiness with the goods and services handed down to them by the administration, why should they insist on different institutions for a different production

---

[1] "Free" time, not "leisure" time. The latter thrives in advanced industrial society, but it is unfree to the extent to which it is administered by business and politics.

of different goods and services? And if the individuals are pre-conditioned so that the satisfying goods also include thoughts, feelings, aspirations, why should they wish to think, feel, and imagine for themselves? True, the material and mental commodities offered may be bad, wasteful, rubbish—but *Geist* and knowledge are no telling arguments against satisfaction of needs.

The critique of the Welfare State in terms of liberalism and conservatism (with or without the prefix "neo-") rests, for its validity, on the existence of the very conditions which the Welfare State has surpassed—namely, a lower degree of social wealth and technology. The sinister aspects of this critique show forth in the fight against comprehensive social legislation and adequate government expenditures for services other than those of military defence.

Denunciation of the oppressive capabilities of the Welfare State thus serves to protect the oppressive capabilities of the society *prior* to the Welfare State. At the most advanced stage of capitalism, this society is a system of subdued pluralism, in which the competing institutions concur in solidifying the power of the whole over the individual. Still, for the administered individual, pluralistic administration is far better than total administration. One institution might protect him against the other; one organization might mitigate the impact of the other; possibilities of escape and redress can be calculated. The rule of law, no matter how restricted, is still infinitely safer than rule above or without law.

However, in view of prevailing tendencies, the question must be raised whether this form of pluralism does not accelerate the destruction of pluralism. Advanced industrial society is indeed a system of countervailing powers. But these forces cancel each other out in a higher unification—in the common interest to defend and extend the established position, to combat the historical alternatives, to contain qualitative change. The countervailing powers do not include those which counter the whole.[1] They tend to make the whole immune

against negation from within as well as without; the foreign policy of containment appears as an extension of the domestic policy of containment.

The reality of pluralism becomes ideological, deceptive. It seems to extend rather than reduce manipulation and coordination, to promote rather than counteract the fateful integration. Free institutions compete with authoritarian ones in making the Enemy a deadly force *within* the system. And this deadly force stimulates growth and initiative, not by virtue of the magnitude and economic impact of the defence "sector," but by virtue of the fact that the society as a whole becomes a defence society. For the Enemy is permanent. He is not in the emergency situation but in the normal state of affairs. He threatens in peace as much as in war (and perhaps more than in war); he is thus being built into the system as a cohesive power.

Neither the growing productivity nor the high standard of living depend on the threat from without, but their use for the containment of social change and perpetuation of servitude does. The Enemy is the common denominator of all doing and undoing. And the Enemy is not identical with actual communism or actual capitalism—he is, in both cases, the real spectre of liberation.

Once again: the insanity of the whole absolves the particular insanities and turns the crimes against humanity into a rational enterprise. When the people, aptly stimulated by the public and private authorities, prepare for lives of total mobilization, they are sensible not only because of the present Enemy, but also because of the investment and employment possibilities in industry and entertainment. Even the most insane calculations are rational: the annihilation of five million people is preferable to that of ten million, twenty million, and so on. It is hopeless to argue that a civilization which justifies its defence by such a calculus proclaims its own end.

Under these circumstances, even the existing liberties and escapes fall in place within the organized whole. At this stage of the regi-

---

[1] For a critical and realistic appraisal of Galbraith's ideological concept see Earl Latham, "The Body Politic of the Corporation," in: E.S. Mason, *The Corporation in Modern Society* (Cambridge: Harvard University Press, 1959), p. 223, 235 f.

mented market, is competition alleviating or intensifying the race for bigger and faster turnover and obsolescence? Are the political parties competing for pacification or for a stronger and more costly armament industry? Is the production of "affluence" promoting or delaying the satisfaction of still unfulfilled vital needs? If the first alternatives are true, the contemporary form of pluralism would strengthen the potential for the containment of qualitative change, and thus prevent rather than impel the "catastrophe" of self-determination. Democracy would appear to be the most efficient system of domination.

The image of the Welfare State sketched in the preceding paragraphs is that of a historical freak between organized capitalism and socialism, servitude and freedom, totalitarianism and happiness. Its possibility is sufficiently indicated by prevalent tendencies of technical progress, and sufficiently threatened by explosive forces. The most powerful, of course, is the danger that preparation for total nuclear war may turn into its realization: the deterrent also serves to deter efforts to eliminate the *need* for the deterrent. Other factors are at play which may preclude the pleasant juncture of totalitarianism and happiness, manipulation and democracy, heteronomy and autonomy—in short, the perpetuation of the preestablished harmony between organized and spontaneous behaviour, preconditioned and free thought, expediency and conviction.

Even the most highly organized capitalism retains the social need for private appropriation and distribution of profit as the regulator of the economy. That is, it continues to link the realization of the general interest to that of particular vested interests. In doing so, it continues to face the conflict between the growing potential of pacifying the struggle for existence, and the need for intensifying this struggle; between the progressive "abolition of labour" and the need for preserving labour as the source of profit. The conflict perpetuates the inhuman existence of those who form the human base of the social pyramid—the outsiders and the poor, the unemployed and un-

employable, the persecuted coloured races, the inmates of prisons and mental institutions.

In contemporary communist societies, the enemy without, backwardness, and the legacy of terror perpetuate the oppressive features of "catching up with and surpassing" the achievements of capitalism. The priority of the means over the end is thereby aggravated—a priority which could be broken only if pacification is achieved—and capitalism and communism continue to compete without military force, on a global scale and through global institutions. This pacification would mean the emergence of a genuine world economy—the demise of the nation state, the national interest, national business together with their international alliances. And this is precisely the possibility against which the present world is mobilized:

> Ignorance and unconsciousness are such that nationalism continues to flourish. Neither twentieth century armaments nor industry allow "fatherlands" to insure their security and their existence except through organisations which carry weight on a world wide scale in military and economic matters. But in the East as well as in the West, collective beliefs don't adapt themselves to real changes. The great powers shape their empires or repair the architecture thereof without accepting changes in the economic and political regime which would give effectiveness and meaning to one or the other of the coalitions.
> *(and:)*
> Duped by the nation and duped by the class, the suffering masses are everywhere involved in the harshness of conflict in which their only enemies are masters who knowingly use the mystifications of industry and power.
> The collusion of modern industry and territorial power is a vice which is more profoundly real than capitalist and communist institutions and structures and which no necessary dialectic necessarily eradicates.[1]

The fateful interdependence of the only two "sovereign" social systems in the contemporary world is expressive of the fact that the conflict between progress and politics, between man and his masters has become total. When capitalism meets the challenge of communism, it meets its own capabilities: spectacular development of all productive forces after

---

[1] François Perroux, *La Coexistence pacifique* (Paris: Presses Universitaires, 1958), vol. III, p. 631–632; 633. (In translation.)

the subordination of the private interests in profitability which arrest such development. When communism meets the challenge of capitalism, it too meets its own capabilities: spectacular comforts, liberties, and alleviation of the burden of life. Both systems have these capabilities distorted beyond recognition and, in both cases, the reason is in the last analysis the same—the struggle against a form of life which would dissolve the basis for domination.

Herbert Marcuse. *One Dimensional Man*. London: Routledege and Kegan Paul, Boston: Beacon Press, 1964.

Marx's Response to Hegel

D. F. B. Tucker

D.F.B. TUCKER *is a lecturer in the Department of Political Science, Melbourne University. His writings include* Marxism and Individualism.

Marx rejects Hegel's optimistic teleological approach as metaphysical. It is wrong, he argues, to see the state (or the institution of bourgeois property upheld by the state) as functional to the goals of "Reason" or "Spirit" (conceived as something imposed by history, apart from the specific interests of particular classes).[1] He argues that the important lesson to be learned from an analysis of Rousseau's contribution (especially in the light of Hegel's response) is that it is necessary to reach an understanding of the ways in which institutional practices can help or hinder personal development. In his *Early Manuscripts*[2] he tries to show how Rousseau's insight into the alienating effects of the property claims made by private individuals can be combined with Hegel's sense of historical progress to provide a more adequate account of alienation.[3] What Marx emphasizes is that history has no meaning (in the sense that we cannot say that there are designs or purposes at work which are independent of human actors), but that the impact of institutional practices on individuals is something which can best be understood as resulting from the unintended consequences of those choices that the majority of individuals are likely to make in any given set of circumstances. In the light of this analysis, Marx suggests that what we need is an account which traces the way in which specific roles and relations come to be established, starting

from the premise that the enterprise of producing history results from the impact of the choices of many individuals. Such an approach is important, he tells us, because it is these very relations of production which, in turn, inhibit human development by setting up particular interests that conflict with collective goals. Marx believes that if we are to understand the relationships involved here, we must devote part of our attention at least to the acting individuals in order to see what happens to them within the social enterprise of production. In this regard he concludes that the particular interests of individuals should not confront collectively imposed goals and interests as something alien. Unfortunately, in practice (especially under capitalist relations of production) the relations between individuals seeking to realize their particular human needs and the claims of society with which they are confronted are contradictory. This is partly because social interests represent the negation of the aspiration to develop human potentiality, and because the goals of individuals serve in turn to undermine the debilitating structures imposed by the collectivity. The reason for this, Marx tells us, is that market resource allocation requires that the power of labour be sold as a commodity. In such circumstances it becomes possible, even imperative, for those who own the means of production to extract a surplus by competing with other owners, and they must, therefore, extract the largest possible contribution from their employees. What outrages Marx about this situation is the dehumanization which, he argues, takes place when labour is treated as a

---

[1] See Marx's "Critique of Hegel's Doctrine of the State" (1843), in *Early Writings* (Harmondsworth, Penguin, 1975). For commentary, see S. Avineri, "The Hegelian Origins of Marx's Political Thought," in Avineri (ed.), *Marx's Socialism* (New York, Lieber-Atherton, 1973); *The Social and Political Thought of Karl Marx* (Cambridge, Cambridge University Press, 1968), ch. 2.

[2] Bottomore (ed.), *Early Writings*.

[3] For a recent statement see H. Braverman, *Labour and Monopoly Capital* (New York, Monthly Review Press, 1974).

commodity. He is, of course, concerned about the poverty which he believes results from unbridled competition between capitalists and about the psychological harm caused by the brutalization of work under the capitalist mode of production. These are, however, consequences which Marx takes to be inevitable, given the nature of the system of production he describes in *Capital*. It is, therefore, in Marx's view, quite pointless to complain that the capitalist owners cheat the workers, for they do pay the market price of labour power (which, Marx suggests, reflects the cost of producing the labourer—that is, a wage sufficient to support a family); it is also unhelpful, Marx tells us, to appeal to the better sentiments of humanity in the hope of inspiring social change. Thus, he tells us, moral outrage, in itself and without supporting theories explaining the causes of social evils, is hardly worth expressing.[1]

Marx claims to have located the fundamental problem (the primary cause of the alienation of humanity) in the fact that social choices are made by private individuals whose strategies are dictated by the exigencies of market competition. In sharp contrast to Hegel, who saw modernity as progressively increasing our human capacities, Marx (like Rousseau) believes that this is not necessarily so. Indeed, he is able to show that, contrary to Hegel's optimistic prognosis, under capitalism the vast bulk of humanity is forced to abandon its human dignity by selling itself as a commodity. Furthermore, he argues that the state has always represented the interests of particular classes and should not be presented as the agency of a universal or collective interest. Marx explains that what is required, if we are to transcend the alienation which inhibits human development under capitalism, is that the tyranny of the market be replaced by a system in which social resources can be controlled collectively, and that the imperatives established through competition for profit be replaced by democratic controls which will enable mankind to work constructively towards the realization of truly human goals. He optimistically believes that these goals will be achieved after the capitalist mode of production is replaced by a system based on social ownership of the means of production.

D.F.B. Tucker. *Marxism and Individualism*. New York: St. Martin's Press, 1980.

---

[1] Marx makes this point most forcefully in *The German Ideology* and *Critique of the Gotha Programme*.

Beyond Marx, Beyond Weber

Harold J. Berman

HAROLD J. BERMAN *(1918–) was educated at
Dartmouth College, Yale University, and the
London School of Economics. He is currently
Story Professor of Law at Harvard University. His
has been a prolific writer. Among his notable
works are* The Soviet Criminal Law and
Procedure, Interaction of Law and Religion,
and Law and Revolution.

The social theorists of the nineteenth and
early twentieth centuries were especially
concerned to explain the revolutions which
had periodically interrupted the course of social evolution. Marx, in particular, had a comprehensive concept of revolution, which is
followed in this study; he saw revolution as a
total social, economic, political, legal, and
ideological transformation, and, indeed, a
transformation of man himself.[1] However,
Marx's historical materialism led to over-sim-
plified explanations of the causes of the great
European revolutions and to a limited definition of social classes based on their relationship to the means of production. Thus he
misconceived the Protestant Reformation and
he missed the Papal Revolution entirely. Moreover, Marx extrapolated directly from the history of the European nations to the history of
mankind, without sufficiently taking into account the importance of intermediate cultures
such as the Western, the Islamic, the Chinese.
As Robert Tucker notes, "For Marx the real
social unit is the species, the human collectivity...all social revolutions are world revolutions."[2] Thus Marx unconsciously identified
the history of the West with the history of the
world. His famous statement, "Revolutions
are the locomotives of history," which was

true of the West, was not true of non-Western
cultures when he made it; partly because he
did make it, it has since become true of some
non-Western cultures.

Notwithstanding their rebellion against
conventional historiography, the social theorists simply accepted the prevailing periodiza-
tion of Western history into a Middle Ages
that had begun at some uncertain time in the
past and a Modern Age that had commenced
roughly in the sixteenth (or possibly seventeenth or eighteenth) century. To this they
added, however, a premonition that the modern period of Western history was about to be
superseded by a new age.

The social theorists gave a specific content
to the social-economic formation of the Middle Ages. They called it the age of "feudalism." The Modern Age, in contrast, came to be
viewed as an era of "individualism" or of
"capitalism," depending on whether social
values or economic values were considered
primary. The social theorists sought to analyze
these successive types of social order and to
explain how and why they had come into
being. They used an historical and comparative method in order to create a universal science of social evolution. Marx contended that
every society tends to pass from an "Asiatic"
or slave economy to feudalism, from feudalism to capitalism, and from capitalism to socialism. This progression was seen by him as
an inevitable consequence of the dynamics of
class struggle. The concept of feudalism was
critical to this theory, which postulates that
out of the conflict between a peasantry bound
to the land and a feudal ruling class there
arose, eventually, a new conflict between an
industrial proletariat and a capitalist ruling

---

[1] See Robert C. Tucker, "The Marxian Revolutionary Idea," in *Revolution*, ed. Carl Friedrich, *Nomos*, no. 8(1966), pp.
217–246, esp. p. 219.
[2] *Ibid.*, pp. 223–224.

class, and that out of that conflict there is destined to arise a socialist classless society.

Many non-Marxists have also attributed a universal character to feudalism, seeing it as a stage in the development of many cultures. The Japanese and Russian cultures, in particular, are seen as having experienced feudalism during the "medieval" period of their history. The cross-cultural study of feudalism has yielded interesting and valuable insights; yet it is deceptively cosmopolitan. Behind it lurks the ethnocentric question, "Which features of medieval Western societies are essential to a universal definition of feudalism?" Most social and economic historians have stressed four such features: a subject peasantry bound to the land (serfdom), a specialized military class (knighthood), a fragmented public authority in the hands of a nobility dispersed on landed estates (lordship), and a distribution of power and privileges among the nobility through a system of vassalage and dependent land tenure (fiefs). They have then looked for parallels in other cultures. This might be called a form of academic imperialism.

Omitted from most of the conventional definitions of feudalism is any reference to (1) the belief systems of people living under feudalism, (2) the relation between ecclesiastical and secular authorities in feudal systems, and (3) the types of legal theories and legal institutions that prevail in feudal societies. These omissions leave one without any guidance concerning the general significance of ideology, politics, and law under feudalism—although, at least in regard to Western feudalism, there is no doubt that all three played an extremely important part in the social order as a whole. Even if, as most historical materialists postulate, ideology, politics, and law in the Middle Ages are to be viewed as a superstructure built on the economic base of the feudal mode of production, the crucial question remains, "How and why did Western feudalism produce a very different kind of superstructure from that produced by Japanese or Russian feudalism?"

For Marx the essential elements of feudalism were, first, small-scale agriculture with dependent land tenure ("the petty mode of production"), and second, a subject peasantry bound to the land (serfdom). These made it possible for the feudal ruling class to take the surplus value of the peasants' labor. Other aspects of feudal land tenure as it existed in the West in its heyday, such as vassalage, knighthood, and fragmented public authority, were not, for Marx, defining features of feudalism. He saw feudalism, as he saw capitalism, in terms of its conflicts, not in terms of its cohesion. Moreover, Marx was not interested in the fact that money and commerce played an important part in the economy of the feudal age in the West, and that in the twelfth and thirteenth centuries a flourishing urban civilization, with thousands of cities, coexisted alongside the petty mode of production. Contemporary Marxists, at least, do not—they cannot—deny that this is so, but they generally do deny that it has any great significance. They continue to rely on Marx's postulate of an unremitting antagonism between more or less static, self-sufficient rural economics and commercially expanding urban economies, resulting eventually in the overthrow of the former ("feudalism") by the latter ("capitalism").

Unfortunately for this Marxian analysis, the "feudal mode of production"—that is, the manorial system—had broken down by the end of the fourteenth century, all over Europe, and the "capitalist" mode of production, as defined by Marx, only came into being in the eighteenth, or at the earliest the seventeenth century. This leaves a "transition" period of some three or four centuries during which a central state power developed, namely, the absolute monarchies of Europe. It was the function of the new national states, according to Marxist theory, to repress the peasantry, "since the local organs of feudal power no longer survived."[1] Thus it is argued that although the political system changed completely, the social-economic system remained the same. "The ruling class," says a leading Marxist historian, "remained the same, just as a republic, a constitutional monarchy, and a fascist dicta-

---

[1] Christopher Hill, "A Comment," in Rodney Hilton, ed., *The Transition from Feudalism to Capitalism* (London, 1976), p. 121.

torship can all be forms of the rule of the bourgeoisie."[1] This view paints history with a very broad brush indeed!...

The English economic historian Perry Anderson has attempted to explain, from a Marxist point of view, the fact that only in Europe did capitalism arise out of feudalism. He attributes that development to distinctive features of European feudalism that are often considered by other Marxists to have been part of the superstructure rather than of the economic base. Anderson argues that the distinction between superstructure and base is not applicable to feudalism. In precapitalist societies, he states, "the 'superstructures' of kinship, religion, law, or the state necessarily enter into the constitutive structure of the mode of production."[2]

The recognition of the integration of law and economy in feudal Europe seems, at first, to threaten the whole Marxian analysis. Perhaps, however, the Marxian distinction between base and superstructure can be saved by another means, namely, by limiting its applicability to times of breakdown in the social structure. Perhaps Marxists could agree that normally—in all societies—economic and legal institutions entirely overlap. For example, property (ownership) has normally both an economic and a legal aspect, which are inextricably interrelated. But at certain times the two aspects may split apart, and Marx may have had such times in mind when he distinguished property in an economic sense namely, economic power, from property in a legal sense, namely, economic right. Indeed, the clue to a proper understanding of Marx's social theory may be that he interpreted all history in light of a theory intended to be applicable chiefly to times of revolution.

This would also help to explain Marx's transfer of nineteenth-century ideas of causation, derived from the natural sciences, to historical developments. He searched for scientific laws of history analogous to the scientific laws of physics and chemistry. He found such laws in historical materialism—for example, the law that in every society the mode of production determines class relations between owners and nonowners of the means of production, which in turn determine the political development of the society. This monistic formula, which seems to be an extremely oversimplified method of explaining complex events in normal social life, served two important functions in Marxian thought: it explained the revolutionary origins of existing institutions and beliefs, and it provided a basis for a revolutionary attack upon them. Today, however, ideas of causation even in physics and chemistry are more complex, and in social history it has become less and less possible to speak of laws of causation at all. It is both more accurate and more useful to speak of the interaction of politics, economics, law, religion, art, ideas—without separating these inextricably interrelated aspects of social life into "cause" compartments and "effect" compartments. This is not to deny that some kinds of concerns and interests are more important, and more influential, than others. It is not necessary to retreat from a position of determinism to a position of relativism. The truth, however, seems to be that economic factors are of greater importance in some times and places, political factors in others, religious factors in others, legal factors in others, and so forth; and that of predominant importance in all times and places is the mode of interaction of these various factors.

From this point of view, the brilliant though often obscure writings on law by the great German social theorist Max Weber (1864–1920) represent a certain advance over classical Marxist thought. Weber rejected what he called the "evolutionary dogmatism of Marx-

---

[1] *Ibid.*

[2] Perry Anderson, *Lineages of the Absolutist State* (London, 1974), p. 403. The East German Marxist Rudolf Bahro also sees Western feudalism as a unique economic form which had within it "an immanent tendency of transformation" into capitalism. Bahro states: "Feudalism-capitalism is essentially a single development." *The Alternative in Eastern Europe*, trans. David Fernbach (London, 1978), p. 66.

ism,"[1] especially its assertion that all societies tend to pass through successive stages of development from "Asiatic" or slave economies to feudalism, capitalism, and socialism. He also rejected Marxist historical materialism, with its postulate of economic determinism. "If we look at the causal lines," he said in 1910, "we see them run, at one time, from technical to economic and political matters, at another from political to religious and economic ones, etc. There is no resting point. In my opinion, the view of historical materialism, frequently espoused, that the economic is in some sense the ultimate point in the chain of causes is completely finished as a scientific proposition."[2]

Moreover, Weber, in contrast to Marx, stressed the unique character of modern Western society and the "universal significance and validity of its direction of development."[3] He attributed the uniqueness and the significance of modern Western society to unique factors that had already been present in the pre-modern, precapitalist, pre-Protestant period of European history. For Weber, Western feudalism, the medieval Western city, and other features of "traditional" (as contrasted with "rational") medieval Western society con-

tained within themselves forces that were lacking in the traditional societies of other world cultures, forces which were ultimately capable of transforming the West.[4]

Thus Weber was able to perceive the unique character and unique importance of the early development of Western law, as well as its significance for later economic development. Only the Occident, he stated, had experienced a fully developed system of folk justice, a legal regulation of status groups under feudalism, constitutional controls over princely power by the estates, the replacement of a system of personal laws by "natural law," and the successive receptions of Roman law. "All these events...have only the remotest analogies elsewhere in the world," he wrote. "For this reason, the stage of decisively shaping law by trained legal specialists has not been fully reached anywhere outside the Occident."[5] The existence of highly developed, rational, legal institutions was, in Weber's view, a necessary precondition of the emergence of capitalism.

Harold J. Berman. *Law and Revolution*. Cambridge: Harvard University Press, 1983.

---

[1] *Max Weber on Law in Economy and Society*, ed. Max Rheinstein (Cambridge, Mass., 1966), p. 297.

[2] *Proceedings of the First Conference of German Sociologists*, 1910, quoted in Max Weber, *Economy and Society*, ed. Guenther Roth and Claus Wittich (New York, 1968), I, lxiv.

[3] Max Weber, *Gesammelte Aufsatzen zur Religions-soziologie* (Tübingen, 1920), p. 1.

[4] This conclusion can be supported by many quotations from Weber's writings, although other quotations can be found to qualify and even refute it. In fact, Weber's historical writings are quite confused and inconsistent, though his theoretical analysis is just the opposite.

[5] Rheinstein, *Max Weber*, p. 304.

Part VII

Democratic Socialism

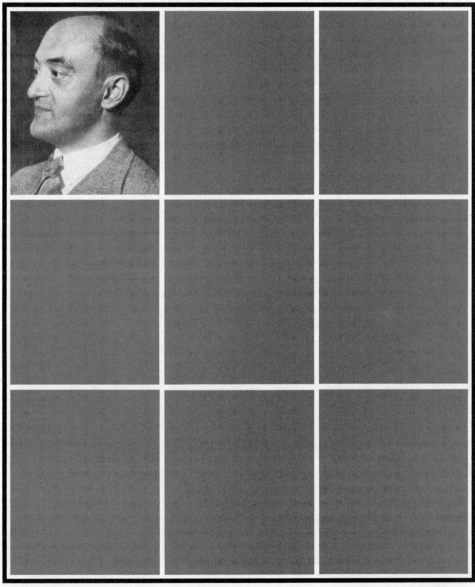

JOSEPH A. SCHUMPETER

The following essays were all written over the past fifty years in different historical conditions, but all share misgivings about capitalism and political systems dominated by it. It is interesting to note how varied and how persistent these misgivings are.

Historically, democratic socialism saw itself as being distinct from Marxism on the one hand and liberalism on the other. In his essay, Charles Taylor speaks of the necessity of socialism—indebted though it be to Marx—to undergo transformation. This transformation is occasioned by the breakdown of one of the main supporting structures of our civilization, the self-image of the present industrial society as a vast productive machine which is linked in various ways to our propensity to consume. According to Taylor, one cannot hope to build a socialist society (i.e. a society built on "more humane priorities") without making more sane our desires to consume. But to do this requires as the foundation of our technological society a new self-image.

In terms much more sweeping than those of Taylor, Joseph Schumpeter indicts capitalism as an enterprise which leads to bureaucratic giants that not only oust the entrepreneur but also expropriate the bourgeois class. Defending socialism, he goes on to maintain that capitalism affected the institutional framework that protected the upper strata of society. Like Marx, Schumpeter includes among the effects of capitalism the destruction of certain arrangements in the feudal world, the rise of the capitalist bourgeoisie, the preservation of political power in the hands of the aristocracy, and, finally, the inability of the bourgeois class to face domestic or international problems.

The emphasis of the Students for a Democratic Society is upon matters less theoretical and deliberately more concrete than those raised by either Taylor or Schumpeter. In its *Port Huron Statement*, the SDS, as it is called, speaks in support of a more open, participatory society at all levels and speaks in defense of a re-examination of fundamental human values in a technological society. In this statement, one sees vividly the ideals of democratic socialism protruding clearly through the surface of a political perspective that is too often burdened by historical considerations and by theoretical observations.

In ways more trenchant and analytic than those of the SDS movement, Alec Nove examines in his essay the economics of feasible socialism. Focusing upon monopoly power, vulnerability and alienation, Nove discusses sectional interests, unions, inflation, monetarism, and externalities. Furthermore, and much to his credit, Nove carries off his discussion without slipping into either dogmatism or question-begging phrases. Instead, he makes a persuasive plea for the consideration of a socialism that would work. Nove's essay ends rather fittingly with a quote from Charles Taylor—a quote which reflects Nove and Taylor's concern over the fetishism surrounding commodities.

The Agony of Economic Man

Charles Taylor

CHARLES TAYLOR *(1931–) is a well-known Canadian socialist philosopher and political scientist. He currently is Professor of Political Science at McGill University. He has contributed numerous articles to journals and has written a number of books including* The Explanation of Behaviour, Hegel, *and* Philosophical Papers: Vol. I Human Agency and Language; Vol. II Philosophy and the Human Sciences.

In the coming years the thought and program of socialism will have to be worked out afresh. Of course, socialism is always rethinking itself, but the present transformation will have to be the most far-reaching in the past century—since the appearance of *Das Kapital* in 1867.

The occasion for this rethinking is a breakdown of one of the props of our civilization, a prop of capitalist civilization to be sure, but one on which socialists counted for the transition to a higher form of society. This breakdown can perhaps best be thought of as a crisis of legitimacy, a crucial weakening of the set of beliefs, practices, and collective representations that help to hold society together. Of course, modern western societies—like all societies beyond the most primitive—have been held together by a variety of legitimating ideas. Nationalism has been one such powerful idea, and no one can claim that it is on the wane. But one of the most important foundations of legitimacy has been the self-image of modern industrial society as a vast productive engine based on creative work, disciplined and rational effort, and the division of labour.

We are so used to this idea that we fail to notice it. Above all, we fail to appreciate how unprecedented it is in human history. It is not that previous societies have not had some shadowy notion of their economic organization, but no society before the rise of modern commercial-industry civilization has ever founded its sense of its own fundamental value on this economic organization (or even on an idealized version of what it is supposed to be). The idea would have appeared grotesque to earlier civilizations. For the Greeks, the "economic" was concerned with the maintenance of life, a pre-condition for politics, which was what really distinguished human society from that of gregarious beasts. To be concerned one's whole life only with the economic was to be in effect a slave. In the Middle Ages what was important in society was that its hierarchical order reflected and connected with the order of things in the universe.

Modern society singled itself out in that its paradigm justifying self-image was that of a productive association bent on transforming the surrounding natural world to meet the needs and fulfil the ends of man. So powerful was this justifying image that moderns were impelled to project it onto other, earlier civilizations. Thus, for Marxism, the real motive force of change in history has always been the tensions within the economic organization of societies. Nascent nineteenth century anthropology interpreted primitive magic as a first, muddled attempt at technological control of the environment. Even today American political science gives us theories of "development" which assume the universality of our modern economic based categories.

The malaise of our time arises partly from the fact that this justifying image has rather suddenly ceased to justify in the eyes of a growing number of people. The image of a society dedicated to constantly increasing production, to greater and greater prodigies of technology, suddenly seems tawdry and senseless. The constant rise in the G.N.P. goes along with an increasing demand for consumer goods, so that increasing social wealth seems to have no impact on the pool of poverty and material want which persists in contemporary industrial society. Seen in the light of humane priorities, we appear to be running as fast as possible in order to stand in the same place. And, to cap it all, this accelerating squirrel-wheel threatens to precipitate an ecological crisis which could be fatal.

This type of criticism of modern society is pretty standard stuff on the left these days. But its implications are not really thought through, and to do so properly requires much more than some minor retouching of socialist theory. To begin with, two facts have failed to register with their full impact: that the decline of its economic justifying image really could threaten our civilization with breakdown, and that socialism has traditionally defined itself in terms of its own version of the productive society, hence its own economic justifying image. It cannot just shrug off the challenge implicit in the fact that all such economic images are under attack today...

Socialism in its present definitions is closely tied up with the economic self-image which it has borrowed from capitalist civilization. Perhaps it would be truer to say that both visions spring from the same civilization, born of the Enlightenment and the growth of industrial society. A really adequate socialist alternative has to be rethought from the ground up.

The socialist economic vision of society is not identical with the capitalist one. In fact, traditional socialism incorporates some strands of the romantic rebellion against the economic vision. But this synthesis is an unstable one; it is a synthesis in wish only, and it cannot withstand the test of practice. This can best be illustrated from the case of Marxism, which after a hundred years still remains the basis of the most coherent and influential conceptions of socialism. On one hand, Marxism offers a vision of socialism as the fulfilment of the productive vocation of capitalism. Socialism will overcome the contradictions of capitalism, the forms of which have become fetters which prevent the immense productive powers of human society from giving their full measure. This has remained a theme of socialist rhetoric for over a century, that capitalism is inherently inefficient and wasteful, that socialism is ultimately the only rational organi-

zation of the economy.

This critique is not simple and univocal: it can mean that capitalism is inefficient in its own terms; or it can mean that socialists are applying a different standard of efficiency—effectiveness in meeting real human need—as against abstract production targets, growing profits, greater potential armaments production, and so on. In practice, socialists have usually meant both, though the accent has varied from context to context. But insofar as the second, more fundamental criticism is salient, we have gone beyond a simple reliance on the economic model; production is now seen as undertaken for the sake of some higher goal, at least potentially.

The question of the re-definition of socialism in our time turns on the definition of that higher goal or goals and the relation of the productive organization of society to it. And here traditional socialism is full of half-clarities and wishful thinking. Basically there are two answers, neither of them satisfactory. Both can be found in Marxism, which here as elsewhere retains its predominant influence.

The first answer is that in socialist or communist society, the distinction between productive work and creation will disappear. All production will take on the intensity, the freedom, the self-expressive power, the playfulness of artistic creation at its most untrammeled. Production will not thus be just a means, which has usurped the role of an end, as many people now experience it in capitalist society, a senseless squirrel-wheel. It will merge with intense self-fulfilment, with the true end of life.

But this perspective is unfortunately as implausible as it is attractive. Artistic creation itself is only free and untrammeled at privileged moments; these moments pre-suppose long hours and months of disciplined work. Even so, we would gladly settle for a world in which all productive labour could have the same creative goal and motivation as the work of artists does today. But although much could be done to relieve men from drudgery and to heighten the significance of many jobs for those who hold them by increasing their participation in the direction of the whole enterprise, it would be utopian to look forward to a society in which there was no more labour which was not an antechamber to creation.

This hard fact is the basis of the second answer of traditional socialism to the alienation of productive labour: that socialist society will profit from technological advance and investment to reduce the hours of work dramatically, thus liberating men for free, creative activity. This answer accepts the continued distinction between creation and productive labour; it proposes to reduce one, perhaps ultimately to the vanishing point, at the expense of the other. We can see this solution as offering in a sense a return to the Greek polis, as it was idealized by its most fortunate citizens: a life of creative action and of full participation in public life. But where with the Greeks the material basis for this life of creative leisure was assured by slave labour, in the future socialist society machines would fill the helot role.

This is probably the most commonly held view among socialists today who are concerned with the shape of a future socialist society; and it is a perspective which many non-socialists also espouse at least in part. It looks deceptively simple: we just apply our increasing productive power to liberating men from drudgery and we open a new era of human history. We truly relegate production to a subordinate role, and one to which we need give less and less time, in order to devote ourselves to the true ends of life.

This idyllic prospect ignores certain stubborn realities. To begin with, we have to admit that we are not proceeding in this direction at all, that the immense wealth and productive power accumulated to date has not served to liberate more and more people for a life of creative leisure. On the contrary, we are probably the hardest working civilization in history. It is true that we have reduced the work week from the horrendous sixty to seventy hours that it was in the last century to more humane proportions. But reductions in the work week today do not usually mean significant reductions in the number of hours worked, but rather an increase in the number of workers for whom overtime is paid. And many people feel obliged to moonlight and thus still work sixty or seventy hours.

Why? The quick answer, which raises all the questions, is that we are absorbing our increased productivity in more and more refined consumer goods. With each rise of productive potential something new is invented which we feel we must have, and the race for this product, together with the efforts of those who haven't yet obtained the last wave of inventions, keeps the squirrel-wheel turning.

The standard socialist response is to lay the blame at the door of the contemporary corporate capitalist system and its essential ancillary of consumer management. But the elements of truth in this charge easily distract attention from the crucial illusion underlying it. The corporate system is built on this endless drive for consumer goods; it provides its focus, determines its pace, and above all entrenches its priorities in the decisions which shape the development of the economy. The corporate system has entrenched the power of these priorities, but it does not itself create these priorities, they do not exist only because of the power of manipulation. Any movement which wishes to change our economic goals in a fundamental way must fight the present hegemony of the large corporation over our society, but the corporation is not the only prop on which this consumer civilization rests. To believe that it is means accepting a naive, demonological, manipulative view of history. No institution creates the spiritual conditions for its own existence; it may intensify them, give them permanence, but it does not bring them into being.

The simple answer which lays the drive for consumer goods at the door of the corporate system cannot be taken seriously. Another equally simple answer is given by apologists for the present system: that men naturally want to possess things, and that given a productive potential which increases indefinitely there will naturally and inevitably follow a desire to possess which also increases indefinitely. Any other view of human nature, it is implied, is naively altruistic.

One does not need to have a wildly altruistic vision of man to question this theory. Men have desired prosperity throughout the ages and, given the chance, riches. But this wealth has not always, or even most often, been defined so exclusively in terms of the possession of things, in particular things, many of which have no intrinsic beauty. The problem of the ends of life cannot be so easily settled. Even if one concedes that men generally desire wealth, the important problems reappear when one tries to define what the life of a wealthy man consists in: and in particular, is wealth desirable because it is the only basis for a life of creative leisure, or is it desirable because it permits an increasing variety of possessions?

Once we set aside both vulgar socialism and corporate apologetics, we have to admit that we have not begun to understand the background to our endless propensity to consume, although such understanding has become an essential part of any adequate socialist theory. We cannot hope to change this propensity without an understanding of it, and we cannot hope to build a socialist society, one founded on more humane priorities, or one in which endless production would not be an end in itself, unless we can bring our urge to consume back into sane proportions.

I cannot claim to have the key to this mystery, but I think it is time that we engaged in some basic speculation about this problem as an indispensable prelude to more sober analysis. In this regard, there are a couple of hypotheses which seem worth exploring. First, we find it very hard to redirect our productive powers from endless consumption to creative leisure because in fact these powers are much less our servants than we like to think. The analogy with ancient Greece might again be appropriate here. Slave labour emancipates the free for other pursuits, but it subjects them to other servitudes, those which are inseparable from life in a slave society: the brutality, the abuse of power, the perpetual fear of revolt. The same is possibly true of our technological civilization. It requires us to acquire certain skills, submit to certain disciplines, integrate ourselves in certain forms of organization, adopt certain attitudes to change, and some of these requirements may be intensified as we try to substitute automated production for human labour.

The picture of machines as the pliant servants of humanity with all options open is more a childish dream of omnipotence than a realistic prospect. Machines are extensions of our own powers, but as such they require that we be moulded to operate them effectively. The mere hardware of a modern economy is nothing without the work discipline, the bureaucratic culture, the habits of innovation which make it operational. This is not to say that we must accept holus-bolus theories of technological determinism which paint a picture of inexorable development of a society dominated by machines. Socialists have rightly been sceptical of such theories. But they are no more schematic and implausible than the theories of human omnipotence. The interesting, and useful enterprise is to identify the limited but significant degrees of freedom which a technological society allows us.

Our endless drive to consume is not accidentally connected to a society founded on the economic justifying image described above. A society which sees its ultimate significance in being a productive engine of unparalleled power must celebrate this by continually renewed tangible expression of this power. It must in some form or other glorify its products. The consumer society which we live in is one variant of this glorification. The society renews itself by recurrently giving birth to an array of "new," freshly designed, supposedly improved products. With the renewal of our consumer durables, we are being sold renewed potency, happiness, a way of life. The hypothesis I am putting forward is that this apotheosis of the compleat consumer is not just an adventitious creation of the advertising-man, it is closely bound up with our basic images of our society and of its ultimate value.

Of course, the glorification of our products doesn't have to take the form of the consumer society. We can also glorify our collective products. This seems to be the path taken by orthodox Soviet Marxism. Here, too, society is defined economically, but the accent is on the collective achievements of "the people," prodigies of productive growth, technological wonders, targets met. Even capitalist societies have taken up this celebration of collective effort, as with the American moon shot.

This is a fatally inadequate vision of socialism. To substitute the glorification of collective products for that of individual products is to remain with the same economic image of society. But it is this image which is losing the allegiance of contemporary man. If socialism is to provide a creative alternative to the decay of capitalist civilization, it could not choose a worse or a more ineffective model.

Additional corroboration of this fact comes from the history of communist societies themselves. They can only maintain the pace of collective endeavour by rigid control from the top. There is pressure within these societies from the base to give more emphasis to consumer goods. This pressure, to be sure, has a very different meaning in a society where things which are by any reckoning essentials are in short supply. But one cannot help suspecting that if consumer demand in these countries were given its head it would show the same endless, insatiable character that it has here.

The collective celebration of productive power has not worked in communist societies. They do not seem to command autonomously the allegiance and enthusiasm to sustain themselves in a less repressive climate. This suggests another connection between modern economically defined society and the drive for consumption. The collective celebrations of this society do not call forth a deep response in men. Only when a modern community defines itself as a nation do its collective acts and symbols strike a deep chord. Modern nationalism is powerful as a public religion; the modern cult of production is not. Hence the public environments of modern industrial societies tend to be drab, if not positively injurious. The centres of modern industrial cities exercise an immense force of repulsion on their citizens, which itself contributes to their degradation. There is thus a powerful drift in modern society towards privatization, the creation of a private space of happiness and personal meaning. The products in which our society celebrates its power thus tend to be private consumption goods.

Seen from another angle, the connection is this: the cult of production projects a vision of man as dominating, transforming the surrounding world and enjoying the fruits of this transformation. It is because we place ultimate value on this form of human life that we are ready to make production the central function of modern society. But, in order to participate in this cult, individuals have to have some tangible part in the process of transform-ing/enjoying. The problem is that just being part of a vast production team, even one which realizes some important achievement, is too abstract; the connection with the end result is too tenuous. The ethos of modern society stresses dominance, control; but the man in the production line feels much more controlled than controlling. It has been a constant theme of socialist aspiration to remedy this by some form of workers' participation in management. But unless some formula of this kind can transform the worker's relation to the whole process of production, the only way in which the average man can have a sense of control is as a consumer, a possessor of things, one who enjoys the fruits of production. This is the only universally available mode of participation in the cult of production. Hence the poor in contemporary affluent societies suffer not just from material deprivation, but from a stigma. They are excommunicated, as it were, from the dominant cult of modern society.

The drive to consumption is therefore no adventitious fad, no product of clever manipulation. It will not be easy to contain. It is tied up with the economic self-image of modern society, and this in turn is linked to a set of powerfully entrenched conceptions of what the value of human life consists in. This is why it is not realistic to treat the infra-structure of technological society as an instrument which we can use at will for any ends we choose. Rather, as long as technological society is held together and given its legitimacy and cohesion by this economic self-image, it will tend to remain fixed on its present goals, the perpetual increase in production and the ever-widening bonanza of consumption. If we are to build a society with radically different priorities, one which will not be driven by this mania of consumption, then we have to evolve a different foundation for technological society, a quite different self-definition to serve as the basis of its cohesion.

This is no easy matter. We might at first be encouraged by the fact that the economic justifying image is losing its grip, but by itself this is no cause for rejoicing. This breakdown could simply render technological society more unlivable in that the only basis for its cohesion would be the widespread use of force. There is no providence, no ineluctable force, which assures us that the breakdown of the cult of production must be followed by another viable foundation for a technological society. Whether this is so or not depends on a number of things, but partly on what is offered as a socialist alternative.

The preceding discussion should allow us to measure a little better what is involved in rethinking socialism for our time. For socialist thought has to tackle this central problem of evolving a different foundation for technological society if the socialist alternative is to be fully relevant to our time. To date the socialist tradition is woefully inadequate to this task. As an alternative to the cult of production it offers mainly the idyll in which productive labour is swallowed up in artistic creation, or the hope that labour can be almost entirely done away with, liberating man for leisure. But the first prospect is impossible; and the second is offered without any idea of how we can overcome the obstacles to it. Without a genuine alternative to the economic image, socialism in the West will be condemned either to offer alternative variants of the cult of production, which will certainly be ignored, or to stand by inactive in the foolish hope that any destruction of the present order will inaugurate a socialist era.

But what would be involved in elaborating such a genuine alternative? I cannot claim to have the answer. But one or two things can be said about what such an alternative would have to be.

The economic model has at its centre the notion of man as producer, as transformer of nature. Man is pure agent. Its Achilles heel is that this offers men a goal which is ultimately empty. The drive to increase production starts with certain goals—to overcome poverty, to provide education for the masses and freedom of choice. But as the production oriented society takes over, it sets its own priorities, and these end up being those of production for its own sake, a glorification of the products. When the hold of this image wanes men have the feeling that this vast and diversified activity is to no purpose, that it is all dressed up with the most prodigious means, yet with nowhere to go. Hence the dominant feeling in this period of decline of the economic image is one of emptiness. The challenge to the current

model is coming from young people who cannot find a satisfactory identity in its vision of the future. It offers no form of life which makes sense.

The failure of the economic model is the condemnation of all models of human society which are based purely on an image of man as agent. Man is also a being to whom things happen, to whom things occur, who sees, hears, and feels. There is a genus of human activities in which what happens to us, or what we simply observe, is given human meaning for us, not changed for our purposes, but taken in, understood, interpreted. For the ancients, the most important of these activities was contemplation: for Aristotle this was the highest activity of man. But in modern time this contemplative function, whereby we take in and come to terms with reality, has been largely assumed by art. One of the signs of malaise in our civilization is that much of contemporary art is infected by the disease of the surrounding social reality, that it tries, half desperately, to become pure action, and wants to escape the exigencies of attentiveness.

In our present society the priorities governing the uses of technology and its development are almost entirely dominated by the goals of production. In an alternative society, they would be dominated, although not so one-sidedly, by a contemplative aspiration. In our present society our man made environment and artifacts are designed chiefly for some function, and then secondarily for "aesthetic appeal." But we rarely think of them in terms of what they express about our vision of things. They do indeed express something, but this is the latent, the forgotten dimension. Exactly the opposite is the case, for instance, with Chartres cathedral, to take a very spectacular example. There beauty and function are secondary to statement. Of course it is out of the question that there be another such total, confident statement in our day. We are more tentative, but we have not ceased wondering, imagining, thinking, in short, contemplating. It is just that we have abandoned one of our paradigm languages. We have let our architecture, and our world of useful objects, go dumb.

A civilization which recovered contemplation would have very different priorities in technology. The rage for obsolescence makes sense in our society because functional objects must be frequently replaced. But expressive objects are kept as long as possible, if they really speak. The priority would be not on serviceable materials and objects but on those which could be lived with for a long time. In such an alternative society, learning would not be confined to a preparatory phase but would be a major occupation for great numbers of people, who would return to it for prolonged periods at different points in their lives. This means that the society would commit a great part of its resources to supporting disinterested, non-functional study.

No one can say whether an alternative mode of technological society, principally organized around the goals of contemplation, would really be viable, whether it could claim men's allegiance as the productive model did in its hey-day and still does for many today.

But only some such alternative can provide a creative denouement to the crisis which our contemporary capitalist civilization is entering. That such an alternative would have to be socialist—that is, based on planning and a high degree of common ownership—must be obvious, but the converse is not true: socialism does not necessarily offer this kind of alternative.

We therefore need a rewriting of socialist theory as complete and far-reaching as that of Karl Marx a hundred years ago. The greatest of socialist theories then was born out of an acute sense of crisis. Perhaps we will be lucky enough to repeat this exploit once more.

Charles Taylor. "The Agony of Economic Man." In *Essays on the Left*. Edited by L. Lapierre, Jack McLeod, Charles Taylor, and Walter Young. Toronto: McClelland and Stewart, 1971.

Crumbling Walls

Joseph A. Schumpeter

JOSEPH A. SCHUMPETER *(1883–1950) was born in Triesch, Czechoslovakia. He practised law in Vienna and was Professor of Economics at two Austrian universities. For two years he was the Austrian Minister of Finance before moving on to the University of Bonn and Harvard University. One of his best known works is* Capitalism, Socialism, and Democracy.

I. The Obsolescence of the Entrepreneurial Function

...To sum up this part of our argument: if capitalist evolution—"progress"—either ceases or becomes completely automatic, the economic basis of the industrial bourgeoisie will be reduced eventually to wages such as are paid for current administrative work excepting remnants of quasi-rents and monopoloid gains that may be expected to linger on for some time. Since capitalist enterprise, by its very achievements, tends to automatize progress, we conclude that it tends to make itself superfluous—to break to pieces under the pressure of its own success. The perfectly bureaucratized giant industrial unit not only ousts the small or medium-sized firm and "expropriates" its owners, but in the end it also ousts the entrepreneur and expropriates the bourgeoisie as a class which in the process stands to lose not only its income but also what is infinitely more important, its function. The true pacemakers of socialism were not the intellectuals or agitators who preached it but the Vanderbilts, Carnegies and Rockefellers. This result may not in every respect be to the taste of Marxian socialists, still less to the taste of socialists of a more popular (Marx would have said, vulgar) description. But so far as prognosis goes, it does not differ from theirs.

II. The Destruction of the Protecting Strata

So far we have been considering the effects of the capitalist process upon the economic bases of the upper strata of capitalist society and upon their social position and prestige. But effects further extend to the institutional framework that protected them. In showing this we shall take the term in its widest acceptance so as to include not only legal institutions but also attitudes of the public mind and policies.

1. Capitalist evolution first of all destroyed, or went far toward destroying, the institutional arrangements of the feudal world—the manor, the village, the craft guild. The facts and mechanisms of this process are too familiar to detain us. Destruction was wrought in three ways. The world of the artisan was destroyed primarily by the automatic effects of the competition that came from the capitalist entrepreneur; political action in removing atrophic organizations and regulations only registered results. The world of the lord and the peasant was destroyed primarily by political—in some cases revolutionary—action and capitalism merely presided over adaptive transformations say, of the German manorial organizations into large-scale agricultural units of production. But along with these industrial and agrarian revolutions went a no less revolutionary change in the general attitude of legislative authority and public opinion. Together with the old economic organization vanished the economic and political privileges of the classes or groups that used to play the leading role in it, particularly the tax exemptions and the political prerogatives of the landed nobility and gentry and of the clergy.

Economically all this meant for the bourgeoisie the breaking of so many fetters and the removal of so many barriers. Politically it meant the replacement of an order in which the bourgeois was a humble subject by another that was more congenial to his rationalist mind and to his immediate interests. But, surveying that process from the standpoint of today, the observer might well wonder whether in the end such complete emancipation was good for the bourgeois and his world. For those fetters not only hampered, they also sheltered. Before proceeding further we must carefully clarify and appraise this point.

2. The related processes of the rise of the capitalist bourgeoisie and of the rise of national states produced, in the sixteenth, seventeenth and eighteenth centuries, a social structure that may seem to us amphibial though it was no more amphibial or transitional than any other. Consider the outstanding instance that is afforded by the monarchy of Louis XIV. The royal power had subjugated the landed aristocracy and at the same time conciliated it by proffering employment and pensions and by conditionally accepting its claim to a ruling or leading class position. The same royal power had subjugated and allied itself with the clergy.[1] It had finally strengthened its sway over the bourgeoisie, its old ally in the struggle with the territorial magnates, protecting and propelling its enterprise in order to exploit it the more effectively in turn. Peasants and the (small) industrial proletariat were likewise managed, exploited and protected by public authority—though the protection was in the case of the French *ancien régime* very much less in evidence than for instance in the Austria of Maria Theresa or of Joseph II—and, vicariously, by landlords or industrialists. This was not simply a government in the sense of nineteenth-century liberalism, i.e., a social agency existing for the performance of a few limited functions to be financed by a minimum of revenue. On principle, the monarchy managed everything, from consciences to the patterns of the silk fabrics of Lyons, and financially it aimed at a maximum of revenue. Though the king was never really absolute, public authority was all-comprehensive.

Correct diagnosis of this pattern is of the utmost importance for our subject. The king, the court, the army, the church and the bureaucracy lived to an increasing extent on revenue created by the capitalist process, even purely feudal sources of income being swelled in consequence of contemporaneous capitalist developments. To an increasing extent also, domestic and foreign policies and institutional changes were shaped to suit and propel that development. *As far as that goes*, the feudal elements in the structure of the so-called absolute monarchy come in only under the heading of atavisms which in fact is the diagnosis one would naturally adopt at first sight.

Looking more closely, however, we realize that those elements meant more than that. The steel frame of that structure still consisted of the human material of feudal society and this material still behaved according to precapitalist patterns. It filled the offices of state, officered the army, devised policies—it functioned as a *classe dirigente* and, though taking account of bourgeois interests, it took care to distance itself from the bourgeoisie. The centerpiece, the king, was king by the grace of God, and the root of his position was feudal, not only in the historical but also in the sociological sense, however much he availed himself of the economic possibilities offered by capitalism. All this was more than atavism. It was an active symbiosis of two social strata, one of which no doubt supported the other economically but was in turn supported by the other politically. Whatever we may think of the achievements or shortcomings of this arrangement, whatever the bourgeois himself may have thought of it at the time or later— and of the aristocratic scapegrace or idler—it was of the essence of that society.

3. Of *that* society only? The subsequent course of things, best exemplified by the English case, suggests the answer. The aristocratic element continued to rule the roost *right to the end of the period of intact and vital capitalism*. No doubt that element—though nowhere so effectively as in England—currently absorbed the brains from other strata that drifted into politics: it made itself the representative of bourgeois interests and fought the battles of

---

[1] Gallicanism was nothing else but the ideological reflex of this.

the bourgeoisie; it had to surrender its last legal privileges; but with these qualifications, and for ends no longer its own, it continued to man the political engine, to manage the state, to govern.

The economically operative part of the bourgeois strata did not offer much opposition to this. On the whole, that kind of division of labor suited them and they liked it. Where they did revolt against it or where they got into the political saddle without having to revolt, they did not make a conspicuous success of ruling and did not prove able to hold their own. The question arises whether it is really safe to assume that these failures were merely due to lack of opportunity to acquire experience and, with experience, the attitudes of a politically ruling class.

It is not. There is a more fundamental reason for those failures such as are instanced by the French or German experiences with bourgeois attempts at ruling—a reason which again will best be visualized by contrasting the figure of the industrialist or merchant with that of the medieval lord. The latter's "profession" not only qualified him admirably for the defense of his own class interest—he was not only able to fight for it physically—but it also cast a halo around him and made of him a ruler of men. The first was important, but more so were the mystic glamour and the lordly attitude—that ability and habit to command and to be obeyed that carried prestige with all classes of society and in every walk of life. That prestige was so great and that attitude so useful that the class position outlived the social and technological conditions which had given rise to it and proved adaptable, by means of a transformation of the class function, to quite different social and economic conditions. With the utmost case and grace the lords and knights metamorphosed themselves into courtiers, administrators, diplomats, politicians and into military officers of a type that had nothing whatever to do with that of the medieval knight. And—most astonishing phenomenon when we come to think of it—a remnant of that old prestige survives even to this day, and not only with our ladies.

Of the industrialist and merchant the opposite is true. There is surely no trace of any mystic glamour about him which is what

counts in the ruling of men. The stock exchange is a poor substitute for the Holy Grail. We have seen that the industrialist and merchant, as far as they are entrepreneurs, also fill a function of leadership. But economic leadership of this type does not readily expand, like the medieval lord's military leadership, into the leadership of nations. On the contrary, the ledger and the cost calculation absorb and confine.

I have called the bourgeois rationalist and unheroic. He can only use rationalist and unheroic means to defend his position or to bend a nation to his will. He can impress by what people may expect from his economic performance, he can argue his case, he can promise to pay out money or threaten to withhold it, he can hire the treacherous services of a *condottiere* or politician or journalist. But that is all and all of it is greatly overrated as to its political value. Nor are his experiences and habits of life of the kind that develop personal fascination. A genius in the business office may be, and often is, utterly unable outside of it to say boo to a goose—both in the drawing room and on the platform. Knowing this he wants to be left alone and to leave politics alone.

Again exceptions will occur to the reader. But again they do not amount to much. Aptitude for, and interest and success in, city management is the only important exception in Europe, and this will be found to strengthen our case instead of weakening it. Before the advent of the modern metropolis, which is no longer a bourgeois affair, city management was akin to business management. Grasp of its problems and authority within its precincts came naturally to the manufacturer and trader, and the local interests of manufacturing and trading supplied most of the subject matter of its politics which therefore lent itself to treatment by the methods and in the spirit of the business office. Under exceptionally favorable conditions, exceptional developments sprouted from those roots, such as the developments of the Venetian or Genoese republics. The case of the Low Countries enters into the same pattern, but it is particularly instructive by virtue of the fact that the merchants' republic invariably failed in the great game of international politics and that in practically every emergency it had to hand over the reins to a warlord of feudal complexion. As regards the United States, it would be easy to list the uniquely favorable circumstances—rapidly waning—that explain its case.

4. The inference is obvious: barring such exceptional conditions, the bourgeois class is ill equipped to face the problems, both domestic and international, that have normally to be faced by a country of any importance. The bourgeois themselves feel this in spite of all the phraseology that seems to deny it, and so do the masses. Within a protecting framework not made of bourgeois material, the bourgeoisie may be successful, not only in the political defensive but also in the offensive, especially as an opposition. For a time it felt so safe as to be able to afford the luxury of attacking the protective frame itself; such bourgeois opposition as there was in imperial Germany illustrates this to perfection. But without protection by some non-bourgeois group, the bourgeoisie is politically helpless and unable not only to lead its nation but even to take care of its particular class interest. Which amounts to saying that it needs a master.

But the capitalist process, both by its economic mechanics and by its psycho-sociological effects, did away with this protecting master or, as in this country, never gave him, or a substitute for him, a chance to develop. The implications of this are strengthened by another consequence of the same process. Capitalist evolution eliminates not only the king *Dei Gratia* but also the political entrenchments that, had they proved tenable, would have been formed by the village and the craft guild. Of course, neither organization was tenable in the precise shape in which capitalism found it. But capitalist policies wrought destruction much beyond what was unavoidable. They attacked the artisan in reservations in which he could have survived for an indefinite time. They forced upon the peasant all the blessings of early liberalism—the free and unsheltered holding and all the individualist rope he needed in order to hang himself.

In breaking down the pre-capitalist framework of society, capitalism thus broke not only barriers that impeded its progress but also flying buttresses that prevented its collapse. That process, impressive in its relentless necessity, was not merely a matter of removing institutional deadwood, but of removing partners of the capitalist stratum, symbiosis with whom was an essential element of the capitalist schema. Having discovered this fact which so many slogans obscure, we might well wonder whether it is quite correct to look upon capitalism as a social form *sui generis* or, in fact, as anything else but the last stage of the decomposition of what we have called feudalism. On the whole, I am inclined to believe that its peculiarities suffice to make a type and to accept that symbiosis of classes which owe their existence to different epochs and processes as the rule rather than as an exception—at least it has been the rule these 6000 years, i.e., ever since primitive tillers of the soil became the subjects of mounted nomads. But there is no great objection that I can see against the opposite view alluded to.

Joseph A. Schumpeter. *Capitalism, Socialism, and Democracy,* 3rd edition. New York: Harper and Row, 1950.

The Port Huron Statement: Values

Students for a Democratic Society

THE STUDENTS FOR A DEMOCRATIC SOCIETY *appeared in the USA in the latter 1960s. It encouraged young Americans to study and participate in the struggle for social change. On various campuses throughout America, the SDS organized effective political opposition to the war in Vietnam.*

Making values explicit—an initial task in establishing alternatives—is an activity that has been devalued and corrupted. The conventional moral terms of the age, the politician moralities—"free world," "people's democracies"—reflect realities poorly, if at all, and seem to function more as ruling myths than as descriptive principles. But neither has our experience in the universities brought us moral enlightenment. Our professors and administrators sacrifice controversy to public relations; their curriculums change more slowly than the living events of the world; their skills and silence are purchased by investors in the arms race; passion is called unscholastic. The questions we might want raised—what is really important? can we live in a different and better way? if we wanted to change society, how would we do it?—are not thought to be questions of a "fruitful, empirical nature," and thus are brushed aside.

Unlike youth in other countries we are used to moral leadership being exercised and moral dimensions being clarified by our elders. But today, for us, not even the liberal and socialist preachments of the past seem adequate to the forms of the present. Consider the old slogans: Capitalism Cannot Reform Itself, United Front Against Fascism, General Strike, All Out on May Day. Or, more recently, No Cooperation with Commies and Fellow Travellers, Ideolo-gies are Exhausted, Bipartisanship, No Utopias. These are incomplete, and there are few new prophets. It has been said that our liberal and socialist predecessors were plagued by vision without program, while our own generation is plagued by program without vision. All around us there is astute grasp of method, technique—the committee, the ad hoc group, the lobbyist, the hard and soft sell, the make, the projected image—but, if pressed critically, such expertise is incompetent to explain its implicit ideals. It is highly fashionable to identify oneself by old categories, or by naming a respected political figure, or by explaining "how we would vote" on various issues.

Theoretic chaos has replaced the idealistic thinking of old—and, unable to reconstitute theoretic order, men have condemned idealism itself. Doubt has replaced hopefulness—and men act out a defeatism that is labelled realistic. The decline of utopia and hope is in fact one of the defining features of social life today. The reasons are various: the dreams of the older left were perverted by Stalinism and never recreated; the congressional stalemate makes men narrow their view of the possible; the specialization of human activity leaves little room for sweeping thought; the horrors of the twentieth century, symbolized in the gas-ovens and concentration camps and atom bombs, have blasted hopefulness. To be idealistic is to be considered apocalyptic, deluded. To have no serious aspirations, on the contrary, is to be "toughminded."

In suggesting social goals and values, therefore, we are aware of entering a sphere of some disrepute. Perhaps matured by the past, we have no sure formulas, no closed theories—but that does not mean values are beyond discussion and tentative determination. A first task of any social movement is to convince people that the search for orienting theories and the creation of human values is complex but worthwhile. We are aware that to avoid platitudes we must analyze the concrete conditions of social order. But to direct such an analysis we must use the guideposts of basic principles. Our own social values involve conceptions of human beings, human relationships, and social systems.

We regard *men* as infinitely precious and possessed of unfulfilled capacities for reason, freedom, and love. In affirming these principles we are aware of countering perhaps the dominant conceptions of man in the twentieth century, that he is a thing to be manipulated, and that he is inherently incapable of directing his own affairs. We oppose the depersonalization that reduces human beings to the status of things—if anything, the brutalities of the twentieth century teach that means and ends are intimately related, that vague appeals to "posterity" cannot justify the mutilations of the present. We oppose, too, the doctrine of human incompetence because it rests essentially on the modern fact that men have been "competently" manipulated into incompetence—we see little reason why men cannot meet with increasing skill the complexities and responsibilities of their situation, if society is organized not for minority, but for majority, participation in decision-making.

Men have unrealized potential for self-cultivation, self-direction, self-understanding, and creativity. It is this potential that we regard as crucial and to which we appeal, not to the human potentiality for violence, unreason, and submission to authority. The goal of man and society should be human independence: a concern not with image of popularity but with finding a meaning in life that is personally authentic; a quality of mind not compulsively driven by a sense of powerlessness, nor one which unthinkingly adopts status values, nor one which represses all threats to its habits, but one which has full, spontaneous access to present and past experiences, one which easily unites the fragmented parts of personal history, one which openly faces problems which are troubling and unresolved; one with an intuitive awareness of possibilities, an active sense of curiosity, an ability and willingness to learn.

This kind of independence does not mean egotistic individualism—the object is not to have one's way so much as it is to have a way that is one's own. Nor do we defy man—we merely have faith in his potential.

Human relationships should involve fraternity and honesty. Human interdependence is contemporary fact; human brotherhood must be willed, however, as a condition of future survival and as the most appropriate form of social relations. Personal links between man and man are needed, especially to go beyond the partial and fragmentary bonds of function that bind men only as worker to worker, employer to employee, teacher to student, American to Russian.

Loneliness, estrangement, isolation describe the vast distance between man and man today. These dominant tendencies cannot be overcome by better personnel management, nor by improved gadgets, but only when a love of man overcomes the idolatrous worship of things by man. As the individualism we affirm is not egoism, the selflessness we affirm is not self-elimination. On the contrary, we believe in generosity of a kind that imprints one's unique individual qualities in the relation to other men, and to all human activity. Further, to dislike isolation is not to favor the abolition of privacy; the latter differs from isolation in that [it] occurs or is abolished according to individual will.

We would replace power rooted in possession, privileged, or circumstance by power and uniqueness rooted in love, reflectiveness, reason and creativity. As a *social system* we seek the establishment of a democracy of individual participation, governed by two central aims: that the individual share in those social decisions determining the quality and direction of his life; that society be organized to encourage independence in men and provide the media for their common participation.

In a participatory democracy, the political life would be based in several root principles:

- that decision-making of basic social consequence be carried on by public groupings;
- that politics be seen positively, as the art of collectively creating an acceptable pattern of social relations;
- that politics has the function of bringing

people out of isolation and into community, thus being a necessary, though not sufficient, means of finding meaning in personal life;

- that the political order should serve to clarify problems in a way instrumental to their solution; it should provide outlets for the expression of personal grievance and aspiration; opposing views should be organized so as to illuminate choices and facilitate the attainment of goals; channels should be commonly available to relate men to knowledge and to power so that private problems—from bad recreation facilities to personal alienation—are formulated as general issues.

The economic sphere would have as its basis the principles:

- that work should involve incentives worthier than money or survival. It should be educative, not stultifying; creative, not mechanical; self-directed, not manipulated, encouraging independence, a respect for others, a sense of dignity and a willingness to accept social responsibility, since it is this experience that has crucial influence on habits, perceptions and individual ethics;
- that the economic experience is so personally decisive that the individual must share in its full determination;
- that the economy itself is of such social importance that its major resources and means of production should be open to democratic participation and subject to democratic social regulation.

Like the political and economic ones, major social institutions—cultural, educational, rehabilitative, and others—should be generally organized with the well-being an dignity of man as the essential measure of success.

In social change or interchange, we find violence to be abhorrent because it requires generally the transformation of the target, be it a human being or a community of people, into a depersonalized object of hate. It is imperative that the means of violence be abolished and the institutions—local, national, international—that encourage non-violence as a condition of conflict be developed.

These are our central values, in skeletal form. It remains vital to understand their denial or attainment in the context of the modern world.

The Port Huron Statement. Chicago: Students for a Democratic Society, 1962.

Socialism—Why?

Alec Nove

ALEC NOVE *is Emeritus Professor of Economics at the University of Glasgow.* Stalinism and After, Political Economy and Soviet Socialism, *and* The Economics of Feasible Socialism *are some of his books.*

This book is about "feasible socialism." Its author must therefore declare his interest. Why write about this theme? Is the author intending to mount an attack on socialism in the name of efficient allocation of resources, Pareto optimality and the virtues of free enterprise? And what "socialism" does he have in mind?

Let us leave this last and very important question aside for the present: one reason for writing this book is precisely to help to arrive at a definition of a socialism that is feasible, that could work with reasonable effectiveness (since a socialism that does not function can be of little help to anyone). Let me put a few cards on the table, by explaining my motives and my starting point. In doing so I shall make some very sweeping generalisations. The reader will, I trust, forgive me if I do not write a long essay defending each general statement and modifying it to fit the many exceptions and modifications that it doubtless needs.

First, it appears to me that the basic assumptions of liberal capitalism are ceasing to be true. At one time it really was the case that the pursuit of personal and sectional interest, on balance, was the way to obtain the best available approximation to the general interest. Of course, there were many exceptions—there always are—but the rationality of a free market economy tended to prevail, and appeared superior to any possible alternative arrangement of our society. To Hayek or Friedman it seems still to be the case today. However, several factors are now working against the efficacy, or even the survival, of the liberal-capitalist model. Many of these have to do with the consequences of *scale* and of *specialisation.* The polarisation of society into a small group of super-monopoly-capitalists and impoverished proletarians foreseen by Marx has not come to pass, and there are indeed a multitude of small businesses, while large packets of shares in big business are held by pension funds and insurance companies, representing aggregations of predominantly small savings. But, when all allowance is made for this, the fact remains that enormous business corporations and conglomerates dominate a whole series of vital industries, and many of the small businesses are highly dependent upon being subcontractors to the giants. Some interesting theories about the motivations of managers of large corporations have developed in the last few decades, which put into question some axioms such as profit "maximisation," but this aspect we will leave aside. The important points in the present context are:

(a) monopoly power and its social-economic consequences,

(b) vulnerability,

(c) alienation.

Monopoly is, of course, almost always relative. There will usually be close substitutes, or some species of monopsony or monopolistic competition. It is not my purpose to enter into controversy on the relative efficiency of the large corporation, its contribution to innovation, and so on. Its decisions affect many thousands of people and could cause grave distress to whole conurbations which rely on it for employment. Its sheer size and the remoteness of its headquarters—in another country in the case of multinationals—complicate labour relations, and can lead to damaging disputes. The greater the degree of monopoly power, the more it is possible to increase profits at the expense of the customer or of quality or of choice, for the less is the importance of the customer's goodwill (a point too easily overlooked by those who try to devise criteria for nationalised monopolies in Britain, for instance). The small number of giants and the power they wield has led to a reconsideration of an economic theory based upon an infinite number of competing units, a theory of the "firm" which, at its worst (in the words of Shubik), sees no difference between General Motors and a corner ice-cream shop. There has been recourse to games theory, and much research on business behaviour and on how prices are actually determined or "administered." Joan Robinson's and Chamberlin's insights about imperfect competition have been deepened. Side by side with mathematically elegant and abstract general-equilibrium models, we have seen growing concern with the consequences of increasing returns, and their converse, increasing unit costs when production declines, leading to higher (cost-based) prices at a time of falling demand. Monopoly power also has its political aspects: both government control over monopolies, and the power of large corporations over government.

There is also the monopoly power of trade unions, which has increased *pari passu* with the vulnerability of the economy to attack from sectional interest groups. We all know that a quite small group of key workers in one component factory can cause enormous damage to industry. Specialisation by plant and by trade has added greatly to this power. Rightwing analysts stress, understandably, the harm trade unions can do to productivity, competitiveness and, ultimately, to the living standards of the union members themselves. In so far as this is indeed so, it is another illustration of the thesis advanced above: that the pursuit of sectional interest has ceased to be compatible with the general interest, including in some cases that of the group pursuing the sectional interest. Lest the words "general interest" upset the orthodox left ("What about the class struggle?"), let me at once explain that the above statement remains valid even if confined to the working class as a whole. Surely it cannot be seriously disputed that repeated work stoppages, plus a variety of restrictive practices, must adversely affect

productivity, and it is a naive socialist indeed who fails to note that there is some connection between productivity and the level of real wages. Yes, I am aware that productivity is affected also by the quality of management and the level (and nature) of investments. Perhaps it can also be recognised that industrial relations are not a zero-sum game, that when (as in West Germany and Japan) there is industrial peace and efficient management, both managers and workers reap the benefit. All this is not an argument for "reformism," just a simple statement of fact. Industrial strife could be the deliberate aim of those who wish to "bash the unions," and certainly is the deliberate aim of revolutionary groups who desire to destabilise and overthrow existing society. However, the essential feature of the situation does not relate to plots of ultra-right or ultra-left: groups pressing their demands, their "just claims," may be of no political colouring, and the disruption of the economy is usually the consequence of what is believed to be self-interest, justified by the fact that the basic ideology of society is the pursuit of self-interest ("Look after Number One," "I'm all right, Jack," and other modern proverbs).

There is taking place in many Western countries a breakdown in traditional deference, in the willingness to obey the boss because he is the boss, which is due to more than simply a greater sense of security. Income inequalities formerly taken for granted come to be resented—and this can happen in a stratified communist-ruled country such as Poland, as well as in, say, Italy or Sweden. Some forms of inequality or privilege are indeed irrational, or can easily and reasonably seem so.

I find it hard to accept that merely allowing others to use my money, or my land, is a "productive" activity, on a par with actually working—though naturally management is work, too, and of course it should be efficient. Why should vast riches go to those who have had the luck to own some oil-bearing land, or to have forebears who were given land in exchange for services rendered (sometimes in bed) to some long-dead monarch? This has nothing whatever to do with any contribution to production or welfare in any sense, and makes it seem more than a little silly to urge "wage restraint" at a time when the very rich do not need to work at all. Industrial leadership, company directorships, too often go to those with the right birth, connections and shareholdings, and they may or may not be the most efficient at their job. In Britain at least the breakdown in deference is accompanied, in some cases deservedly, by lack of respect for the competence of senior management. This is combined with a sense of alienation: large-scale units are run by virtually unknown bosses; the outcome of the work, and its organisation, is none of the business of the workforce. Their lack of interest and commitment can affect not only their job-satisfaction but also efficiency and productivity. Conversely, pride in work, a sense of achievement and identity, has a positive economic effect, too often ignored in textbooks on microeconomics. One has only to study a country in which, for reasons not easily understood by Europeans, this effect seems to have been achieved: Japan.

All this is connected also with inflation. Powerful groups in society ask for more. This leads to *excess demands*. Purely monetarist "explanations" of inflation seem remarkably superficial. There have always, of course, been people who have wanted more—more wages, more social benefits, more defence spending, or whatever. History provides numerous examples of debasing coinage, printing too much money, and so on. But it is surely significant that worldwide inflation, affecting countries under very different political parties and regimes, or widely differing levels of development, should have become so universal, so difficult to combat. Needless to say, these pressures and demands do lead to an increase in the money supply (so Friedman is not "wrong," but the real causes remain unanalysed by him).

Inflation has effects on economic behaviour which move it far from the paths of rationality. Ota Sik has argued that society's investments should not be an incidental consequence of the struggle to divide up the national income. It is one of the less satisfactory features of the neo-Ricardian or "Sraffa" models that, even though they assume that investment is wholly financed from profits, real wages are seen as the result of the class struggle: what labour does not get the capitalists do, and vice versa.

This is a sophisticated version of the zero-sum-game approach, and seems to me remarkably undynamic: even in the medium run, real wages can scarcely rise significantly without investments! Imagine a situation in which, by powerful class struggle, the workers reduce net profits to zero. There is then in the model no net investment, therefore no growth, because investment is assumed to be financed out of profits, directly or indirectly; increased production of consumers' goods could scarcely occur under these circumstances. But individuals or groups, understandably, see only their own individual or group interests. Nor is it a matter of stupidity or blinkered vision. It is impossible to demonstrate that any one segment of a complex society which demands more for its own consumption is thereby hindering the process of growth which could be financed by others. (Thus members of the Association of University Teachers quite reasonably ask for higher salaries, and would vote for lower taxes too, although their salaries are paid out of taxes, since there could always be less spent on something else, and their salaries represent a tiny percentage of the state budget.) So, although demanding more for current consumption, people may in fact be acting against their own best interests, but, from where they are situated, this *cannot* be seen. In a world in which each freely takes what he or she can, it is in the interest of any individual or group to pursue its own narrowly defined advantage, because others are doing so. (Perhaps instead of the "prisoner's dilemma" we should speak of a free man's dilemma!)

But at the same time those who invest seek, understandably enough, a hedge against inflation, shelter from the prevailing uncertainty. This leads to a concentration on the short term, reflected in and reflecting the high rate of interest. It is quite logical, as in the case of the railway union pension fund, to "invest" in old masters and to keep the paintings in a secret vault. It may pay the individual to keep money in Zurich. So, apart from the question of how much *should* be invested, the choices between investment alternatives are twisted out of shape, with a short time-horizon plus security as dominant aims. Of course, an element of risk-taking, the need to cope with uncertainty and imperfect information, always existed, and mistakes were made, gambles taken. But the decision-maker today is presented with a remarkably unclear and confused set of signals. It is hard enough to guess what the costs of materials, labour, the rate of interest, will be in six months' time, let alone six years' time (and it takes that long to build any large factory). At least all this sets up the presumption that rational investment decisions would represent a remarkable coincidence, rather than being the normal outcome of the institutional and economic circumstances.

Another aspect of "rational" investments relates to their effects on employment. In the more developed countries there is increasing danger that labour-saving innovations will be introduced at a rate far exceeding the possibility of providing alternative jobs, with serious chronic unemployment as the consequence—and this apart from and in addition to unemployment that arises out of cyclical trends or deflationary policies. There is likely to exist a contradiction between the profitability of labour-saving at microeconomic levels and the macro and/or social consequences. There might have to be organised work-sharing, with much shorter hours, but neither the employers nor the trade unions seem able to focus on the problems of implementing such a strategy. Matters are exacerbated by the possibility—or perhaps even the likelihood—of material shortages which obstruct growth in output. To mention this does not imply the acceptance of a full gloom-and-doom scenario à la Club of Rome. But the energy crisis appears to be long-lasting, the troubles and disruptions among Third World producers of materials and fuels are all too likely to persist, and we can face various unpredictable bottlenecks. Some products, say, cocoa and iron ore, could be in ample supply, but demand for them would be constrained by production difficulties and recession occasioned by shortage of, say, oil and non-ferrous metals. Conventional economic analysis and the normal market mechanism are not well attuned to handling physical shortage. This is no doubt one reason why central controls are usually imposed in wartime. Or take another example: fish in the North Sea. Shortage causes higher

prices, which stimulates further efforts to catch fish, which makes the shortage worse, and so on, until there are no fish. A higher profit is supposed to act as a stimulus to higher output, on the implied assumption that this does not run into physical limits which make higher output impossible. This is why, in the case of fish, government regulation is necessary. Such instances could become more common in the future, as issues of environmental protection have become already. (NB: I appreciate that in, for example, the USSR, scarce resources have been wastefully exploited, and the rivers and atmosphere polluted. The point is that this mode of behaviour can be quite consistent with private profit-making, whereas at least the *model* of a socialist planning system implies that such things should not happen. Why they *do* happen will be analysed later in this book).

In general, socialists should be stressing the importance of *externalities*, these being circumstances in which effects external to the given transaction are sufficiently important to be taken into consideration. In a sense, every action has *some* external effects, but they are mostly insignificant, and the cost of taking them into account would be totally prohibitive. However, instances exist, and are recognised by all schools and ideologies, in which externalities matter: diseconomies, such as pollution, ugliness, congestion, noise, the killing of bees by insecticides, and so on; economies, such as the advantage obtained by third parties, or society in general, from efficient urban transportation, reliable postal services, or the planting of attractive flowers in a neighbour's garden. In our modern world the number of instances in which externalities matter seems to be increasing. So, therefore, does the number of occasions in which private or sectional interest can conflict with a more general interest.

Reverting to the earlier example of employment and unemployment, one sees this particularly vividly in the so-called Third World. The reasons are sometimes obscured by rhetoric. Thus the fact that, in many Third World countries, industrial investment is labour-saving when labour is overabundant is blamed on multinational corporations. This question I discussed in an article many years ago, under the heading of "The explosive model."[1] The problem is not in fact due to the machinations of multinationals, imperialists, or foreign investors. For a number of reasons which this is not the place to examine, modern labour-saving technology is in fact profitable to use even where wages of unskilled labour are low. Thus a bulldozer saves so much labour that it would be cheaper to use it even if the labourers it replaced were paid at bare subsistence rates. Domestic capitalists also find that it pays to substitute capital for labour, not only in industry but also in agriculture. The "explosive" nature of this model arises from the fact that, with high population growth, this leads to a growth of underemployed or unemployed *marginados*, a source of social disorder and human misery.

This is but one of the issues that arise in developing countries which incline many of them to opt for what they believe to be a "socialist" road. That for many this turns into a disastrous blind alley is not in dispute, at least not by me. What does seem clear is that there are powerful reasons why the capitalist road is rejected. Some relate to traditional attitudes of a pre-capitalist kind. These were strong in pre-revolutionary Russia. Among aristocrats, intellectuals (whether conservative, like Dostoevsky, or radical-revolutionary, such as Lenin or Gorky) and peasants, there was a kind of gut reaction against the mercantile spirit of Western capitalism. Thus the peasants had to have the notion of private property in land forced upon them by the Stolypin reforms of 1906–11, and promptly undid the bulk of these reforms in the chaos of revolution, reverting spontaneously to quasi-medieval forms of communal tenure. These attitudes were among the causes which shaped the Russian revolution. More recently we have seen in Iran the militantly conservative-traditionalist rejection of Western-style capitalist development. One sees, in varying degrees, the social-political unacceptability of rapid transformation of societies in the name of private profit, where highly imperfect markets and uneven development enable some individuals to grow very rich indeed while the very poor remain very poor.

Again, this is a huge subject, with (I know) much to be said on both sides. All I wish to do at this point is to note that there exists an ideology of developmental socialism, often confused and naive, but anti-capitalist. Maybe, as Lord Harris would doubtless argue, development would be speeded if these countries all adopted the policies which produced good results in South Korea (though the latest reports on political repression there are not exactly encouraging). But it may be no more meaningful to advise Algeria to adopt the South Korean economic model than to instruct Great Britain to introduce Japanese-style labour relations. In all societies there must be a minimum of consensus, of acceptance of the political and economic basis of society. Without it there could be chaos, or organised repression, whether of the Stalin or the right-wing militarist variety. Economic development involving rapid structural change not only provides huge opportunities for (often undeserved) private profit, but also stimulates strong opposition.

It is sometimes said that private ownership of the means of production is a necessary condition for political democracy. Maybe. But it most certainly is not a sufficient condition. The experience of many (most?) developing countries suggests a reverse correlation: the capitalist development road requires the maintenance of order by a powerful repressive apparatus, a military or one-party regime. Or one could look at the question another way. Rapid, destabilising structural change hurts many people, upsets traditional modes of life, often involves sacrifice. This must be in the name of something, a principle, an ideology. It is surely no accident that this ideology is so frequently socialist in its language, though nationalism is also a potent force. So we will have to pay some attention to the logic (and dangers too) of "developmental socialism."

There is a point of more general application. Contrary to the belief of many economists, "no social system can work which is based exclusively upon a network of free con-

---

[1] A. Nove, *Review of Development Studies*, October 1966.

tracts between (legally) equal contracting parties, and in which everyone is supposed to be guided by nothing except his own short-run utilitarian interest." The quotation is from Schumpeter; [1] it can be reinforced by a similar one from Joan Robinson, and I have already cited Pareto in a similar vein. Societies concerned *only* with profit will fall to pieces. Corruption, in the literal and the figurative sense, can flourish where the making of money becomes the primary aspiration, the dominant criterion of success.

As will become clear in the course of this book, I am aware that human acquisitiveness is a force which cannot be ignored, which indeed must be harnessed in the search for efficiency. But it hardly requires to be stimulated, by advertising and militant commercialisation. There is something genuinely repulsive in the amount of money to be made by pandering to the lowest common denominator, in the mass communication industry, with some of the highest incomes going to presenters of shows, or disc-jockeys. The very concept of "show business" can hardly fail to offend anyone seriously concerned about culture. Concern for quality of life frequently collides with the profit motive. Galbraith's "public squalor" is a consequence of the concentration of attention on commercially meaningful activities, on private wealth. In my own city of Glasgow an excellent parks department has built a splendid walkway along a river, and maintains fine botanic gardens, available to the public free. It is not obvious that expenditure for such purposes generates less human satisfaction than private spending on girlie magazines, or on advertising detergents and deodorants.

"Socialism" is thought of as an alternative to a society still based largely on private ownership and private profit. Generations of reformers and revolutionaries envisaged a world in which there would be no great inequalities of income and wealth, where common ownership would prevail, where economic (and political) power would be more evenly distributed, where ordinary people would have greater control over their lives and over the conditions of their work, in which deliberate planning for the common good of society would replace (at least in part) the elemental forces of the marketplace. In the preceding pages I have tried to put forward a *prima facie* case for taking all this seriously, without using familiar (and question-begging) phrases about the contradictions of capitalism, its final crisis, exploitation, misery, and so on. As I stressed at the beginning, I know that there are counter-arguments. The system that now exists in the West differs greatly from the *laissez-faire* capitalism analysed by Marx. The Soviet system generates many of the same deficiencies and distortions, and some specific to itself, for reasons that will be discussed later. Some, at least, of the negative aspects of contemporary society may relate more to large-scale industrialism than to private ownership as such. There is much that is vague, confused, impractical, in socialist economic ideas, whether or not derived from Marx, and it will be the principal task of this book to discuss and analyse these ideas in a critical spirit. Indeed, the very definition of "socialism" raises serious difficulties. One must recognise that it is a great deal easier to point to blemishes in existing societies than to find effective remedies, to devise an alternative model that actually works. Authors of pedestrian textbooks can confine their analysis to a "world" of perfect competition, perfect markets and perfect knowledge, in which the initial axioms and definitions eliminate all the problems of real life. Socialists, understandably, have little patience with such models. They, in their turn, cannot substitute for them an equally unreal model of their own, in which all-knowing "democratic" planners provide all that is needed for the good of society, and in which the (predictable) difficulties which these planners will face are assumed not to exist. To use Peter Wiles's phrase, perfect competition and perfect computation are alike in being perfect (and equal in their unreality). Marx has provided a powerful critique of capitalist society. But did he indicate a feasible alternative? It is to this question that the first part of this book will be devoted.

The preceding pages were already written

---

[1] Quoted in W. Brus, *Journal of Comparative Economics*, vol. 4, 1980, p. 53.

when I came across some relevant thoughts on a related theme by Charles Taylor. He wrote: "Societies destroy themselves when they violate the conditions of legitimacy which they themselves tend to posit and inculcate." While denying the validity of "vulgar-Marxism," he points to

> features of industrial society—the meaninglessness and subordination of work; the mindless lack of control over priorities, above all the fetishisation of commodities...(in a non-Marxist sense, endowed magically with the properties of life they subserve)... We see ourselves as playthings of mindless impersonal forces, or worse as victims of a fascination for mere things... There is a crisis of allegiance in our society.

He does not fail to stress "the scramble for income and advantage in which powerful forces competed and maintained their position at the expense of the unorganised through inflation," and he sees "inflation as the visible signs of our disarray." (Compare these observations with the superficial monetarist platitudes!)

"It is a society," Taylor writes, "which is sapping the bases of its own legitimacy." But it does not follow that capitalism is about to destroy itself. He ends his argument by asking: "Is this a self-destruction of *capitalism*? Is it only the capitalist form of society which drives it towards the kind of hypertrophy which provokes a legitimation crisis?" This is a very important point. Is it large-scale industrial society as such that is at the heart of our perplexities and discontents? Are there perhaps other causes too? Should we not be seeking answers to such questions? Taylor's article ends with the words: "Only then will socialist thought be in a position to effect the theoretical renewal it so desperately needs."[1]

Alec Nove. *The Economics of Feasible Socialism*. London: George Allen & Unwin, 1983.

---

[1] Charles Taylor, "Growth, legitimacy and the modern identity," *Praxis International*, July 1981, pp. 111–25.

Part VIII

Fascism

ADOLF HITLER

Some of the following excerpts, notably those of Hitler and Mussolini, present fascism with unavoidable bluntness. If one is seeking forthrightness, one finds it in these tracts. The essays of Chamberlain and Pearson present raw data which are nicely integrated into the historical overview of Hayes. Finally, Brooker's analytical work offers a keen analysis of one principle used in one version of fascism.

On 24 February 1920, Adolf Hitler delivered a speech in Munich in which he introduced his *Twenty-Five Points of the German Workers' Party*. These points were more than intimations of the political line to be pursued by Hitler and his followers in the years to come, for they spoke openly and approvingly of anti-semitism, of the denunciation of the Treaties of Versailles and Saint-Germain, of the *lebensraum* doctrine, and of censorship of the press. Even if it was not a philosophical statement but a rallying cry that could and would be heard by the masses, the *Twenty-Five Points* captured the spirit of the German version of fascism more than any other document.

In contrast to Hitler's Twenty-Five Points stood Mussolini's *The Political and Social Doctrine of Fascism*, which must be seen as a quasi-philosophical statement. Running through Mussolini's comments are, unquestionably, trace elements of the philosophy of Hegel and Nietzsche. In this tract, Mussolini pillages pacifism, Marxism, materialism, individualism, liberalism, and democratic ideology; and he venerates the state, action, discipline, and spirituality.

The essays by Houston Chamberlain and Karl Pearson share common fascist-oriented motifs, in particular the motif of Social Darwinism with its emphasis upon the superiority and inferiority of races. It is not surprising that this theme was drawn into the vortex of fascism in Italy and National Socialism in Germany, and helped give form to the image of human nature which those two political perspectives advocated and defended.

Leaning upon the writings of Chamberlain and Pearson, Paul Hayes gives an effective historical overview of the intellectual forces at work in shaping fascism and National Socialism. Here he highlights the writings of Fichte, Count Gobineau, and Kidd, as well as those of Chamberlain and Pearson, to show how they helped conjoin Social Darwinism with some version of imperialism, not only in Germany but also England.

In the final essay, Paul Brooker gives an original and incisive account of the *Führerprinzip*, the leader principle, in National Socialism. He makes no attempt to analyze this principle in any context other than the German one, but his investigation casts much light upon his subject and is a useful starting point for anyone interested in exploring the principle in the Italian context. Brooker persuasively argues that the leader principle sought, in his words, "a massive quantitative expansion of leadership roles in society" and as such clashed quite directly with the administrative principle of bureaucratic authority suggested by Max Weber. Brooker points out that, notwithstanding its success elsewhere, Hitler's *Führerprinzip* encountered difficulties in the civil service, in big business, and in the churches.

The Twenty-Five Points

Adolf Hitler

ADOLF HITLER (1889–1945) was the leader of Germany during the Third Reich (1933–1945). He was a skillful orator. Mein Kampf *was written by him while in prison for his attempting to overthrow the Government of Germany in 1923.*

The Twenty-Five Points of the German Workers' Party, 1920[1]

The program of the German Workers' Party is limited as to period. The leaders have no intention, once the aims announced in it have been achieved, of setting up fresh ones, merely in order to increase the discontent of the masses artificially, and so ensure the continued existence of the party.

1. We demand the union of all Germans to form a Great Germany on the basis of the right of self-determination enjoyed by nations.

2. We demand equality of rights for the German people in its dealings with other nations, and abolition of the peace treaties of Versailles and Saint-Germain.

3. We demand land and territory (colonies) for the nourishment of our people and for settling our excess population.

4. None but members of the nation may be citizens of the state. None but those of German blood, whatever their creed, may be members of the nation. No Jew, therefore, may be a member of the nation.

5. Anyone who is not a citizen of the state may live in Germany only as a guest and must be regarded as being subject to foreign laws.

6. The right of voting on the leadership and legislation is to be enjoyed by the state alone. We demand therefore that all official appointments, of whatever kind, whether in the Reich, in the country, or in the smaller localities, shall be granted to citizens of the state alone. We oppose the corrupting custom of Parliament of filling posts merely with a view to party considerations, and without reference to character or capacity.

7. We demand that the state shall make it its first duty to promote the industry and livelihood of citizens of the state. If it is not possible to nourish the entire population of the state, foreign nationals (non-citizens of the state) must be excluded from the Reich.

8. All non-German immigration must be prevented...

9. All citizens of the state shall be equal as regards rights and duties.

10. It must be the first duty of each citizen of the state to work with his mind or with his body. The activities of the individual may not clash with the interests of the whole, but must proceed within the frame of the community and be for the general good.

We demand therefore:

11. Abolition of incomes unearned by work.

12. In view of the enormous sacrifice of life and property demanded of a nation by every war, personal enrichment due to a war must be regarded as a crime against the nation. We demand therefore ruthless confiscation of all war gains.

13. We demand nationalization of all businesses (trusts)...

14. We demand that the profits from wholesale trade shall be shared.

15. We demand extensive development of provision for old age.

16. We demand creation and maintenance of a healthy middle class, immediate communalization of wholesale business premises, and their lease at a cheap rate to small traders, and

---

[1] Ed. note: The content of this speech was prepared by Anton Drexler, Gottfried Eckart, and Adolf Hitler. The speech was delivered February 24, 1920, and proclaimed the following day. In August of the same year the name of the Party was changed to the National Socialist German Workers' Party.

that extreme consideration shall be shown to all small purveyors to the state, district authorities, and smaller localities.

17. We demand land reform suitable to our national requirements…

18. We demand ruthless prosecution of those whose activities are injurious to the common interest. Sordid criminals against the nation, usurers, profiteers, etc., must be punished with death, whatever their creed or race.

19. We demand that the Roman Law, which serves the materialistic world order, shall be replaced by a legal system for all Germany.

20. With the aim of opening to every capable and industrious German the possibility of higher education and of thus obtaining advancement, the state must consider a thorough reconstruction of our national system of education…

21. The state must see to raising the standard of health in the nation by protecting mothers and infants, prohibiting child labor, increasing bodily efficiency by obligatory gymnastics and sports laid down by law, and by extensive support of clubs engaged in the bodily development of the young.

22. We demand abolition of a paid army and formation of a national army.

23. We demand legal warfare against conscious political lying and its dissemination in the press. In order to facilitate creation of a German national press we demand:

a) that all editors of newspapers and their assistants, employing the German language, must be members of the nation;

b) that special permission from the state shall be necessary before non-German newspapers may appear. These are not necessarily printed in the German language;

c) that non-Germans shall be prohibited by law from participation financially in or influencing German newspapers…

It must be forbidden to publish papers which do not conduce to the national welfare. We demand legal prosecution of all tendencies in art and literature of a kind likely to disintegrate our life as a nation, and the suppression of institutions which militate against the requirements above-mentioned.

24. We demand liberty for all religious denominations in the state, so far as they are not a danger to it and do not militate against the moral feelings of the German race.

The party, as such, stands for positive Christianity, but does not bind itself in the matter of creed to any particular confession. It combats the Jewish-materialist spirit within us and without us…

25. That all the foregoing may be realized we demand the creation of a strong central power of the state. Unquestioned authority of the politically centralized Parliament over the entire Reich and its organizations; and formation of chambers for classes and occupations for the purpose of carrying out the general laws promulgated by the Reich in the various states of the confederation.

The leaders of the party swear to go straight forward—if necessary to sacrifice their lives—in securing fulfillment of the foregoing points.

Adolf Hitler. *The Twenty-Five Points.* Originally published in 1920.

The Political and Social Doctrine of Fascism

Benito Mussolini

BENITO MUSSOLINI *(1883–1945) was born in central Italy and was leader of that country from 1922 until 1943. His political views are best summed up in* The Political and Social Doctrine of Fascism.

Fascism is now a completely individual thing, not only as a regime but as a doctrine. And this means that to-day Fascism, exercising its critical sense upon itself and upon others, has formed its own distinct and peculiar point of view, to which it can refer and upon which, therefore, it can act in the face of all problems, practical or intellectual, which confront the world.

And above all, Fascism, the more it considers and observes the future and the development of humanity quite apart from political considerations of the moment, believes neither in the possibility nor the utility of perpetual peace. It thus repudiates the doctrine of Pacifism—born of a renunciation of the struggle and an act of cowardice in the face of sacrifice. War alone brings up to its highest tension all human energy and puts the stamp of nobility upon the peoples who have the courage to meet it. All other trials are substitutes, which never really put men into the position where they have to make the great decision—the alternative of life or death. Thus a doctrine which is founded upon this harmful postulate of peace is hostile to Fascism. And thus hostile to the spirit of Fascism, though accepted for what use they can be in dealing with particular political situations, are all the international leagues and societies which, as history will show, can be scattered to the winds when once strong national feeling is aroused by any motive—sentimental, ideal, or practical. This anti-Pacifist spirit is carried by Fascism even

into the life of the individual; the proud motto of the *Squadrista*, "Me ne frego," written on the bandage of the wound, is an act of philosophy not only stoic, the summary of a doctrine not only political—it is the education to combat, the acceptation of the risks which combat implies, and a new way of life for Italy. Thus the Fascist accepts life and loves it, knowing nothing of and despising suicide: he rather conceives of life as duty and struggle and conquest, life which should be high and full, lived for oneself, but above all for others—those who are at hand and those who are far distant, contemporaries, and those who will come after.

This "demographic" policy of the regime is the result of the above premise. Thus the Fascist loves in actual fact his neighbour, but this "neighbour" is not merely a vague and undefined concept, this love for one's neighbour puts no obstacle in the way of necessary educational severity, and still less to differentiation of status and to physical distance. Fascism repudiates any universal embrace, and in order to live worthily in the community of civilized peoples watches its contemporaries with vigilant eyes, takes good note of their state of mind and, in the changing trend of their interests, does not allow itself to be deceived by temporary and fallacious appearances.

Such a conception of life makes Fascism the complete opposite of that doctrine, the base of so-called scientific and Marxian Socialism, the materialist conception of history; according to which the history of human civilization can be explained simply through the conflict of interests among the various social groups and by the change and development in the means and instruments of production. That the changes in the economic field—new discoveries of raw materials, new methods of working them, and the inventions of science—have their importance no one can deny; but that these factors are sufficient to explain the history of humanity excluding all others is an absurd delusion. Fascism, now and always, believes in holiness and in heroism; that is to say, in actions influenced by no economic motive, direct or indirect. And if the economic conception of history be denied, according to which theory men are no more than puppets, carried to and fro by the waves of chance, while the real directing forces are quite out of their control, it follows that the existence of an unchangeable and unchanging class-war is also denied—the natural progeny of the economic conception of history. And above all Fascism denies that class-war can be the preponderant force in the transformation of society. These two fundamental concepts of Socialism being this refuted, nothing is left of it but the sentimental aspiration—as old as humanity itself—towards a social convention in which the sorrows and sufferings of the humblest shall be alleviated. But here again Fascism repudiates the conception of "economic" happiness, to be realized by Socialism and, as it were, at a given moment in economic evolution to assure to everyone the maximum of well-being. Fascism denies the materialist conception of happiness as a possibility, and abandons it to its inventors, the economists of the first half of the nineteenth century: that is to say, Fascism denies the validity of the equation, well-being-happiness, which would reduce men to the level of animals, caring for one thing only—to be fat and well-fed—and would thus degrade humanity to a purely physical existence.

After Socialism, Fascism combats the whole complex system of democratic ideology, and repudiates it, whether in its theoretical premises or in its practical application. Fascism denies that the majority, by the simple fact that it is a majority, can direct human society; it denies that numbers alone can govern by means of a periodical consultation, and it affirms the immutable, beneficial and fruitful inequality of mankind, which can never be permanently levelled through the mere operation of a mechanical process such as universal suffrage. The democratic regime may be defined as from time to time giving the people the illusion of sovereignty, while the real effective sovereignty lies in the hands of other concealed and irresponsible forces. Democracy is a regime nominally without a king, but it is rules by many kings—more absolute, tyrannical and ruinous than one sole king, even though a tyrant. This explains why Fascism, having first in 1922 (for reasons of expediency) assumed an attitude tending towards republicanism, renounced this point of view before the march to Rome; being convinced that the question of political form is not to-day of prime importance, and after having studied the examples of monarchies and republics past and present reached the conclusion that monarchy or republicanism are not to be judged, as it were, by an absolute standard; but that they represent forms in which the evolution—political, historical, traditional or psychological—of a particular country had expressed itself. Fascism supersedes the antithesis monarchy or republicanism, while democracy still tarries beneath the domination of this idea, for ever pointing out the insufficiency of the first and for ever the praising of the second as the perfect regime. To-day, it can be seen that there are republics innately reactionary and absolutist, and also monarchies which incorporate the most ardent social and political hopes of the future.

"Reason and science," says Renan (one of the inspired pre-Fascists) in his philosophical meditations, "are products of humanity, but to expect reason as a direct product of the people and a direct result of their action is to deceive oneself by a chimera. It is not necessary for the existence of reason that everybody should understand it. And in any case, if such a decimation of truth were necessary, it could not be achieved in a low-class democracy, which seems as though it must of its very nature extinguish any kind of noble training. The principle that society exists solely through the well-being and the personal liberty of all the individuals of which it is composed does not appear to be conformable to the plans of nature, in whose workings the race alone seems to be taken into consideration, and the individual sacrificed to it. It is greatly to be feared that the last stage of such a conception of democracy (though I must hasten to point out that the term 'democracy' may be interpreted in various ways) would end in a condition of society in which a degenerate herd would have no other preoccupation but the satisfaction of the lowest desires of common men." Thus Renan. Fascism denies, in democracy, the absurd conventional untruth of political equality dressed out in the garb of collective irresponsibility, and the myth of "happiness" and indefinite progress. But, if democracy may be conceived in diverse forms—that is to say, taking democracy to mean a state of society in which the populace are not reduced to impotence in the State—Fascism may write itself down as "an organized, centralized and authoritative democracy."

Fascism has taken up an attitude of complete opposition to the doctrines of Liberalism, both in the political field and the field of economics. There should be no undue exaggeration (simply with the object of immediate success in controversy) of the importance of Liberalism in the last century, nor should what was but one among many theories which appeared in that period be put forward as a religion for humanity for all time, present and to come. Liberalism only flourished for half a century...

The era of Liberalism, after having accumulated an infinity of Gordian knots, tried to untie them in the slaughter of the World War—and never has any religion demanded of its votaries such a monstrous sacrifice. Perhaps the Liberal Gods were athirst for blood? But now, to-day, the Liberal faith must shut the doors of its deserted temples, deserted because the peoples of the world realize that its worship—agnostic in the field of economics and indifferent in the field of politics and morals—will lead, as it has already led, to certain ruin. In addition to this, let it be pointed out that all the political hopes of the present day are anti-Liberal, and it is therefore supremely ridiculous to try to classify this sole creed as outside the judgment of history, as though history were a hunting ground reserved for the professors of Liberalism alone—as though Liberalism were the final unalterable verdict of civilization.

But the Fascist negation of Socialism, Democracy and Liberalism must not be taken to mean that Fascism desires to lead the world back to the state of affairs before 1789, the date which seems to be indicated as the opening years of the succeeding semi-Liberal century: we do not desire to turn back; Fascism has not chosen De Maistre for its high-priest. Absolute monarchy has been and can never return, any more than blind acceptance of ecclesiastical authority...

The foundation of Fascism is the conception of the State, its character, its duty, and its aim. Fascism conceives of the State as an absolute, in comparison with which all individuals or groups are relative, only to be conceived of in their relation to the State. The conception of the Liberal State is not that of a directing force, guiding the play and development, both material and spiritual, of a collective body, but merely a force limited to the function of recording results: on the other hand, the Fascist State is itself conscious, and has itself a will and a personality—thus it may be called the "ethic" State. In 1929, at the first five-yearly assembly of the Fascist regime, I said:

For us Fascists, the State is not merely a guardian, preoccupied solely with the duty of assuring the personal safety of the citizens; nor is it an organization with purely material aims, such as to guarantee a certain level of well-being and peaceful conditions of life; for a mere council of administration would be sufficient to realize such objects. Nor is it a purely political creation, divorced from all contact with the complex material reality which makes up the life of the individual and the life of the people as a whole. The State, as conceived of and as created by Fascism, is a spiritual and moral fact in itself, since its political, juridical and economic organization of the nation is a concrete thing: and such an organization must be in its origins and development a manifestation of the spirit. The State is the guarantor of security both internal and external, but it is also the custodian and transmitter of the spirit of the people, as it has grown up through the centuries in language, in customs and in faith. And the State is not only a living reality of the present, it is also linked with the past and above all with the future, and thus transcending the brief limits of individual life, it represents the immanent spirit of the nation. The forms in which States express themselves may change, but the necessity for such forms is eternal. It is the State which educated its citizens in civic virtue, gives them a consciousness of their mission and welds them into unity; harmonizing their various interests through justice, and transmitting to future generations the mental conquests of science, of art, of law and the solidarity of humanity. It leads men from primitive tribal life to that highest expression of human power which is Empire: it links up through the centuries the names of those of its members who have died for its existence and in obedience to its laws, it holds up the memory of the leaders who have increased its territory and the geniuses who have illumined it with glory as an example to be followed by future generations. When the conception of the State declines, and disunifying and centrifugal tendencies prevail, whether of individuals or of particular groups, the nations where such phenomena appear are in their decline...

The Fascist State is not indifferent to the fact of religion in general, or to that particular and positive faith which is Italian Catholicism. The State professes no theology, but a morality, and in the Fascist State religion is considered as one of the deepest manifestations of the spirit of man, thus it is not only respected but defended and protected. The Fascist State has never tried to create its own God, as at one moment Robespierre and the wildest extremists of the Convention tried to do; nor does it vainly seek to obliterate religion from the hearts of men as does Bolshevism: Fascism respects the God of the ascetics, the saints and heroes, and equally, God as He is perceived and worshipped by simple people.

The Fascist State is an embodied will to power and government: The Roman tradition is here an ideal of force in action. According to Fascism, government is not so much a thing to be expressed in territorial or military terms as in terms of morality and the spirit. It must be thought of as an Empire—that is to say, a nation which directly or indirectly rules other nations, without the need for conquering a single square yard of territory. For Fascism, the growth of Empire, that is to say the expansion of the nation, is an essential manifestation of vitality, and its opposite a sign of deca-

dence. Peoples which are rising, or rising again after a period of decadence, are always imperialist; any renunciation is a sign of decay and of death. Fascism is the doctrine best adapted to represent the tendencies and the aspirations of a people, like the people of Italy, who are rising again after many centuries of abasement and foreign servitude. But Empire demands discipline, the co-ordination of all forces and a deeply-felt sense of duty and sacrifice; this fact explains many aspects of the practical working of the regime, the character of many forces in the State, and the necessarily severe measures which must be taken against those who would oppose this spontaneous and inevitable movement of Italy in the twentieth century, and would oppose it by recalling the outworn ideology of the nineteenth century—repudiated wheresoever there has been the courage to undertake great experiments of social and political transformation: for never before has the nation stood more in need of authority, of direction and of order. If every age has its own characteristic doctrine, there are a thousand signs which point to Fascism as the characteristic doctrine of our time. For if a doctrine must be a living thing, this is proved by the fact that Fascism has created a living faith; and that this faith is very powerful in the minds of men, is demonstrated by those who have suffered and died for it.

Fascism has henceforth in the world the universality of all those doctrines which, in realizing themselves, have represented a stage in the history of the human spirit.

Benito Mussolini. *The Political and Social Doctrines of Fascism.* Translated by J. Soames. London: Hogarth Press, 1933.

Foundations of the Nineteenth Century

Houston Stewart Chamberlain

HOUSTON STEWART CHAMBERLAIN *(1855–1926) was an Englishman who developed the notion of the genetically superior folk-nation. He made use of Darwinian ideas and applied them to the Aryan race. Most of his thoughts on racial traits are discussed in* Foundations of the Nineteenth Century.

The Jews

At a later time, indeed, a Semitic flood swept once more across the European, Asiatic and African world, a flood such as, but for the destruction of Carthage by Rome, would have swept over Europe a thousand years before, with results which would have been decisive and permanent. But here, too, the Semitic idea—"faith wide, narrow the thought"— proved itself more powerful than its bearers; the Arabs were gradually thrown back and, in contrast to the Jews, not one of them remained on European soil; but where their abstract idolatry had obtained a foothold all possibility of a culture disappeared; the Semitic dogma of materialism, which in this case and in contrast to Christianity had kept itself free of all Aryan admixtures, deprived noble human races of all soul, and excluded them for ever from the "race that strives to reach the light."—Of the Semites only the Jews, as we see, have positively furthered our culture and also shared, as far as their extremely assimilative nature permitted them, in the legacy of antiquity.

The Teutonic Races

The entrance of the Teutonic races into the history of the world forms the counterpart to the spread of this diminutive and yet so influ- ential people. There, too, we see what pure race signifies, at the same time, however, what variety of races is—that great natural principle of many-sidedness, and of dissimilarity of mental gifts, which shallow, venal, ignorant babblers of the present day would fain deny, slavish souls sprung from the chaos of peoples, who feel at ease only in a confused atmosphere of characterlessness and absence of individuality. To this day these two powers— Jews and Teutonic races—stand, wherever the recent spread of the Chaos has not blurred their features, now as friendly, now as hostile, but always as alien forces face to face.

In this book I understand by "Teutonic peoples" the different North-European races, which appear in history as Celts, Teutons (Germanen) and Slavs, and from whom— mostly by indeterminable mingling—the peoples of modern Europe are descended. It is certain that they belonged originally to a single family, as I shall prove in the sixth chapter; but the Teuton in the narrower Tacitean sense of the word has proved himself so intellectually, morally and physically pre-eminent among his kinsmen, that we are entitled to make his name summarily represent the whole family. The Teuton is the soul of our culture. Europe of to-day, with its many branches over the whole world, represents the chequered result of an infinitely manifold mingling of races: what binds us all together and makes an organic unity of us is "Teutonic" blood. If we look around, we see that the importance of each nation as a living power to-day is dependent upon the proportion of genuinely Teutonic blood in its population. Only Teutons sit on the thrones of Europe.— What preceded in the history of the world we may regard as Prolegomena; true history, the history which still controls the rhythm of our hearts and circulates in our veins, inspiring us to new hope and new creation, begins at the moment when the Teuton with his masterful hand lays his grip upon the legacy of antiquity...

Importance of Race

Nothing is so convincing as the consciousness of the possession of Race. The man who belongs to a distinct, pure race, never loses the sense of it. The guardian angel of his lineage is ever at his side, supporting him where he loses his foothold, warning him like the Socratic Daemon where he is in danger of going astray, compelling obedience, and forcing him to undertakings which, deeming them impossible, he would never have dared to attempt. Weak and erring like all that is human, a man of this stamp recognises himself, as others recognise him, by the sureness of his character, and by the fact that his actions are marked by a certain simple and peculiar greatness, which finds its explanation in his distinctly typical and super-personal qualities. Race lifts a man above himself: it endows him with extraordinary—I might almost say supernatural—powers, so entirely does it distinguish him from the individual who springs from the chaotic jumble of peoples drawn from all parts of the world: and should this man of pure origin be perchance gifted above his fellows, then the fact of Race strengthens and elevates him on every hand, and he becomes a genius towering over the rest of mankind, not because he has been thrown upon the earth like a flaming meteor by a freak of nature, but because he soars heavenward like some strong and stately tree, nourished by thousands and thousands of roots—no solitary individual, but the living sum of untold striving for the same goal. He who has eyes to see at once detects Race in animals. It shows itself in the whole habit of the beast, and proclaims itself in a hundred peculiarities which defy analysis: nay more, it proves itself by achievements, for its possession invariably leads to something excessive and out of the common—even to that which is exaggerated and not free from bias. Goethe's dictum, "only that which is extravagant (*überschwänglich*) makes greatness," is well known.[1] That is the very quality which a thoroughbred race reared from superior materials bestows upon its individual descendants—something "extravagant"—and, indeed, what we learn from every racehorse, every thoroughbred fox-terrier, every Cochin China fowl, is the very lesson which the history of mankind so eloquently teaches us! Is not the Greek in the fulness of his glory an unparalleled example of this "extravagance"? And do we not see this "extravagance" first make its appearance when immigration from the North has ceased, and the various strong breeds of men, isolated on the peninsula once for all, begin to fuse into a new race, brighter and more brilliant, where, as in Athens, the racial blood flows from many sources—simpler and more resisting where, as in Lacedemon, even this mixture of blood had been barred out. Is the race not as it were extinguished, as soon as fate wrests the land from its proud exclusiveness and incorporates it in a greater whole?[2] Does not Rome teach us the same lesson? Has not in this case also a special mixture of blood produced an abso-

---

[1] *Materialien zur Geschichte der Farbenlehre*, the part dealing with Newton's personality.

[2] It is well known that it was but gradually extinguished, and that in spite of a political situation, which must assuredly have brought speedy destruction on everything Hellenic, had not race qualities here had a decisive influence. Till late in the Christian era Athens remained the centre of intellectual life for mankind; Alexandria was more talked of, the strong Semitic contingent saw to that; but any one who wished to study in earnest travelled to Athens, till Christian narrow-mindedness for ever closed the schools there in the year 529, and we learn that as late as this even the man of the people was distinguished in Athens "by the liveliness of his intellect, the correctness of his language and the sureness of his taste" (Gibbon, chap. xl.). There is in George Finlay's book, *Medieval Greece*, chap. i., a complete and very interesting and clear account of the gradual destruction of the Hellenic race by reign immigration. One after the other colonies of Roman soldiers from all parts of the Empire, then Celts, Teutonic peoples, Slavonians, Bulgarians. Wallachians, Albanesians, etc., had moved into the country and mixed with the original population. The Zaconians, who were numerous even in the fifteenth century, but have now almost died out, are said to be the only pure Hellenes.

lutely new race, similar in qualities and capacities to no later one, endowed with exuberant power? And does not victory in this case effect what disaster did in that, but only much more quickly? Like a cataract the stream of strange blood overflooded the almost depopulated Rome and at once the Romans ceased to be. Would one small tribe from among all the Semites have become a world-embracing power had it not made "purity of race" its inflexible fundamental law? In days when so much nonsense is talked concerning this question, let Disraeli teach us that the whole significance of judaism lies in its purity of race, that this alone gives it power and duration, and just as it has outlived the people of antiquity, so, thanks to its knowledge of this law of nature, will it outlive the constantly mingling races of to-day.[1]

What is the use of detailed scientific investigations as to whether there are distinguishable races? whether race has a worth? how this is possible? and so on. We turn the tables and say: it is evident that there are such races: it is a fact of direct experience that the quality of the race is of vital importance; your province is only to find out the how and the wherefore, not to deny the facts themselves in order to indulge your ignorance. One of the greatest ethnologists of the present day, Adolf Bastian, testifies that, "what we see in history is not a transformation, a passing of one race into another, but entirely new and perfect creations, which the ever-youthful productivity of nature sends forth from the invisible realm of Hades."[2] Whoever travels the short distance between Calais and Dover, feels almost as if he had reached a different planet, so great is the difference between the English and French, despite their many points of relationship. The observer can also see from this instance the value of purer "inbreeding." England is practically cut off by its insular po-

sition: the last (not very extensive) invasion took place 800 years ago; since than only a few thousands from the Netherlands, and later a few thousand Huguenots have crossed over (all of the same origin), and thus has been reared that race which at the present moment is unquestionably the strongest in Europe.[3]

Direct experience, however, offers us a series of quite different observations on race, all of which may gradually contribute to the extension of our knowledge as well as to its definiteness. In contrast to the new, growing, Anglo-Saxon race, look, for instance, at the Sephardim, the so-called "Spanish Jews"; here we find how a genuine race can by purity keep itself noble for centuries and tens of centuries, but at the same time how very necessary it is to distinguish between the nobly reared portions of a nation and the rest. In England, Holland and Italy there are still genuine Sephardim but very few, since they can scarcely any longer avoid crossing with the Ashkenazim (the so-called "German Jews"). Thus, for example, the Montefiores of the present generation have all without exception married German Jewesses. But every one who has travelled in the East of Europe, where the genuine Sephardim still as far as possible avoid all intercourse with German Jews, for whom they have an almost comical repugnance, will agree with me when I say that it is only when one sees these men and has intercourse with them that one begins to comprehend the significance of Judaism in the history of the world. This is nobility in the fullest sense of the world, genuine nobility of race! Beautiful figures, noble heads, dignity in speech and bearing.

Houston Stewart Chamberlain. *Foundations of the Nineteenth Century*. New York: John Lane, London: The Bodley Head, 1912.

---

[1] See the novels *Tancred* and *Coningsby*. In the latter Sidonia says: "Race is everything; there is no other truth. And every race must fall which carelessly suffers its blood to become mixed."

[2] *Das Beständige in den Menschenrassen und die Spielweite ihrer Veränderlichkeit*, 1868, p. 26.

[3] Mention should also be made of Japan, where likewise a felicitous crossing and afterwards insular isolation have contributed to the production of a very remarkable race, much stronger and (within the Mongoloid sphere of possibility) much more profoundly endowed than most Europeans imagine. Perhaps the only books in which one gets to know the Japanese soul are those of Lafcadio Hearn: *Kokoro, Hints and Echoes of Japanese Inner Life; Gleanings in Buddha Fields*, and others.

National Life from the Standpoint of Science

Karl Pearson

KARL PEARSON (1857–1936) was Professor of
Applied Mathematics and Mechanics and later
Galton Professor of National Eugenics, both at the
University of London. He applied mathematics to
general biology and national character traits,
among many other subjects. He laid special
emphasis upon the idea of the tribe rather than the
individual and attempted to relate this idea to that
of bad stock and lower races. His popular works
include National Life and The Grammar of
Science.

Now, if we once realize that this law of inheritance is as inevitable as the law of gravity, we shall cease to struggle against it. This does not mean a fatal resignation to the presence of bad stock, but a conscious attempt to modify the percentage of it in our own community and in the world at large. Let me illustrate what I mean. A showman takes a wolf and, by aid of training and nurture, a more or less judicious administration of food and whip, makes it apparently docile and friendly as a dog. But one day, when the whip is not there, it is quite possible that the wolf will turn upon its keeper, or upon somebody else. Even if it does not, its offspring will not benefit by the parental education. I don't believe that the showman's way can be a permanent success; I believe, however, that you might completely domesticate the wolf, as the dog has been domesticated, by steadily selecting the more docile members of the community through several generations, and breeding only from these, rejecting the remainder. Now, if you have once realized the force of heredity, you will see in natural selection—the choice of the physically and mentally fitter to be the parents of the next generation—a most munificent provision for the progress of all forms of

life. Nurture and education may immensely aid the social machine, but they must be repeated generation by generation; they will not in themselves reduce the tendency to the production of bad stock. Conscious or unconscious selection can alone bring that about.

What I have said about bad stock seems to me to hold for the lower races of man. How many centuries, how many thousand of years, have the Kaffir or the negro held large districts in Africa undisturbed by the white man? Yet their intertribal struggles have not yet produced a civilization in the least comparable with the Aryan. Educate and nurture them as you will, I do not believe that you will succeed in modifying the stock. History shows me one way, and one way only, in which a high state of civilization has been produced, namely, the struggle of race with race, and the survival of the physically and mentally fitter race. If you want to know whether the lower races of man can evolve a higher type, I fear the only course is to leave them to fight it out among themselves, and even then the struggle for existence between individual and individual, between tribe and tribe, may not be supported by that physical selection due to a particular climate on which probably so much of the Aryan's success depended.

If you bring the white man into contact with the black, you too often suspend the very process of natural selection on which the evolution of a higher type depends. You get superior and inferior races living on the same soil, and that coexistence is demoralizing for both. They naturally sink into the position of master and servant, if not admittedly or covertly into that of slave-owner and slave. Frequently they intercross, and if the bad stock be raised the good is lowered. Even in the case of Eurasians, of whom I have met mentally and physically fine specimens, I have felt how much better they would have been had they been pure Asiatics or pure Europeans. Thus it comes about that when the struggle for existence between races is suspended, the solution of great problems may be unnaturally postponed; instead of the slow, stern processes of evolution, cataclysmal solutions are prepared for the future. Such problems in suspense, it appears to me, are to be found in the negro population of the Southern States of America, in the large admixture of Indian blood in some of the South American races, but, above all, in the Kaffir factor in South Africa.

You may possibly think that I am straying from my subject, but I want to justify natural selection to you. I want you to see selection as something which renders the inexorable law of heredity a source of progress which produces the good through suffering, an infinitely greater good which far outbalances the very obvious pain and evil. Let us suppose the alternative were possible. Let us suppose we could prevent the white man, if we liked, from going to lands of which the agriculture and mineral resources are not worked to the full; then I should say a thousand times better for him that he should not go than that he should settle down and live alongside the inferior race. The only healthy alternative is that he should go and completely drive out the inferior race. That is practically what the white man has done in North America. We sometimes forget the light that chapter of history throws on more recent experiences. Some 250 years ago there was a man who fought in our country against taxation without representation, and another man who did not mind going to prison for the sake of his religious opinions. As Englishmen we are proud of them both, but we sometimes forget that they were both considerable capitalists for their age, and started chartered companies in another continent. Well, a good deal went on in the plantations they founded, if not with their knowledge, with that at least of their servants and of their successors, which would shock us all at the present day. But I venture to say that no man calmly judging will wish either that the whites had never gone to America, or would desire the whites and Red Indians were today living alongside each other as negro and white in Southern States, as Kaffir

and European in South Africa, still less that they had mixed their blood as Spaniard and Indian in South America. The civilization of the white man is a civilization dependent upon free white labour, and when that element of stability is removed it will collapse like those of Greece and Rome. I venture to assert, then, that the struggle for existence between white and red man, painful and even terrible as it was in its details, has given us a good far outbalancing its immediate evil. In place of the red man, contributing practically nothing to the work and thought of the world, we have a great nation, mistress of many arts, and able, with its youthful imagination and fresh, untrammelled impulses, to contribute much to the common stock of civilized man. Against that we have only to put the romantic sympathy for the Red Indian generated by the novels of Cooper and the poems of Longfellow, and then—see how little it weights in the balance!

But America is but one case in which we have to mark a masterful human progress following an inter-racial struggle. The Australian nation is another case of great civilization supplanting a lower race unable to work to the full the land and its resources. Further back in history you find the same tale with almost every European nation. Sometimes when the conquering race is not too diverse in civilization and in type of energy there is an amalgamation of races, as when Norman and Anglo-Saxon ultimately blended; at other times the inferior race is driven out before the superior, as the Celt drove out the Iberian. The struggle means suffering, intense suffering, while it is in progress; but that struggle and that suffering have been the stages by which the white man has reached his present stage of development, and they account for the fact that he no longer lives in caves and feeds on roots and nuts. This dependence of progress on the survival of the fitter race, terribly black as it may seem to some of you, gives the struggle for existence its redeeming features; it is the fiery crucible out of which comes the finer metal. You may hope for a time when the sword shall be turned into the ploughshare, when American and German and English traders shall no longer compete in the markets of the world for their raw material and for their food supply, when the white man and the dark shall share the soil between them, and each till it as he lists. But, believe me, when that day comes mankind will no longer progress; there will be nothing to check the fertility of inferior stock; the relentless law of heredity will not be controlled and guided by natural selection. Man will stagnate; and unless he ceases to multiply, the catastrophe will come again; famine and pestilence, as we see them in the East, physical selection instead of the struggle of race against race, will do the work more relentlessly, and, to judge from India and China, far less efficiently than of old.

Karl Pearson. *National Life from the Standpoint of Science*. Originally published in 1901.

The Myth of Race

Paul M. Hayes

PAUL M. HAYES *is a Fellow of Keble College, Oxford University. His writings include* Quisling: The Career and Political Ideas of Vidkun Quisling *and* Fascism.

"The physical development and racial improvement of the people form the necessary basis of lasting progress." Vidkun Quisling, *Russian and Ourselves.*

The concept of racial superiority was a constituent part of fascist ideology. Because of the particular forms racial theory took during the period of Nazi ascendancy on the continent of Europe—the campaigns for the systematic elimination of the Jews and the Slavs—the myth of race is perhaps the most widely known fascist theory. It overlapped at several points with the idea of élitist government and also with more common national and military objectives. It is often stated that there was much that was essentially German rather than fascist in these theories. The Italians, for example, on the whole showed little enthusiasm for the idea of racial superiority, except under German pressure in the years immediately preceding the outbreak of the Second World War. However, even among the Italians there were firm believers in racial superiority, not only among the full-blown fascists such as Farinacci but also among nationalists. In a letter of 1895 D'Annunzio[1] wrote: "I glory in the fact that I am a Latin, and I recognize a barbarian in every man of non-Latin blood... If the Latin races are to preserve themselves, it is time they returned to the healthy prejudice which created the grandeur of Greece and Rome—to believe that all others are barbarians."[2] The step from D'Annunzio to Rosenberg was but small.

In fact, the notion of racial superiority was of a much older vintage than the close of the nineteenth century. At the beginning of the century, under pressure from the aggressive French nationalism spearheaded by Napoleon, many Germans responded by consoling themselves for the defeat of Austria and Prussia with the thought that Germans were bound to triumph over disaster in the long run through their natural superiority as a race. Thus the term "Volk" came to have a particular meaning for Germans—one which was associated with endeavour, struggle, reward and domination. As the German paradoxically gained rather than lost ground.

One of the earliest enthusiasts for the concept of racial superiority was Fichte[3] who, in 1807, declared in a lecture at Berlin that not only were the Germans an *"Urvolk"* (original folk) but furthermore it was "quite plain that only the German...truly has a folk and is entitled to depend on one; he only is able to feel real and rational love for his nation."[4] This theme was to be taken up by many other Germans, even among his contemporaries. Some of these were men of real ability, others crude and uneducated. Most prominent among the latter group was Jahn[5] who combined his

---

[1] Gabriele D'Annunzio (1863–1938), Italian poet and novelist.

[2] D'Annunzio to Hérelle (his French translator), 1895. Quoted in *The Poet as Superman* by Anthony Rhodes, p. 50.

[3] Johann Fichte (1762–1814), a German philosopher, frequently accused of atheism.

[4] *Reden an die deutsche Nation.* Part IV.

[5] Friedrich Jahn (1778–1852), the German "founder of gymnastics."

opinions of the physical and mental attributes of the German people into a strange and incoherent philosophy of race. On a more sophisticated level, Arndt[1] (an early believer in the destiny of the Nordic races) and von der Marwitz[2] (an early campaigner against the Jews) brought many members of the educated classes, particularly in Prussia, over to Fichte's views.

The propagation of Fichte's ideas, albeit in a more complex form, owed much to the ability of Görres,[3] a publicist and author. His main work was *Das Wachstum der Historie* in which he elaborated the concept of the myth of the folk. At one time he was editor of the *Rheinischer Merkur*, using his position to campaign for a greater, united Germany. His views were not, however, merely nationalist but also racialist—he was a firm believer in the purity and strength of the German race: "Like cannot dissociate itself from like, nor can blood of the same mixture belie itself, even though it may have branched off from the main stream into smaller vessels."[4] His work was repeated by many minor figures during the following decades.

By the middle of the nineteenth century the concept of racial superiority was well established in the European cultural tradition, although, curiously, most of the thinkers who had embraced the doctrine fervently had been German. It is thus easy to see why for so many Germans the concept of the *"Herrenvolk,"* delineated by Hitler in the 1920s and 1930s, should have been so attractive. It was familiar—a part of the German literary and historical tradition. It had become a doctrine sedulously fostered by generations of instructors, in the schools, universities and in the armed forces. The concept had received further reinforcement from the military victories of 1866 and 1870–1 and the economic prosperity of the following half century. The chosen race was that of Germany.

However, the leading apostle of race theory was not a German, but a French diplomat, Count Arthur Gobineau. Gobineau stressed the importance of race as the essential factor in the process of civilization, although many of his opinions were later distorted by twentieth-century fascists in order to suit their own purposes. He was a man of intensely pessimistic social outlook, viewing the decadence of contemporary society with resignation and loathing. His opinions of the virtues of certain races was never very consistent, varying according to his mood and his diplomatic postings. For example, early in his career he declared in the *Essai sur l'inégalité des races humaines* that society in Latin America was decadent, principally because of miscegenation between Europeans and natives. Yet a few years later, when in correspondence with Pedro II of Brazil, he took a very different stand.[5] Again, he was at first sympathetic to Prussia, later to Austria. His work was thus neither consistent nor systematic.

It was Gobineau's view of the hierarchical structure of races that was to have so much influence upon later writers. He believed that the most important peoples were to be found among the white races, followed by the yellow races and then the black. Among the white races were some of great ethnic purity which, therefore, had considerable potential for the development of civilization. There were others of different stock within the white races whose main capacity was the ability to transmit ethnic decay and hence to accelerate the collapse of civilization. The race which possessed the maximum potential for civilization was that of the Teutons. The most degenerate were the Slavs and the Celts. The preferred race of Teutons varied according to his moods, being at different times the Germans, the Scandinavians and the English.

Many of Gobineau's ideas were ignored or glossed over by later writers. He was not particularly anti-Semitic, believing that the debasement of the Jews arose from

---

[1] Ernst Arndt (1769–1860), German poet and patriot.

[2] Friedrich von der Marwitz (1777–1837), Prussian general.

[3] Joseph von Görres (1776–1848), German Catholic writer.

[4] *Das Wachstum der Historie.*

[5] For further discussion see *Father of Racist Ideology: the social and political thought of Count Gobineau* by M.D. Biddiss.

miscegenation with the black races rather than from racial faults inherent in themselves. This aspect of his thought was studiously ignored by Rosenberg and many other devotees. Similarly, he was hostile to slavery, but even in his own lifetime two American publicists—Henry Hotz and Josiah Nott—perverted his views for their own propaganda purposes. More predictably, he was anti-egalitarian and anti-democratic. He believed in an ordered, hierarchical society. He was hostile to materialism and cherished the institutions of the family and aristocracy. He regarded an élite as essential to the preservation of a civilized society. The influence of these and other ideas among the Junkers and other members of the educated classes in Germany was particular strong and bred many imitators.

Within Germany the concept of race was further strengthened by the writings of Schemann, the founder of the Gobineau Society in 1893, Wagner,[1] Dühring[2] and Lagarde.[3] All of these men flourished in the second half of the nineteenth century and some were very influential, Wagner in particular, because his appeal stretched beyond the literary circles in which his contemporaries were almost exclusively active. Strangely enough, the views of these men had in part been stimulated by the progress of scientific analysis. Darwin's ideas and researches, which were of inestimable scientific importance, soon acquired a political dimension when they were claimed by the apostles of race. A new and more powerful form of racialism arose—dubbed Social-Darwinism.

Enthusiasts for this cult were by no means confined to Germany. Indeed, three leading writers were of English origin—Houston Chamberlain, Pearson[4] and Kidd.[5] Chamberlain developed the concept of the folk-nation, destined to triumph because of its superior genetic gifts. His devotion to the Aryan race, in particular the German branch, was extraordinary. He was frequently guilty of grossly inaccurate historical statements in defence of his ideas. He believed, for example, that the Renaissance had been the result of an upsurge in the German spirit. The unfortunate fact that many of the earliest Renaissance scholars and artists had come from Italy was explained in terms of the heavy preponderance of Teutonic blood in northern Italy (settled by the Lombards, Franks and Goths). Chamberlain's views thus antedated those of Farinacci by some forty years. Furthermore, Chamberlain regarded physical and mental superiority as complementary attributes: "...horses and dogs give us every chance of observing that the intellectual gifts go hand in hand with the physical; this is specially true of the moral qualities; a mongrel is frequently very clever, but never reliable; morally he is always a weed."[6] Chamberlain thus helped create a strange and perverted mixture of the theories of Darwin and Gobineau. He found a highly receptive audience in Imperial Germany.

While Chamberlain's ideas fell on fruitful soil in Germany, Pearson was engaged upon similar work in England. In 1905 he wrote that "A nation...is an organized whole...kept up to a high pitch of external efficiency by contest, chiefly by way of war with inferior races, and with equal races by the struggle for trade-routes and for the sources of raw material and of food supply."[7] Pearson's contribution to the

---

[1] Richard Wagner (1813–83), German composer whose music reflected his political views. Prominent believer in racial myths.

[2] Eugen Dühring (1833–1921), German political economist and philosopher.

[3] Paul Lagarde (1827–91), German biblical and oriental scholar who was a professor at Göttingen.

[4] Karl Pearson (1857–1936), English mathematician and statistician.

[5] Benjamin Kidd (1858–1916), English sociologist who was originally a minor civil servant. Chiefly famous for *Social Evolution*.

[6] *Grundzüge des neunzehnten Jahrhunderts*. Quoted in *The Roots of National Socialism, 1783–1933* by R. D'O. Butler, p. 168.

[7] *National Life from the Standpoint of Science* by K. Pearson, p. 46.

theory of race was to emphasize the importance of the "tribute" as distinct from the "individual." In the 1890s his ideas gained ground not only against the orthodox views of Darwin but also perversions of those views by Germans such as Haeckel.[1] Pearson's main rival in Britain was Kidd, whose major contribution to racial theory was his *Social Evolution* of 1894. Kidd was not liked or respected by Pearson, for he was not only anti-socialist (and Pearson claimed to be socialist) but also a devout Christian. However, they both agreed that it was essential for the Empire to be maintained, if necessary at the expense of inferior peoples. Kidd had written that "In the North American Continent, in the plains of Australia, in New Zealand, and South Africa, the representatives of this vigorous and virile race are at last in full possession."[2] Pearson echoed these sentiments when, at the height of the Boer War, he declared: "This dependence of progress on the survival of the fitter race, terribly black as it may seem to some of you, gives the struggle for existence its redeeming features; it is the fiery crucible out of which comes the finer metal."[3]

The myth of race found powerful allies in the period preceding the First World War. The economic and social pressures generated in Europe by changing industrial patterns found a ready outlet in the drive towards imperialism. Powerful groups in Germany and England adopted the arguments of the racial theorist to suit their own political ends. Similar movements existed in both France and Italy, but they were less strong, perhaps because of the checks to imperial policies sustained by these countries at Fashoda in 1898 and Adowa in 1896.

It was in England and Germany (and later the United States) that the influence of the concept of race, conjoined with imperialism, rose to a peak. A number of otherwise apparently incompatible ideas became united in a strange combination of Social-Darwinism Social-Imperialism, religious mysticism and the theories of racial destiny. Politicians and writers were carried away by the heady doctrine. It is easy to see how Sorel's views on the importance of myths in history were developed during these years of frenzied activity...

In Germany anti-Semitism soon became part of the racial myth. All the failures of German policy, the inability to transform economic into political domination, could be attributed to the pollution of Aryan society by the Jews. It was at this level that the theories of Darwin and the eccentric views of Gobineau became popularized in bastard versions. Anti-Semites ranged from men of the people, like Stöcker,[4] to intellectuals such as Dühring, Houston Chamberlain, Driesmans and Wilser. Dühring's *Die Judenfrage als Racen-, Sitten-, und Kulturfrage* was the classic exposition of anti-Semitic theory. Beside this massive work of excoriation the attempts of men like Wilser to prove Aryan supremacy by means of genetic analysis paled into insignificance. Dühring asserted that "society is in many places so paralysed by moral poison that it can no longer stir its limbs to reaction... Now what part have the Jews played in this corruption? ... Where the Jews are to the fore, there is there most corruption. This is a basic fact of all cultural history and cultural geography."[5] Dühring's viewpoint was to some extent formed by his hatred of France and England, in which countries Gambetta and Disraeli were influential, and the press, in which Jews were frequently very powerfully established. Dühring's economic views, which were hostile to free trade, further reinforced these sentiments. In fact some of his suggestions merely antedate Hitler's actions by half a century— "the commonplace and short-sighted pretext of toleration is no longer relevant...[there should be]...social defence against marriage with those belonging to the Jewish race... Req-

---

[1] Ernest Haeckel (1834–1919), German biologist who had his own ideas about evolution.

[2] *Social Revolution* by B. Kidd. Quoted in *Imperialism and Social Reform* by B. Semmel, p. 33.

[3] In November 1900. *National Life from the Standpoint of Science*, pp. 26–7.

[4] Adolf Stöcker (1835–1909), German priest and political agitator.

[5] *Die Judenfrage als Racen-, Sitten-, und Kulturfrage* by E. Dühring.

uisites of an effective agitation with the reduction and extinction of the powers of the Jews as the final target."[1]

Dühring's crude anti-Semitism was shared by Wagner and many other influential Germans. Houston Chamberlain, however, was hostile to the Jews not because of a belief in their racial impurity but rather because they formed a major obstacle to German domination of Europe, through their economic and industrial influence. The views of others were less sophisticated, being based on greed, envy, religious intolerance or any of a number of other social factors.

If anti-Semitism was rife in Germany, Russia and their Eastern European dependencies it also existed outside these areas. In Austria, where many Jews had settled, Schoenerer[2] and Lueger[3] made political capital out of anti-Semitism. In Romania, Bulgaria and Serbia the Jews faced regular attacks from right-wing, nationalist bodies. At the end of the nineteenth century the small Jewish community in France came under hostile public inspection because of the false allegations against Dreyfus. Leading the anti-Semitic agitation was Drumont,[4] whose political influence did not decline until the Dreyfus Affair had been finally settled in favour of the accused. Even in Britain, where the Jews were exceptionally well integrated, strange anti-Semitic echoes were occasionally heard. During the constitutional crisis of 1909–11 Belloc[5] described the House of Lords as "by its constitution a committee for the protection of the Anglo-Judaic plutocracy."[6]

It was, however, the collapse of German society in 1918 and the following years which gave new life to anti-semitism. To the minds of the general public, right-wing propaganda about Jewish betrayal seemed a plausible explanation for the misfortunes which had overtaken Germany. The prominence of Jews amid the ranks of the Social Democrats in Germany and among the Bolsheviks in Russia confirmed these beliefs. The economic and social problems that faced industrialized Europe after 1918 paved the way for a general revival of hostility to the Jews.

It was in this period that Drexler,[7] soon to be succeeded as leader by Hitler, founded the Nazi Party and adopted a policy of systematic anti-Semitism. The Fatherland Party of Tirpitz held similar views, as well as a whole host of splinter groups. Soon Hitler's anti-Semitism began to attract important recruits, Ludendorff[8] and Houston Chamberlain. Keyserling, while declaring that anti-Semitism might appear irrational, suggested that "it must have some justification, for Jews are, as they always have been, equally despised throughout the world."[9] Von Beck's bogus *Protocols of the Elders of Sion* strongly influenced Rosenberg and Streicher.[10] Moeller van den Bruck[11] linked Marxism and Judaism with the formation of anti-German combinations in Europe. In anti-Semitism Hitler and the Nazis found the well-nigh perfect weapon, combining the strength of mass working-class support with intellectual and upper- and mid-

---

[1] *Ibid.*

[2] Georg von Schoenerer (1842–1921), Austrian politician and writer.

[3] Karl Lueger (1844–1910), controversial Austrian politician of uncertain affiliation.

[4] Édouard Drumont (1844–1917), French writer and deputy.

[5] Hilaire Belloc (1870–1953), British writer, poet and historian.

[6] *Annual Register*, 1910, p. 25.

[7] Anton Drexler (1884–1942), German locksmith, founder of what was to become the Nazi Party.

[8] Erich Ludendorff (1865–1937), German general, famous for his victories in the First World War.

[9] *The World in the Making* by H. Keyserling. Hermann Keyserling (1880–1946) was of aristocratic origin and had been greatly influenced by Houston Chamberlain.

[10] Julius Streicher (1885–1946), German propagandist and pornographer.

[11] Artur Moeller van der Bruck (1876–1925), German writer and thinker, chiefly remembered for *Das Dritte Reich*.

dle-class prejudices, with which to attack and destroy the weak structure of German democracy.

The theories of race thus were spread through many lands, though flourishing most strongly in Germany. The apostles of race could be found among all classes of men, in conditions of economic strength and of economic weakness. The theories derived strength from popular misinterpretation of important scientific discoveries and from resolution born of defeat. The desire for a pure Aryan race seems to have gained ground in Germany despite the defeat of 1918. Race theory embraced snippets of many different ideas; it was derived from nationalism, militarism, Darwinism, socialism, élitism and romanticism. Those who supported the theories ranged from pillars of society, like Milner,[1] to those who believed in a new form of social dynamism, like Hitler. The element of the irrational was very strong, as of course it needed to be, and thus belief continued for some long time after favourable evidence had ceased to exist. Perhaps examination of this subject may be concluded with one final example—despite widespread hostility to racial theory in the 1930s in Britain, Mosley[2] was able to suggest (and expect the public to believe) that "We have created the Empire without race mixture or pollution... It should only be necessary by education and propaganda to teach the British that racial mixtures are bad."[3] In the same pamphlet he also asserted that it would become necessary to breed children in order to protect the national interest. Race theory was by no means just *"le vice allemand"* as so many of the post-war generation would like to think.

Paul Hayes. *Fascism*. New York: The Free Press, 1973.

---

[1] First Viscount Milner (1854–1925), English politician.

[2] Sir Oswald Mosley (1896–), English politician of changeable political views.

[3] *Fascism: 100 Questions, No. 93*, by Sir O. Mosley. His views on birth control are given in the answer to Question 76.

The Nazi Fuehrerprinzip: A Weberian Analysis

Paul Brooker

PAUL BROOKER *is a professor at the University of Canterbury, New Zealand.*

The popular image of Nazi ideology tends to overlook some ideological social concepts which had a major effect on the Nazi regime's domestic policies. Perhaps the most important of these concepts was that of *Volksgemeinschaft*, or "community of the *Volk*," which was an example of what Durkheim described as mechanical solidarity.[1] But another important ideological concept was that of the *Fuehrerprinzip*, or "leader principle," which unfortunately has been given only slight attention in many of the modern works in English on the Nazi regime. What I shall be attempting to do in this paper is, firstly, to give some insight into the nature of the Nazi *Fuehrerprinzip* and the degree to which the Nazi regime propagated it throughout German society. (I shall be dealing only peripherally with the complicated question of the extent to which outward conformity to the norms of the *Fuehrerprinzip* was matched by an inner acceptance of the principle.) Secondly, as it clearly involves a theory of legitimacy, I shall attempt to analyse the *Fuehrerprinzip* in terms of Weber's traditional-charismatic-legal typology of legitimacy.

The *Fuehrerprinzip*

The Nazi party ideologists regarded the *Fuehrerprinzip* as representing, like the ideo-logical concept of the *Volksgemeinschaft*, an attack upon the nature of modern society as it had been displayed under the Weimar Republic. Just as the spiritual *Volksgemeinschaft* stood opposed to the rootless, egotistical individualism and the materialist class struggle of Weimar society, so the *Fuehrerprinzip* stood opposed to the anonymity and lack of personal responsibility characteristic of Weimar society's parliamentary and bureaucratic forms of politics and administration.

There are definite similarities in this attack to some of the criticisms Weber had made in newspaper articles in 1917 of the workings of the monarchical-bureaucratic regime which had preceded the Weimar Republic. Weber argued that for all its famous administrative expertise the state bureaucracy lacked a sense of direction, which could be provided only by a political leader who, on condition that he was given the degree of personal authority which he needed, would accept personal responsibility for the direction in which he led the state. Weber admitted that the bureaucratic official often made independent decisions and showed organisational imagination but he argued that the official's responsibility was of a different kind; it was bound up with the ethos of *office* which obligated him to carry out even those directives he considered wrong as if they "corresponded to his innermost conviction."[2] At the time that he wrote, Weber believed that these political leaders, whom he refers to as "plebiscitary" leaders, could be

---

[1] P.A.M. Brooker. *A Durkheimian Theory of Fascism: Germany, Italy and Japan.* (Unpublished Oxford University D.Phil Thesis. 1983). pp. 5–8.

[2] M. Weber, *Economy and Society*, Vol III (New York, Bedminster Press, 1968). Appendix II, pp. 1403–1405.

produced by parliament, as Lloyd George had been in Britain, but a few weeks' experience of the first German post-wa. democratic parliament and its economic horse-trading convinced him that a directly elected President with extensive powers offered the only hope for Germany of creating a plebiscitary democracy[1]—a type of democracy which is described by Weber in his sociological theorising as one where "democracy is combined with an important role of leadership" to form what he calls a *Fuehrerdemokratie*.[2]

The National Socialist critique, however, went beyond attacking the parliamentary democracy of the Weimar Republic and its inability to give direction to the bureaucracy. The Nazis also argued that bureaucratic administration and the secret ballot of even a plebiscitary democracy ensured that the great mass of administrators and citizens both escaped from the burdens and were denied the privileges of personal responsibility. The *Fuehrerprinzip* sought a massive quantitative expansion of leadership roles in society and, in so far as it clashed with the contrasting administrative principle of bureaucratic authority, it clashed with Weber's argument that modern bureaucracy was the most appropriate means for administrating an industrialised society. The Nazi belief that the impersonal, office-based and rule-governed bureaucratic authority should be replaced at all levels of administration by the personal responsibility of a (sub-) leadership role, one which in Hitler's words allowed "unconditional authority and freedom of action downward, but...unlimited responsibility upward" would have appeared quite incongruous to Weber.[3]

This is not to say that he would have found the Nazi conception of Hitler's position as political *Fuehrer* any more satisfactory—significantly, the term used by legal experts and

other propagandists to describe the Nazi regime was *Fuehrerstaat* not *Fuehrerdemokratie*. Hitler certainly received all of the powers necessary to lead the German state and people in whichever direction he chose. His claim to "the pre- and extragovernmental, even supragovernmental, powers personified by the 'Leader' as the carrier of the historic mission of National Socialism" was reflected in his position as supreme legislator, supreme administrator and supreme judge.[4] These powers were buttressed by a personal oath of obedience to "Adolf Hitler, *Fuehrer* of the German Reich and people" demanded from all soldiers, cabinet ministers, civil servants and judges.[5] His word was regarded quite literally as law by legal experts—"Even his speeches were considered as binding sources of legislation and had the force of law when deemed expedient."[6] Although Hitler's claim to be the representative of the German people was used by legal theorists as the justification for his supra-constitutional powers, there was no mention of any means, such as elections, by which this relationship was to be periodically confirmed or indeed through which his personal responsibility for failure could result in the revocation of his powers. He was apparently *Fuehrer* for life. When the outbreak of war turned his mind to the question of the succession to his position as *Fuehrer*, he simply designated Goering as his first successor and Hess as his second successor. Admittedly, plebiscites were used by Hitler but, with the exception of the referendum of 19 August 1934 on the law combining the newly vacant office of President with Hitler's office of Chancellor to form the novel legal office of "*Fuehrer* and Chancellor" (reduced to just "*Fuehrer*" in July 1939), they were linked to foreign policy issues that allowed the people's patriotism to be exploited. Thus the 12 November 1933 election

[1] D. Beetham, *Max Weber and the Theory of Modern Politics*, (London. George Allen and Unwin. 1974), pp. 232–237.

[2] M. Weber, *The Theory of Social and Economic Organisation*, (New York, The Free Press, 1964), pp. 387–388 and 389, note 61.

[3] Adolf Hitler, *Mein Kampf*, (London, Hutchinson. 1974), p. 543.

[4] K.D. Bracher. *The German Dictatorship*. (Harmondsworth, England. Penguin Books. 1978). p. 424.

[5] F. Neumann *Behemoth*. (London, Victor Gollancz 1942). p. 25. Bracher. *The German Dictatorship* p. 428.

[6] Bracher. *The German Dictatorship*. p. 428.

of a new *Reichstag* on the basis of accepting or rejecting "The *Fuehrer's* List" of candidates, the first occasion on which Hitler could claim direct plebiscitary backing rather than just leadership of the majority party in a governing coalition, was coupled with the issue of Germany's withdrawal from the League of Nations. However, the essential point is that "experts all agree that the Leader is not bound by the popular decision. 'Even if the voting public turns against him, he remains the one who represents the objective mission of the people.'"[1]

In seeking to apply the *Fuehrerprinzip* to the rest of German society, the Nazi party was able to use its own organisation as a model of a huge pyramid of sub-leaders (each layer of leaders appointing their trusted personal followers to leadership positions in the level below) exercising delegated functional or territorial authority from Reich level down to that of the street block leader—in 1935 there were nearly 300,000 territorial sub-leaders alone. This pattern was duplicated in organisations affiliated with the party or under its direct influence. The National Socialist Women's League (N.S. *Frauenschaft*), the German Labour Front (DAF) and the National Socialist People's (NSV) were all multi-million-member organisations (the DAF had some 25 million members) with a leadership structure extending down to the block level. The dozen or more other affiliates did not extend down to the local territorial level but demonstrated the *Fuehrerprinzip* to the various professions in their care, e.g. teaching, the civil service, law. The leader principle was experienced by youth in the compulsory Hitler Youth (HJ) and Reich Labour Service (RAD) and in the National Socialist League of German Students (NSDStB). Although both the Hitler Youth, after 1935, and the RAD were officially state organisations, this did not prevent their being saturated with Nazi party doctrine and practice. Similarly, the Reich Food Estate was a compulsory *economic* or-

ganisation of all those engaged in food production and marketing but was strongly influenced by the party and was organised according to the *Fuehrerprinzip*, with a pyramid of delegated authority extending from the Reich leader appointed by Hitler to the local village leader. "The National Peasants" Leader delegates or "entrusts" "duties" to his inferior designees; these delegate or "entrust" duties to other inferior officers. At the bottom of the scale the peasant is "delegated" or "entrusted" the duties of cultivating the land to the maximum advantage of "the people."[2] Another new public organisation which used the *Fuehrerprinzip* as the basis of authority was the Reich Chamber of Culture. Subdivided into separate Chambers for music, art, theatre, literature, press, radio and film which extended down to regional and local levels, it was similar to the Reich Food Estate in demanding the compulsory membership (in this case as a means of ideological rather than economic control) of all engaged in producing or marketing its product. The officials of the Reich Chamber of Culture "are personally responsible to him [Goebbels, the Minister of Propaganda and Public Enlightenment] for the conduct of their offices, all the business and professional affairs over which each office has charge, and can be removed or overruled by him for any cause at any time as he may see fit. The same powers are conferred on each officer under him, so far as the authority of this delegated 'Leader' may extend as defined by decree."[3]

However, the Nazis, not surprisingly, ran into problems when trying to introduce the *Fuehrerprinzip* into one of the other components of Hitler's administrative staff, the civil service. The Nazi Minister of Interior, Frick, and the National Socialist League of Civil Servants wanted to use the *Fuehrerprinzip* to help fulfil their ambition of creating a Nazified civil service that would provide the National Socialist state with a leadership corps which would take on more responsible and creative

[1] Neumann, *Behemoth*, p. 52.

[2] R. A. Brady. *The Spirit and Structure of German Fascism*, (London, Victor Gollancz, 1937), p. 233.

[3] Brady. *The Spirit and Structure of German Fascism*, p. 90.

duties than had previously been allotted to the civil service. They hoped to create an "administration leader" by concentrating unconditionally on ability and introducing a more pragmatic and political training than the purely legal training which had always characterised the German civil service.[1] To give more scope for this administrative leadership there was a call for simultaneously decentralising and concentrating the control of the specialist state departments by subordinating all of them to the head of the Interior administration at each level of state authority (Reich, *Laender*, provinces, *Regierungsbezirke* and *Landkreise*). This ambitious programme never made any progress against the weight of bureaucratic resistance and in the absence of the support from Hitler which would have been necessary to overcome this resistance. For all of Hitler's emphasis on the "leadership of men," rather than the administration of rules, and his desire for a "government without administration,"[2] in practice he was not enthusiastic about any sweeping and therefore disruptive reorganisation of the civil service. The party faithful had to be content instead with introducing the *Fuehrerprinzip* into the 51,000 municipalities by replacing local self-government with an appointed mayor—appointed jointly by state and party—as the solely responsible "leader" of his community.

Nevertheless, the *Fuehrerprinzip* still played an important role as an ideological symbol in the internal disputes which bedevilled the Nazi civil service. There are some interesting examples of this role in the dozen or so references to the "Fuehrer principle" to be found in Peterson's Reich-to-village sample of Hitler's administration. In trying just to maintain the status quo in the position of the Interior administration versus the established specialist state departments and the plethora of new agencies being created by Hitler, Frick had to

resort to "Using the NS slogan of the Fuehrer principle, i.e. one person with full command and responsibility," and his State Secretary tried "hiding behind the sacred 'Fuehrer principle'" when requesting at a meeting of Reich State Secretaries from other departments that Reich ministries stop taking over the specialist departments of the *Laender*, the former constituent states of the formerly federal Reich.[3] The *Fuehrerprinzip* was also used to justify suggestions for a decentralisation of power within the Interior administration down to the regional level, where it tended to be dominated by the party's regional boss, the *Gauleiter*. One of them argued that the state should follow the party model of emphasising the role of regional leaders, who had close contact with the people, and so ensure the dominance of the "Germanic Fuehrer principle" rather than the "Roman bureaucratic principle."[4] The *Fuehrerprinzip* could, though, provide protection for the state bureaucrat against party intervention. "A part of the Nazi ideology assisted the bureaucrat trying to avoid publicity; the Fuehrer principle meant that one should obey one's superior, i.e. bureaucrat, and not the party."[5] And even an opponent of the regime, actively trying to sabotage the Nazi cause, "was aided by the 'Fuehrer principle' supposed to be used in the new order. His powers as school superintendent were nearly dictatorial."[6]

The propagation of the *Fuehrerprinzip* beyond the boundaries of Hitler's administrative staff and into that "private" sphere where leaders would not be appointed by Hitler or by one of his sub-leaders met with a similar mixture of success and failure.

Big business was able to blunt some of the more radical applications of the *Fuehrerprinzip* to its organizations. The most important victory was keeping the *Fuehrerprinzip* out of the business equivalent of the civil service bureau-

[1] Broszat. *The Hitler State*, pp. 241–242.

[2] H. Mommsen. "National Socialism: Continuity and Change." in W. Laqueur (ed). *Fascism: A Reader's Guide*, (Harmondsworth, England, Penguin Books, 1979). p. 176.

[3] E.N. Peterson. *The Limits of Hitler's Power*. (Princeton, New Jersey, Princeton University Press. 1969), p. 107. p. 109.

[4] Peterson. *The Limits of Hitler's Power*, p. 111.

[5] Peterson. *The Limits of Hitler's Power*. p. 440.

[6] Peterson. *The Limits of Hitler's Power*. p. 371.

cracy. The clerical staff of German firms had been modelled on the Prussian civil service, to the extent that these non-manual employees liked to refer to themselves as *Privatbeamten*, "private civil servants," and during the Nazi era there doesn't appear to have been any greater capitulation to the *Fuehrerprinzip* in these private bureaucracies than there was in the public civil service. The heads of businesses, though, were in a more vulnerable position when they tried to resist an ideological attempt to turn them into a sort of business *Fuehrer*. If they did not publicly adopt *Fuehrer* roles, it would appear that the application of the *Fuehrerprinzip* stopped at the boundary of the business sector, which would represent not only a source of frustration for the Nazi ideologists but also a blow to the regime's pretence to have created a unified, Nazified German society. Even so, concessions could still be won by businessmen.[1] While having to accept the introduction of the *Fuehrerprinzip* into the complicated array of national groups and chambers of industry set up by the Nazi regime as the supposedly autonomous political organisation of German business, representatives of big business were able to veto the provisions of a draft law of 1934 which sought to introduce the *Fuehrerprinzip* into the running of big corporations by excluding the shareholders from executive responsibilities and by demanding that the president of the board of directors should also exercise the role of managing director. The battle was rejoined in 1937 over another draft law on business corporations which the Academy of German Law, for one, hoped would introduce the *Fuehrerprinzip*—albeit in the shape of an elected (presumably by the shareholders) rather than an appointed leader. The eventual law did not go so far and was content with strengthening the position of the board of directors against the mass of "irresponsible shareholders."[2]

If the ideologists were unable to force the shareholder-director-manager relationship into the *Fuehrer* mould, they had more success with the employer-employee relation. The Law for the Ordering of National Labour of 1934 decreed that the individual plant was to be the basic unit of industrial relations and subdivided this "plant community" (*Betriebsgemeinschaft*) into leader (*Betriebsfuehrer*), the employer, and "followers" or "retinue" (*Gefolgschaft*), his employees. "This was the economic translation of the Führerprinzip (leader principle) dear to the party's ideologists and a derivative of their antipathy to the divided responsibilities and authority of modern industrial organisation."[3] The working day now began with a military-style parade of both manual and non-manual workers which included singing a Nazi or patriotic song, raising the German flag and perhaps listening to a short speech by the *Betriebsfuehrer*.[4] The ceremony was obviously aimed at personalising the employer's authority and giving him a brief opportunity to display his leadership qualities. Although these early morning ceremonies may have proved irksome to the owner or manager deemed leader of the plant, his formal control over his employees was significantly extended by the new leader-follower conception of industrial relations. Section 2 of the National Socialist Charter of Labour declared: "The leader of the plant de-

---

[1] Neumann, *Behemoth*, pp. 197–201, p. 236. Schoenbaum, *Hitler's Social Revolution*. pp. 124–125.

[2] On the other hand, big business could not prevent the more gradual but also fundamental campaign begun in 1934 to convert the anonymous joint stock company owned by numerous shareholders into the more personal form of ownership represented by partnership or sole proprietorship. By 1940 nearly two thousand joint stock companies and more than eighteen thousand limited liability companies had made the change, whether encouraged by tax concessions, forced by legal restrictions on the minimum size of shareholdings and joint stock companies or persuaded by propaganda.

[3] Schoenbaum, *Hitler's Social Revolution*. p. 86.

[4] T. W. Mason. *National Socialist Policies Toward the German Working Classes,*. 1925–1939. (Unpublished Oxford University D.Phil. Thesis, 1971) p. 122.

cides as against the followers in all matters pertaining to the plant in so far as they are regulated by statute. He shall look after the well-being of the followers, while the latter shall keep faith with him, based on the plant community."[1] Nazi propagandists laid great stress on the fact that the relationship between plant leader and follower was a "Germanic" relationship of faith, honour and care, not a "Romanistic" materialistic labour contract which treated labour as a commodity. But in reality the official interpretation of the leader's moral obligation, as demanded by his sense of "honour," to care for his followers did not impose any new burdens not already demanded by Weimar labour law, while the official interpretation of the follower's obligation to keep faith with his leader was so open-ended that even that minimum of protection afforded by simply the rational, rights-duties *form* of a labour contract would have been welcomed by workers.[2]

Among the other "private" rather than "staff" organisations were the host of occupational or leisure groups which, in many cases enthusiastically, aligned themselves with the Nazi regime and its ideology. One of the more obvious ways of doing so was by adopting the *Fuehrerprinzip* as the basis for running the association. As in the example of the German Mathematical Association, the leader was usually elected by the membership. In September 1933 its President stated in his address: "But we also know that even in a merely advisory capacity, we are in a position to be heard only if in external matters, too, we adapt ourselves to the demands of the movement. Hence, we decided to submit these three points for your approval: 1. The leadership principle. You are to elect a leader, who is to bear the sole responsibility. 2. The leader then is to appoint his assistants, and especially the members of a leader's council... 3. The Association's board

is to be dissolved. It is the prerogative of the leader to organise that institution in a new form..."[3]

The most important of these associations, however, were the Churches and though the Catholic Church resisted Nazi influences, the desire of many Protestants for a Reich Bishop seems to have been directly related to the public prominence being given to the *Fuehrerprinzip*. These Protestants were favourably disposed to Nazi-backed plans for the creation of a unified Protestant Church under the authority of a Reich Bishop and an array of provincial bishops. "The argument used [within the churches] was that the church needed spiritual leaders in authority and not mere administrators, but it is difficult to believe that the demand for bishops was not also inspired by the *Führerprinzip* (the Führer model) prevalent in politics."[4] In fact, the argument for spiritual *leaders* instead of *administrators* was itself an application of the *Fuehrerprinzip* to the religious sphere. What is particularly interesting is that this new proposed leadership structure and the accompanying hostility to "parliamentism" in church administration were supported not only by the avowed Nazi sympathizers in the church, who called themselves the "German Christians," but also by what might be termed "orthodox Christians"—"there was a general feeling, especially among young theologians, that a new era had dawned which offered great opportunities after a long period of retreat. If the church were to reap the harvest it needed to be open to new ideas and new men."[5] But the ambitious plan was never fulfilled in practice, as the doctrinal indiscretions of the radicals among the "German Christians" inspired a resistance to change among more conservative Protestants. Hitler refused to support the radicals against this resistance and so, although a Reich Bishop was actually

---

[1] Neumann. *Behemoth.* p. 343.

[2] Neumann, *Behemoth.* pp. 342–344. There were labour courts established to ensure that leaders and followers did not violate their honour by, respectively, exploitation or disloyalty but these courts were basically propaganda devices and offered no real protection for employees.

[3] J. Remak (ed). *The Nazi Years: A Documentary History* (Englewood Cliffs, New Jersey, Prentice-Hall. 1969). p. 56.

[4] J.R.C. Wright. *"Above Parties": The Political Attitudes of the German Protestant Church Leadership 1918–1933.* (Oxford, Oxford University Press. 1974). p. 120.

[5] Wright. *"Above Parties,"* p. 120.

elected in September 1933, by the end of 1935 he was ignored by everyone, including the Nazis themselves.

Therefore, even leaving aside the special case of the army's autonomy from Nazism, the ideological campaign to spread the *Fuehrerprinzip* throughout German society ran into political difficulties when dealing with the civil service, big business and the churches. Hitler was prepared to allow other factors, such as short-term administrative effectiveness or popular support, to overrule the ambitions of Nazi ideologists. Nevertheless, these limitations should not obscure the successes of the campaign to propagate the *Fuehrerprinzip*. Millions of Germans now had the opportunity to experience the personal responsibility and absolutism of a *Fuehrer*. "Germany had become a nation of leaders. Although all had to obey, many could at least also give orders somewhere, could share in the leader principle..."[1]

Paul Brooker. "The Nazi Fuehrerprinzip: A Weberian Analysis." *Political Science.* 37 (1985): 50–58.

---

[1] Bracher. *The German Dictatorship*, p. 433.

Part IX

Anarchism

PETER KROPOTKIN

As an ideology, anarchism stands alone in that it is impossible for it to be implemented. Yet this has not discouraged able minds from sketching its implications, thereby giving form to its utopian dream. Even those persons who have not felt moved by the dream of the anarchist have nonetheless felt indebted to the dream for forcing them to clarify and sharpen their own political intuitions.

Like John Locke before him, William Godwin the anarchist recognizes the significance to a political philosophy of the institution of property-keeping. For this reason, he subjects the institution to analysis, recognizing three degrees of property: the permanent right to things which, being vested in one person, result in a greater sum of benefit than would have resulted from their being otherwise appropriated; the entitlement each person has to the produce of his own industry; and, the system of disposing of another man's industry.

Godwin distinguishes between the first two of these and the last, the former being beneficial and the latter being perverse and destructive. Furthermore, he openly acknowledges the connection between property and positive law. In rounding out his discussion, Godwin curiously ties the institution of property to the indefeasible right of private judgement, a right which he alleges is the first object of government. Godwin would thus seem to take us in a libertarian direction.

Almost a full century after Godwin, there appeared in Russia another anarchist, Peter Kropotkin. In words that are more scathing and uncompromising than those of his predecessor, Kropotkin mounts a bold attack upon the state and its laws, particularly the laws dealing with property. He maintains that law,

rather than being a compendium of customs for the preservation of society, is but an instrument for the continuance of the exploitation and domination of the toiling masses. Dividing laws into those dealing with the protection of property, persons, and government, he says half of the laws deal with the first of these three categories. He proceeds, in the name of anarchism, to criticize sweepingly all of these types of law, advocating in their place liberty, equality, and practical human sympathy.

In an effective essay, A. Bradney presents an overview of Kropotkin's anarchistic ideas as they pertain to law. He indicates that Kropotkin draws a distinction between customary and written law, viewing the former as encapsulating the irreducible minimum of ways of acting necessary for social life and the latter as providing tools of domination. Whereas the former support mutual aid, the latter support mutual suspicion. And as Bradney reads Kropotkin, mutual aid in turn supports individual self-assertion, whereas mutual suspicion supports egoistical individualism. Bradney correctly points out that Kropotkin favours individual self-assertion rather than egoistical individualism, but he calls upon Kropotkin to explain the difference between these kinds of individualism.

Richard Falk picks up some of the threads running throughout Godwin and Kropotkin, and then asks three questions of anarchists. First, are not the preconditions for anarchist success insurmountable? Second, isn't the anarchist prospect too remote in time? Third, does the receptivity of anarchism to violence undermine the moral basis of its claim to provide an ideology for global reform? These questions are central to his discussion of the erosion of the state-system.

There is a logical tension in anarchists' writings in their ideas on the state and the individual, on the proper view of human nature as social or autonomous, on desirable and undesirable individualism, and on liberty and authority. Moreover, this tension is not simply between one anarchist and another but is intrinsic to the writings of particular anarchists. Still, it would be regrettable and shortsighted of us to dismiss anarchists. Two things support this claim: first, the fact that anarchism has demonstrated a staying power even during difficult times, and second, the burgeoning demographic and ecological problems besetting mankind that are not being met by less extreme philosophies and ideologies. The following essays should capture our attention for these reasons alone.

Of Property

William Godwin

WILLIAM GODWIN (1756–1836) was born in
England and was both a libertarian and anarchist
who argued against the tyranny of tradition and
authority. Central to his ideas was his attack upon
the institution of property. His ideas are most
clearly expressed in Enquiry Concerning
Political Justice.

Principles of Property

Having considered at large the question of
the person entitled to the use of the means of
benefit or pleasure, it is time that we proceed
to the second question, of the person, in
whose hands the preservation and distribution of any of these means, will be most justly
and beneficially vested...

Of property there are three degrees.

The first and simplest degree, is that of my
permanent right in those things, the use of
which being attributed to me, a greater sum of
benefit or pleasure will result, than could have
arisen from their being otherwise appropriated. It is of no consequence, in this case, how
I came into possession of them, the only necessary conditions being, their superior usefulness to me, and that my title to them is such as
is generally acquiesced in, by the community
in which I live. Every man is unjust, who conducts himself in such a manner respecting
these things, as to infringe, in any degree,
upon my power of using them, at the time
when the using them will be of real importance to me.

It has already appeared[1] that one of the
most essential of the rights of man, is my right
to the forbearance of others; not merely that
they shall refrain from everything that may, by
direct consequence, affect my life, or the pos-

session of my powers, but that they shall refrain from usurping upon my understanding,
and shall leave me a certain equal sphere for
the exercise of my private judgement. This is
necessary, because it is possible for them to be
wrong, as well as for me to be so, because the
exercise of the understanding is essential to
the improvement of man, and because the
pain and interruption I suffer, are as real,
when they infringe, in my conception only,
upon what is of importance to me, as if the
infringement had been, in the utmost degree,
palpable. Hence it follows, that no man may,
in ordinary cases, make use of my apartment,
furniture or garments, or of my food, in the
way of barter or loan, without having first obtained my consent.

The second degree of property, is the empire to which every man is entitled, over the
produce of his own industry, even that part of
it the use of which ought not to be appropriated to himself. It has been repeatedly shown
that all the rights of man which are of this
description, are passive.[2] He has no right of
option in the disposal of anything which may
fall into his hands. Every shilling of his property, and even every, the minutest, exertion of
his powers, have received their destination
from the decrees of justice. He is only the
steward. But still he is the steward. These
things must be trusted to his award, checked
only by the censorial power that is vested, in
the general sense, and favourable or un-
favourable opinion, of that portion of mankind among whom he resides. Man is
changed, from the capable subject of illimit-
able excellence, into the vilest and most despi-
cable thing that imagination can conceive,
when he is restrained from acting upon the

---

[1] II. v and vi. [Ed. note: Godwin refers here to Book II, Chapters V and VI wherein he discusses rights and the right of
private judgement.]

[2] II. v.

dictates of his understanding. All men cannot individually be entitled to exercise compulsion on each other, for this would produce universal anarchy. All men cannot collectively be entitled to exercise unbounded compulsion, for this would produce universal slavery: the interference of government, however impartially vested, is, no doubt, only to be resorted to, upon occasions of rare occurrence, and indispensable urgency.

It will readily be perceived, that this second species of property, is in a less rigorous sense fundamental, than the first. It is, in one point of view, a sort of usurpation. It vests in me the preservation and dispensing of that, which in point of complete and absolute right belongs to you.

The third degree of property, is that which occupies the most vigilant attention in the civilized states of Europe. It is a system, in whatever manner established, by which one man enters into the faculty of disposing of the produce of another man's industry. There is scarcely any species of wealth, expenditure or splendour, existing in any civilized country, that is not, in some way, produced, by the express manual labour, and corporeal industry, of the inhabitants of that country. The spontaneous productions of the earth are few, and contribute little to wealth, expenditure or splendour. Every man may calculate, in every glass of wine he drinks, and every ornament he annexes to his person, how many individuals have been condemned to slavery and sweat, incessant drudgery, unwholesome food, continual hardships, deplorable ignorance, and brutal insensibility, that he may be supplied with these luxuries. It is a gross imposition, that men are accustomed to put upon themselves, when they talk of the property bequeathed to them by their ancestors. The property is produced by the daily labour of men who are now in existence. All that their ancestors bequeathed to them, was a mouldy patent, which they show, as a title to extort from their neighbours what the labour of those neighbours has produced.

It is clear therefore that the third species of property, is in direct contradiction to the second.

The most desirable state of human society would require, that the quantity of manual labour and corporeal industry to be exerted, and particularly that part of it which is not the uninfluenced choice of our own judgement, but is imposed upon each individual by the necessity of his affairs, should be reduced within as narrow limits as possible. For any man to enjoy the most trivial accommodation, while, at the same time, a similar accommodation is not accessible to every other member of the community, is, absolutely speaking, wrong. All refinements of luxury, all inventions that tend to give employment to a great number of labouring hands, are directly adverse to the propagation of happiness. Every additional tax that is laid on, every new channel that is opened for the expenditure of the public money, unless it be compensated (which is scarcely ever the case) by an equivalent deduction from the luxuries of the rich, is so much added to the general stock of ignorance, drudgery and hardship. The country gentleman who, by levelling an eminence, or introducing a sheet of water into his park, finds work for hundreds of industrious poor, is the enemy, and not, as has commonly been imagined, the friend, of his species. Let us suppose that, in any country, there is now ten times as much industry and manual labour, as there was three centuries ago. Except so far as this is applied to maintain an increased population, it is expended in the more costly indulgences of the rich. Very little indeed is employed to increase the happiness or conveniences of the poor. They barely subsist at present, and they did as much at the remoter period of which we speak. Those who, by fraud or force, have usurped the power of buying and selling the labour of the great mass of the community, are sufficiently disposed to take care that they should never do more than subsist. An object of industry added to or taken from the general stock, produces a momentary difference, but things speedily fall back into their former state. If every labouring inhabitant of Great Britain were able and willing today to double the quantity of his industry, for a short time he would derive some advantage from the increased stock of commodities produced. But the rich would speedily discover the means of monopolizing this produce, as they had done the former. A small part of it only, could consist in commodities essential to the subsistence of man, or be fairly distributed through the community. All that is luxury and superfluity, would increase the accommodations of the rich, and perhaps, by reducing the price of luxuries, augment the number of those to whom such accommodations were accessible. But it would afford no alleviation to the great mass of the community. Its more favoured members would give their inferiors no greater wages for twenty hours' labour, suppose, than they now do for ten.

What reason is there then that this species of property should be respected? Because, ill as the system is, it will perhaps be found, that it is better than any other, which, by any means, except those of reason, the love of distinction, or the love of justice, can be substituted in its place. It is not easy to say whether misery or absurdity would be most conspicuous, in a plan which should invite every man to seize, upon everything he conceived himself to want. If, by positive institution, the property of every man were equalized today, without a contemporary change in men's dispositions and sentiments, it would become unequal tomorrow. The same evils would spring up with a rapid growth; and we should have gained nothing, by a project, which, while it violated every man's habits, and many men's inclinations, would render thousands miserable. We have already shown,[1] and shall have occasion to show more at large,[2] how pernicious the consequences would be, if government were to take the whole permanently into their hands, and dispense to every man his daily bread. It may even be suspected that agrarian laws, and others of a similar tendency, which have been invented for the purpose of keeping down the spirit of accumulation, deserve to be regarded, as remedies, more pernicious, than the disease they are intended to cure.[3]

An interesting question suggests itself in this stage of the discussion. How far is the idea of property to be considered as the off-spring of positive institution? The decision of this question may prove extremely essential to the point upon which we are engaged. The regulation of property by positive laws may be a very exceptionable means of reforming its present inequality, at the same time that an equal objection may by no means lie, against a proceeding, the object of which shall be merely to supersede positive laws, or such positive laws as are peculiarly exceptionable.

In pursuing this enquiry, it is necessary to institute a distinction, between such positive laws, or established practices (which are often found little less efficacious than laws), as are peculiar to certain ages and countries, and such laws or practices, as are common to all civilized communities, and may therefore be perhaps interwoven with the existence of society.

The idea of property, or permanent empire, in those things which ought to be applied to our personal use, and still more in the produce of our industry, unavoidably suggests the idea of some species of law or practice by which it is guaranteed. Without this, property could not exist. Yet we have endeavoured to show that the maintenance of these two kinds of property is highly beneficial. Let us consider the consequences that grow out of this position.

Every man should be urged to the performance of his duty, as much as possible, by the instigations of reason alone.[4] Compulsion to be exercised by one human being over another, whether individually, or in the name of the community, if in any case to be resorted to, is at least to be resorted to only in cases of indispensable urgency. It is not therefore to be called in, for the purpose of causing one individual to exert a little more, or another a little less, of productive industry. Neither is it to be called in, for the purpose of causing the industrious individual to make the precise distribution of his produce which he ought to make. Hence it follows that, while the present erroneous opinions and prejudices respecting ac-

---

[1] VI, viii, p. 237. [Ed. note: Book VI deals with Opinion As A Subject, and c. viii with National Education.]

[2] Ch. viii.

[3] VI. i, p. 224. [Ed. note: the subject of this is the Political Superintendence of Opinion.]

[4] II. vi; Book VII, *passim*. [Ed. note: Book VII deals with Crimes and Punishments.]

cumulation continue, actual accumulation will, in some degree, take place.

For, let it be observed that, not only no well-informed community will interfere with the quantity of any man's industry, or the disposal of its produce, but the members of every such well-informed community will exert themselves, to turn aside the purpose of any man who shall be inclined, to dictate to, or restrain, his neighbour in this respect.

The most destructive of all excesses, is that, where one man shall dictate to another, or undertake to compel him to do, or refrain from doing, anything (except, as was before stated, in cases of the most indispensable urgency), otherwise than with his own consent. Hence it follows that the distribution of wealth in every community, must be left to depend upon the sentiments of the individuals of that community. If, in any society, wealth be estimated at its true value, and accumulation and monopoly be regarded as the seals of mischief, injustice and dishonour, instead of being treated as titles to attention and deference, in that society the accommodations of human life will tend to their level, and the inequality of conditions will be destroyed.[1] A revolution of opinions is the only means of attaining to this inestimable benefit. Every attempt to effect this purpose by means of regulation, will probably be found ill conceived and abortive. Be this as it will, every attempt to correct the distribution of wealth by individual violence, is certainly to be regarded as hostile to the first principles of public security...

There is another circumstance necessary to be stated, by way of qualification to the preceding conclusion. Evils often exist in a community, which, though mere excrescences at first, at length become so incorporated with the principle of social existence, that they cannot suddenly be separated, without the risk of involving the most dreadful calamities... The inequalities of property perhaps constituted a state, through which it was at least necessary for us to pass, and which constituted the true original excitement to the unfolding the pow-

ers of the human mind. ... Yet, were they to be suddenly and instantly abolished, two evils would necessarily follow. First, the abrupt reduction of thousands to a condition, the reverse of that to which they had hitherto been accustomed, a condition, perhaps the most auspicious to human talent and felicity, but for which habit had wholly unfitted them, and which would be to them a continual source of dejection and suffering. It may be doubted, whether the genuine cause of reform ever demands, that, in its name, we should sentence whole classes of men to wretchedness. Secondly, an attempt abruptly to abolish practices, which had originally no apology to plead for their introduction, would be attended with as dreadful convulsions, and as melancholy a series of public calamities, as an attack upon the first principles of society itself. All the reasonings therefore, which were formerly adduced under the head of revolutions,[2] are applicable to the present case.

Having now accomplished what was last proposed,[3] and endeavoured to ascertain in what particulars the present system of property is to be considered as the capricious offspring of positive institution, let us return to the point which led us to that enquiry, the question concerning the degree of respect to which property in general is entitled. And here it is only necessary that we should recollect the principle in which the doctrine of property is founded, the sacred and indefeasible right of private judgement. There are but two objects for which government can rationally be conceived to have been originated: first, as a treasury of public wisdom, by which individuals might, in all cases, with advantage be directed, and which might actively lead us, with greater certainty, in the path of happiness: or, secondly, instead of being forward to act itself as an umpire, that the community might fill the humbler office of guardian of the rights of private judgement, and never interpose, but when one man appeared, in this respect, alarmingly to encroach upon another. All the arguments of this work have tended to

---

[1] Ch. i, [Ed. note: Here Godwin refers to c.i in Book VIII, which deals with Property.]

[2] IV. ii, [Ed. note: Book IV deals with The Operation of Opinion in Societies and Individuals, and c. ii with Revolutions.]

[3] [Ed. note: Godwin refers here to Book VIII which covers the Subject Property, and c. ii which touches the Principles of Property.]

that the latter, and not the former, is the true end of civil institution. The first idea of property then, is a deduction from the right of private judgement; the first object of government, is the preservation of this right. Without permitting to every man, to a considerable degree, the exercise of his own discretion, there can be no independence, no improvement, no virtue and no happiness. This is a privilege in the highest degree sacred; for its maintenance, no exertions and sacrifices can be too great. Thus deep is the foundation of the doctrine of property. It is, in the last resort, the palladium of all that ought to be dear to us, and must never be approached but with awe and veneration. He that seeks to loosen the hold of this principle upon our minds, and that would lead us to sanction any exceptions to it without the most deliberate and impartial consideration, however right may be his intentions, is, in that instance, an enemy to the whole. A condition indispensably necessary to every species of excellence, is security. Unless I can foresee, in a considerable degree, the treatment I shall receive from my species, and am able to predict, to a certain extent, what will be the limits of their irregularity and caprice, I can engage in no valuable undertaking. Civil society maintains a greater proportion of security among men, than can be found in the savage state: this is one of the reasons why, under the shade of civil society, arts have been invented, sciences perfected, and the nature of man, in his individual and relative capacity, gradually developed.

William Godwin. *Of Property*. Originally published in 1793.

Law and Authority

Peter Kropotkin

PETER KROPOTKIN *(1840–1921) was born into an aristocratic family in Russia. He eventually turned his back upon a promising military and academic career to explore his developing anarchistic ideas and attempt to put them into practice. His most famous writing was* Mutual Aid.

The protection of the person, which is put forward as the true mission of law, occupies an imperceptible space among them, for, in existing society, assaults upon the person directly dictated by hatred and brutality tend to disappear. Nowadays, if anyone is murdered, it is generally for the sake of robbing him; rarely because of personal vengeance. But if this class of crimes and misdemeanors is continually diminishing, we certainly do not owe the change to legislation. It is due to the growth of humanitarianism in our societies, to our increasingly social habits rather than to the prescriptions of our laws. Repeal tomorrow every law dealing with the protection of the person, and tomorrow stop all proceedings for assault, and the number of attempts dictated by personal vengeance and by brutality would not be augmented by one single instance.

It will perhaps be objected that during the last fifty years, a good many liberal laws have been enacted. But, if these laws are analyzed, it will be discovered that this liberal legislation consists in the repeal of the laws bequeathed to us by the barbarism of preceding centuries. Every liberal law, every radical program, may be summed up in these words,—abolition of laws grown irksome to the middle-class itself, and return and extension to all citizens of liberties enjoyed by the townships of the twelfth century. The abolition of capital punishment, trial by jury of all "crimes" (there was a more liberal jury in the twelfth century), the election of magistrates, the right of bringing public officials to trial, the abolition of standing armies, free instruction, etc., everything that is pointed out as an invention of modern liberalism, is but a return to the freedom which existed before church and king had laid hands upon every manifestation of human life.

Thus the protection of exploitation directly by laws on property, and indirectly by the maintenance of the State is both the spirit and the substance of our modern codes, and the one function of our costly legislative machinery. But it is time we gave up being satisfied with mere phrases, and learned to appreciate their real significance. The law, which on its first appearance presented itself as a compendium of customs useful for the preservation of society, is now perceived to be nothing but an instrument for the maintenance of exploitation and the domination of the toiling masses by rich idlers. At the present day its civilizing mission is *nil*; it has but one object,—to bolster up exploitation.

This is what is told us by history as to the development of law. Is it in virtue of this history that we are called upon to respect it? Certainly not. It has no more title to respect than capital, the fruit of pillage. And the first duty of the revolution will be to make a bonfire of all existing laws as it will of all titles to property.

IV

The millions of laws which exist for the regulation of humanity appear upon investigation to be divided into three principal categories: protection of property, protection of persons, protection of government. And by analyzing each of these three categories, we arrive at the same logical and necessary conclusion: *the uselessness and hurtfulness of law.*

Socialists know what is meant by protection of property. Laws on property are not made to guarantee either to the individual or to society the enjoyment of the produce of their own labor. On the contrary, they are made to rob the producer of a part of what he has created, and to secure to certain other people that portion of the produce which they have stolen either from the producer or from society as a whole. When, for example, the law establishes Mr. So-and-So's right to a house, it is not establishing his right to a cottage he has built for himself, or to a house he has erected with the help of some of his friends. In that case no one would have disputed his right. On the contrary, the law is establishing his right to a house which is not the product of his labor; first of all because he has had it built for him by others to whom he has not paid the full value of their work, and next because that house represents a social value which he could not have produced for himself. The law is establishing his right to what belongs to everybody in general and to nobody in particular. The same house built in the midst of Siberia would not have the value it possesses in a large town, and, as we know, that value arises from the labor of something like fifty generations of men who have built the town, beautified it, supplied it with water and gas, fine promenades, colleges, theatres, shops, railways, and roads leading in all directions. Thus, by recognizing the right of Mr. So-and-So to a particular house in Paris, London, or Rouen, the law is unjustly appropriating to him a certain portion of the produce of the labor of mankind in general. And it is precisely because this appropriation and all other forms of property bearing the same character are a crying injustice, that a whole arsenal of laws and a whole army of soldiers, policemen, and judges are needed to maintain it against the good sense and just feeling inherent in humanity.

Half our laws,—the civil code in each country,—serves no other purpose than to maintain this appropriation, this monopoly for the benefit of certain individuals against the whole of mankind. Three-fourths of the causes decided by the tribunals are nothing but quarrels between monopolists—two robbers disputing over their booty. And a great many of our criminal laws have the same object in view, their end being to keep the workman in a sub-ordinate position towards his employer, and thus afford security for exploitation.

As for guaranteeing the product of his labor to the producer, there are no laws which even attempt such a thing. It is so simple and natural, so much a part of the manners and customs of mankind, that law has not given it so much as a thought. Open brigandage, sword in hand, is no feature of our age. Neither does one workman ever come and dispute the produce of his labor with another. If they have a misunderstanding they settle it by calling in a third person, without having recourse to law. The only person who exacts from another what that other has produced, is the proprietor, who comes in and deducts the lion's share. As for humanity in general, it everywhere respects the right of each to what he has created, without the interposition of any special laws.

As all the laws about property which make up thick volumes of codes and are the delight of our lawyers have no other object than to protect the unjust appropriation of human labor by certain monopolists, there is no reason for their existence, and, on the day of the revolution, social revolutionists are thoroughly determined to put an end to them. Indeed, a bonfire might be made with perfect justice of all laws bearing upon the so-called "rights of property." All title-deeds, all registers, in a word, of all that is in any way connected with an institution which will soon be looked upon as a blot in the history of humanity, as humiliating as the slavery and serfdom of past ages.

The remarks just made upon laws concerning property are quite as applicable to the second category of laws; those for the maintenance of government, i.e., constitutional law.

It again is a complete arsenal of laws, decrees, ordinances, orders in council, and what not, all serving to protect the diverse forms of representative government, delegated or usurped, beneath which humanity is writhing. We know very well—anarchists have often enough pointed out in their perpetual criticism of the various forms of government—that the mission of all governments, monarchical, constitutional, or republican, is to protect and maintain by force the privileges of the classes in possession, the aristocracy, clergy, and traders. A good third of our laws—and each country possesses some tens of thousands of them—the fundamental laws on taxes, excise duties, the organization of ministerial departments and their offices, of the army, the police, the church, etc., have no other end than to maintain, patch up, and develop the administrative machine. And this machine in its turn serves almost entirely to protect the privileges of the possessing classes. Analyze all these laws, observe them in action day by day, and you will discover that not one is worth preserving.

About such laws there can be no two opinions. Not only anarchists, but more or less revolutionary radicals also, are agreed that the only use to be made of laws concerning the organization of government is to fling them into the fire.

The third category of law still remains to be considered; that relating to the protection of the person and the detection and prevention of "crime." This is the most important because most prejudices attach to it; because, if law enjoys a certain amount of consideration, it is in consequence of the belief that this species of law is absolutely indispensable to the maintenance of security in our societies. These are laws developed from the nucleus of customs useful to human communities, which have been turned to account by rulers to sanctify their own domination. The authority of the chiefs of tribes, of rich families in towns, and of the king, depended upon their judicial functions, and even down to the present day, whenever the necessity of government is spoken of, its function as supreme judge is the thing implied. "Without a government men would tear one another to pieces," argues the village orator. "The ultimate end of all government is to secure twelve honest jurymen to every accused person," said Burke.

Well, in spite of all the prejudices existing on this subject, it is quite time that anarchists should boldly declare this category of laws as useless and injurious as the preceding ones.

First of all, as to so-called "crimes"—assaults upon persons—it is well known that two-thirds, and often as many as three-fourths, of such "crimes" are instigated by the desire to obtain possession of someone's wealth. This immense class of so-called "crimes and misdemeanors" will disappear on the day on which private property ceases to exist. "But," it will be said, "there will always be brutes who will attempt the lives of their fellow citizens, who will lay their hands to a knife in every quarrel, and revenge the slightest offense by murder, if there are no laws to restrain and punishments to withhold them." This refrain is repeated every time the right of society to *punish* is called in question.

Yet there is one fact concerning this head which at the present time is thoroughly established; the severity of punishment does not diminish the amount of crime. Hang, and, if you like, quarter murderers, and the number of murders will not decrease by one. On the other hand, abolish the penalty of death, and there will not be one murder more; there will be fewer. Statistics prove it. But if the harvest is good, and bread cheap, and the weather fine, the number of murders immediately decreases. This again is proved by statistics. The amount of crime always augments and diminishes in proportion to the price of provisions and the state of the weather. Not that all murderers are actuated by hunger. That is not the case. But when the harvest is good, and provisions are at an obtainable price, and when the sun shines, men, lighter-hearted and less miserable than usual, do not give way to gloomy passions, do not from trivial motives plunge a knife into the bosom of a fellow creature.

Moreover, it is also a well known fact that the fear of punishment has never stopped a single murderer. He who kills his neighbor from revenge or misery does not reason much about consequences; and there have been few murderers who were not firmly convinced that they should escape prosecution.

Without speaking of a society in which a man will receive a better education, in which the development of all his faculties, and the possibility of exercising them, will procure him so many enjoyments that he will not seek to poison them by remorse—even in our society, even with those sad products of misery whom we see today in the public houses of great cities—on the day when no punishment is inflicted upon murderers, the number of murders will not be augmented by a single case. And it is extremely probable that it will be, on the contrary, diminished by all those cases which are due at present to habitual criminals, who have been brutalized in prisons.

We are continually being told of the benefits conferred by law, and the beneficial effect of penalties, but have the speakers ever attempted to strike a balance between the benefits attributed to laws and penalties, and the degrading effect of these penalties upon humanity? Only calculate all the evil passions awakened in mankind by the atrocious punishments formerly inflicted in our streets! Man is the cruelest animal upon earth. And who has pampered and developed the cruel instincts unknown, even among monkeys, if it is not the king, the judge, and the priests, armed with law, who caused flesh to be torn off in strips, boiling pitch to be poured into wounds, limbs to be dislocated, bones to be crushed, men to be sawn asunder to maintain their authority? Only estimate the torrent of depravity let loose in human society by the "informing" which is countenanced by judges, and paid in hard cash by governments, under pretext of assisting in the discovery of "crime." Only go into the jails and study what man becomes when he is deprived of freedom and shut up with other depraved beings, steeped in the vice and corruption which oozes from the very walls of our existing prisons. Only remember that the more these prisons are reformed, the more detestable they become. Our model modern penitentiaries are a hundredfold more abominable than the dungeons of the middle ages. Finally, consider what corruption, what depravity of mind is kept up among men by the idea of obedience, the very essence of law; of chastisement; of authority having the right to punish, to judge irrespective of our conscience and the esteem of our friends; of the necessity for executioners, jailers, and informers—in a word, by all the attributes of law and authority. Consider all this, and you will assuredly agree with us in saying that a law inflicting penalties is an abomination which should cease to exist.

Peoples without political organization, and therefore less depraved than ourselves, have perfectly understood that the man who is called "criminal" is simply unfortunate; that the remedy is not to flog him, to chain him up, or to kill him on the scaffold or in prison, but to help him by the most brotherly care, by treatment based on equality, by the usages of life among honest men. In the next revolution we hope that this cry will go forth:

> Burn the guillotines; demolish the prisons; drive away the judges, policemen and informers—the impurest race upon the face of the earth; treat as a brother the man who has been led by passion to do ill to his fellow; above all, take from the ignoble products of middle-class idleness the possibility of displaying their vices in attractive colors; and be sure that but few crimes will mar our society.

The main supports of crime are idleness, law and authority; laws about property, laws about government, laws about penalties and misdemeanors: and authority, which takes upon itself to manufacture these laws and to apply them.

No more laws! No more judges! Liberty, equality, and practical human sympathy are the only effectual barriers we can oppose to the anti-social instincts of certain among us.

Peter Kropotkin. "Law and Authority." Originally published in 1886.

Taking Law Less Seriously—An Anarchist Legal Theory

A. Bradney

A. BRADNEY *is Lecturer in Law at the University of Leicester, England.*

Kropotkin's theory of law

In analysing theories of law convention demands that discussion begins with a definition of law. In relation to Kropotkin this convention is of especial importance. On the one hand Kropotkin writes of law,

> The confused mass of rules of conduct called law...has taken the place of those stone monsters, before whom human victims used to be immolated, and whom slavish savages dared not even touch lest they should be slain by the thunderbolts of heaven.[1]

On the other hand he writes of "the masses,"

> [They had] their own social organization, which was based upon their own conceptions of equity, mutual aid, and mutual support—of common law, in a word...[2]

When investigating what he identifies as the three principal categories of law Kropotkin argues that "we arrive at the same logical and necessary conclusion: *the uselessness and hurtfulness of law*" (emphasis in the original)[3]. Despite this, in the same article, Kropotkin commends the "customary law" of primitive communities, "that suffices to maintain cordial relations between the inhabitants of the village, the members of the tribe or community." Kropotkin is it seems both irredeemably hostile to law and yet willing to promote it as a mechanism for maintaining social harmony. Can a definition of law explain this discordant approach?

Kropotkin's concept of law distinguishes between two forms, written law and customary law. The distinction between these two forms is conceived by reference to the history of the forms which points in turn to fundamental differences in the relationship between the forms and the people to whom they refer.

Kropotkin identifies customary law with anthropologist's descriptions of social life amongst primitive peoples and his own observations of such life in Siberia. He equates such law (which he sometimes refers to as common law) with social habits, "which are useful for the preservation of society and the propagation of the race." Although he writes that such habits are "anterior to all law" it is clear that he means by this that they are anterior to all written law. Customary law is "spontaneously developed by the very nature of things, like those habits in animals which men call instinct." Such law is not the result of individual innovation or creation. For each tribe it is "an infinite series of unwritten rules of propriety which are the fruit of their common experience."[4] Kropotkin observes that,

> Wherever we go we find the same sociable manners, the same spirit of solidarity. And when we endeavour to penetrate into the darkness of post ages, we find the same tribal life, the same associ-

---

[1] *Revolutionary Pamphlets*, p. 198. [Ed. note: The citation here is to the Pamphlets as edited by R. Baldwin (1970).]

[2] *Mutual Aid*, p. 114. [Ed. note: Bradney does not say which edition he is referring to.]

[3] *Revolutionary Pamphlets*, p. 212

[4] *Mutual Aid*. p. 111.

ations of men, however primitive, for mutual support.

Customary law is an expression of a general sense of the necessity for mutual aid.

...life in societies would be utterly impossible without a corresponding development of social feelings, and, especially, of a certain collective sense of justice growing to be a habit. If every individual was constantly abusing its personal advantages without others interfering in favour of the wronged, no society-life would be possible. And feelings of justice develop, more or less, with all gregarious animals.[1]

Customary law is thus a communal expression of a biological instinct found in all social animals. It relates to patterns of behaviour necessary for the continuance of society. Human beings do not obey such law, in the sense of having it imposed upon them either as law as such or as a rule in practice; rather they recognise and follow it. "His [the savage's] common law is his religion; it is his very habit of being."[2]

Part of Kropotkin's argument is the denial of the possibility of an individual alone, outside society. Humanity is a social species and a study of all social species of animal shows, *"the co-ordination of the individual will* with the will and purpose of the whole, and this co-ordination has already become an hereditary habit, i.e. an instinct."[3] The provenance of customary law is similar to, and evidenced by, the herd instinct of social animals. Customary law is the irreducible minimum of ways of acting necessary for social life; custom the penumbra of such ways of acting that differentiate one society from another.

Written law, in contrast, arises only at a particular point in the evolution of human societies. Customs and habits necessary for the preservation of societies are not the only ones that will arise in any society. They reflect only one side of human nature. "[T]wo sets of diametrically opposed feelings...exist in man."

Alongside the tendency to mutual aid there run, "feelings which induce man to subdue other men in order to utilize them for his individual ends."[4] Kropotkin argues that, "[t]he priest and the warrior," influenced by such desires, "have succeeded in imposing upon primitive societies customs advantageous to both of them."[5] Partially in consequence of this, "society becomes more and more divided into two hostile classes, one seeking to establish its domination, and the other struggling to escape..."

It is at this point that written law (which is not necessarily "written," this being a convenient short-hand word identifying the form) will rise. Written law does not represent simply "a collection of prescriptions serviceable to rulers" for, if it did, there would be some difficulty in the minority that are rulers ensuring the acceptance and obedience of the majority that are the ruled. Written law contains "confounded in one code, the two currents of custom,"

Its character is the skilful commingling of customs useful to society, customs which have no need of written law to insure respect, with other customs useful only to rulers, injurious to the mass of people, and maintained only by the fear of punishment.

"Do not kill," says the code, and hastens to add, "And pay tithes to the priests".

Such law is imposed upon the mass of people as much by deceit as to the nature of its content as by the imposition of sanction. Written law is however, no matter what the content of the particular rule, force.

The character of written law may not always be apparent. The presence of necessary social habits within the written law serves to disguise it. There is also a natural tendency to obedience, a

tendency to run in a groove... In children and all savages it attains striking proportions... Man, when he is at all superstitious, is always afraid to

---

[1] *Ibid.*, p. 58.
[2] *Mutual Aid.* p. 112.
[3] *Ethics.* pp. 64–65. [Ed. note: Bradney refers here to the edition (no date) translated by L.S. Friedland and J.R. Pizoshnikoff.]
[4] *Ibid.*, p. 22.
[5] *Revolutionary Pamphlets*, p. 203.

introduce any sort of change into existing conditions; he generally venerates what is ancient.[1]

Humanity, led by education, exhortation and individual inertia to move with the current that is law, never perceives the strength of that current.

The forms of law which Kropotkin describes are forms linked mainly by title. Upon close analysis customary law bears little relationship to the kind of law found in the municipal legal systems of modern, complex societies. Kropotkin's usage of the term "law" in reference to both forms is merely an acknowledgement of the historical success of efforts to confuse notions of the nature of the two.

Thus far Kropotkin's work is descriptive. However Kropotkin's purpose was not merely descriptive; with Marx, Kropotkin believed that the point was not merely to describe the world but to change it. There is therefore an ethical and evaluative side to his theory. His proposition is,

No more laws! No more judges! Liberty, equality, and practical human sympathy are the only effectual barriers we can oppose to the anti-social instincts of certain among us.[2]

This rejection is of written law in favour of customary law, "practical human sympathy," because it is the latter which contributes to, whilst the former detracts from, the continued evolution of humanity.

Although Kropotkin's conclusion is polemical the arguments he adduces for it are as rigorous as those he puts forward in his description of forms of law.

We come into this world as beings already endowed with the rudiments of morality; but we can become moral men only through the development of our moral rudiments...morality as the joint product of instinct, feeling, and reason exists only in man. It developed gradually, it is developing now, and will continue to grow.[3]

For Kropotkin written law's failing was that it had no place in this evolutionary process.

As an arithmetical matter Kropotkin saw most rules of law as being concerned with matters which encouraged individualism at the expense of society as a whole. The greatest single category of laws were those concerned with the protection of property. "...(A)ll the laws about property...have no other object than to protect the unjust appropriation of human labour by certain monopolists..."[4] Since people live within society their actions can rarely be broken down so as to ascribe purely individual responsibility; the manufacturer, whose inventive genius is seen to justify his large profit, relies on the abilities and efforts of his workers;[5] the owner of property in a city derives the value of that property from the fact of the life and work of those around. "The same house built in the midst of Siberia would not have the value it possesses in a large town."[6] Property laws ascribe to one that which is the result of the labour of many; they are a way of dividing the indivisible to the benefit of the few. As such they encourage not mutual aid but mutual suspicion.

Although many laws are plainly concerned with the protection of property a smaller number of legal rules in any society have no direct connection with property. Kropotkin classifies these laws as those being concerned with the protection of persons and those being concerned with the protection of government.

Despite the relatively small number of legal rules concerned with the protection of persons the category is, Kropotkin argues, of great importance. "[I]f law enjoys a certain amount of consideration, it is in consequence of the belief that this species of law is absolutely indispensable to the maintenance of security in our societies."[7] Kropotkin argues however that such laws are as "useless and injurious" as any

[1] *Ibid.*, p. 205.
[2] *Ibid.*, p. 218.
[3] *Ethics.* p. 252.
[4] *Revolutionary Pamphlets.* p. 43.
[5] *Ibid.*, p. 58.
[6] *Ibid.*, p. 213.
[7] *Ibid.*, pp. 214–215.

other example of written law. Most crimes, however their overt motivation, are caused by a desire for wealth. Therefore if the notion of property is abandoned such crimes will lose their *raison d'être*. A small residual number of offences may still exist when the motive for the crime is entirely unrelated to property. In relation to these offences Kropotkin observes that the reason for the criminal law is its power to punish. However, no evidence exists to show that punishment prevents crime. Kropotkin argues that the correct correlation to be drawn is between the crime-rate and the socio-economic conditions of the society. Violent crime will not occur if a society is so organised as to allow all its members an education and the facilities to develop their faculties to the full. Conversely, if the problem the criminal law is concerned with is cruelty and depravity, then is not the criminal law and the criminal justice system an example of just such cruelty and depravity?

> [C]onsider what corruption, what depravity of mind is kept up among men by the idea of obedience, the very essence of law; of chastisement; of authority having the right to punish, to judge irrespective of our conscience and the esteem of friends; of the necessity for executions, jailers and friends...[1]

The criminal law works by means of force and thus reinforces the very motivation which it is supposed to reform.

The final category of laws are those concerned with the protection of government. These can only be justified if the end of government is in itself good, but Kropotkin sees government as merely another example by which a small minority can subjugate the majority within society for their own ends. Thus the ends of all laws are in themselves undesirable.

The undesirable ends of law are perhaps less important for Kropotkin than the undesirable means. "...[W]e are so perverted by this existence under the ferrule of law...we shall lose all initiative, all habit of thinking for ourselves."[2] The form of written law encourages a tendency to unthinking obedience. As Kropotkin notes elsewhere, "[i]t is so easy to hang a man...and it relieves us of thinking of the causes of crime."[3] So, *mutatis mutandis*, with all laws. In the short term the spirit of mutual aid may be encouraged or discouraged by the socio-economic conditions of a society. In the long term the tendency to mutual aid must prevail. However law is ethically undesirable because, by discouraging habits of social awareness, it mitigates against the tendency to mutual aid. Written law is not an argument directing the population to the reasons for certain actions. Rather the law calls for immediate obedience and a willingness to disregard thought of self or others in favour of regard for law for its own sake.

The theory assessed

The strength of Kropotkin's theory depends on a number of different factors. Internal coherence is necessary but not sufficient for the theory to be correct. The theory must have an appropriate relationship with the reality which it purports to describe. However it would be naive to ask whether the theory is in accord with the various studies of law, human personalities and society, expecting that an answer which tended to the negative would invalidate the theory. Descriptions of the world, or a particular part of it, do not take place in a vacuum. Theories held, even if unconscious and ill-formed, help dictate vision. An analogy used by the American poet and literary critic Yvor Winters in a similar context illustrates the point.

> The breeders who devised the standard and created the breed, however, started with neither a perfect standard nor perfect specimens; they started with a general idea of what they wanted and a multiplicity of variously made specimens with which to begin their breeding. One improves one's understanding of the general by examining the particular; one improves the particular by referring to the general.[4]

So it is with theory and evidence. Theory

1 *Revolutionary Pamphlets*. p. 217.

2 *Ibid.*, p. 197.

3 *Ibid.*, p. 135.

4 Quoted in D. Davis *Wisdom and Wilderness* (1983), pp. 156–157.

informs evidence and evidence informs theory, each changing the other.

Seeing humanity as an animal species, Kropotkin argues that there is a tendency to mutual aid in the human species which is a part of the general history of evolution. This observation, however, runs counter to the usual perception that history, and therefore human nature, is a matter of competition and dispute. This common view, Kropotkin argues, is a matter not only of a partial reading of history but also a partial recording of history.

> Thousands of volumes have been written to record the acts of governments; the most trifling amelioration due to law has been recorded; its good effects have been exaggerated, its bad effects passed by in silence. But where is the book recording what has been achieved by the free co-operation of well-inspired men? [1]

Just as some have argued that the working-class, women, religious and ethnic minorities have been excluded from recorded history, so Kropotkin argues that examples of the co-operative inclinations of humanity have been excluded. A concentration on dispute has led to a misunderstanding of the place that dispute plays in society. What is at worst a perversion of human nature and at most a single facet of it has come to be regarded as the dominant characteristic.

Merely to allege a hidden history is not to prove it. However, in the latter half of this century, the evidence which Kropotkin did not provide has become increasingly available. Prompted by studies in social anthropology, sociologists and social anthropologists have looked at their own cultures with new eyes. The emergence, particularly in the USA, of urban anthropology has provided an impetus to the study of co-operative social networks within cultures.[2] Analysis of communities within cities has concentrated on the symbiotic links that lead to social coherence. The hidden history of mutual aid is not only the history of institutions like Trinity House,

where good works are done on the basis of co-operation rather than coercion, but also the discovery that people live much of their lives wholly within small social groups even when they are apparently full members of a complex society.[3] The state system of law can be seen as only one form of regulation in society. Moreover when these other forms are revealed it is clear that, as Kropotkin predicted, they do not reflect the coercive and divisive nature of written law. Thus, for example, in his study *Justice Without Law*, Auerbach argues of dispute settlement in the USA,

> Historically arbitration and mediation were the preferred alternatives. They expressed an ideology of communitarian justice without formal law, an equitable process based on reciprocal access and trust among community members.[4]

Auerbach's book is a study of various examples of just this spirit.

A simple denial of the notion of mutual aid on the basis of commonsense, historically derived notions of human nature may be, as Kropotkin suggests, illegitimate. However, this does not in itself support Kropotkin's thesis. The search for positive evidence to buttress his theory poses several difficulties. Firstly, even work which may produce evidence in support of Kropotkin's view has been done using different conceptual apparatus to that of Kropotkin. This necessitates adjusting terminology, and thus results, if that evidence is to be used. There are not inconsiderable intellectual dangers and difficulties involved in this process. Work can be used directly only on its own terms. What it has not said, it has not said. Even the most careful translation of terms may be regarded as, and may necessarily be, distorting. It is equally difficult to use work to support and to rebut arguments produced in different conceptual terms. Pursued to its ultimate logical conclusion all forms of scholarly argument become impossible when what one author said at one time cannot be used in connection with what another author said at a different time for fear that one disre-

---

[1] *Revolutionary Pamphlets.* p. 66.

[2] See, for example. R. Basham *Urban Anthropology* (1973).

[3] See, for example. K. Pryer *Endless Pressure* (1979).

[4] J. Auerbach *Justice Without Law* (1983), p. 4.

gards the nuances of language in both. Secondly, Kropotkin's thesis involves a wide range of argument. Evidence will tend to support not the thesis but parts of it. Finally, evidence must be taken from the various disciplines upon which Kropotkin's work touches. There are inherent in this process the dangers of eclecticism and arbitrariness. Pieces of work, wrenched out of context, may take on an apparent significance which they do not possess viewed in relation to the broad range of work in their area. Nevertheless, there are within modern scholarship a number of important pieces of work which may be taken to lend support to Kropotkin's views.

If Kropotkin's views on the nature of customary law and the character of the human species as animal are correct, then it is possible to deduce the conclusion that some form of customary law must be found amongst the species of social animals. If customary law constitutes a reflection of a minimum level of sociability, and if this sociability, this tendency to mutual aid, is common to all social animals, then something approximating to common law should be found amongst social animals. To this extent observations of social animals constitute a test of Kropotkin's speculations on human nature in general and his views on customary law in particular.

For many years animal behaviour was seen as a mechanical matter. Just as anthropologists had once described the behaviour of primitive peoples in terms of fixed patterns and predetermined reactions to the environment so animal behaviour was seen in the same way. Such descriptions did not allow for even the minimal degree of individuality demanded by Kropotkin's description of customary law. However, even when such views were at their most dominant, countervailing observations were made. Eugene Marais, both an ethologist and a lawyer, studied baboons in South Africa. During his observations he noted,

At first hazily and ill-defined, but later more clearly and more obviously we noticed in the ba-

boon troops "laws," "order," "government," "culture," or whatever we may wish to call that which more definitely distinguishes human from animal society.

...it is certain that without the observance of certain fixed "moral" laws they, the baboons, could not exist a week... The existence of the troop was possible only because of the observance of certain laws.[1]

Marais's perception of "law" and "government" amongst baboons was based upon an increasing awareness of the individuality of the animals, of their position as beings with personality and individual motivations. A general increase in the awareness of the degree of individuality amongst animals in a particular species has recently led to more sophisticated, though basically similar, observations. Thus, for example, Frans de Waal has concluded, on the basis of observations made at Burger's Zoo in Arnhem, that, amongst chimpanzees,

Every community develops its own social traditions. On the other hand, such variations always revolve around certain fundamental themes, which are characteristic for the species.[2]

and elsewhere that,

When Aristotle referred to man as a *political animal* he could not know just how near the mark he was. Our political activity seems to be a part of our evolutionary heritage we share with our close relatives.[3]

De Waal's observations of shifting power relations in a framework of accepted obligations seem to accord with Kropotkin's views. Nor is it possible to dismiss de Waal's work as an aberrant exception to the general trend within the field of ethology. Thomas Hinde, widely acknowledged as a leading figure in the field, reviewing de Waal's book, welcomed it as an example of a new trend producing results that would surprise some, though not all, ethologists. It was clear, he wrote, "that ethologists have often tended to underestimate the abilities of the animals they studied..."[4] On the basis of such evidence it is possible to argue that there is a biological ten-

---

[1]   E. Marais *My Friends the Baboons* (1975), p. 101.

[2]   F. de Waal *Chimpanzee Politics* (1982). p. 210.

[3]   de Waal *op. cit.* n 2 above, p. 211.

[4]   T. Hinde, "The Apes of Arnhem" (1982) *Times Literary Supplement*, p. 1124.

dency which produces a minimum form of social ordering common to all social animals including man and that within these relationships one sees the origins of law. From this one can go on to argue that any theory of law must take account of this genesis.

Evidence which will support Kropotkin's thesis about the origins of law supports only half of his argument. The other half is that concerned with the deleterious effects of written law. As has been seen Kropotkin's concern is not mainly with the direct prohibitive effects of law (although these are of consequence) but rather with the spirit that written law engenders within people. Law in creating patterns of obedience enhances what Erich Fromm termed "the fear of freedom." In his book of that title Fromm wrote that, "we are fascinated by the growth of freedom from powers *outside* ourselves and are blinded to the fact of *inner* restraints, compulsions, and fears..."[1] The feeling of powerlessness as an individual has as a corollary an ideology which dictates obedience to law and, indeed, all authority. This feeling is both encouraged and calmed by the notion that the determination of an individual's actions (and thus the responsibility for those actions) lies not in the individual themselves but in the imperatives of legal rules.

The immediate response to such a position as that above is that Kropotkin exaggerates both people's propensity to obedience and the harm that results from such obedience. However a series of experiments by Stanley Milgram appear to indicate that Kropotkin's arguments and conclusions are substantially correct. In Milgram's experiments volunteer subjects were led to believe that they were helping in investigations in the psychology of learning. An experimenter told subjects to read lists of paired words to a "victim." Single words were then read back to the "victim" who was required to respond with the correct paired word. Failure on the part of the "victim" to respond correctly meant that the subject had to give him an electric shock increasing in intensity from switches marked "Slight Shock" to those marked "Danger: Severe Shock" and finally those marked "XXX." The "victim" was a collaborator in the experiment, a professional actor, instructed to give wrong answers and to simulate pain and distress when "shocked." At higher levels of shock the "victims" would ask for the experiment to be terminated, talk of cardiac problems and eventually simulate death. The point at which the subject was unwilling to continue giving "shocks" to the "victim" varied according to the subject and the precise conditions of the experiment. In most experiments the mean average response of subjects was that they were willing to give shocks to the level of "Intense Shock" or "Extreme Intensity Shock." At this level the "victim" had already passed the stage of saying that he no longer wished to take part in the experiment and was giving screams of "agonised pain." In a number of cases subjects were willing to give the "victim" shocks up to and beyond the point where they believed the "victim" to be dead. Milgram says in conclusion that the difficulty in the experiment was finding a limit to obedience; in finding a point at which subjects would do not just what they were told but what they believed to be right. His conclusion was that,

A substantial proportion of people do what they are told, irrespective of the content of the act and without limitations of conscience, so long as they perceive that the command comes from legitimate authority.[2]

Law is of course an archetypal form of legitimate authority. Kropotkin's strictures thus seem well-supported by Milgram's experimental evidence.

The work quoted above is of course merely illustrative of parts of Kropotkin's thesis. A theory which has the compass that his does can neither be proved nor disproved in an essay of this form. However the work quoted is sufficient to suggest that Kropotkin's thesis is both serious and substantial enough to warrant further study.

---

[1] E. Fromm *The Fear of Freedom* (1960), p. 91.

[2] S. Milgram *Obedience to Authority* (1974), p. 189.

The strength of Kropotkin's thesis lies in his perception of the tendency that law has to create, in Bankowski's phrase, "the automatic man necessary for the automatic processes of modern capitalism."[1] There is however at this point a potential weakness in Kropotkin's thesis. Kropotkin's attack upon law is based upon a defence of the autonomy, and value, of the individual. Written law is deficient because it fails to serve the needs of the individual. This is in keeping with an analysis which argues that,

> A most important condition which a modern ethical system is bound to satisfy is that it must not fetter individual initiative, *be it for so high a purpose as the welfare of the commonwealth or species.*[2] (emphasis added)

Yet Kropotkin also seems to promote a different form of automatic person. "Primitive folk...," he writes, "so much identify their lives with that of the tribe, that each of their acts, however insignificant, is considered a tribal affair."[3] Later he writes, "...the savage obeys the prescriptions of the common law [of the tribe]...even more blindly than the civilized man obeys the prescriptions of written law..."[4] In suggesting that this common law is a reflection of a biological tendency to mutual aid Kropotkin appears approving, or at least accepting, that very form of "automatism" that he decries in contemporary society.

The promotion of the individual is certainly not an absolute good in Kropotkin's philosophy. He writes that,

> ...individual self-assertion which is desirable has often been, and continually is, something quite different from, and far larger and deeper than, the petty, unintelligent narrowmindedness, which, with a large class of writers, goes for "individualism" and "self-assertion"...[5]

Elsewhere he characterises the individualism of the nineteenth century as "the egoistic turn of mind given to the public mind" and contrasts it unfavourably with the communistic tendency.[6] However Kropotkin never fully explains what is the difference between the undesirable egoistic turn of mind and the desirable individual self-assertion.

In part the problem may result from Kropotkin having differing emphasis at different stages in his life. In particular *Ethics* seems to show a deeper regard for the position of the individual at the expense of society as a whole. This may reflect the fact that *Ethics*, which remained uncompleted at the time of Kropotkin's death, was written after the Russian Revolution. In 1919 Kropotkin wrote, "[w]e are learning in Russia how *not* to introduce communism."[7] His view of individuality may have changed in consequence of this. However this could not explain the earlier passages in *Mutual Aid* which seems to be the result of an unresolved contradiction in thought.

Kropotkin's paradoxical views on the desirability of individuality are potentially more damaging to his theory than problems concerned with the empirical backing for it. Consideration of the empirical fit of his theory requires further scholarship and probably further research. However, this is merely an expansion on work already done. In the case of Kropotkin's views of individuality what is required is not exegesis but change. Kropotkin's theory must be amended so as to provide a coherence it does not currently have.

A. Bradney. "Taking Law Less Seriously—An Anarchist Legal Theory." *Legal Studies.* V. (1985): 138–149.

---

[1] Bankowski *op. cit.* n 1 above.

[2] Kropotkin *Ethics.* p.27.

[3] *Mutual Aid*, p. 111.

[4] *Ibid.*, p. 110.

[5] *Ibid.*, p. xvi.

[6] *Revolutionary Pamphlets*, p. 60.

[7] *Ibid.*, p. 254.

Anarchism and World Order

Richard A. Falk

RICHARD A. FALK *is Albert G. Milbank Professor of International Law and Practice, Center of International Studies, Princeton University.*

Three Hard Questions For Anarchists

1. *Are not the preconditions for anarchist success insurmountable?* The great anarchist success stories have been episodic, short-lived (e.g., the Paris Commune of 1871, the anarchist collectives in parts of Spain during the 1939s, the May uprising in Paris in 1968). Nowhere have anarchists enjoyed a period of sustained success. Generally, anarchist success has generated an overpowering reaction of repression, as when the mercenary soldiery of Versailles crushed and massacred the Paris Communards in May 1871 only weeks after their extraordinary triumph. Anarchists view such failures as inevitable "first attempts"; Kropotkin calls "the Commune of Paris, the child of a period of transition...doomed to perish" but "the forerunner of social revolution."[1] Murray Bookchin and Daniel Guérin make a similar assessment of the Paris uprising of 1968, regarding its occurrence as proof of the anarchist critique, its collapse as evidence that "the molecular movement below that prepares the condition for revolution" had not yet carried far enough.[2]

On a deeper level, anarchists understand that the prerequisite for anarchist success *anywhere* is its success *everywhere*. It is this vital precondition that is at once so convincing and so formidable as to call into question whether the anarchist position can in fact be taken seriously as a progressive alternative to state socialism.

Bakunin expressed the anarchist demand and rationale with clarity:

A federalist in the internal affairs of the country, he desires an international confederation, first of all in the spirit of justice, and second because he is convinced that the economic and social revolution, transcending all the artificial and pernicious barriers between states, can only be brought about, in part at least, by the solidarity in action, if not of all, then at least of the majority of the nations constituting the civilized world today, so that sooner or later all nations must join together.[3]

Or, as Daniel Guérin expressed it: "An isolated national revolution cannot succeed. The social revolution inevitably becomes a world revolution."[4]

In essence, not only is it difficult for anarchists to attain power, but once they manage to do so their "organic institutions" seem incapable of holding it. Their movements will be liquidated ruthlessly by statists of "the left" of "the right."[5] Given such vulnerability, it may even be a betrayal of one's followers to expose them to slaughter by mounting a challenge

[1] *Kropotkin*, p. 127. [Ed. note: Falk cites here Kropotkin, "The Commons of Paris" in Martin A. Miller, ed. *Selected Writings on Anarchism and Revolution* by P.A. Kropotkin (Cambridge, Mass.: MIT Press, 1970).]

[2] Bookchin, *Post-Scarcity Anarchism*, p. 258. [Ed. note: Falk cites here M. Bookchin, *Post-Scarcity Anarchism* (Berkeley, Calif.: Ramport Press, 1971).]

[3] *Bakunin.* p. 118. [Ed. note: Falk's reference is to Sam Dolgoff, ed. *Bakunin on Anarchy* (New York: Anchor, 1973).]

[4] Guérin, *Anarchism: From Theory to Practice* (New York: Monthly Review Press, 1970), p. 69.

[5] George Woodstock, *Anarchism* (New York: World Publishing Co., 1962), pp. 275–424.

against the entrenched forces of statism in the absence of either the will or the capabilities to protect the challengers.[1]

There is a report of a fascinating conversation between Lenin and Kropotkin in May 1919 in which Lenin mounts such an argument in two ways. First, he makes his familiar point that "You can't make a revolution wearing white gloves. We know perfectly well that we have made and will make a great many mistakes... But it is impossible not to make mistakes during a revolution. Not to make them means to renounce life entirely and do nothing at all. But we have preferred to make errors and thus to act... We want to act and we will, despite all the mistakes, and will bring our socialist revolution to the final and inevitably victorious end."[2] Lenin here in effect acknowledges the errors that flow from using state power to secure the revolutionary victory from external and internal enemies, and he rebuffs the anarchist view that state power can be dissolved. Lenin's second rebuff of the anarchist position is his condescending view of its revolutionary power: "Do you really think that the capitalist world will submit to the path of the cooperative movement?... You will pardon me, but this is all nonsense! We need direct action of the masses, revolutionary action of the masses, that activity which seizes the capitalist world by the throat and brings it down."[3] Of anarchist concepts of "social revolution," Lenin says "these are children's playthings, idle chatter, having no realist soil underneath, no force, no means, and almost nothing approaching our socialist

goals... We don't need the struggle and violent acts of separate persons. It is high time that the anarchists understood this and stopped scattering their revolutionary energy on utterly useless affairs."[4] In sum, Lenin is arguing that the ends of anarchists must be pursued by mass violent revolution and secured through state power. The anarchist response is, of course, that the choice of such means perverts and dooms the ends. The antagonism of anarchists toward the Bolshevik Revolution has been vindicated many times over.[5] On the level of their discussion, it seems that both Lenin and Kropotkin are correct,[6]— Lenin in saying that there is no other way to succeed, the anarchists by contending that such success is as bad as, if not worse than, defeat.

But, in my view, the strongest case for the feasibility of the anarchist position still remains to be argued. It is implicit, perhaps, in Kropotkin's own work on the origins of the modern state and on its feudal antecedents in the European cities of the eleventh and twelfth centuries.[7] Kropotkin's argument rests on the historical claim that a vital society of communes and free cities created by brotherhoods, guilds, and individual initiative existed earlier: "...it is shown by an immense documentation from many sources, that never, either before or since, has mankind known a period of relative well-being for all as in the cities of the Middle Ages. The poverty, insecurity, and physical exploitation of labor that exist in our times were then unknown."[8] Drawing on non-Western experience as well, Kropotkin argues

---

[1] Such allegations have been made with respect to Salvador Allende's efforts in the early 1970s to transform the societal base of Chile without dismantling the state apparatus with its strong links to the vested interests of the older order.

[2] *Kropotkin*, p. 328.

[3] *Kropotkin*. pp. 329–30.

[4] *Kropotkin*. p. 330.

[5] One of the earliest and most eloquent anarchist critics of the Soviet experience was Emma Goldmann. See her *My Disillusionment with Russia* (Garden City, New York: Doubleday, 1923).

[6] Kropotkin's position can be extrapolated from his general anarchist writings; he did not state the anarchist case in his conversations with Lenin.

[7] See Kropotkin's excellent essay, "The State: Its Historic Rule," in *Kropotkin*, pp. 211–64.

[8] *Kropotkin* p. 231.

in effect that societal well-being and security based on anarchist conceptions of organic institutions (of a cooperative character) were immensely successful over a wide geographical and cultural expanse until crushed by the emergent states of the fifteenth and sixteenth centuries. Thus, there is a kind of *prima facie* case for plausibility of the anarchist model, although in a prestatal context.

But evidence of the anarchist potential for "success" does not end with medieval Europe. The direction of contemporary China, especially its antiparty, populist phase that culminated in the Cultural Revolution, contains strong anarchist elements.[1] Indeed, it was precisely on these grounds of repudiating "organization" and "bureaucracy" as a basis for communist discipline that China made itself so offensive to communist ideologues in the Kremlin.[2] China is, of course, a mixed case. In its foreign policy it places great stress on statist prerogatives. Nevertheless, in its domestic patterns the Chinese example lends some credibility to Bakunin's and Kropotkin's claim that there are nonbureaucratic roads to socialism, and gives the anarchist orientation renewed plausibility as a serious political alternative.[3]

Such plausibility can, it seems to me, be extrapolated in a poststatal context. Here, my argument, sustained by sources as dissimilar as Saul Mendlovitz and Henry Kissinger, is that we are undergoing a profound historical transformation that is destroying the organizational matrix of a global system based on territorial states.[4] That is, we are entering a poststatal period, although its character remains highly conjectural. Whatever the outcome, however, the anarchist stress on nonterritorial associations and communal consciousness seems highly relevant because of

its basic compatibility with the inevitable shift in the relation of forces.

In sum, the anarchist case for radical reform (i.e., for social revolution) was *chimerical within* the confines of the state system. However, the state system is now being superseded. In this context, one set of plausible possibilities is the globalization of societal life in a way that allows cooperative organizational forms to flourish. That is, the anarchist vision (as epitomized in Bakunin's writings) of a fusion between a universal confederation and organic societal forms of a communal character lies at the very center of the *only* hopeful prospect for the future of world order.[5] Needless to say, such a prospect has slim chances for success, but at least the possibility is no longer chimerical, given the change of objective circumstances. The state system is not an implacable foe, for many economic, political, technological, and sociological forces are everywhere undermining its bases of potency, if unevenly and at an uncertain rate. Therefore, although the political precondition of scale imposed by anarchism still remains formidable, it may yet prove historically surmountable. It may be surmountable because the preparatory processes going on throughout the world during this historical period are creating more favorable global conditions for the anarchist cause than have hitherto existed for several centuries. This assessment arises from several distinct developments. Perhaps the most significant is the growing disenchantment with the values, goals, and methods of industrial society. This sense of disenchantment is coming to be shared by increasing numbers of citizens, particularly in the developed nations of the West, and is finding various forms of expression that reflect revised notions of necessity based on "limits to growth," notions of

[1] See perceptive discussion, in Schurmann, *Logic of World Power* (New York: Pantheon, 1974), pp. 369–80.

[2] Schurmann, *Logic of World Power*. p. 380.

[3] For a skeptical interpretation of China's domestic experience see Donald Zagoria, "China by Daylight," *Dissent* (Spring 1975), pp. 135–47.

[4] For opposing interpretations on the durability of the state and the state system see Saul H. Mendlovitz, Introduction, in Saul H. Mendlovitz, ed., *On the Creation of a Just World Order* (New York: Free Press, 1975), pp. vii–xvii, and Stanley Hoffmann, "Obstinate or Obsolete? The Fate of the Nation-State and the Case of Western Europe," *Daedalus* (Summer 1966), pp. 862–915.

[5] A general interpretation can be found in Robert Heilbroner, *An Inquiry into the Human Prospect* (New York: Norton, 1974); see also Falk, *A Study of Future Worlds* (New York: Free Press, 1975), pp. 417–37; Richard A. Falk, "A New Paradigm for International Legal Studies: Prospects and Proposals," *Yale Law Journal 84*: 969–1021 (1975).

well-being based on intermediate technology and small-scale institutions, and notions of personal transcendence based on a new spiritual energy that repudiates both conventional religion and secular humanism. In this setting, the quest for an appropriate politics converges rather dramatically with the central tenets of anarchist belief. This modern sensibility realizes, at last, that the state is simultaneously *too large* to satisfy human needs and *too small* to cope with the requirements of guidance for an increasingly interdependent planet. This realization is temporarily offset by a rising tide of statism in many other parts of the world, where political independence is a forbidden fruit only recently tasted, but where the fruit will be poisoned, as everywhere else, by a world of nuclear weapons, ecological decay, and mass economic privation. The main *problematique* of our age is whether an appropriate politics of global reform, combining a centralized form of functional guidance with decentralized economic, social, and political structures, can be shaped by voluntary action, or whether it must be formed in a crucible of tragedy and catastrophe. Attentiveness to the anarchist tradition can be one part of an effort to achieve an appropriate politics *this* side of catastrophe. Obviously, the objective conditions which require such a reassessment of political forms are not by themselves sufficient to effect a transformation. Indeed, the very relevance of these ideas may lead their powerful opponents to regard them as even more dangerous now than in the past. Prudence and patience are essential in these circumstances. The crises of the state system may yet require several decades to develop to the point where eruptions of spontaneous anarchistic energies would not unleash a variety of devastating backlashes.

2. *Given the urgency of global reform, isn't the anarchist prospect too remote in time?* Even accepting the optimistic assessment of the preceding section, namely, that the hour of anarchism may coincide with the collapse of statism, restructuring of the world system would still appear to be developed for an un-

necessarily and dangerously long period of several decades or more. Just as the emergence of the state system was a matter of centuries, so might the consolidation of a new system of political order require hundreds of years.[1] Two sets of questions call for judgment based on imponderables. First, how serious and pressing is the crisis? Is the fire close at hand, or still barely visible on a distant horizon? How can we know? Second, are any alternative means available through which the principal goals of global reform could be attained more reliably and rapidly than through anarchism? Do we have any responsible basis for selecting or rejecting these alternatives? In part, we are forced here to confront the most fundamental issues of politics, knowledge, and action. In the abstract, we do not know enough to choose or to act. Of course this same limitation bears on every school of political thought, including those that defend the status quo or incline toward gradualism. But it has even greater bearing on a political position that proposes radical tactics and goals, especially if large-scale violence is likely to ensue. On the other hand, this line of reasoning may be deceptive. In a moment of crisis, to do nothing may be the most risky of all postures toward the future. It is generally better to jump from a sinking ship than it is to stay on board, even if one knows nothing about the prospects of rescue from the waters below. The collective situation of human society cannot be cast in such deceptive simplicity. The veil of ignorance is thick indeed when it comes to assessing policy alternatives for the future of world society.

But the argument from ignorance cuts the other way as well. We have no real way to assess the degrees of progress along the transition path. Perhaps the collapse of statism is closer than we think. As Paul Goodman wrote:

> It will be said that there is no time. Yes, probably. But let me cite a remark of Tocqueville. In his last work, *L'Ancien Régime*, he notes "with terror," as he says, how throughout the eighteenth century writer after writer and expert after expert pointed out that this and that detail of the Old Regime was

---

[1] See Joseph R. Strayer, *On the Medieval Origins of the Modern State* (Princeton University Press, 1970).

unviable and could not possibly survive; added up, they proved that the entire Old Regime was doomed and must soon collapse; and yet *there was not a single man who foretold that there would be a mighty revolution.*[1]

In the face of such uncertainty, compounded by the many evidences of pressure on the state system, it makes political as well as moral sense to pursue a *principled set of conclusions* even if their realization cannot be immediately foreseen. In one sense Herbert Read is correct in saying that "the task of the anarchist philosopher is not to prove the imminence of a Golden Age, but to justify the value of believing in its possibility."[2]

Such a value depends on some degree of plausibility, but also on whether or not there are any preferable alternatives. Given the established bankruptcy of statist solutions on the right and left, given the vulnerability of the state system as a whole to catastrophic and, quite possibly, irreversible damage, and given the insufficiency of gradualist strategies of amelioration, the case for some variant of radical anarchism seems strong despite the inability of the anarchist to provide skeptics with a credible timetable.

In essence, the issue of urgency reinforces the anarchist case. The primary world order need is to find an alternative to statism. Anarchism, despite its limited political success during the statist era, provides the most coherent, widespread, and persistent tradition of anti-statist thought. It is also a tradition that has generally been inclined toward world-order values: peace, economic equity, civil liberties, ecological defense. As such, it represents the most normatively acceptable sequel to the state system. Other sequels include imperial consolidation; world state; regional federation; intergovernmental functionalism.[3]

To affirm the relevance of the anarchist tradition is not to accept the adequacy of its current formulations but only of its general orientation. Advocates of an anarchist approach need to formulate the globalist implications of anarchism in a manner responsive to the current world-order crisis. As far as I know, this has not yet been done. Indeed, anarchism suffers from the tendency of other traditions of philosophical speculation generated during the statist era, namely, to concentrate upon the national question and to assume that the global question will disappear when all nations have correctly resolved their own domestic problems. As I have suggested, anarchists are more dependent than other reformers on supportive transnational developments; but their analysis of international events is usually identical to that of Marxists, on the level of critique, and highly impressionistic when it comes to making specific proposals. Thus, the claims of anarchism are not weakened by the urgency of the world crisis, but the need for a more historically sensitive interpretation and for a globally oriented formulation of anarchist response is essential.

3. *Does the receptivity of anarchism to violence undermine the moral basis of its claim to provide an ideology for global reform?* I am not discussing here the anarchist as "bomb-thrower," but neither do I identify anarchism with pacifist ethics. As a philosophical position anarchism adopts an equivocal view of violence as an agent of change. Although anarchists tend to rely on spontaneous militancy of a nonviolent character—most typically, the general strike or other forms of unarmed struggle and resistance—there is no prevailing anarchist view on the role of violence.

I think Howard Zinn has sympathetically, but reliably, presented the anarchist position on violence in this assessment:

Some anarchists—like other revolutionaries throughout history...have emphasized violent uprising. Some have advocated, and tried, assassination and terror... What makes anarchists unique among revolutionaries, however, is that most of them see revolution as a cultural, ideological, creative process, in which violence would be as inci-

---

[1] Goodman, "Ambiguities of Pacifist Politics," in Leonard I. Krimerman and Lewis Perry, eds. *Patterns of Anarchy* (New York: Anchor, 1966), p. 136; see also *Kropotkin*, pp. 121–24.

[2] Read, *Anarchy and Order* (Boston: Beacon Press, 1971), p. 14.

[3] For consideration of world order option see Falk, *Future Worlds*, pp. 150–276; Falk, "A New Paradigm..." pp. 999–1017.

dental as the outcries of mother and baby in child-birth. It might be unavoidable—given the natural resistance to change—but something to be kept at a minimum while more important things happen.[1]

The question is whether, given the technology of destruction and the ruthlessness of statist leadership, this view of violence is adequate. It can be attacked from either side, as underestimating the role of violence for any serious revolutionary position, or as too willing to accept the moral Trojan Horse of political violence.

Mainstream Marxists and neo-Marxists generally contend that revolution depends upon mass-based armed struggle. A recent formulation is "the political statement of the Weather Underground" released under the title *Prairie Fire*:

It's an illusion that imperialism will decay peacefully. Imperialism has meant constant war. Imperialists defend their control of the means of life with terrible force. There is no reason to believe they will become humane or relinquish power... To not prepare the people for this struggle is to disarm them ideologically and physically and to perpetrate a cruel hoax.[2]

The cruel hoax is, of course, the illusion that revolution can occur without armed struggle, that a revolution can be made with white gloves. But as Kropotkin soon perceived, once the white gloves have been thrown away, it becomes all too easy to adopt terror and torture.[3] In my view, the abuse of state power by socialism has reversed the presumption that violence is a necessary concomitant of revolution. On the contrary, it now seems a cruel hoax to promise humane outcomes from any revolutionary process that embraces violence with anything other than the utmost reluctance. Any genuinely radical position that purports moral (as well as political) credibility must, above all else, reject a cult of violence, and justify the use of specific forms of violence in the most careful and conditional manner.

Richard A. Falk. "Anarchism and World Order." In *Anarchism: Nomos XIX*. Edited by J. Roland Pennock and John W. Chapman. New York: New York University Press, 1978.

---

[1] Zinn, Introduction, Read, *Anarchy and Order*. p. xvii.

[2] *Prairie Fire*, Political Statement of the Weather Underground, 1974. p. 3.

[3] See Kropotkin letter to Lenin date 21 December 1920, in *Kropotkin*. pp. 338–39.

Part X

Fundamentalism

AYATOLLAH KHOMEINI

In recent years fundamentalism in Islam, Christianity, and Judaism, has grown to be a significant political force. Not only has this renewed fundamentalism imposed a unique political perspective upon events in the Middle East as well as in North America, it now seems about to impose the same perspective upon events in the USSR. Certainly, if we wish to stay abreast of developments in domestic and international politics, we can hardly afford to be indifferent to the history, present impact, and future potential of this rising force of fundamentalism. In this respect, the five articles and interviews reprinted in this chapter offer the reader some valuable insight into the history and growing influence of Islamic, Judaic, and Christian fundamentalism.

In his historic overview of Islamic fundamentalism, Hamid Enayat concentrates primarily on the movement of the Islamic Brothers in Egypt. Enayat credits Hasan al-Bannā' with founding the Egyptian movement in 1928. This movement (or "Society" as Enayat calls it) saw itself as the inheritor of the active elements in the Sunnī tradition and stressed the liberation of Egypt from foreign control as well as the creation of a free Islamic government. In tracing the movement's development in Egypt, Enayat goes on to highlight the importance of the Palestinian crisis with its accompanying Arab-Israeli conflicts. Enayat concludes his article by emphasising the Brothers' concept of the Islamic state as one "advanced by militant and armed movement."

In ways complementary to those of Enayat, James Piscatori singles out four factors contributing to the revival of Islam. These are: the defeat of Egypt, Syria, and Jordan in the 1967 war with Israel which shattered the morale of most Muslims; the

process of development; the universal crisis of modernity in which Muslim societies find themselves; and finally, the emphasis placed upon Islam by political developments in particular societies. In making these comments, Piscatori speaks not just of the Brotherhood and the Sunnīs but of the Shi'a as well. Moreover, Piscatori sees important similarities between born-again Christians and veiled-again Muslims, impliedly referring to their fundamentalistic common denominator.

Another insight into Islamic fundamentalism, this time of a Shi'ite variety, is provided by Ayatollah Khomeini in his 1980 New Year's address. He denounces both Westernization and Easternization and calls upon his fellow Iranians to follow the path of Islam. Urging his listeners to confront the world with "our ideology," Khomeini proceeds to give his blessings to Palestine, Lebanon, and Afghanistan. Further, he mentions several specific points which his followers should heed, notably the need for compliance with Islamic religious regulations and manners, the desirability of purging from the universities all professors who have had contact with either the East or the West, the attractiveness of the removal of pro-Shah or deviant elements from radio and television, and finally the importance of a pro-clerical attitude in furthering independence, freedom, and Islam in Iran.

In the USA, fundamentalism has been of a Christian variety with Jerry Falwell as one of its central leaders. In the following interview and brief article, we see his commitment to the Moral Majority, a group which he helped found as a Christian agency of change in a corrupted society. Falwell reveals his belief that the nuclear freeze movement endangers the freedoms which Americans cherish, that the reform movement of President Botha in South Africa will bring participatory government, and that the real hope for influencing the world lies in training young people "in those things vital to the cause of world evangelization." In the interview with Falwell, we perceive clearly a man who is dedicated to conservative Christianity, the institution of the church, and the institution of the family. In addition we perceive readily his own awareness of mechanisms that will aid him in attaining his fundamentalist goals, including speaking tours, the use of television and radio, and the establishment of his own university.

Like Christianity, Judaism is also experiencing a revival of fundamentalism, a movement that, like Jerry Falwell's Moral Majority, is both spiritual and political in its thrust. In his article, Robert Friedman reviews the ideas of Rabbi Meir Kahane, an Orthodox Jew and founder of the Jewish Defense League. According to Friedman, Kahane believes any act is acceptable if it is permitted by the *halakah*, Jewish religious law. Among the acts which Kahane has allegedly condoned or advocated are: the expulsion of the Arabs from Israel, the criminalization of sex between Arab men and Jewish women, the enforced prohibition of insults aimed at Judaism or Jewish people, and the de-struction of the Dome of the Rock Mosque. Friedman makes clear both the strong Messianic expectations which Kahane holds and the considerable political expertise which he brings to the Kach Party in Israel. According to Friedman, Kahane's apocalyptic imagery as well as his appeal to the Sephardim, the Jews who have come to Israel from Arab lands, make him the purveyor of an influential ideological message that today confronts Israelis, both Jewish and Arab.

As a movement, fundamentalism is certainly not entirely new; however, in domestic and international politics it has achieved new prominence. Indeed, modern fundamentalism has become a force to be reckoned with. In its religious garb, one of its basic characteristics is its reactionary nature. It aims to return to the solid values of the past as they are found in the "sacred" book, whether that be the *Koran*, the *Bible*, or the *Torah*. And at times fundamentalism in its present form recaptures the Manichaean dualism of the past in which the powerful force of good wages an epic struggle with the powerful force of evil. As with Manichaeanism, so too with fundamentalism, its adherents see the forces of good and evil as being always clearly discernible. Furthermore, modern fundamentalists believe that the strategy of good gaining victory over evil is always readily ascertainable.

Fundamentalism

Hamid Enayat

HAMID ENAYAT *was formerly professor of political science at Tehran University. He is currently a Fellow at St. Antony's College, Oxford University.*

The movement of the Muslim Brothers, although forming so far the only organised Islamic trend which has had a following all over the Muslim world—particularly Egypt, Syria, Pakistan, Indonesia and Malaysia—by no means presents a homogeneous front. Its ideology, temper and style of activity in each country have been largely determined by the strategy and requirements of the national struggle, whether for independence, democracy or redeeming the vanished identity of the national culture. Accordingly, the strength of its demand for the Islamic state, and the motives and reasons for this demand, have varied greatly from country to country. Before the Islamic Revolution of 1979 in Iran, the strongest appeal came from Pakistan where the idea of the Islamic state has always generally exerted a compelling attraction, for the simple reason that it was Islam that brought Pakistan into existence as a state. The drive in Egypt and Iran had been no less vigorous, but it was often distracted by the powerful competition of secular ideologies—nationalism, liberalism, socialism and Communism. The degree of intellectual sophistication in the formulation of the demand has similarly not been uniform— with Pakistan again taking the lead. Here we consider some of the broad characteristics of the movement in Egypt, Iran and Pakistan as examples of modern Islamic fundamentalism—in contradistinction to the traditional type exemplified by the Saudi model.

The Brothers' movement in Egypt, founded in 1928 by Hasan al-Banna' (d. 1949), was the product of one of the most complex phases of its modern history. This complexity, in the words of Banna' himself, resulted from the "disputed control of Egypt between the Wafd and Liberal Constitutionalist parties, and the vociferous political debating, with the consequence of 'disunity', which followed in the wake of the revolution of 1919; the post-war 'orientations to apostasy and nihilisms' which were engulfing the Muslim world; the attacks on tradition and orthodoxy—emboldened by the 'Kemalist revolt' in Turkey—which were organised into a movement for the intellectual and social emancipation of Egypt," and the non-Islamic, secularist and libertarian trends which had pervaded the entire academic and intellectual climate of Egypt.[1] The significance of this statement by Banna' is that, while some fundamentalists today may claim their creed to be a natural outgrowth of the truth and the inherent resilience of Islam, he thus admits to a direct correlation between the Brothers' movement and its surrounding social, cultural and political factors. His own response to this prodigious range of threats to the Islamic character of Egyptian society was at first moral and didactic. He merely strove for a time to awaken his limited audience to the dangers by preaching and writing. But as his Society spread and came into conflict with opposing forces in the country, it moved towards growing militancy and political action. The factors prodding it along this course were again motley, and often sprang from Egypt's internal political development, especially its struggle against British imperialism before and after the Second World War. But one factor requires special mention here because it figures with unfailing regularity in the history of the Brothers' movement in most other

---

[1] Richard P. Mitchell, *The Society of Muslim Brothers* (London, 1969) (hereafter cited as Mitchell, *Brothers*) p. 4. See also Ra'ūf Shalabī, *Ash-Shaykh Hasan al-Banna' wa madrasatuh 'Al-Ikhwan al-Muslimun* (Cairo, 1978) pp. 133–9.

Muslim countries as well. This was the impact of the Palestinian crisis, and the ensuing Arab-Israeli hostilities. The simultaneity of a number of turning-points in the history of the expansion of the Society with those in the drama of the Arab-Zionist conflict furnish yet another proof of the truism that political radicalism thrives on nothing better than the threat of an external enemy. This became evident on at least three occasions between the date of the creation of the Society, and its dissolution, once in 1948, and again in 1954.

The first was the transformation of the Society from its modest beginnings as a youth club into a potent political force. This coincided with the first phase of the open conflict between the Arabs and the Zionists, culminating in the Arab general strike of 1936–9, which provided the Society with an unprecedented opportunity to relinquish its pious campaign of "propaganda, communication, and information" in favour of political activism. The Brothers' contribution to the Arab cause in Palestine must have played a decisive role in encouraging Bannā' to decide in 1939 on turning the Society into a political organisation. What is of more interest to us is that the Brothers redefined their ideology for the next phase in a way which stressed the ability of Islam to become a total ideology, since they now declared their programme to be based on three principles: "(a) Islam is a comprehensive, self-evolving (*murtakamil bi-dhatihi*) system; it is the ultimate path of life, in all its spheres; (b) Islam emanates from, and is based on, two fundamental sources, the Qur'ān, and the Prophetic Tradition; (c) Islam is applicable to all times and places."[1] Bannā' then declared his movement to be the inheritor, and catalyst, of the most activist elements in the Sunnī traditionalist and reformist thinking by describing it as "a *Salafiyyah* message, a Sunnī way, a Sūfī truth, a political organisation, an athletic group, a scientific and cultural link, an eco-nomic enterprise and a social idea."[2] The programme of the Society consisted of two items. One was the "internationalisation" of the movement: it stressed the necessity of a struggle not only to liberate Egypt, but the whole of "the Islamic homeland" from foreign control. The other was the duty "to institute in this homeland a free Islamic government, practising the principles of Islam, applying its social system, propounding its solid fundamentals, and transmitting its wise call to the people." It then went on to add that "so long as this government is not established, the Muslims are all of them guilty before God Almighty of having failed to install it." This betrayal, in "the bewildering circumstances" of the time, was a betrayal, not only of Muslims, but of all humanity.[3] The Brothers could hardly be more explicit in their demand for an Islamic state.

The second instance of the impact of the Palestinian crisis had an even more radicalising influence on the Brothers' political ideology and activity. It was precipitated by the United Nations' resolution on the partition of Palestine in November 1947, and the first Arab-Israeli war. Even before that, with the increasing bitterness of the political mood of the country, and the sharpening of the struggle against the British, violence had become a normal feature of political life, with various groups using it both against one another and the Government. The stresses and frustrations caused by the war, and the Arab defeat of 1948, incited the activists to fresh violence inside Egypt, but most of the blame for this was put on the Brothers, whose society was consequently dissolved in December 1948.[4] After the assassination of Bannā' in 1949, the moderate wing of the Society tried to retrieve its legal status by electing as its leader Hasan Ismā'īl Hudaybī, a judge of more than twenty years standing, and an outspoken opponent of violence and terrorism. But this was a temporary diversion, and the militants soon took

---

[1] Zakariyyā Sulaymān Bayyūmī, *Al-ikhwan al-Muslimum* (Cairo, 1979) (hereafter cited as Bayyūmī, *Al-ikhwan*) p. 90.

[2] *Ibid.*, p. 90, footnote 2; also Mitchell, *Brothers*, p. 14.

[3] Bayyūmī, *Al-ikhwan*, p. 91.

[4] *Ibid.*, p. 118.

over again. The first war with Israel affected the fate of the Brothers—and through them, Egyptian politics—in another way too: it put them in touch with the Free Officers, the nationalist group in the Egyptian army which overthrew the monarchy in 1952. Although marred at times by an ambiguity that characterised the Society's position towards all political groups, these links were of a special nature, forged as they were by the common hardships of the two groups at the Battle of Falūjah. Apparently, while the Brothers helped to indoctrinate the Free Officers, the latter helped the Brothers with military education (Nāsir was once accused of having trained the Brothers in the use of arms).[1] One reason for such intimacy may have been the fact that while the Society's tactical co-operation with political circles was often planned and effected "from above," its alliance with the Free Officers was made possible by the shared idealism, and joint action "at the bottom." This rift between the leadership and the rank and file—which is perhaps an inherent disability of all political parties committed to ideologies—later on badly damaged the Society as Egypt's political crisis deepened. However, the common feelings and experiences of the past must have aroused among the Brothers an expectation that, with the Free Officers establishing themselves as rulers of Egypt, the realisation of Islamic ideals was within easy reach. When the Officers proved to be much less doctrinaire than they had appeared on the battle field, and too pragmatic for the Brothers' taste, conflict developed fast, and with all the intensity and violence that mark the feuds between erstwhile comrades. Such reversals turn out to be less puzzling when one notes that the rift between the leadership and the rank and file in the Society widened after 1952, as circumstances became temporarily more favourable to its activities. While at

least some of the leaders seemed inclined to co-operate with the regime, and consented to a gradualist approach, the rank and file were becoming increasingly impatient with the slow pace of reforms, and suspicious of the Officers. It was thus that an unsuccessful attempt was made by the more militant Brothers on Nāsir's life in October 1954, following which the Society was once again dissolved, and a number of its leaders and activists were executed, or condemned to long terms of imprisonment.[2] It is difficult to conceive how the relationship between the Brothers and the Free Officers could have followed such a tortuous course without the Palestinian crisis having acted as a major catalyst in the growing radicalisation of the Brothers' political thinking.

One can go on pointing to still more examples of the continuing link between the Brothers' radicalism and the Arab-Israeli conflict after 1954: the traumatic effects of the Arab defeat in the Six-Day War of 1967, however disastrous for Nāsirism, were highly beneficial for the Brothers and their ideology. They dealt a mortal blow to the semi-secular Arab socialism, and created the right collective psyche for new attempts at vindicating the truth of suppressed or neglected traditional beliefs. This is what happens, thundered the review of al-Azhar, when Muslims discard their glorious heritage, and allow themselves to be enticed by fleeting, exotic ideas—a rebuke which would have had greater moral force if al-Azhar itself had not been obediently toeing the official line during the previous decade.[3] Although in the past al-Azhar had shared the Brothers' absolute faith in the unsurpassed ability of Islam to solve the social and political problems of Muslims, this was the first time after a long period that, in addressing the rulers, it was restating the same faith in the annoyed tone of a guide who

---

[1] Mitchell, *Brothers*, pp. 89, 99: also Anwar el-Sadat, *In Search of Identity* (London, 1978) pp. 22–4; for Sadat's less inhibited accounts of the Free Officers' relations with the Brothers, see his *Revolt on the Nile* (London, 1957) pp. 26 ff., 30, 43 ff., 61 ff.; also Ishaq Musa Husaini, *The Moslem Brethren* (Beirut, 1956) p. 118.

[2] Mitchell, *Brothers*. pp. 151–62.

[3] Editorials of the *Majallat' al-Azhar*, issues of February and October, vol. XL (1968).

had long suffered the aberrations of his way-ward disciples. Like the Brothers, some of the Azharites interpreted the Arab-Israeli war in terms of a conflict between Islam and Judaism, and appealed for intensified religious education of the people as the most effective way of fighting Israel.[1] Both the Brothers and al-Azhar were helped in their bid for self-assertion by the religious fervour which was aroused in response to some of the consequences of the Arab defeat: the decision of the Israeli Government to declare the irrevocable annexation of Jerusalem, which is equally sacred for Muslims, the fire at al-Aqsā Mosque, and the emergence of messianic vision and religious feelings in Israel itself. As if to concede the justice of the orthodox admonitions, the Egyptian Government released several hundred Brothers from prisons in April 1968, an act which marked a general relaxation of controls on the fundamentalist groups, at least for the time being.

The Brothers' concept of the Islamic state is an accentuated form of Rashīd Ridā's. But its real distinguishing mark is that, as Nadav Safran rightly says, it is advanced by a militant and armed movement which does not simply "express pious boasting or devotional cant," but reflects a "messianic vision" which the Brothers seek to bring into being "sword in hand."[2] But this interpretation reveals only half the truth in so far as it does not take full account of the fact that the Brothers' political outlook was at least partly a reaction against what the Arab masses regarded as Israeli expansionism since 1948. Safran bases part of his stimulating criticism of the Brothers' doctrines on a well-known book, Min huna na'lam (From Here We Learn), published in 1948 by one of their prominent leaders, Muhammad Ghazzālī, who later defected from their ranks, but the ideas he expressed in that particular book and some of his other publications can

still be treated as representative of the fundamentalist perception of the Islamic state. It is noteworthy that one of the arguments which Ghazzālī puts forward in this book to prove the case for the Islamic state—to which Safran makes no reference—is the example set by Israel. The Israelis, Ghazzālī muses with admiration, "could have called their country the Jewish Republic, or the Jewish Socialist Union, just as their Arab neighbours have named their countries after the ruling families—[such as] the Mutawakkilite State of the Yemen, or Hashimite Jordan, or Saudi Arabia." But they called it Israel "which is the symbol of their attachment to their religion and reminiscences, and of their respect for their sacred values. The Jews who have done this are masters of wealth and knowledge and leaders of politics and economy, and there have been people from among them who have taken part in effecting the nuclear fission, and in many inventions. Nevertheless, they have felt no shame in ascribing themselves to their religion and have not thought of shirking their obligations."[3] This tendency to taunt the Muslims for not emulating the Israelis in blending religion with politics must have received further moral stimulus from the later growth of the Judaic influences in Israel's political, military and educational institutions, as the new state consolidated itself.

At the other end of the spectrum, there are authors like Richard Mitchell, who have tried to make the Brothers' political doctrines less distasteful to Western audiences by denying that they ever aimed at installing an Islamic state, in the sense of the Caliphate or a theocracy. Mitchell's argument is that one should distinguish in the Brothers' political writings between the concept of the Islamic state and that of the Islamic order (an nizam al-islami): according to him the Brothers merely sought the former and not the latter.[4] This view can-

---

[1] Ibid., especially the October issue, articles entitled "The Jewish Attitude towards Islam and the Muslims in the 'Initial Era' [al-'asr al-awwal]," "The Jewish Role in the Hostility against the Foundation of Islam," and 'Isra 'iliyyat in Qur'ānic Commentaries and the Hadith'.

[2] Nadav Safran, Egypt in Search of Political Community (Cambridge, Mass., 1961) p. 234.

[3] Muhammad Ghazzālī, Min huna na'lam (Cairo, 1948) (hereafter cited as Ghazzālī, Min huna) p. 49 (English translation by Isma'il el-Faruqi entitled Our Beginning in Wisdom (New York, 1975) p. 21).

[4] Mitchell, Brothers, pp. 234–5.

not be reconciled with the kinds of statement that we quoted earlier from the Brothers' programme of 1939. But it is true that under Bannā's leadership, so long as there was any hope of achieving power through constitutional means, the Society, either out of wavering or for purposes of camouflage or politicking, often avoided a stance which would indicate a revolutionary rejection of the *status quo*. It is with respect to such vacillations that one is inclined to agree with the Egyptian critic of the Brothers. Raf'at as-Sa'īd, in describing their ideology as "politics without programme."[1] But as prospects for their imminent accession to power receded, both as a result of official suppression and the tremendous popularity of Nāsirism from the Suez crisis of 1956 onwards, their ideas became more and more rigid and lucid. This process was strengthened by external factors as well: the more the West and Israel appeared to be aggressive the more strongly the Brothers felt confident to fall back on the neglected Islamic heritage, and to delineate the state that should be grounded on it. So in the eyes of the new theorists of the movement, the silver lining to all its setbacks was the greater receptivity of the "real" public to their protests and aspirations. The extent to which they perceived the psychological climate to have changed in their favour can be gauged by their attitude to the Caliphate. If in 1924, as we saw before, Rashīd Ridā lauded the Turkish measures against the Caliphate as a timely exercise of the religiously sanctioned right to revolt against unjust rulers, in 1950 Ghazzālī deprecated the abolition of the Caliphate as a cowardly submission to the desires of the imperialist West which was aware of the symbolic value of that institution for millions of Muslims scattered all over the world.[2] For him, the Western hostility to Islam is a continuation of the Crusades. Some people, he says, are misled by appearances, and believe that the Europeans have discarded religion altogether; they therefore doubt that Europe's stand against Islam is motivated by Crusader feelings. But the truth is otherwise, "the official title of the British sovereign is the Defender of the Faith, and the first item on the programme of the Conservative Party is the establishment of a Christian civilisation, and the ruling party at the moment in Italy...is the Christian Democratic Party."[3] All this amounts to a negative justification of the necessity of the Islamic state. Muslims should set up such a state, so Ghazzālī seems to be arguing, because Israel and the West are clinging to their religions, hellbent on the destruction of Islam. True, Ghazzālī also offers positive justifications, although these are largely the repetitions of the arguments already quoted from Rashīd Ridā, and the critics of 'Abd ar-Rāziq. But even these assertions are studded with frequent references to European history—to the example of the French and Russian revolutionaries: just as they did not rest content with mere preaching of their egalitarian ideals but proceeded to attain political power as a necessary goal of their activities, so too Muslims cannot divorce their spiritual and moral values from politics without depriving themselves of the possibility of promoting those values.[4]

Hamid Enayat. *Modern Islamic Political Thought*. Austin: University of Texas Press, 1982.

---

[1] Raf'at as-Sa'īd, *Hasan al-Banna* (Cairo, 1977) pp. 83 ff.

[2] Ghazzālī, *Kifah din*, 3rd ed. (Cairo, 1965) pp. 133–9.

[3] Ghazzālī, *Min huna*, p. 25.

[4] *Ibid.*, pp. 22–3.

The Nature of the Islamic Revival

James P. Piscatori

JAMES P. PISCATORI *is a Research Fellow at the Royal Institute of International Affairs in London.*

Reasons for the revival

In looking for an explanation of the [Islamic] revival, therefore, we must take a somewhat longer view. Four broad reasons come into sight.

First, the defeat of Egypt, Syria, and Jordan in the 1967 war with Israel shattered the morale not only of the Arabs, who lost in a head-to-head fight with the enemy, but also of most Muslims, who lost the holy city of Jerusalem. This was not just a defeat or a loss, it was *al-nakba,* "*the* disaster"—the culmination of a long series of setbacks and humiliations which stretched back in modern times to the first militarily unsuccessful encounters that the Ottoman Muslims had with the Europeans. These defeats had given rise to a sense of inferiority, which at first was based on an appreciation of technological, though not theological, inadequacy. But now, in the mid-twentieth century, the loss of sacred territory led many Muslims to conclude either one of two things—either that Islam was an inferior religion, or that they were inadequate believers who had not lived up to the ideals of Islam and therefore deserved their fate.

Most Muslims seem to have concluded that they—or at least their governments—had gone astray, although by and large they did not work out the implication of their failure: that the other side, the enemy, had done something right. This inability or unwillingness to grasp the nettle was the despair of many intellectuals, but, probably because of its simplic-ity, the popular conclusion concentrated the emotions: Muslims needed to be better Muslims, and their governments more Islamic, if God was to spare them further calamity, or if they were ever to have a chance of recapturing Jerusalem. At the very least the Israeli occupation outraged them, and in the common outrage Muslims everywhere found a stronger identification with each other than had existed previously in the modern era. Some Arab Muslims, in particular, came to see a certain hollowness in Nasirism, the ideology that had seemed the panacea for the Arabs' problems, and were prompted to search for an ideology and programme that could be both coherent and effective. Even before the war, some had come to regard 'Abd al-Nasir as an impious and incompetent tyrant, and as such a greater enemy than the Israelis.[1] But, when it came, the catastrophe of 1967 forced many others to reconsider basic principles and to look for an Islamic ideology.

It is all the more ironic, then, that in 1985, less than twenty years after the 1967 war, many Muslim—mainly Shi'i—activists in Lebanon came to see the Palestinians as an obstacle to their own Islamic revolution. They reached this conclusion as a consequence of disputes, over power and territorial control in Lebanon, and these disputes, along with the generally heightened awareness of Islam since the Iranian revolution, led them to de-emphasize the Palestinian struggle *per se* while putting more stress on liberating Jerusalem, the third holiest city of Islam. For whatever reason, then—the defeat of the Arabs by Israel or the conflict between Palestinians and Shi'i groups in Lebanon—a new sense of Islamic

---

[1] See, for example, 'Ali Jirisha, *'Indama yakhuma al-tughah* (Cairo, Dar al-I'tisam, 1975), pp. 48–50.

commitment has emerged out of the general Arab-Israeli imbroglio.

Second, the process of development has been a contributing factor. It has stimulated the revival in two main ways: (a) it has often strained the social and political fabric, thereby leading people to turn to traditional symbols and rites as a way of comforting and orienting themselves; and (b) it has provided the means of speedy communication and easy dissemination of both domestic and international information.

(a) The most important dimension to the first point is the unsettling and unrelieved exodus of people from the countryside to the cities. For example, between 1960 and 1975 the rate of increase in the urban population exceeded the growth of the industrial labour force in Egypt by 2 per cent, Iran by 3 per cent, Iraq by 8 per cent, Jordan by 18 per cent, Kuwait by 14 percent, Lebanon by 3 per cent, Morocco by 10 per cent, Saudi Arabia by 11 per cent, Syria by 3 per cent, and South Yemen by 13 per cent.[1] More recent data would undoubtedly show this trend continuing. Most rural migrants quickly become the urban poor, victims of their own hope, swallowed by the very process which they believed would liberate them. Unscrupulous contractors exploit the members of this seemingly inexhaustible labour pool in order to build as cheaply as possible the new buildings that dot the urban landscape, and government is often unwilling or unable to protect them and to give them basic shelter. In countries such as India and Nigeria, they are also subjected to ethnic or racial discrimination and made to feel that they do not belong and that they probably never will. Many of their children are likely to be forgotten, escaping the educational net and remaining largely unprotected against serious disease.

I must not leave the simplistic impression that these rural migrants have the same destiny or produce the same effect everywhere that they settle. These obviously differ with the culture, the state of the economy, and the size of the city. With regard to the last point, for example, migrants are able to spread rural attitudes more widely in small provincial towns than in the large cities, and not simply because of the difference in size. As Serif Mardin shows in the case of Turkey, the provincial towns provide fertile ground for Islamic sentiment because the petty-bourgeois merchants and the small-scale farmers feel exploited by the large capitalists and alienated from their Europeanized culture.[2] But there does seem to be a general connection between the sense of not belonging and the turn to religion. In places where Sufi *tariqas*, or brotherhoods, are present, such as Morocco or Senegal, the mystical assimilation of a local saint's grace (*baraka*) is a powerful antidote to the joylessness of everyday life. In some societies, such as Iran, where well-established religious institutions provide some degree of financial assistance, or at least cushion the move from the countryside, migrants naturally come into close contact with the religious officials. In Lebanon the Shi'a who have migrated from the south or the Beqaa Valley to Beirut do not seem to lose their sectarian identification. If anything, they become more aware of it. In the city and suburbs, as outsiders needing the patronage of families to which they do not belong, they feel that they have incurred dishonour and lowered the status that they had in the countryside. In such an alien environment, the political point of reference is no longer family, as it was in the village, but sect.[3] In other societies, such as Nigeria, where extreme economic imbalance and a climate of religious tension prevail, the migrants become natural recruits of millenarian movements. The official report on the Kano disturbances in December 1980, in which the followers of the self-proclaimed prophet known as Maitatsine wreaked horren-

---

[1] Lewis W. Snider, "Political Instability and Social Change in the Middle East," *Korea and World Affairs*, 8 (Summer, 1984), 288.

[2] Serif Mardin, "Religion and Politics in Modern Turkey," in Piscatori (ed.), *Islam in the Political Process*, p. 154.

[3] Fuad I. Khuri, "Sectarian Loyalty Among Rural Migrants in Two Lebanese Suburbs: A Stage Between Family and National Allegiance," in Richard Antoun and Iliya Harik (eds), *Rural Politics and Social Change in the Middle East* (Bloomington and London, Indiana University Press, 1972), pp. 204–10.

dous devastation, explained this phenomenon well:

> We have earlier made mention of his [Maitatsine's] application for a piece of land to erect temporary structures. His intention, we believe, was to provide accommodation for these men coming from the rural areas since he knew very well that the first problem they would face on arrival at Kano was accommodation... These fanatics who have been brought up in extreme poverty, generally had a grudge against privileged people in the society, whose alleged ostentatious way of living often annoyed them. Because of the very wide gap between the rich and the poor in our society and coupled with the teaching of Muhammad Marwa [Maitatsine], they were more than prepared to rise against the society at the slightest opportunity. After all they did not have much to lose... They did not own more than the clothes they wore. They had nothing to fall back to.[1]

In every case, the migration from the countryside has helped to spread rural attitudes in the cities, particularly a pronounced emphasis on Islamic tradition. It has thus given impetus to the urban Islamic revival.

The effects are less dramatic among the middle classes, but many of these, too, are unhappy with the process of development. As sophisticated education has become increasingly available, technicians, lawyers, engineers, and teachers have become the new "productive" middle class in place of the old bazaaris and landowners. These latter resent the loss of status and influence and are suspicious of the Western advisers, suddenly indiscreetly visible, who are purportedly exemplars of a different lifestyle and set of values, and

are supposed to show the local people the way to a more efficient and prosperous future. The former, the members of the "new" middle class, are impatient with the old ideology and anxious to better their position socially and politically.

Poverty and deprivation affect the attitudes of the rural migrants and, equally true, greater wealth and an improved social position affect the attitudes of the middle classes. It is precisely because the middle classes are better off that they are dissatisfied; their appetite has been whetted and they want more. This is particularly true of the lower middle class. According to Saad Eddin Ibrahim's profile of Egyptian Islamic militants, over 70 per cent were from modest, not poor, backgrounds and were first-generation city-dwellers.[2] Nazih Ayubi shows further that there is a difference in social background between those who attend al-Azhar and those who attend the secular universities, and that it is this latter, upwardly mobile and largely non-peasant, group that yields more of the new activists than we might have guessed. In fact, there is nothing new in this pattern: for example, of the 1,950 members of the main assembly of the Egyptian Muslim Brotherhood (al-Ikhwan al-Muslimun) in 1953, only 22 were not of the educated urban middle classes.[3]

For many urban Muslims, however, the sense of not belonging, of being neither fully modern nor suitably traditional, has been the price of success. A 1971 study of middle-class Egyptians indicated that a high proportion did not feel integrated into society and in fact

[1] Federal Republic of Nigeria, *Report of Tribunal of Inquiry on Kano Disturbances* (Lagos, Federal Government Press, 1981), p. 79.

[2] Saad Eddin Ibrahim, "Anatomy of Egypt's Militant Islamic Groups: Methodological Note and Preliminary Findings," *International Journal of Middle East Studies*, 12 (December 1980), 438–9; "Militant Islam Joins and Mainstream," *Arabia: the Islamic World Review* (April 1984), p. 68.

[3] In 1966, for example, 5.8 per cent of the students at Cairo University were *fallahin*, or of rural background, whereas 45.5 per cent of al-Azhar University's students were *fallahin*: Nazih Nasif al-Ayubi, *Siyasat al-ta'lim fi misr: dirasa siyasiyya wa idariyya* (Cairo, Markaz al-Dirasat al-Siyasiyya wa'l-Istratijiyya [al-Ahram], May 1978), p. 72. Also see his "The Political Revival of Islam: The Case of Egypt," *International Journal of Middle East Studies*, 12 (December 1980), 493.

regarded their relations with other people in terms of hostility and even conflict.[1] Religion may not hold the answer for these people, but they are automatically attracted to it because the religious instinct runs deep and because such secular ideologies as Nasirism and Ba'thism have seemed so obviously wanting—both materially and spiritually. Most members of the middle classes will express their religious feeling through the state-controlled religious establishment and will oppose a radical challenge to it.[2] Yet some will turn to more radical alternatives as they sense that the religious establishment is indistinguishable from a regime whose policies appear to close doors to them, even as they open doors to foreign political and business elites. (President al-Sadat's economic policy of attracting outside investment was called *infitah*, or "opening.") These Muslims will take to radical and often violent activity as they shout "Allahu Akhbar!" ("God is most great!"), but they have something in common with those others who feel at sea. Islam, not clearly defined but keenly felt, is their mooring. The metaphor is different in a short story by the Egyptian writer Alifa Rifaat, but the point is the same: for the middle-class woman trying to come to terms with her new sexual assertiveness, "the five daily prayers were like punctuation marks that divided up and gave meaning to her life."[3]

(b) The other way in which the process of development has stimulated a sense of renewal is by advancing the dissemination of information throughout the developing world. Despite the static plight of the sub-proletariat or *lumpenproletariat*,[4] there have been substantial improvements in literacy among the rest of the population; moreover, radios have become a common possession. As a result, people are now more in touch with what is going on in the rest of the world, and are anxious to formulate Islamic positions on current political, economic, and social issues—or, in other words, to think of the world's problems in Islamic terms. At the same time, Muslims come to know how dissatisfaction and protest against injustices can be and have been, in other places, framed by reference to Islam.

The fast and efficient distribution within Iran of Ayatullah Khumayni's sermons, delivered in exile and recorded on cassettes—"revolution-by-cassette" demonstrates further how modern information technology can help people focus their discontent and build their identity around one set of ideas, even though the exponent of those ideas is far removed. To put it the other way around, it shows how religious leaders can use popular feelings by appealing to traditional values, even when they are not physically present: this projection is the powerful extension of the mosque sermon (*khutba*).

Khumayni provides the most celebrated example, but there are others. Cassettes of the sermons of Shaykh 'Abd al-Hamid Kishk, an Egyptian *'alim*, are played throughout the Middle East. Young people are particularly attracted by them, as young people throughout Malaysia are attracted by recordings of the *khutbas* of Haji Hadi Awang, who, from his base in rural Trengganu, rails—impartially—

---

[1] Study by Fu'ad al-Bahi al-Sayyid in L.K. Malika (ed.), *Qira' at fi'ilm al-nafs al-ijtima'i fi'l-watan al-'arabi*, vol. 3 (Cairo, Al-Hay'a al-Misriyya al-'Amma li'l-Kitab, 1979).

[2] Dale F. Eickelman shows how the Moroccan bourgeoisie benefited from French encouragement of non-Sherqawi brotherhoods and, later, the Sultan's encouragement of "scripturalist" Muslim authorities. Accordingly, its religious attitudes were accommodating to those of the official establishment: *Moroccan Islam: Tradition and Society in a Pilgrimage Center* (Austin and London, University of Texas Press, 1976), pp. 222–32.

[3] Alifa Rifaat, *Distant View of a Minaret*, trans. by Denys Johnson-Davies (London, Quartet Books, 1983), p. 3.

[4] Marxists make a distinction between the two. For example, the Iranian Bizhan Jazani speaks of the sub-proletariat as the shanty-town urban poor who are potential revolutionaries, whereas the *lumpenproletariat* are thieves, hooligans, and prostitutes who are inevitably "depraved," "classless," and reactionary: *Capitalism and Revolution in Iran* (London, Zed Press, 1980), pp. 141–3.

against infidels and half-hearted Muslims alike. Because of the emphasis on community, the importance of the mosque as a central meeting-place, the gathering together of Muslims from all over the world during the Pilgrimage, and the respect given to such official interpreters as the 'ulama, Islam constitutes a vigorous communication system of its own and is what Marshal Lyautey called "a sounding board."[1] Modern technology has dramatically enhanced this capability.

The third general reason for the present revival, in addition to the intellectual and spiritual malaise since the 1967 war and the effects of the development process, is that Muslim societies have been caught up in the universal crisis of modernity. Most Muslims, like virtually everyone else in the developed and developing world, are feeling ill at ease with a way of life that places less and less emphasis on loyalties to the family and seems to find religious institutions increasingly irrelevant. In the past century a discernible shift towards the individual has taken place within societies—i.e. towards lessening the individual's dependence on the extended family (even in such socially conservative Gulf shaykhdoms as Qatar),[2] weakening parental authority, liberating women, and questioning the authority of the clergy. No direct causal relationship exists of course, but this period has also seen an alarming increase in divorce, alcohol and drug addiction, nerve disorders, and crime. It is not surprising, therefore, that "dropping-out," or "evaporation" (johatsu) as the Japanese say, has come to seem attractive to many. At the very least, modernism has led to a diminution of belief: "After the dizzying history of the last fifty years, the world has grown strange, and people floated."[3] Iranian writers, for example, are now beginning to talk about modernity, not modernization, as the problem, and the notion that something is missing in one's life seems to have generated a time of "secular discontents,"[4] leading many to wonder whether the age has lost its way and to ask, "What is it, after all, to be modern?"

Modernity gives rise to a basic search for identity, in which many people accept that knowing oneself comes through associating with the crowd rather than seeking to rise above it. This search is in fact an individual act of self-discovery, but because of Islam's intense association of the individual believer with the whole community of believers, it seems as if it is an act of self-abnegation. Muslims in a sense are looking for what Daniel Bell called "new rites of incorporation," which link today's deracinated individual to a community and a history.[5] And yet, in another sense, this is wrong: they are looking, rather, for old rites of incorporation that appear to be new even as they are familiar. Religion, precisely because in the past it answered questions on life and death and provided its followers with moral links to each other, becomes the means by which individuals hope to answer the new question of what it is to be modern, and, in so doing, to gain perhaps a reassuring, common world-view. In this respect, born-again Christians and veiled-again Muslims are responding to the same broad phenomenon.

Islam supplies a particularly powerful rite of incorporation because it puts great emphasis on the idea of community and on the Prophet's time as the model for the organization of society. Prior to the revelation that Muhammad received, the people of the Arabian peninsula had worshipped several gods and organized themselves according to tribal, blood ties. But it was the radical innovation of Islam to insist that each person is to be subservient to the one true God and to look upon every other person as brother. This community is based on the bonds of morality, not blood or tribal custom or expediency, and involves the acceptance of responsibilities to-

---

[1] Quoted in Charles-André Julien, "Crisis and Reform in French North Africa," Foreign Affairs, 29 (April 1951), 455.

[2] In Qatar, by 1975, only 37 per cent of families living close to each other were related, and since then the trend towards the nuclear family as the primary social unit has continued: Levon H. Melikian and Juhaina S. El-Easa, "Oil and Social Change in the Gulf," Journal of Arab Affairs, I (October 1981), 83.

[3] V.S. Naipaul, Among the Believers: An Islamic Journey, (London, Deutsch, 1981), p. 285.

[4] James Finn, "Secular Discontents," Worldview, 24 (March 1981), 5–8.

[5] Daniel Bell, The Cultural Contradictions of Capitalism (London, Heinemann, 2nd edn. 1979), p. 170.

wards God and men. Although the *umma* incorporates all the believers, it will eventually become universal and include all mankind. In the meantime, Muslims are to follow the example of the Prophet and, in the case of the Sunnis, his four immediate successor, "the rightly guided Caliphs," or, in the case of the Shi'a, the Imams. It is this perception of fraternity, and of a glorious past, that gives all Muslims—Sunnis and Shi'a—a powerful sense of belonging.

Finally, the fourth general reason for the revival is that the conditions of political development in these societies have tended to heighten the importance of Islam as a political ideology. Because most of these societies are poor in institutions and dominated by unelected rulers, it is natural for those in power to look for a way of legitimating themselves. Legitimation may perhaps be too grand a word to convey what I mean: rulers seek evidence of approval from the ruled or, at least, evidence of acquiescence or the absence of outright opposition. Several monarchies are especially adept at using Islamic symbols for this purpose: the Moroccan king makes much of his traditional title, Commander of the Faithful (*amir al-mu'minin*); the Saudi king finds a naturally sympathetic response when he speaks of his role as protector of Mecca and Medina; and the Jordanian king is careful to emphasize his descent from the Prophet. Monarchs probably always need reassurance, but the need in the case of these leaders has certainly become greater and more definite since the unleashing by the Iranian revolution of a violent ideological storm whose avowed purpose has been to overcome all the remaining shahs of the Muslim world. The fact that development schemes seem to be losing momentum or running into trouble has further contributed to the uneasy climate.

This defensiveness on the part of the existing leaders has been apparent not only in the traditional monarchies, but also in the republics, where such leaders as al-Sadat and Mubarak of Egypt and al-Numayri of the Sudan have faced considerable opposition to their rule and have found it expedient to put

Islam to their service. Al-Sadat, for example, found it useful—although it was extremely controversial—to have a *fatwa* from al-Azhar supporting his peace treaty with Israel; Mubarak has created an official Islamic publication, *al-Liwa al-Islami* (*The Islamic Standard*), to rival the popular and often censorious Muslim Brotherhood publication *al-Da'wa* (*The Call*); and al-Numayri courted Sufi leaders and made concessions to the Muslim Brothers, such as the introduction of Islamic law. In Malaysia as well, the government, although keenly aware of the multi-ethnic composition of the population, has increasingly affirmed its Islamic credentials, and the ruling part, the United Malays' National Organization (UMNO), has claimed that it is the largest Islamic party in the country.

In all these countries governments have been able to use Islam with such ease because, as an ideology, it is vague in content yet highly charged: people instinctively respond to it as a general symbol but also as a guide to their loyalties. Its vocabulary, too, is thoroughly familiar to everyone, thereby guaranteeing that the government's message cannot be missed. Napoleon recognized the value and ease—of using Islamic symbolism at the time of this invasion of Egypt in 1798. His proclamation to the people of Egypt began with the standard Muslim invocation of "God, the Merciful, the Compassionate" (*bismallah*), and went on to say "I worship God (may He be exalted) far more than the Mamlukes do, and respect His Prophet and Glorious Quran... [T]he French also are sincere Muslims."[1]

Governments have also been able to use Islam to their own ends because it lends itself readily to nationalization: or, to express it differently, they have been able to make it part of the bureaucracy. Even the Malaysian federal government, which is sensitive to states' rights, pre-eminently including the right to regulate religion, has moved to bureaucratize Islam. It has not only created such coordinating bodies as the National Council for Islamic Affairs, the National Fatwa Council, and the Religious Affairs Division of the Prime

---

[1] Quoted in Albert Hourani, *Arabic Thought in the Liberal Age, 1798–1939* (London, Oxford University Press, 1970), p. 30.

Minister's office, but has also taken over a number of religious schools in the states. In effect, then, governments have recognized the power of Islam and sought to harness it to their own ends.

But just as Islam can be used to legitimate, so can it be used to express opposition. And there are signs that this use has been increasing too. The increase has come about partly as a result of the Shah's overthrow, but also because in many countries in which there are no regular outlets for political expression Islam has been found to be an effective and relatively safe way of making a political stand. Governments have been hesitant to suppress groups speaking in the name of Islam because of the need to appear orthodox themselves, in order either to forestall domestic opposition or to attract aid from Muslim "patrons" such as Saudi Arabia. As a result, many Muslim groups have been relatively free to criticize their governments, albeit in a circumspect way. The Muslim Brotherhood has been doing this in Jordan, where it has been tolerated as long as it remains a loyal opposition; this pattern was also true of the Brotherhood in the Sudan for most of the al-Numayri regime. Furthermore, it has happened in Algeria and Tunisia, where Muslim groups have acted as a kind of pressure group that tries to influence policies rather than to replace the regime.

In regimes so repressive that they brook no dissent and regard Muslim criticism of any sort as a threat to their survival, the "Islamic alternative" almost invariably has become more radical. It has become a kind of party, whose aim is to replace the regime, rather than a pressure group. This radicalization of a political alternative of course happens in any repressive society, as it did in Poland, where Solidarity may be thought of as the opposition party. It even happens in societies perceived by only a small minority to be repressive, such as West Germany, which is totalitarian in the eyes of the Baader-Meinhoff gang. My point is not to demonstrate the uniqueness of Muslim societies but merely to indicate that in the Muslim case, too, ostensibly ideological—or religious—groups may become politically radicalized in certain circumstances.

Islam might acquire an even more contentious political centrality, a revolutionary character, if social and economic conditions were dire. This would be the case if there were a marked division between the haves and have-nots, or, to use the terminology at once Qur'anic and secular of the Iranian revolution, between the "oppressors" (*mustakburun*) (16:22–3) and the "oppressed" (*mustad'afun*)(4:97). The rural poor and new urban immigrants would constitute the "oppressed" (or the "disinherited," as is said in Lebanon),[1] and the large landowners and urban middle-class professionals would constitute the "oppressors." In this situation, as was the case in Iran, politics would become increasingly polarized and vicious as all were caught up in a double revolution of expectations: peasants expecting the good life in the dazzling capitals; professionals and intellectuals expecting greater influence, status, and political participation. Both sides would be destined for disappointment, and would inevitably see each other as obstacles. The professionals and intellectuals would come to regard the urban immigrants as a drain on scarce resources; and, more importantly, given the role played by street politics in the increasingly city-dominated developing countries, the "disinherited" would come to regard members of the new professional middle class as new oppressors, who used Islam as a tactic to gain mass support but who really cared only about advancing their own narrow self-interest. Moreover, those who said they wanted to make Islam relevant to the conditions of the modern world would be seen as having sold out to, or at least compromised with, the Westernized, secularizing leadership. It is in this way that "modernist" groups, such as the Masyumi party in Indonesia, lose ground to more "traditionalist" ones, such as the Nahdatul Ulama.

In effect, then, a revolution of *falling* expectations would take place, particularly among the rural poor and urban immigrants. Seeing a

---

[1] In 1974 Shi'i authorities, particularly Musa al-Sadr, established Harakat al-Mahrumin (Movement of the Disinherited) in Lebanon in order to advance Shi'i rights. A military wing, Amal (an acronym meaning "hope"), was set up the following year.

prosperous future recede on the horizon, they would naturally cling to the only comfort of the present, the pillar of traditional faith, and, in doing so, would give political expression to the frustration and indignities of living on the margin of the society. It is a phenomenon that Soviet writers have come to regard as inevitable: "It is natural for them, therefore, to ex-press their socio-political aspirations and protest against colonial and imperialist oppression in religious form."[1]

James P. Piscatori. *Islam in a World of Nation-States.* Cambridge: Cambridge University Press, 1986.

---

[1] A. Vasilyev, "Islam in the Present-Day World," *International Affairs* (Moscow), no. II (November 1981), p. 53.

We Shall Confront the World with Our Ideology

Ayatollah Khomeini

AYATOLLAH KHOMEINI (1900–) took on his
surname in 1930 in honour of his birthplace,
Khomein, Iran. He assumed the title "ayatollah"
when he had gained enough of a following to merit
the designation. After fourteen years in exile he
returned to Iran after the fall of the Shah,
replacing the monarchy with a theocracy.

In the name of God, the compassionate, the merciful, let me congratulate all oppressed people and the noble Iranian nation on the occasion of the new year, whose present is the consolidation of the foundation of the Islamic Republic. The will of almighty God, may He be praised, decreed the release of this oppressed nation from the yoke of the tyranny and crimes of the satanical regime and from the yoke of the domination of oppressive powers, especially the government of the world-devouring America, and to unfurl the banner of Islamic justice over our beloved country. It is our duty to stand up to the superpowers and we have the ability to stand up against them, provided that our intellectuals give up their fascination with Westernization or Easternization and follow the straight path of Islam and nationalism.

We are fighting against international communism to the same degree that we are fighting against the Western world—devourers led by America, Israel and Zionism. My dear friends, you should know that the danger from the communist powers is not less than America and the danger of America is such that if we show the slightest negligence we shall be destroyed. Both superpowers have risen for the obliteration of the oppressed na-

tions and we should support the oppressed people of the world. [shouts of "God is great"]

We should try hard to export our revolution to the world, and should set aside the thought that we do not export our revolution, because Islam does not regard various Islamic countries differently and is the supporter of all the oppressed people of the world. On the other hand, all the superpowers and all the powers have risen to destroy us. If we remain in an enclosed environment we shall definitely face defeat. We should clearly settle our accounts with the powers and superpowers and should demonstrate to them that, despite all the grave difficulties that we have, we shall confront the world with our ideology.

My dear youth, who are the object of my attention, take the Koran in one hand and the weapon in the other and so defend your dignity and honor that you can deprive them of the power of thinking and plotting against you. [shouts of approval]

Be so merciful to your friends that you do not cease from bestowing upon them all that you possess. Be aware that today's world is the world of oppressed people and that, sooner or later, theirs is the victory. [shouts of approval] The oppressed are the ones who shall inherit the earth and shall govern by God's decree.

Once again, I announce my support for all movements, fronts, and groups which are fighting in order to escape from the claws of the Eastern or Western superpowers. I announce my support for beloved Palestine and beloved Lebanon. Once again, I strongly condemn the dastardly occupation of Afghanistan by the plunderers and occupiers of the aggressive East. [shouts of "God is great"] I hope that the Muslim and noble people of Afghanistan will as soon as possible achieve true victory and independence and be released from the grip of these so-called supporters of the working classes. [shouts of "God is great"]

The noble nation should know that the entire victory was achieved through the will of almighty God and by means of transformation which came about throughout the country, and through the spirit of faith and a spirit of self-sacrifice, which was manifested in the decisive majority of the nation. Turning toward God and the unity of expression was the basis of our victory. If we forget the secret of victory and we turn away from great Islam and its holy teachings and if we follow the path of disunity and dissension, there is the danger that the bounty of God almighty may cease and the path may be laid open for the oppressors, and that the deceits and plots of the satanical powers may put our beloved nation in bondage and waste the pure blood which has been shed on the path of independence and freedom and spoil the hardships which our dear young and old have endured, and that our Islamic country may forever endure that which passed during the satanical regime, and that those who were defeated as a result of the Islamic revolution may do to us that which they did and continue to do to the deprived and oppressed people of the world.

Therefore, being conscious of my divine and religious duty, I remind you of certain points. And his excellency the president and the Revolutionary Council and the government and the security forces are emphatically entrusted with the execution of these points. [shouts of support] I ask the entire nation, with all its power and with its strong allegiance to beloved Islam, to seriously support them throughout the country.

I see that the plots of the anti-revolutionary satans aimed at providing opportunities for the East or the West are increasing. It is the divine, human and national duty of our government and nation to prevent these plots, with all of our ability.

Now I point out certain issues: [shouts of "God is great"]

1. This year is a year in which security should return to Iran [shouts of "God is great"] and the noble people live in utmost comfort. Once again, I announce my support

for the noble Iranian Armed Forces. [shouts of "God is great"] However, the Armed Forces of the Islamic Republic should fully observe all laws and regulations. His excellency, the president, who has been appointed commander in chief of the Armed Forces on my behalf, is duty-bound to severely punish anyone, regardless of his position and grade, who wishes to create disruption in the army or organize strikes or indulge in slowdowns or violate army discipline and regulations or rebel against army regulations. As soon as an offense has been determined, the president should immediately expel the guilty individual from the Armed Forces and begin legal proceedings against him. I shall no longer tolerate disorder within the army in any form. Whoever causes disruption in the work of the Armed Forces will be presented to the nation as a counterrevolutionary, so that the dear nation may settle its account with the remnants of the criminal Shah's army. [shouts of "God is great"]

My dear military brothers, O you who turned your backs on the vile Shah and his plundering agents and joined the ranks of the nation. Today is the day of service to the nation and to beloved Iran. You should try to save this country from the enemies of Islam and Iran through hard work and endeavor.

2. Once again, I announce my support for the Guards Corps, and I remind them and their commanders that the lightest violation will lead to prosecution. If, God forbid, you do something which may cause disruption in the discipline of the corps, you will be immediately expelled. All that I said about the army will also be carried out concerning them. My revolutionary children, be sure that you deal with all people with kindness and with Islamic manners. [shouts of "God is great"]

3. The police and the gendarmerie of the country should observe order. As I have been informed, there are a great number of slowdowns at police stations. Those who do not have good records should strive to show greater harmony with the people and in order to establish order throughout Iran. They should regard themselves as part of the nation. I hope that in the future a fundamental reorganization be carried out in the gendarmerie and the police. The security forces

should regard themselves as belonging to Islam and the Muslims. The explosions in the south have greatly aggrieved me; why do not the corps and the police and gendarmerie clearly identify and punish a group of ungodly persons dependent on the former regime, corrupt, foreign and dependent on America? These people are guilty of sowing corruption on earth, both those who directly take part in such actions and those who guide the affairs from afar. Their conviction as those who are guilty of sowing corruption on earth is clear. The Revolution Courts should show greater decisiveness, so that they may uproot them. [shouts of "God is great"]

4. Revolution Courts throughout the country should be perfect examples of the implementation of God's religion. They should try not to be diverted from the teachings of God almighty, even by one step. They should observe complete care. They should sit in justice with revolutionary patience. The courts have no right to have armed forces of their own. They should act according to the constitution and gradually the Islamic judicial system should take over the responsibilities of the courts. Therefore, they should prevent wrongdoings with utmost decisiveness and if, God forbid, a person has violated God's teachings, this should immediately be made known to the nation and he should be punished. [shouts of "God is great"]

5. The government is duty-bound to provide the means of labor and production for workers, farmers and laborers. However, they too should know that strikes and slowdowns will not only strengthen the superpowers, but also cause the hope of the oppressed people in the Islamic and non-Islamic countries who have risen to be turned into despair. The people of each city, as soon as they learn of a strike at a factory, should go to that place and see what they want. You should identify the counterrevolutionaries and make them known to the people. The noble people of Iran can no longer pay unearned salaries to a number of ungodly people. [shouts of approval]

My dear workers, you should know that those who every day create tumult in a corner of the country and who basically come to the field with the logic of force are your headstrong enemies and wish to turn you away from the path of the revolution. They are dictators, who if they ever come to power will not allow anyone to breathe. You should fight against them in all fields and identify them to the public as your number one enemy and reveal their connection and dependence upon the aggressive East or the colonial West. The government is duty-bound to severely punish those who are involved in such actions. [shouts of approval]

6. I do not understand why the government is not reactivating the wheels of industry, which have stopped and are in the interest of the public. The government should, as soon as possible, implement the projects which have been stopped and are in the interest of the nation, as well as some new projects, so that the economic situation of our country may be set right. [shouts of "God is great"]

7. In government departments, all government employees must obey the government elected by the people; otherwise, harsh actions are needed. Anybody who wishes to disrupt a government department should be expelled immediately and should be made known to the nation. I am amazed at how the responsible officials are not making use of the strength of the people. The people themselves will settle their accounts with the counterrevolutionaries and expose them. [shouts of "God is great"]

8. The confiscation of the property of the oppressors by unauthorized individuals or unqualified courts is strongly condemned. All confiscations should be carried out according to religious regulations, with the verdict of the prosecutor or the court judges. No one else has any right to interfere in such actions. The violators should be severely punished. [shouts of "God is great"]

9. The distribution of land should be carried out according to religious regulations; and when it is proved that somebody's land should be distributed, only the qualified courts have the right to seize the land. No one else has any right to trespass on anybody's land, place of residence or orchard and, basically, unqualified individuals have no right to interfere in such actions. However, they can pass to responsible officials information concerning the land, house or orchards of members of the satanical regime who have

wrongfully usurped other people's property. If anybody commits an action contrary to Islamic principles and regulations, he will be vigorously prosecuted. [shouts of "God is great"]

10. The Housing Foundation and the Foundation of the Oppressed should produce as soon as possible the balance sheets of their actions so that the people may be informed of the activities of these two revolutionary organs. The Housing Foundation should clarify how much work it has performed; and the Foundation of the Oppressed should clearly publish the list of movable and real property of the satanical people, especially the Shah, his family and his filthy lackeys throughout Iran and should announce what they have carried out so far. They should say to whom they have given the property of the traitorous Shah.

Is it true that the foundation of the Oppressed has been turned into the foundation of the oppressors? If this is so, purging is necessary and to neglect this important matter is forbidden. These two foundations should clearly explain to the people why they have not been able to carry out their duties faster. If some people are committing evil deeds in the name of the oppressed, it is the duty of all the courts throughout Iran to act with speed. [shouts of "God is great"]

11. Revolution should come about in all the universities throughout Iran, so that the professors who are in contact with the East or the West will be purged, and so that the universities may become healthy places for the study of higher Islamic teachings. The false teachings of the former regime should be abruptly stopped in universities throughout Iran because all the misery of the Iranian society during the reign of this father and son was due to these false teachings. If we had a proper set-up in our universities, we would have never had a university-educated intelligentsia who during Iran's most critical period are engaged in conflict and schism among themselves and are cut off from the people and are so negligent of what happens to the people, as though they do not live in Iran. [shouts of "God is great"] All of our backwardness is due to the lack of proper understanding by most of the university intellectuals of the Islamic society

of Iran. Unfortunately, the same thing is still true. Most of the deadly blows which have been delivered to this society have been due to the majority of these university-educated intellectuals who have always regarded—and still regard—themselves as being great and have always said things—and still continue to say things—which only their other intellectual friends can understand, regardless of whether the people understand them or not. Because the public is of no significance to them and all that is important to them is themselves. This is due to the fact that false university education during the reign of the Shah so trained university-educated intellectuals that they attached no value whatsoever to the oppressed masses. Unfortunately, even now it is the same.

Committed and responsible intellectuals, you should set aside dissension and schism and should think of the people and you should free yourselves from the evil of the "isms" and "ists" of the East or the West, for the sake of the salvation of the people, who have given martyrs. You should stand on your own feet and should refrain from relying on foreigners. The students of religious teaching and university students should carefully study Islamic principles and should set aside the slogans of deviant groups and should replace all deviationist thinking with beloved and genuine Islam. Religion students and university students should know that Islam is itself a rich school, which is never in need of grafting any other ideologies to it. All you should know that mixed thinking is a betrayal of Islam and the Muslims [shouts of "God is great"] and the bitter results of such thinking will become apparent in future years.

Most regrettably, at times it can be seen that due to the lack of the proper and precise understanding of Islamic issues, some people have mixed Islamic ideas with Marxist ideas and have created a concoction which is in no way in accordance with the progressive teachings of Islam. Dear students, do not follow the wrong path of the uncommitted university intellectuals and do not separate yourselves from the people.

12. Another issue is the press and the mass media. Once again, I ask all the press throughout Iran to come and join hands and freely write about the issues, but not to engage in

plots. I have repeatedly said that the press should be independent and free.

But unfortunately and with great amazement I have seen a number of them engaged in implementing the evil designs of the right or the left, most unjustly, in Iran; and they are still doing it. In every country the press plays an essential role in the creation of a healthy or unhealthy atmosphere. I hope that they will engage in service to God and the people. Also, radio and television should be independent and free and should broadcast every kind of criticism with complete impartiality, so that once again we will not see the radio and television from the time of the deposed Shah. Radio and television should be purged of its pro-Shah or deviant elements. [shouts of "God is great"]

13. These days, through the agents of the Shah and his lackeys, attacks have increased on the true clergy, who in fact, both at the time of the Shah and at the time of his father, were among the most distinguished strata of the nation, who through their numerous uprisings against the corruption of the regime engaged in struggle and divulged the crimes of the regime. Throughout the rightful struggles of the noble nation against the Shah and America, the clergy led the struggles that led to victory. Exactly at the time when the clergy started its irrepressible struggle against the traitorous Shah in the years 1962 and 1963, the Shah called the committed and responsible clergy black reactionaries, because the only serious threat to him and to his rule came from the struggling clergy, who had roots in the depth of the souls of the people and stood up against him and against his oppression. Now, the agents of the Shah have again put the word reaction into the mouths of my children who are unaware of the depth of the issues, in order to crush the clergy, who are the foundation of independence and freedom of this country. My beloved and revolutionary children: Today the insulting and the weakening of the role of the clergy is a blow against independence, freedom and Islam. Today, it is treason to follow the path of the traitorous Shah and use the word treason concerning this respected class, who are among the most distinguished strata, not accepting either the yoke of the East or that of the West.

My dear sisters and brothers, you should know that those people who regard the clergy as reactionary are, ultimately, following the path of the Shah and America. [shouts of "God is great"] The noble Iranian nation, by supporting the genuine and committed Iranian clergy, who have always been the guardians and protectors of this country, will remit their debts to Islam and will cut off the hands of all of history's oppressors of their country.

On the other hand, I announce to the respected clergy, wherever they are, that it is possible that the satans and their agents may engage in hostile propaganda against the dear youth, especially the university students. The clergy should know that today all strata of the nation especially these two respected strata, who are the intellectual power of the nation, should join hands and fight against satanic forces and the oppressors and advance the Islamic movement in united ranks and protect independence and freedom as they would their own dear lives. It was the plan of the world-devourers and their agents to separate these two effective and thinking strata from one another during the satanic regime; and, unfortunately, they were successful and they ruined the country. This plan is once again being implemented and with the slightest negligence we shall be ruined.

I hope that all strata of the nation, especially these two respected strata, will not be negligent of plots and conspiracies in the new year and will nullify the evil plans through their unity of expression. [shouts of "God is great"]

Finally, after praying for forgiveness for the martyrs of the Islamic Revolution and expressing gratitude for their self-sacrifice, it is necessary on this new year to express my congratulations to their relatives, to their mothers and fathers and congratulate them on their being able to train such lions and lionesses. Also, I wish to congratulate the injured and the crippled of the revolution, who were pioneers in the advancement of the movement of the nation and the establishment of the Islamic Republic. Verily, our Islamic revolution is indebted to the self-sacrifice of these two beloved groups. I and the nation will not forget their brave deeds and will honor their memory.

I beseech almighty God for the greatness of Islam and the Muslims. God's greetings and blessings be upon you.

Ayatollah Khomeini. "We Shall Confront the World with Our Ideology." *Middle East Research and Information Project Reports.* 88 (1980): 22–25.

Blessed Are the Peacemakers

Jerry Falwell

JERRY FALWELL (1933–) is the President of the
Moral Majority, which he helped found in 1979.
He is also the Chancellor of Liberty Baptist
College, Lynchburg, Virginia.

Jesus said, "Blessed are the peacemakers."
President Reagan, with his "Peace Through
Strength" initiative believes that the moral
and military strength of the United States is an
absolutely essential deterrent to war. I and
thousands of ministers and lay people agree
with the President on his position.

The role of the schools of America relative
to teaching students the facts about nuclear
peril and the issues raised by this nuclear peril
should be a clearly educational one. Students
have a right to be informed about nuclear
peril and about the different views on how
this peril may be avoided.

I, President Reagan, and most of the military experts in our nation's government, believe the freedoms we cherish so highly in this
nation are endangered by the nuclear freeze
movement. On the other hand, there are many
well-meaning, sincere, genuinely frightened
individuals who believe that we can best
avoid a nuclear holocaust by accomplishing a
freeze of one kind or another. It is my wish
that the schools of the nation would teach students the facts about the nuclear peril and
would then allow those students to decide for
themselves.

First, we should ask why not a freeze? Because in theory, the idea of freezing all production of nuclear weapons sounds like a
laudable goal when, in actuality, a freeze
would prove detrimental to our national security. A nuclear freeze at this time would, for
example, lock an already existing Soviet advantage in nuclear weapons. A freeze would
reward the Soviets for their massive buildup
and would lock in their advantages. A freeze
would prevent the United States from improving the survivability of their already rapidly
aging strategic force and would make our military apparatus increasingly vulnerable to Soviet attack.

The freeze would also not allow us to maintain our antiquated B-52 bomber force in top
shape.

Just last year, we deployed the first ballistic
missile submarine in 15 years. Our present
fleet of submarines is approximately 15–20
years old. A nuclear freeze would not allow
these subs to be replaced.

A nuclear freeze would halt the development of an MX missile, a Trident SSBN, Trident 1SLBM, Trident 2SLBM, B-1 bomber, air
launch cruise missiles, sea launch cruise missiles, Pershing 2 missile, ground launch cruise
missiles.

In summary, the overall impact of a freeze
would be to seriously reduce U.S. chances of
survival in the event of a nuclear first strike by
the Soviets. This undermines the deterrent factor that has kept the Soviet Union at bay in the
past and would, in turn, increase the risk of
war.

A nuclear freeze would be a step backward
from our serious negotiations with the Soviet
Union in Geneva where U.S. negotiators are
seeking deep and verifiable reductions in the
most destabilizing nuclear forces of both sides.

Thus, a freeze is a vote to ignore reality
since freezing current forces now would make
us less, not more, secure. It would undercut
our reductions and negotiations, and reward
the Soviets for their massive buildup in the
last decade, while preventing the U.S. from
taking steps necessary to modernize our aging
and increasingly vulnerable deterrence systems.

Jerry Falwell. "Blessed are the Peacemakers." Social
Education. November/December 1983: 488–89.

Where Is Jerry Falwell Headed?

Interview with *Christianity Today*

Shedding his earlier opposition to political involvement, Jerry Falwell helped found Moral Majority in 1979. The group was organized to oppose abortion and to support traditional family values, a strong national defense, and the State of Israel.

Moral Majority enabled fundamentalists to join forces with those from other religious traditions in addressing social and moral issues. Falwell says Catholics make up the largest constituency in Moral Majority, accounting for some 30 percent of its adherents. The organization also includes evangelicals, Jews, and Mormons.

Last month, Falwell announced the formation of Liberty Federation, an umbrella organization that will address a broader range of public policy issues (CT, February 7, 1986, p. 60). Among other issues, the organization will speak out on the strategic defense initiative, the spread of communism, and American foreign policy toward South Africa and the Philippines. Moral Majority is functioning as a subsidiary of Liberty Federation. Another subsidiary, Liberty Alliance, operates as the educational and political lobbying arm of Liberty Federation.

Christianity Today asked Falwell to assess the Religious Right in 1986. He also outlines his goals for the future, and tells how he has changed after seven years of political activism.

Has the New Right's political power crested, or will it continue to grow?

The New Right has been very successful, and its influence is growing rapidly. There is a perception across the country that with Ronald Reagan in the White House, the moral issues are on the front burner, the country is moving to the Right, and we have won the battle.

However, most people in the New Right would tell you they are having difficulty raising funds. That is true for two reasons. First, so many more organizations are raising funds out of the same pool. Second, the perception of safety, which our success has created, hurts fund-raising efforts. You don't do well in fund raising unless you are in trouble.

Organizations in the political Right are realizing that there are X number of people interested in supporting conservative causes, and they are all asking those same people for money. One of my friends receives at least 30 letters a day from political and conservative organizations. The number of organizations needing money is growing faster than the head count of conservative supporters. So some of these organizations are going to die out.

But these factors have not affected the Christian Right. Our supporters back us out of a spiritual motivation, rather than political motivation. Our budget is $100 million—the largest ever. Our supporters are giving continuously, regardless of who is in the White House.

The New Right has had a positive influence on the Christian Right. They have educated us on many of the issues, giving us political savvy in a hurry. And groups like Moral Majority have spawned hundreds of groups of conservative Christians who are now registered voters. They are speaking to the issues, and they are politically involved. The next step for us is challenging our people to run for office. We probably have 90 to 100 running this year.

Your statements last fall opposing economic sanctions against South Africa raised the ire of many Americans, including religious leaders. Isn't this a problem that has no simple theological answer?

I don't know any reasonable Christian who supports apartheid. So we begin from a point of agreement. But there is tremendous diversity on how to solve the problem. I have fundamentalist friends who disagree with my position on South Africa.

I want to see every one of the 30 million residents of South Africa participating in the political process there. And I want to see it happen as quickly as possible. But I don't want South Africa to go the route of Mozambique, Zimbabwe, and Angola. When colonialism became history in Africa and Europeans moved out instantly, bloodbaths occurred. The citizens of those countries had not had time to develop the expertise to operate a fair and reasonable government.

The gradual move toward reform that South African President P.W. Botha is committed to will eventually bring a participatory government. It will bring an end to apartheid, and provide prosperity without bloodshed.

Now, the African National Congress (ANC) and its arm inside the country, the United Democratic Front, are advocating violence. Half of the 800 people who have died have been blacks killed by blacks. There has been brutality, and you can't excuse all the conduct of the South African government any more than you can the ANC.

Change can take place. But intervention from outside—from the Soviets or the United States—will create havoc. We need to use economic pressure and a lot of restraint to give them time to do in a few years what it took America 170 years to accomplish.

Your stands on political matters give rise to criticism from both the Right and the Left. How do you live with that kind of tension?

I have a relative position of safety as pastor of Thomas Road Baptist Church in Lynchburg, Virginia. We have 21,000 members who have grown up with me since the inception of the church 30 years ago. They know where I'm coming from. They have seen my views develop.

Many of them were here when we were a part of the segregated South and had no black members. They were here when our first black member was baptized. They saw our philosophy change and they saw our commitment to non-involvement in political issues reversed.

They were here long enough to hear the rationale and to see that change is not always bad.

They see the weeks and weeks of information and experience that lead up to the public positions I take. As a result, no matter what may be printed in the newspapers, when I come home I have no reaction to calm down. And with no intention of ever running for political office, I don't have to worry about opinion polls.

When you espouse a position that you know will be criticized, are you prepared to respond to your opponents?

As a younger preacher, I was far more sensitive to public opinion and criticism. There are two college professors who for 15 or 20 years have taped every message I have preached. They try to find some contradiction or ethnic bias or something. Every time they think they find something, they run to the *Washington Post*. There were days when I responded to them. But one day I realized that no matter who said what it didn't hurt me. My response to this garbage did me far more damage than what my critics said or did to me. So I stopped responding long ago, I operate totally on offense now.

Criticism can help keep us accountable. Who carries out that function in your life?

First, I am accountable to God. Next, I am accountable to a local congregation. As a pastor, I can't have any scandals. And I can't have a financial debacle because my congregation must have confidence in me. Third, as an organization, we are accountable to our donors. We are audited by an outside accounting firm every year. All of our donors have access to our financial statements.

How has your role changed since you founded Moral Majority?

Before Moral Majority was formed, I had more freedom to express my opinions. Since then, I've had to gradually pull in the ropes and be very cautious on making statements until I've weighed the impact on our own camp. The South African debate is probably the most volatile one we have been involved in because there are really good people on both sides of the issue.

I've had to pull in my tendency to shoot from the hip. I've also had to learn that I can't talk to anybody outside my own family about sensitive subjects, because my comments invariably appear in print. That's a hard lesson for a very public, extroverted person like myself.

In Lynchburg, I can stop at a hot-dog joint and talk with the guys I went to high school with. That doesn't mean I don't have detractors here. I do. But in this town I'm just Jerry.

It's totally different when I leave Lynchburg. My high visibility has made me become what I don't like to be: a private person outside of my home town. That is the most painful consequence of what I do.

Liberty University is a special concern of yours. What are your hopes and dreams for that school?

Liberty University is my way of carrying out the dream and vision God has given me. That vision is to give the gospel to the world in my generation. Television and radio are effective; the local church here is effective; our speaking tours are effective. But my hope for making an impact on the world with this generation and generations to come is to train young people in the things that are vital to the cause of world evangelization.

Now in our fifteenth year, we have 6,900 students. We have 75 majors, and we are fully accredited. Our master's program is in place, and our doctoral program begins this fall. We're also planning to start a law school. When you include our elementary and high school, we have 8,500 students. We have a dream of 50,000 students shortly after the first of the century.

There are several areas where Liberty University can reverse the trends that have corrupted society. We have trained 1,000 preachers. We have also trained journalists. We have a large business major, and a large education major. Our students who major in political science are required to work as in-

terns in Washington for senators and congressmen. One of our graduates is running for Congress this fall. One day we will be doing what Harvard has done. We'll have hundreds of our graduates running for office.

How is God moving you further along the ministry path he has set for you?

At age 52, my spiritual growth is as important as it was 34 years ago when I became a Christian. The study of the Word of God, my personal relationship with God, and my time in fellowship and prayer are as vital, if not more so, now as in the past.

I read a lot—not only the Bible and books about the Bible and men and women of God—but also books like *Iacocca* and *Losing Ground*. I try to read all the best sellers that are coming out so the world doesn't walk past us. I probably read two books a week. I have to make some sacrifices in order to find the time to do that. I'm trying to improve myself. I'm trying to learn. I'm trying as hard to grow now as I did 30 years ago so that I am capable of leading the people that God has put under my ministry.

What would you like your legacy to be?

I'd like to be remembered as a good husband, father, and pastor. That is my first calling. I've got three children in school. Two of them are in college, and one is in law school. We do everything together. I may fail in a lot of areas, but, God willing, it won't be at home.

Likewise, as pastor of Thomas Road Baptist Church, I'm always here on Sunday morning, Sunday night, and Wednesday morning. I won't miss two Wednesday nights a year. And I don't miss any Sunday mornings.

"Where is Jerry Falwell Headed in 1986?" (Interview). *Christianity Today*. February 21, 1986: 39–41.

The Sayings of Rabbi Kahane

Robert I. Friedman

ROBERT I. FRIEDMAN *is a writer on Middle Eastern affairs and an occasional contributor to the* The New York Review of Books.

I first talked with Rabbi Meir Kahane in December 1979, at his Jerusalem headquarters, which he calls the Museum of the Potential Holocaust. The "museum" was filled with anti-Semitic literature which he had clipped from American hate-group publications and pasted on display boards. At the time, Kahane was a political pariah. His followers in Israel consisted of no more than a few dozen American teen-agers who had belonged to the Jewish Defense League in the United States. "Numbers aren't important," Kahane told me. "How many Macabees fought the Greeks?"

Today Kahane's followers are far more numerous. In August 1984, he won a Knesset seat with 25,907 votes, 1.2 percent of the electorate. A poll conducted last summer by the prestigious Van Leer Institute in Jerusalem found that 40 percent of Israelis between the ages of fifteen and eighteen (excluding kibbutz youth) agreed with Kahane's fiercely anti-Arab views, and that 11 percent of the young Israelis surveyed would vote for him. The results so shocked the institute that it did not release them; but *Ha'aretz* uncovered the findings and published them in a front-page story (June 6, 1985). On August 27, *Ma'ariv* published the results of another poll that predicted Kahane's Kach ("Thus") party would, with about 9 percent of the electorate, win eleven seats (out of 120) in the Knesset if early elections were held, making it the third largest party in Israel.

More recently, on December 6, 1985, *Ma'ariv* published a poll indicating that Kahane's support had dropped to about 4 percent of the electorate—still enough for five seats. According to Hanoch Smith, a public opinion expert whose polls are published in *Davar* and the *Jerusalem Post*, Kahane's support fluctuates in relation to the level of Arab terrorism directed against Jews in Israel. Smith believes Kahane has a steady "band of support" of around 4 to 5 percent of the electorate, making him a "weighty political force" in future elections.

Though much has been written about Kahane, the man and his views have been obscured by the controversy surrounding his remarkable political success. What follows is a selection of Meir Kahane's own statements— remarks that he has made to me and to others, about people, events, and the ideas that have influenced him.[1]

The Rabbi from Brooklyn

Kahane was born in Brooklyn in 1932. He has one brother, Nachman, a rabbi who now heads a yeshiva in the Muslim quarter of Jerusalem's Old City. Kahane's father was a highly respected rabbi, a fervent Zionist, and a member of the right-wing Revisionist movement headed by Ze'ev Jabotinsky, who Meir remembers once came to dinner with the Kahanes in Brooklyn.

Kahane, who was trained at the Orthodox Yeshiva Mirrer in Brooklyn, became an ordained rabbi in the late 1950s. At about that time he graduated with a law degree from New York University, from which he later received a master of arts degree in international law. In 1958 he married a young woman from New York, Libby Blum, and soon after began serving as the rabbi of the Howard Beach Synagogue in a middle-class section of Queens. He was fired, he told me, when he "turned the synagogue president's son into an observant Jew." He really didn't mind being fired, he

---

[1] I include some of his statements quoted in my article on him in *Present Tense* (August, 1980).

said, because he didn't like being a traditional rabbi, and he hated the nouveaux riches Jews in his congregation "who lived in $100,000 homes without furniture."

In 1962 Kahane moved to Israel, leaving his wife and four children in Queens. He told relatives that he would soon become a member of the Israeli cabinet. "He thought Ben-Gurion was going to meet him at the docks," his uncle, Rabbi Isaac Trainin, who is the director of religious affairs for New York's Federation of Jewish Philanthropies, said. Kahane returned to the United States four months later, broke and unemployed.

The Underground Years

In 1963, Kahane and a childhood friend, Joseph Churba, formed a think tank called Consultant Research Association, which collected information for US intelligence agencies and other organizations. (Churba, an ordained rabbi, later became a Middle East specialist for Air Force intelligence and a foreign affairs adviser to Ronald Reagan during the 1980 campaign.) Churba and Kahane rented an apartment on New York's upper East Side under the name of Michael King, a byline Kahane sometimes used when he wrote occasional sports stories for the Brooklyn Daily.

By his own account, Kahane spent much of the next two years leading a double life. He would leave his house in Laurelton, Queens, on Monday for Washington or Manhattan, and return for the Sabbath on Friday. He posed variously as a foreign correspondent, a college professor, or a well-to-do bachelor. He spent one summer in the Hamptons at Churba's house. A New York public relations woman told The New York Times in 1971 that she remembered running into Kahane at a party on Long Island. "I knew him only as Michael King," she told the Times. "He told me he had been a correspondent for a wire service in Africa and I recall at one point he volunteered that he was a Presbyterian." On July 31, 1966, a Gentile woman with whom Kahane was reportedly having an affair, jumped to her death from the Queensboro Bridge. According to the Times story, Kahane, deeply depressed, attended her funeral in Connecticut and, in the years after her death, would sometimes place roses on her grave. In

1984 Kahane told the Jewish World that "there is no truth to the allegations" that he and the woman were lovers. "I make it a rule never to debase myself by responding to these kind of charges."

Sometime in 1963, Kahane told me, the FBI asked if the Consultant Research Association would infiltrate the then little-known John Birch Society to find out the source of its funds. (An FBI spokesman in New York says Kahane never worked for the FBI. Kahane says, "If the FBI says it isn't so, then they have their reasons.")

Kahane claims he went underground using the name Michael King because, he told me, "naturally, Meir Kahane with a yarmulke wouldn't have gotten very far." For many months he travelled through Southern California and the Southwest. It was in this bastion of right-wing conservatism, he says, that he was first exposed to virulent anti-Semitism. "It was a very dangerous job," Kahane recalled. "I rooted out the moneyed Birchers, then the FBI went in and leaned on them."

Kahane says he stopped these activities for the FBI in 1965, when he and Churba set up the Fourth of July Movement. This organization tried to create cells on American college campuses to support the Vietnam War. According to Kahane, the movement received "seed money" from the government "and certain groups within the labor movement," including George Meany. But it failed after less than a month because "we never got the amount of money we needed. My concern with the Birchers and with the left-wing student movement was always a Jewish one. I saw a growing sense of isolation on the part of Americans from world affairs. To keep our noses out of world affairs is not good for Jews."

In 1968, he and Churba wrote a book, The Jewish Stake in Vietnam, which argued that if the US reneged on its commitment to South Vietnam it would do the same to Israel. It was therefore vital for American Jews to support the war. The Jewish Stake was published by Crossroads Publishing at 2 West Twenty-third Street in New York. Kahane told me Crossroads Publishing had been set up by "the government" solely to distribute its pro-Vietnam polemic.

"After Vietnam, I knew the days of American Jewry were numbered," Kahane said, "America was a paper tiger. It would never fight for Israel."

The Jewish Defense League

People often ask me why I started the JDL—was it a personal trauma? No, I had an extremely pleasant life. I loved my neighborhood, and my Jewish and Italian friends. I spent hours roaming the streets, hanging out on the corner and playing games. I was a great baseball player.

By the late 1960s, however, Kahane became obsessed with the likelihood of an impending Holocaust. He told me that the newsroom of the *Jewish Press* in Brooklyn, where he worked as an associate editor in 1967 and 1968, was flooded with disturbing items about anti-Semitic acts all over the country—including, Kahane said, acts of violence by blacks and Puerto Ricans against Jews too old or too poor to leave the decaying inner cities.

When he expressed his concern about growing black anti-Semitism to leaders of major Jewish organizations, Kahane claims they told him to suppress the news to avoid aggravating the situation. In 1968 *Jewish Press* publisher Sholom Klass fired Kahane for using the paper to attack John Lindsay, then running for reelection as mayor of New York, as an anti-Semite. "Nineteen sixty-eight was a bad year," Kahane remembered. "I lost my job. I was also very upset that young Jews didn't give a damn about being Jewish anymore. They were fighting for blacks, for the Vietcong, for Cubans, for lettuce, but not for themselves." That year he took a small advertisement in the *Jewish Press*, seeking youths interested in "Jewish pride"—the first step in organizing the JDL. "Thirty-five people showed up and it took off."

Preaching Jewish pride and Jewish power, Kahane captured the imagination of thousands of young Jews. His slogans were "Never Again" and "Every Jew a 22." In 1969, he set up a weapons and martial arts training camp in the Catskill Mountains. By 1970 the JDL reportedly had some ten thousand members. Soon JDL members were arrested for bombing Russian and Arab property in the US and beating and harassing Russian and Arab diplomats. In July 1971, Kahane himself was convicted in a New York federal court for taking part in a conspiracy to manufacture firebombs. He was given a five-year suspended sentence and placed on probation for five years.

By the fall of 1971, JDL attacks against Soviet targets in the US had become so numerous that President Nixon became concerned Kahane would wreck the Strategic Arms Limitations Talks. The Soviet press had been filled with lurid accounts of Kahane's anti-Soviet actions and held Nixon personally responsible for the "Zionist hooligan." A confidential State Department memo at the time urged the Justice Department to secure indictments against JDL troublemakers, arguing it would "measurably improve the ability of the United States to deal with the Soviet Union on substantive foreign policy issues."

In 1972 the JDL claimed its first victim—a Jew. That year the offices of the Jewish impresario Sol Hurok, who was bringing Soviet talent to the US, were bombed by the JDL, killing a twenty-seven-year-old secretary. Kahane, then in Israel, deplored the act. "I once asked Begin how he felt when he learned that thirty or forty Jews were killed in the [Irgun] bombing of the King David Hotel," Kahane said during an interview in Jerusalem in 1979. "Begin told me he felt horrible. That's exactly how I felt after the Hurok bombing."

But Kahane was soon urging his associates to assassinate some of the people he opposed.

Kahane and the Mob

The JDL worked with other right-wing groups such as the American-Italian Civil Rights League, founded by the New York City mob boss Joseph Colombo, Sr., to instill pride in Italian-Americans and to counteract the notion that Italians in America were gangsters. Colombo's lawyer Barry Ivan Slotnick, who was recently hired as the lawyer for Bernhard Goetz, told Colombo about Kahane. At a dinner in 1971, Slotnick mentioned to Colombo that he was representing Kahane at his arraignment on bomb-making charges. Slotnick said Kahane didn't have much money and would probably have to fight his case from jail.

Colombo, who according to Slotnick was attracted to Kahane's tough Jewish image, showed up in court the next morning with a bondsman to pay the rabbi's $25,000 bail. Later, during an impromptu press conference with Colombo, Kahane told reporters that he welcomed the mob boss's support, and promised to "picket the offices of the FBI if Mr. Colombo asks our [JDL] help."

Asked by a *New York Times* reporter to discuss the implications of an alliance between the JDL and the Italian-American Civil Rights League, Kahane replied: "It's human brotherhood. People of other faiths and backgrounds have come to help. It's the kind of thing which, had it been blacks helping Jews, it would have drawn raves. The Italians are no worse than the blacks."

In the months that followed Kahane and Colombo became, Slotnick says, "close and good friends." In 1971, for example, Colombo helped Kahane organize a demonstration in Washington to protest the persecution of Soviet Jews. The demonstration, which Colombo and sixty of his followers attended, resulted in more than thirteen hundred arrests. Kahane told me Colombo paid bail and provided lawyers for some of those arrested. After the rally, Colombo "went on ABC/TV and said 'We Italian-Americans demand that the American government cut relations with the Russians unless they let the Jews go,'" Kahane told me. "I wanted to kiss him."

Kahane and Colombo were often seen together. Kahane took the mobster to his favorite kosher deli on the lower East Side and Colombo took the rabbi to his country club on Long Island to play golf. Kahane told critics, "I'll march with anyone if I think I can help a Jew." When Colombo was shot in the head by assassins while he was leading an Italian-American Unity Day rally in Columbus Circle, Kahane, who was to be a featured speaker, rushed to the hospital to visit his dying friend. "Colombo was a beautiful man and a friend of the Jewish people," Kahane later told me.

Kahane in Israel

In September 1971, Kahane moved to Israel. "It was impossible for me to tell Jews to go to Israel without going myself," he told me. At the time, Kahane told the Israeli press that he had no intention of entering local politics. He said he wanted to start his own *kirya* (or Jewish educational center). American Jewish graduates of the center, he told me, were to return to US college campuses and form student groups that would counteract Jewish left-wing activism in academia. Kahane had been given $100,000 by well-to-do New Yorkers to set up the center.

Later, Murray Wilson, a wealthy New York businessman who had given Kahane fifty thousand dollars, accused him of taking the money meant for the school and using it to finance a campaign for the Knesset. "We worked like dogs this spring and summer—with a *minimum* of help—to put out the best summer program Israel has ever had," Kahane wrote Wilson. "If...you are disillusioned, tell me now, so I will know how to function. This school is going to put out Jewish leaders the way we want them." Kahane sent Wilson a canceled check for three thousand dollars drawn on his personal bank account and made out to the school—a sum Kahane wrote represented his "total personal savings."

The school soon collapsed and in 1973 Kahane ran for the Knesset as the head of the Kach party. At that time Kahane was getting much favorable attention in the Israeli press for his work on behalf of Soviet Jews. He polled 12,811 votes, just a few hundred short of the number required to obtain a Knesset seat. Kahane's activities became more extreme, in part, he says, to gain publicity and win new followers. But his strategy backfired. When he ran again in 1977 and 1981, he lost by wide margins.

Meanwhile, Kahane was directing JDL activities in America. Following the murder of eleven Israeli athletes at the 1972 Munich Olympics, Kahane ordered his followers to step up their violent activities in America. On May 17, 1973, Kahane, from his Jerusalem office, wrote the following letter to an associate in New York:

Dear Josh: If we can't find some Jew(s) willing to blow up the Iraqui Embassy in Washington...and if we can't get someone to *shoot* a Russian diplomat (anyone) we are Jewish pigs and deserve what we get.

P.S. for this you can try to get money from Joe Alster, Stern etc. *You* don't go but send someone trustworthy with this letter—then burn it!

In another letter, Kahane outlined his plan to sabotage détente between the US and the Soviet Union.

All possible efforts have to be made to stop Brezhnev's trip to America or, failing that, to ruin it. A successful visit will make détente an unstoppable thing and the Russians will then turn on their Jews... I suggest an immediate kidnapping or shooting of a diplomat.

Kahane names the Soviet diplomat, his Virginia address, and the model, make, year, and license-plate number of his car.

Kahane ordered a JDL member to place "a bomb at the offices of Occidental Petroleum to warn Armand Hammer and any other people against deals with the Russians. Similarly, at a Chase Manhattan Bank since David Rockefeller opened a bank in Moscow."

Kahane also ordered a shooting attack on the Soviet embassy in Washington. He instructed an American Jewish high-school student who belonged to the JDL to have her teacher invite a Soviet diplomat to speak to her class so the JDL could assassinate him. "This is urgent for the survival of...Jews or else I would never ask you to risk things. After anything is done," Kahane cautioned, "wait to hear the news broadcast and if no innocent person is killed, phone the press."

The letters never reached their destination. They were intercepted by Shin Bet (Israel's internal security service) and forwarded to the FBI. Although Kahane's lawyers urged him to remain in Israel, in 1974 he returned to New York and was arrested on charges of violating the probation that had been granted after his 1971 conviction for conspiring to manufacture explosives. On February 21, 1975, the US government used the letters to revoke his probation.

"The letters—all the violence that the JDL...has used...was not a mindless violence or a heedless violence," Kahane said to the Court before sentencing. "It was a lesson in political logic." The letters had been written in response to Munich, which "struck at the very spirit of what people like to call The New Jew," and against détente, which, he said, "doomed" Soviet Jews.

What I did I did, but I certainly never did it with a contempt for law, never. I did what I did. I will do what I may do again, because I love the law and

there must be law with justice and there must be law with freedom and there must be law for all the people. If I ever stopped doing what I have to do, my wife would break up the family. I have the most wonderful wife and I spoke to her last Friday by telephone. She said, "Whatever happens, you just do what you have to do."

So I can only end by saying that I don't envy you, Your Honor. I did what the Government says I did and I violated probation and you will have to do what you have to do and do it with a good conscience and know that which I did I did with a good conscience.

Kahane was sentenced to one year in prison. He served four months in jail in New York City and eight months in a minimum security federal penitentiary in Allenwood, Pennsylvania.

"Prison was a real joy," he told me. "I read the Torah all day."

Front Groups/Funding

According to one of the founders of the JDL and others who have worked with Kahane, the rabbi has set up numerous front groups that were to serve primarily as a means for both Kahane and the JDL to collect funds. In 1981, the Anti-Defamation League identified fifteen fictitious businesses soliciting funds for Jewish "causes" that were associated with the JDL in California. The ADL found that the businesses were no more than a name and a postbox.

Other fronts included SOIL (Save Our Israeli Land), which was set up by Kahane in 1974, and placed under the control of Dov Hikind, currently the New York assemblyman from the Forty-eighth District, which includes Boro Park in Brooklyn. SOIL, a group that demonstrated against returning Arab land captured by the Israeli Army in the 1967 Six Day War, was intended to attract people who wouldn't want to be associated with the JDL. "The use of front groups should be encouraged within limitations," Kahane wrote a JDL board member in 1974.

SOIL, under Dov H. is a good example of what can be done. I think Dov should be invited to the next Board meeting to explain what has been done and what is being done. All SOIL names should be discreetly funneled to JDL which in turn should be careful to contact these people only many weeks later and without saying that they were gotten from SOIL. Work closely with Dov; I told him that he is to listen.

Assemblyman Hikind denies that Kahane controlled SOIL.

In the same letter, Kahane recommended the formation of a JDL front group to be named Yiud (destiny) as a way of attracting young people between the ages of ten and seventeen who would be more stable emotionally than many of the members of the JDL. Kahane also suggested that the JDL organize a *shul* (temple). He explained: "A *shul* is never bothered by the IRS and it can be held in a store front in Brooklyn... It is a great investment because then tax deductible contributions can be made with no trouble and the store can be used for meetings."

Kahane travels to the US four or five times a year to raise money. He has collected millions of dollars from American Jewish businessmen since founding the JDL in 1968. Among the well-to-do Jews who have supported the JDL are Reuben Mattus, the founder and president of Haagen-Dazs ice cream, and Bob Jacobs, an accountant from Staten Island, who has also raised money on behalf of convicted Jewish terrorists in Israel. (Mattus told me he has ceased to contribute.) Kahane told me that donations to him have increased, "especially from Jewish millionaires," since his election to the Knesset. "Everybody loves a winner," he said.

Palestinians

Shortly after he arrived in Israel, Kahane turned his attention to Palestinian Arabs. In 1974 he first proposed the idea of setting up a Jewish anti-Arab terrorist underground. In his book *The Jewish Idea*, published in 1974, he wrote that

> a world-wide Jewish anti-terror group be established and that this group must be organized and aided in exactly the same way as the terrorists are aided by Arab governments. With a serious face, the government of Israel must deny any connection with the group, even while allowing the same training bases on its soil as the Arab states allow the terrorists.

On June 13, 1980, he wrote in his weekly column in the *Jewish Press*, "Hundred(s) of Jewish lives will be lost, G-d forbid, unless the

government immediately moves to...create a terror-against-terror group that will spread fear and shatter the souls of the Arabs in Eretz Yisrael."

The Rabin government was not receptive to Kahane's views on terrorism. Many of his young followers were. Sometime in 1975, according to Israeli police officials, Kahane began to build an anti-Arab terrorist underground calling itself TNT (Terror Against Terror) in Jerusalem and the occupied West Bank. Police sources in Israel I talked to say Kahane was usually very careful not to become directly involved in planning or carrying out terrorist acts. "He created the climate for his supporters to act in," an Israeli police official told me. In May 1975, TNT struck for the first time, firebombing an empty Arab bus in an Arab suburb of East Jerusalem. A month later, four members of Kach were arrested for firebombing an East Jerusalem mosque. TNT struck sporadically during the next few years. After Begin was elected prime minister in 1977, the attacks grew more frequent and deadly.

In March 1984, five young JDL members from America who had trained with automatic weapons in a JDL training camp in the Catskills machine-gunned a bus filled with Arab workers near Jerusalem, wounding eight of them. Yehuda Richter, who came from Los Angeles and was Kahane's deputy in Kach, was sentenced to eight years in prison for the attack. In October 1984, a young Sephardic Jew from a Jerusalem slum fired a US-made anti-tank rocket at an Arab bus, killing one and wounding many more. Kahane made the man an honorary member of Kach, paid for his lawyer, and said his act was "sanctified by God."

Kahane himself has been arrested in Israel more than twenty times on charges ranging from sedition to inciting riots, which often occur when he and his followers visit an Arab village. On May 12, 1980, in an unprecedented action, former defense minister Ezer Weizman ordered Kahane to be detained for six months under the Emergency Powers Law of 1945 for purportedly plotting to blow up the Dome of the Rock Mosque in East Jerusalem—the third holiest shrine in Islam. Kahane was the first Jew to be arrested in the Jewish state under the law which was promulgated during the British Mandate in Palestine and which Israel has since used extensively against Arab terrorists.

Kahane was last arrested in Israel two years ago, on January 5, 1984, when he held a demonstration with about fifteen followers in support of arrested members of TNT. Kahane and two of his supporters were being charged with incitement to riot when they walked out of the West Jerusalem police station while the police were busy filling out forms. Kahane hid in Jerusalem for two days before he gave himself up "but of course, not before I gave a press conference."

Kahane has called Jews who have been arrested for terrorist acts against Arabs "nice Jewish boys" and says they "have fulfilled a holy task." Those in Kach who have been arrested for terrorist violence have been defended by lawyers hired by Kach and supported by Kahane at rallies and fund-raisers in both Israel and America.

In November 1984, when I interviewed Kahane at the Tudor Hotel on East Forty-second Street in New York, I asked him: "You were quoted as having applauded recent Jewish terrorist attacks against Arabs in Israel."

"Yes," he said. "What am I supposed to do? What are we supposed to do when Arabs at their own initiative...kill Jews? What are we supposed to do about that?"

"Did you know in advance of the TNT terrorist attacks or help plan them?" I asked.

"Next question," he replied.

Kahane has often explained his hatred of Arabs. "There are hundreds of unreported incidents of Arabs attacking and sexually molesting Jews [in Israel]," he told me during an interview in Jerusalem in 1979. "And who do you think plants bombs here—the American Boy Scouts? I don't want to live in a state where I have to worry about being blown up in the back of a bus."

"I don't blame the Arabs for hating us," the rabbi said. "This was their land—once. And no matter what the Israeli left says, you can't buy Arab love with indoor toilets and good health care. Israeli Arabs and West Bank Arabs identify with the PLO. They also multiply like rabbits. At their rate of growth they will take over the Knesset in twenty-five years. I am not prepared to sacrifice Zionism to democracy. There is only one solution: the Arabs must leave Israel!"

"Of course it's not nice. Did I say it's nice? Is it nice when Israel bombs the PLO in Lebanon and kills women and children? We have smart bombs, not nice bombs."

"How would you implement these ideas if you were the prime minister of Israel?" I asked.

"I'd go to the Arabs and tell them to leave," he replied. "I'd promise generous compensation. If they refused, I'd force them out."

"How could you do that?" I asked. "Midnight deportations in cattle cars?"

"Yes! I'm not a racist. A racist is a Jew who says Arabs can be equal citizens in a Jewish state."

The Sephardim

Kahane's anti-Arab message has found considerable support among Israel's Sephardim. As early as 1979, in an attempt to broaden Kach's political base, he set up religious and ideological study groups in the slums of Jerusalem and Tel Aviv. He tried to attract young people by offering them karate training if they attended his classes in "Jewish values."

"Once we hook them" he told me, "we emphasize two things. First, Arabs. They don't like Arabs. They come from Arab countries."

"Second, poverty. When we speak of poverty, we speak of spiritual poverty. The reaction to being poor and how one copes with it is different when one has values. The Jews in Mea Sharem [the ultra-Orthodox quarter in Jerusalem] have twelve kids and live in two rooms and they don't go out and commit crimes."

He tries to teach young people from the poor neighborhoods to find their spiritual and emotional center in Judaism. They should, he tells them, move out to the fresh Judean air and build new settlements. He envisions the West Bank filled, one day, with proud Oriental Jews.

Halakah

Kahane believes any act is acceptable if it is dictated by *halakah* (Jewish religious law), which in his view overrides the democratically enacted laws of the state. According to his interpretation of religious law, every Jew must return to Eretz Yisrael and build up the land in preparation for the End of Days and the redemption of mankind. Any act not specifically forbidden by religious law is, for Kahane, permissible to achieve those goals.

"My purpose in life, therefore, is to say the things that no other Jewish leader is saying— that the fate of the Jewish people in the *Galut* (exile) and in Israel rests on their being Jewish again. This can only be done in Israel. Only then will God shine his light on Zion."

Kahane has argued that Messianic redemption would have taken place if the Israeli government had expelled the Arabs, destroyed the Dome of the Rock Mosque, which was built on top of the ruins of the Second Temple, and annexed Judea and Samaria. "Had we acted without considering the Gentile reaction," Kahane has written, "without fear of what he may say or do, the Messiah would have come right through the open door and brought us redemption."

The main question that concerns him about the future, he claims, is how much suffering Jews have to endure before redemption. "A horrible world war is coming," Kahane told me in January 1980. "Tens of millions will die. It will be the Apocalypse. God will punish us for forsaking him. But we must have faith. The Messiah will come. There will be a resurrection of the dead—all the things that Jews believed in before they got so damn sophisticated. The amount of suffering we endure will depend upon what we do between now and the end."

"That's up to us—it's not up to God."

In the Knesset

Kahane has prepared several bills for the Knesset. One calls for the expulsion of Israel's Arabs. Another would make it a crime punishable by two years in jail for a Jewish woman to have sex with an Arab. A third would make it illegal to insult Judaism and the Jewish people. "We state that anyone who declares that any verse or saying in the Bible, the Talmud, or the Commentary isn't true is racist and should be subject to three years in prison," Kahane told me.

"After your election, you promised to drive Israel crazy. Are you doing so?" I asked Kahane during our interview at the Tudor Hotel.

"I am. I get up in the Knesset and say: 'When I'm prime minister no Arab will be hurt by Jewish terrorists because there won't be an Arab left in Israel!' Then everyone rages in the Knesset, and then it's shown on TV, and the attorney general makes his statement condemning racism, then there are demands made all over the place to strip me of my parliamentary immunity. And just when Israeli news editors decide not to give Kahane any more coverage—to keep him off the front pages—I do something outrageous and it's a media event. I'm playing games... Every time I walk into the Knesset, the other 119 members die a thousand deaths!"

Kahane claims that his prospects improved when Prime Minister Menachem Begin left the political scene. When Begin resigned from politics, more of the Sephardim, especially young people, supported Kahane. "Begin could have done anything and the streets would have gone with him. I used to hear from people, 'If I had a second vote, you would have it.' I knew I couldn't beat Begin. So I patiently waited. I wouldn't attack Begin because it was foolish to attack Begin. But his leaving was good for me and it was certainly good for the Jewish people."

"I am an Ashkenazi Orthodox Jewish rabbi leading a mass movement which is predominately Sephardim," Kahane boasted to me. "*I have the streets!* That's what frightens the left."

Kill the Jew

Kahane and his followers have also turned their wrath on Jews. Kach squads have attacked Israeli antiwar demonstrations, assaulted homosexuals and Jewish women who have had relations with Arabs, and threatened liberal politicians, artists, and journalists. Even Israeli government officials are not immune. In September 1984, after Morton Dolinsky, then head of the Israeli Government Press Office, told United Press International that he opposed Kahane's methods, he received a threatening telegram from Boston saying, "You have striven by every means in your power to defame and destroy our movement. Now that we have gained some element of power we intend to deal with you as you have dealt with us." It was signed, "Friends of

Rabbi Meir Kahane."

"The Jewish establishment is not relevant to the Jewish people," Kahane told me in November 1984. "I've said it before, I'll say it again, they are pygmies, they are dwarfs, they are imbeciles... They are ignorant of what Jewish destiny is...and they are in the way, they are in the way."

In his August 31, 1984, column in the *Jewish Press*, Kahane came close to saying that he favored the liquidation of Jews whose views he finds pernicious. "In order to save Israel," he writes, "the Torah says to burn out the evil from our midst. Indeed, the rabbis of the Talmud bring down the verse, 'and thou shalt love thy fellow Jew as thyself' in order to explain why we must kill the Jew who is deserving of death in a humane way."

"Love of Jews? Of course. And sacrifice for them; by all means. But when a Jew rises to challenge fundamentals of God, Jewry and Israel, that Jew must be stopped. And indeed, the punishment that we bring on the wicked Jew goes a long and necessary way to atonement for him in the world to come."

Kahane named some of the Jews he thinks must be stopped: "If Yosi Sarid and Shulamit Aloni[1] and Mapam[2] and Meir Vilner[3] and the whole host of Hellenists, spiritually sick, move to threaten the very existence of Judaism, Jewry, and Israel—there is nothing moral about tolerating it. To the contrary, it is the most immoral and evil of things. Their evil threatens every Jew, their sins will sink the Jewish ship which carries every Jew. If Schindler[4] and Reform Judaism split Jews into two separate camps and threaten the very definition of a Jew with their ignorant arrogance, are we to be 'tolerant' and 'moderate'?"

"It takes great strength to love Jews so much that one fights for them. It takes, perhaps, even more strength to love Jews so much that one fights Jews who would destroy them. The pity is that most Jews are so weak and apathetic that they neither love nor hate enough. They remain indifferent and 'pareve',

seeking to hide from responsibility. But the truth remains that we are in need of the strong Jews. Those strong enough to love and hate and wise enough to know when to do what. 'Any scholar who is not as strong as iron is not a scholar.' Where are the scholars? Where is the strength?"

Minister of Defense

At a speech in Haifa on June 28, 1985, Kahane attacked Jews and Arabs equally. "No one can understand the soul of those (Arab) beasts, those roaches. We shall either cut their throats or throw them out. I only say what you think." According to a report by No'omi Cohen in *Kolbo Haifa*, a local Haifa newspaper, Kahane then directed a stream of obscenities against the mayor of Haifa, Arieh Goral, and Shulamit Aloni and Yosi Sarid, whom he called "scoundrel," "dog," "disgusting," and "Jewish prostitutes who employ Arab pimps."

Cohen concluded her account of the speech by quoting a promise Kahane made to the audience: "In two years time, they (the Arabs) will turn on the radio and hear that Kahane has been named Minister of Defense. Then they will come to me, bow to me, lick my feet, and I will be merciful and will allow them to leave. Whoever does not leave will be slaughtered."

Persona Non Grata

The Israeli government and some private organizations have introduced a number of measures designed to curtail Kahane's growing influence in Israel. On December 25, 1984, in an attempt to limit Kahane's parliamentary immunity, the Knesset voted to allow the police to bar Kahane from entering Arab villages, where he had frequently gone to exhort the Arabs to leave Israel. However, Kahane's other rights of parliamentary immunity, including freedom from persecution, remain intact. The government also has banned Kahane from entering Israeli high schools, and from speaking on radio and television. Further-

---

[1] Sarid and Aloni are members of the Citizens Rights Movement party in the Knesset.

[2] Mapam is a left-wing labor party.

[3] Vilner is the Secretary General of the New Communist Party and a member of the Knesset.

[4] Alexander Schindler is head of the Union of American Hebrew Congregations.

more, the Knesset is considering an amendment to the Basic Law that would forbid a
party that advocates racist views from participating in Knesset elections. Kahane would undoubtedly appeal such an amendment to the
High Court, which previously overturned the
Knesset Rules Committee's attempt to prevent
him from running in the 1984 parliamentary
elections.

This fall the Knesset stopped Kahane from
introducing two bills it considered anti-
democratic—one limiting the rights of non-
Jews in Israel, and the other prohibiting sex
between Jews and Arabs. Kahane appealed to
the High Court. On November 2, 1985, the
High Court ordered the Knesset presidium to
permit Kahane to table his bills. While ac-
knowledging that the bills were reminiscent of
Nazi regulations against the Jews in Germany,
the court ruled that Kahane, as a Knesset
member, had the democratic right to introduce
legislation. The speaker of the Knesset, however, has ignored the ruling, and Kahane has
again appealed to the High Court. (Kahane is
also appealing the State Department's decision of last October to strip him of American
citizenship.)

More recently, on December 1, 1985, the
Anti-Defamation League of the B'nai Brith organization, which has been active in opposing
Kahane in the US, began to sponsor a weekly
public service announcement on Israeli television warning against the danger of Kahane
and his ideology. Meanwhile, anti-Kahane
groups have formed a center-left ad hoc coalition capable of mobilizing thousands of dem-
onstrators to disrupt Kahane's public
speaking engagements. Several such demonstrations took place in 1985.

Kahane's most serious challenge, however,
is from the right. "Until 1984, the religious-na-
tionalist camp did not consider Kahane a challenge," says Dr. Ehud Sprinzak of Hebrew
University, an expert on Israeli extremist
groups. "No effort was made to curtail his influence in Yeshivot and West Bank settlements. This is no longer the case. Electoral
strength in Israel translates into power and
money, and there is little readiness to share
them with Kahane." Ariel Sharon, who his
supporters claim is the strongman Israel needs
to stop Kahane and solve the country's social

and political difficulties, told his followers at a
rally last July that "our danger is not Yosi
Sarid, but rather Kahane, who takes all our
votes."

Yet despite Kahane's legal vulnerability and
the challenges from the right and the left, it is
unlikely that he will disappear soon from the
Israeli parliamentary scene. According to Israeli pollster Hanoch Smith, Kahane has made
impressive gains among his core constituency—the young, poorly educated Sephardim
from Israel's slums and development towns
who compete with Israeli Arabs for low-pay-
ing jobs in a weak economy. "Kahane expressed the Sephardim's hatred of the Arabs
and their frustration with the economy,"
Smith told me. The amount of support he receives from the Sephardic community "is directly related to the level of Arab terrorism
directed against Jews in Israel." When terrorism was high, as it was last summer, Kahane
polled 9 percent of the electorate. But when
economic and political tensions decline, so
does his support—"not because Kahane has
been discredited, but because they (the
Sephardim) feel less threatened," Smith says.
It is possible, on this view, that Kahane's popularity will subside.

Some Israeli observers believe that the
broad opposition to him, combined with his
own extremism, will force him to the margins
of politics. "No doubt, if Kahane poses a
threat in the next election, the Knesset and the
High Court will find a way to keep him from
running," I was told by Nachum Barnea, the
editor of *Koterit Rashit*, a weekly magazine
published in Jerusalem. Kahane's behavior, he
said, has been more circumspect in recent
months because he hears that the High Court
will outlaw his party. "But when he's less pro-
vocative he gets less coverage," and with less
publicity his popularity diminishes.

Nevertheless, Smith says, if Kahane runs
"it's probable" that he will "at least hold his
seat and gain a few more" in the next election.
"He's a threat with even a few seats." If elections are held and there is a stalemate between
Labor and Likud, and Kahane has four or five
seats, he will be in a position of considerable
power. If Likud wanted to form a government
they might have to come to terms with him.
Unfortunately, Smith says, "He's not *persona*

non grata enough" to be excluded from a political deal.

Dr. Sprinzak, who believes Kahane is a "significant political force," points out that if he got the votes of 5 to 6 percent of the electorate (or about six seats) Kahane would be the head of the third largest bloc of votes in Israel. "That would almost certainly mean Kahane would get a cabinet post if there were a Likud government," he says. "Kahane wants the Ministry of Defense. He would never get that. They would give him the Ministry of Interior. He would be in charge of civil rights and minority affairs. Can you imagine what that would mean?"

Kahane would probably agree with much of what Smith and Sprinzak say about him. He sees his power and strength growing as Israeli society itself becomes more deeply polarized along ethnic, social, and political lines. "I always knew I'd get a [Knesset] seat," Kahane told me in November 1984.

And if they hold elections in a year, we will get many, many more seats. If unemployment in a year is as high as we think it will be, and if inflation in a year is as high as we think it will be, and if Ronald Reagan—who of course is a disaster for the Jewish people—pressures the Israeli government to trade land for peace, and there are more Arab terrorist attacks on Jews, it's completely conceivable that we will have eight to ten seats... The worse it gets for Israel, the better it is for me!

Political and economic conditions in Israel are not as bad as Kahane hoped, but throughout the country one finds wall slogans calling for the expulsion of Arabs or the death of various liberal politicians and signed with a Kach logo—a clenched fist exploding through a black Star of David. It seems much too soon to dismiss the threat of Rabbi Meir Kahane.

Robert I. Friedman. "The Sayings of Rabbi Kahane." *The New York Review of Books* 33, No. 2 (February 13, 1986): 15–20.

Part XI
Environmentalism

DAVID SUZUKI

Political ideologies and political philosophies are by no means passé. Nevertheless, the emergence of serious environmental problems including the greenhouse effect, the disposal of radioactive waste, acid rain, and the threatened extinction of species of plants and animals have forced all reasonable persons to rethink their political priorities. As we face these and other environmental issues, our dogmatic slumbers in politics have suddenly come to an abrupt end. The following essays or reports written over the past twenty years make it incumbent on us to re-examine our political perspectives with the hope of finding solutions to some very complex problems. In light of the following contributions, we cannot be sanguine about the possibility of finding these solutions nicely located in the previously examined ideologies and philosophies.

E.F. Schumacher in his article challenges one of the latent assumptions in some of the previously studied ideologies, namely the assumption that the problem of production has been solved. He proceeds convincingly to lay out some of the difficulties associated with the way in which we make use of natural resources. He examines our use of fossil fuels as an example of a resource which we are presently consuming at an alarming rate. He then hints that the solution to this rate of consumption cannot lie in the use of nuclear energy for this solution "solves" one problem by creating a bigger one. Perhaps Schumacher's comments do not now strike us as novel or penetrating, but we should keep in mind that his comments were made some fifteen years ago when environmental concerns were not on the political agenda. One lesson to grasp here is that economic and social criticisms,

even if true, require some lead time for acceptance or serious consideration.

The so-called Brandt Report of 1980 focusses upon North-South relations and the need for a new economic order. As such it does not focus directly upon the environment in a biological sense or resource management sense. However the Report makes a compelling case for directing our attention to environmental matters of an economic nature, i.e. directing our attention to poverty, hunger, commodities, and mineral development, as well as the monetary system. The global uncertainties in these areas create alarming prospects for the future. In unequivocal terms the Report says what is called for are "dynamic new approaches" in the foregoing areas, notwithstanding the extant political principles and political systems.

In the UN report on man's common future (a successor to the Brandt Report), Gro Harlem Brundtland and her colleagues attempt to deal with the problem of sustainable economic growth in the modern world. This problem is examined deliberately and carefully in the context of pollution, natural resources, energy, and population growth. In the following excerpt, the Brundtland Commission asserts that the next few decades are crucial for humanity's future. The Commission adopts a position only intimated by the Brandt Report, namely that developmental and environmental considerations are locked together, requiring a dramatic shift in the approach of individuals and governments in the handling of economic and ecological systems. Owing to this attitudinal shift and to the growing interdependence between sectors of the economy and between nations of the world, the committee claims that the "real world" has issued a challenge for institutional and legal change to meet some of the serious accompanying problems. To this end, the Commission suggests a two-pronged attack upon environmental problems: first, the maintaining and strengthening of governmental policies and agencies that deal with environmental effects, and secondly, the mandating of governmental agencies to sustain the environment upon which social and economic goods depend. The Commission then turns to specific proposals for institutional and legal change at the national, regional, and international levels.

In a keynote address to the American Association for the Advancement of Science, Peter Raven boldly asserts that by dealing with present environmental problems we lay the basis for peace and prosperity. By not doing this we edge towards disaster. According to Raven, the tropics are the centre of some of our more serious ecological problems including record human population growth, acute poverty, and ignorance of agricultural and forestry techniques. Raven then goes on to detail the effect of deforestation in the tropics and elsewhere. This effect embraces such things as the global economy, human migration patterns, global climates, and the erosion of biological diversity. And in words somewhat reminiscent of Schumacher's, but certainly of Brandt's and Brundtland's, Raven adds that new global thinking is necessary to handle the world ecosystem.

In the final essay, David Suzuki examines the "cataclysmic degradation" to the environment that has occurred over the past generation in Canada and other countries. Suzuki says that we seem unable to use our strategy for survival because we cling to allegedly "sacred truths" that obscure our vision of present day problems. This persistent obscurity prevents us from comprehending the limited nature of our understanding of the environment. This in turn gives rise to an unjustified level of confidence that we know what we are doing when we claim to manage the environment. He stresses that we need to rid ourselves of this obscurity and do so by examining critically the above "sacred truths" to which we have subjectively adhered. Suzuki concludes his article by saying that what is needed—and desperately so—is a new model of man's place in nature.

The articles in this chapter make clear that we have reached a serious point in our environmental history. As the Fourteenth Dalai Lama says, the present generation of the human species is "pivotal." As Schumacher, Brandt, Brundtland, and Suzuki argue, man's economic endeavours are ravaging his environment. Each of these writers stresses that the environment must be put back into man's planning, notably his economic planning. The focus of these writings is a new political perspective centred around man's relation with his sensitive environment.

The Problem of Production

E. F. Schumacher

E.F. SCHUMACHER *was a Rhodes scholar in economics, an economic advisor to the British Control Commission in postwar Germany, and for about twenty years prior to 1971 was the top economist at the British Coal Board. His books include* Small Is Beautiful *and* A Guide for the Perplexed.

One of the most fateful errors of our age is the belief that "the problem of production" has been solved. Not only is this belief firmly held by people remote from production and therefore professionally unacquainted with the facts—it is held by virtually all the experts, the captains of industry, the economic managers in the governments of the world, the academic and not-so-academic economists, not to mention the economic journalists. They may disagree on many things but they all agree that the problem of production has been solved; that mankind has at last come of age. For the rich countries, they say, the most important task now is "education for leisure" and, for the poor countries, the "transfer of technology."

That things are not going as well as they ought to be going must be due to human wickedness. We must therefore construct a political system so perfect that human wickedness disappears and everybody behaves well, no matter how much wickedness there may be in him or her. In fact, it is widely held that everybody is born good; if one turns into a criminal or an exploiter, this is the fault of "the system." No doubt "the system" is in many ways bad and must be changed. One of the main reasons why it is bad and why it can still survive in spite of its badness, is this erroneous view that the "problem of production" has been solved. As this error pervades all present-day systems there is at present not much to choose between them.

The arising of this error, so egregious and so firmly rooted, is closely connected with the philosophical, not to say religious, changes during the last three or four centuries in man's attitude to nature. I should perhaps say: Western man's attitude to nature, but since the whole world is now in a process of westernisation, the more generalised statement appears to be justified. Modern man does not experience himself as a part of nature but as an outside force destined to dominate and conquer it. He even talks of a battle with nature, forgetting that, if he won the battle, he would find himself on the losing side. Until quite recently, the battle seemed to go well enough to give him the illusion of unlimited powers, but not so well as to bring the possibility of total victory into view. This has now come into view, and many people, albeit only a minority, are beginning to realise what this means for the continued existence of humanity.

The illusion of unlimited powers, nourished by astonishing scientific and technological achievements, has produced the concurrent illusion of having solved the problem of production. The latter illusion is based on the failure to distinguish between income and capital where this distinction matters most. Every economist and businessman is familiar with the distinction, and applies it conscientiously and with considerable subtlety to all economic affairs—except where it really matters: namely, the irreplaceable capital which man has not made, but simply found, and without which he can do nothing.

A businessman would not consider a firm to have solved its problems of production and to have achieved viability if he saw that it was rapidly consuming its capital. How, then, could we overlook this vital fact when it comes to that very big firm, the economy of Spaceship Earth and, in particular, the economies of its rich passengers?

One reason for overlooking this vital fact is that we are estranged from reality and inclined to treat as valueless everything that we have not made ourselves. Even the great Dr. Marx fell into this devastating error when he formulated the so-called "labour theory of value." Now we have indeed laboured to make some of the capital which today helps us to produce—a large fund of scientific, technological, and other knowledge; an elaborate physical infrastructure; innumerable types of sophisticated capital equipment, etc.—but all this is but a small part of the total capital we are using. Far larger is the capital provided by nature and not by man—and we do not even recognize it as such. This larger part is now being used up at an alarming rate, and that is why it is an absurd and suicidal error to believe, and act on the belief, that the problem of production has been solved.

Let us take a closer look at this "natural capital." First of all, and most obviously, there are the fossil fuels. No one, I am sure, will deny that we are treating them as income items although they are undeniably capital items. If we treated them as capital items, we should be concerned with conservation; we should do everything in our power to try and minimize their current rate of use; we might be saying, for instance, that the money obtained from the realisation of these assets— these irreplaceable assets—must be placed into a special fund to be devoted exclusively to the evolution of production methods and patterns of living which do *not* depend on fossil fuels at all or depend on them only to a very slight extent. These and many other things we should be doing if we treated fossil fuels as capital and not as income. And we do not do any of them, but the exact contrary of every one of them: we are not in the least concerned with conservation; we are maximising, instead of minimising, the current rates of use; and, far from being interested in studying the possibilities of alternative methods of production and patterns of living—so as to get off the collision course on which we are moving with ever-increasing speed—we happily talk of unlimited progress along the beaten track, of "education for leisure" in the rich countries, and of "the transfer of technology" to the poor countries.

The liquidation of these capital assets is proceeding so rapidly that even in the allegedly richest country in the world, the United States of America, there are many worried men, right up to the White House, calling for the massive conversion of coal into oil and gas, demanding ever more gigantic efforts to search for and exploit the remaining treasures of the earth. Look at the figures that are being put forward under the heading "World Fuel Requirements in the Year 2000." If we are now using something like 7000 million tons of coal equivalent, the need in twenty-eight years' time will be three times as large—around 20,000 million tons! What are twenty-eight years? Looking backwards, they take us roughly to the end of World War II, and, of course, since then fuel consumption has trebled; but the trebling involved an increase of less than 5000 million tons of coal equivalent. Now we are calmly talking about an increase three times as large.

People ask: Can it be done? And the answer comes back: It must be done and therefore it shall be done. One might say (with apologies to John Kenneth Galbraith) that it is a case of the bland leading the blind. But why cast aspersions? The question itself is wrong-headed, because it carries the implicit assumption that we are dealing with income and not with capital. What is so special about the year 2000? What about the year 2028, when little children running about today will be planning for their retirement? Another trebling by then? All these questions and answers are seen to be absurd the moment we realise that we are dealing with capital and not with income: fossil fuels are not made by men; they cannot be recycled. Once they are gone they are gone for ever.

But what—it will be asked—about the income fuels? Yes, indeed, what about them? Currently, they contribute (reckoned in calories) less than four per cent to the world total. In the foreseeable future they will have to contribute seventy, eighty, ninety per cent. To do something on a small scale is one thing: to do it on a gigantic scale is quite another, and to make an impact on the world fuel problem, contributions have to be truly gigantic. Who will say that the problem of production has been solved when it comes to income fuels required on a truly gigantic scale?

Fossil fuels are merely a part of the "natural capital" which we steadfastly insist on treating as expendable, as if it were income, and by no means the most important part. If we squander our fossil fuels, we threaten civilisation; but if we squander the capital represented by living nature around us, we threaten life itself. People are waking up to this threat, and they demand that pollution must stop. They think of pollution as a rather nasty habit indulged in by careless or greedy people who, as it were, throw their rubbish over the fence into the neighbour's garden. A more civilised behaviour, they realise, would incur some extra cost, and therefore we need a faster rate of economic growth to be able to pay for it. From now on, they say, we should use at least some of the fruits of our ever-increasing productivity to improve "the quality of life" and not merely to increase the quantity of consumption. All this is fair enough, but it touches only the outer fringe of the problem.

To get to the crux of the matter, we do well to ask why it is that all these terms—pollution, environment, ecology, etc.—have *so suddenly* come into prominence. After all, we have had an industrial system for quite some time, yet only five or ten years ago these words were virtually unknown. Is this a sudden fad, a silly fashion, or perhaps a sudden failure of nerve?

The explanation is not difficult to find. As with fossil fuels, we have indeed been living on the capital of living nature for some time, but at a fairly modest rate. It is only since the end of World War II that we have succeeded in increasing this rate to alarming proportions. In comparison with what is going on now and what has been going on, progressively, during the last quarter of a century, all the industrial activities of mankind up to, and including, World War II are as nothing. The next four or five years are likely to see more industrial production, taking the world as a whole, than all of mankind accomplished up to 1945. In other words, quite recently—so recently that most of us have hardly yet become conscious of it—there has been a unique quantitative jump in industrial production.

Partly as a cause and also as an effect, there has also been a unique qualitative jump. Our

scientists and technologists have learned to compound substances unknown to nature. Against many of them, nature is virtually defenceless. There are no natural agents to attack and break them down. It is as if aborigines were suddenly attacked with machine-gun fire: their bows and arrows are of no avail. These substances, unknown to nature, owe their almost magical effectiveness precisely to nature's defencelessness—and that accounts also for their dangerous ecological impact. It is only in the last twenty years or so that they have made their appearance in *bulk*. Because they have no natural enemies, they tend to accumulate, and the long-term consequences of this accumulation are in many cases known to be extremely dangerous, and in other cases totally unpredictable.

In other words, the changes of the last twenty-five years, both in the quantity and in the quality of man's industrial processes, have produced an entirely new situation—a situation resulting not from our failure but from what we thought were our greatest successes. And this has come so suddenly that we hardly noticed the fact that we were very rapidly using up a certain kind of irreplaceable capital asset, namely the *tolerance margins* which benign nature always provides.

Now let me return to the question of "income fuels" with which I had previously dealt in a somewhat cavalier manner. No one is suggesting that the world-wide industrial system which is being envisaged to operate in the year 2000, a generation ahead, would be sustained primarily by water or wind power. No, we are told that we are moving rapidly into the nuclear age. Of course, this has been the story for quite some time, for over twenty years, and yet, the contribution of nuclear energy to man's total fuel and energy requirements is still minute. In 1970, it amounted to 2.7 per cent in Britain; 0.6 per cent in the European Community; and 0.3 per cent in the United States, to mention only the countries that have gone the furthest. Perhaps we can assume that nature's tolerance margins will be able to cope with such small impositions, although there are many people even today who are deeply worried, and Dr. Edward D. David, President Nixon's Science Adviser, talking about the storage of radioactive wastes, says that "one has a queasy feeling about something that has to stay underground and be pretty well sealed off for 25,000 years before it is harmless."

However that may be, the point I am making is a very simple one: the proposition to replace thousands of millions of tons of fossil fuels, every year, by nuclear energy means to "solve" the fuel problem by creating an environmental and ecological problem of such a monstrous magnitude that Dr. David will not be the only one to have "a queasy feeling." It means solving one problem by shifting it to another sphere—there to create an indefinitely bigger problem.

E.F. Schumacher. *Small is Beautiful*. New York: Perennial Books, 1973.

A Dangerous Future

Willy Brandt

WILLY BRANDT (1913–) *was Mayor of Berlin before moving on to become the Chancellor of West Germany. In his capacity as a global statesman he was given the responsibility of heading up the United Nations Commission investigating the state of North/South relations.* The Report of the Independent Commission on International Development Issues *was the result of this investigation.*

Prospects for the future are alarming. Increased global uncertainties have reduced expectations of economic growth, and the problems of handling surplus oil revenues are accentuating the threat of a grave financial crisis. There is serious doubt as to whether adjustments to international balance of payments problems and the management of world liquidity and debt can be achieved adequately by the existing machinery. Those middle-income countries which are rapidly increasing their industrial exports are generating anxieties and uncertainties among competing industrialists and workers in the North, and governments are failing to agree about rules to allow access to their markets. Investments in exploration for energy and minerals in the South, which is critical for industrial growth in both North and South, has slowed down to a trickle, as a result of political and economic uncertainties. The abolition of poverty is itself not only a moral obligation. It is against everyone's interests to allow poverty to continue, with the insecurity, suffering and destruction which it brings. In the meantime military spending, now at a pace of over $400 billion a year, is wasting still more resources and energies which could be devoted to world development.

With the prospect of even higher unemployment and slower long-term growth many people will instinctively want to protect themselves from the harsh realities of foreign competition, turning instead to their purely domestic responsibilities; this withdrawal has already begun. But there can be no doubt that such a defensive reaction will be disastrous, as it was in the years before the Second World War. Since that time the nations of both the South and the North have become far more interdependent and actions taken by one country can seriously affect countries at the other side of the world. The self-interest of nations can now only be effectively pursued through taking account of mutual interests.

We realize that much of the responsibility for averting catastrophe must lie within nations and regions, both in the North and the South; their governments must set their own programmes based on long-term survival and justice rather than temporary expediency. While developing countries call for social justice internationally, they must not neglect such values at home; nor must they let slip the opportunities at hand for greater cooperation among themselves. The North for its part must not pursue selfish policies, depleting the world of precious resources; it too must find new patterns of growth, more sensitive to the world's needs.

We are also aware that long-term world security and development will depend on the participation of both the East European countries and of China, each of which have their own important experiences of rapid development. Only a reduction of the distrust and fears between East and West can establish a sound and permanent basis for North-South cooperation, and we therefore hope that the eastern governments and their peoples will participate more fully with the rest of the world in joint endeavours to find solutions to the world's problems.

Each of us on the Commission, coming from countries in five continents with very different political systems and principles, has our own perspective and historical experience. But all of us have become convinced that the world community will have to work out dynamic new approaches, both immediately and for the longer run. The debate between North and South has been continuing for some years: it is urgent that both sides should now work together in a programme based on action for a rational and equitable international economic order.

The journey will be long and difficult, but it must begin now if it is to meet the challenge of the next century. We have to set clear goals for solving the most serious and dangerous problems if we are to concentrate our minds, and prevent a retreat into the dead-end which results from the pursuit of short-term interest. We must do so as a matter of common humanity, and also of mutual survival. The poor will not make progress in a world economy characterized by uncertainty, disorder and low rates of growth; it is equally true that the rich cannot prosper without progress by the poor. The world requires a new system of economic relationships that acknowledges these mutual needs and human interests. The challenge for the next decades will not be met by an adversary system of winners and losers—North versus South or East versus West—but only by one founded on human solidarity and international cooperation amongst all.

A new international order will take time to achieve: we have set out the full range of our proposals in our Summary of Recommendations on all the subject matter we have discussed. Here, we outline first the principal tasks for international negotiation and action over the next two decades. But the present world crisis is so acute that we have also felt compelled to draw up an emergency programme, one which would go far to overcome the present *malaise*, while working towards the long-term structural reforms.

Tasks for the 80s and 90s

All countries must be able to participate fully in the world economy in a way which assists genuine development. This will come about in the long run only in an economic environment which enables all developing countries to achieve self-sustaining growth.

Priority Needs of the Poorest

Priority must be given to the needs of the poorest countries and regions. We call for a major initiative in favour of the poverty belts of Africa and Asia. We recognize that the removal of poverty requires both substantial resource transfers from the developed countries and an increased determination of the developing countries to improve economic management and deal with social and economic inequalities.

Abolition of Hunger

The world must aim to abolish hunger and malnutrition by the end of the century through the elimination of absolute poverty. Greater food production, intensified agricultural development, and measures for international food security, are essential. These too require both major additional external assistance and revised priorities in many developing countries.

Commodities

Earnings from commodities must be strengthened so that they can contribute more adequately to the development of Third World countries, most of which are still heavily dependent on primary commodity exports. They should be enabled to process their own raw materials locally and to participate in their international marketing, transport and distribution. Commodity prices should be stabilized at a remunerative level to become less vulnerable to market fluctuations. For these purposes the proposed Common Fund and other relevant institutions need adequate resources. Existing schemes for compensating against instability should be improved and expanded.

Manufactures

The North should reverse the present trend towards protecting its industries against competition from the Third World and promote instead a process of positive, anticipatory restructuring. Industrial adjustment policies affect other countries closely and should be subject to international consultation and surveillance. The codes established by the GATT Tokyo Round which concluded in 1979 will be useful if they are acted upon forcefully, but further work is necessary to link temporary safeguard restrictions to genuine adjustment policies. Developing countries should beware of their own protectionism, which affects the competitiveness of their exports, and curtails the opportunities for trade among themselves which is an essential element in their mutual cooperation.

Transnationals, Technology and Mineral Development

International codes of conduct and effective national laws should be agreed to ensure the broader sharing of technology, to control restrictive business practices and to provide a framework for the activities of transnational corporations. A better international investment regime should both enable developing countries to benefit from the expertise and resources of multinational corporations, and promote stable relationships between these corporations and host governments. It would also encourage greater initiatives and investments for the exploration of minerals and oil in the Third World which are essential for the prospects of world supplies. The weakest countries will require special assistance to permit them to participate effectively in such a regime.

Reform of the Monetary System

The disarray of the international monetary system is one of the key problems of the world economy. A system is needed which will establish more stable exchange rates, symmetry in the burden of adjustment to balance of payments deficits and surpluses, and an orderly expansion of international liquidity. A key element in international policies to increase monetary stability must be to make Special Drawing Rights the principal reserve asset. The issuing of SDRs must be geared solely to the agreed need for international liquidity, and will not create any additional element of international inflation. But we think that the distribution of those SDRs that are issued should also be related to the financial requirements of developing countries.

A New Approach to Development Finance

The objectives we have defined above, together with others we discuss in our Report, will call for a transfer of funds on a very considerable scale. The dangers and hardships which will occur without it are unprecedented. There are pressing needs in food, in mineral and energy exploration and development—needs in the South whose satisfaction is important to the North. The plight of the poorest countries is desperate. A large range of other low-income developing countries need major support from concessional finance to accelerate growth and cope with balance of payments deficits. The middle-income countries have relied extensively on commercial borrowing, and measures are needed to ensure that they can continue to borrow from the market and manage their heavy debt burdens. Basing ourselves on the best available estimates made by a variety of agencies, we have concluded that the achievement of goals with which we could be satisfied will require sums equal to more than a doubling of the current $20 billion of annual official development assistance, together with substantial additional lending on market terms.

Such a substantial stepping-up of the financing of imports that are vital for world development would also serve to maintain and promote world trade on which the welfare of all countries depends. The economies of the North need to regain economic vitality but their intimate dependence on world markets makes it impossible for them to do this by trying to put their own house in order while forgetting about the rest of the world. Public and political leaders in all countries must be aware of the need to take determined action and to mobilize the political will. We envisage a new approach to development finance incorporating the following elements:

1. Funds for development must be recognized as a responsibility of the whole world community, and placed on a predictable and long-term basis. We believe all countries—West and East, and South, excepting the poorest countries—should contribute. Their contribution would be on a sliding scale related to national income, in what would amount to an element of universal taxation.

There is an existing aid target for rich countries to provide 0.7 per cent of their gross national product as aid. For a country with average incomes of $6000, this would amount to $42 per person. The rich countries should commit themselves to a definite timetable for reaching the target, and for advancing towards one per cent before the year 2000.

2. We also believe more funds should be raised from "automatic" sources. We have examined a number of possibilities including levies related to international trade, military expenditures or arms exports, and revenues from the "global commons," especially seabed minerals. Funds accruing from some of these new sources, insofar as they can be attributed to individual countries, would count towards aid targets. We believe that a system of universal and automatic contributions would help to establish the principle of global responsibility, and could be a step towards co-management of the world economy.

3. The World Bank and Regional Development Banks should take new steps to increase their lending. The World Bank is already doubling its capital to $80 billion. We urge that the statutes of the World Bank be amended to change its gearing ratio from 1 to 1 to 2 to 1 which would raise its borrowing capacity to $160 billion. With the record and prestige the Bank has built up, we believe that the change would not affect its market standing. We also call for a higher proportion of financing to be channelled through the Regional Development Banks, which should be similarly strengthened for this purpose.

4. Borrowing for on-lending to developing countries should take place against the collateral of the retained portion of the gold reserves of the IMF, which represents a large resource worth upwards of $40 billion at market prices prevailing towards the end of 1979. The profits from such further sales of this gold as may be agreed should be used to subsidize the cost of borrowing by developing countries.

5. The serious gaps which our Report has found in the present range of financing, particularly the lack of programme lending, must be filled. We believe a different type of relationship and policy discussion is required between borrowers and lenders to permit much greater amounts of such lending side by side

with the funds available for specific investment projects. Consideration should therefore be given to the creation of a new institution— a World Development Fund—based on broader sharing in decision-making and able to attract universal membership. Further, we have expressed our hope that a growing consciousness of worldwide responsibility to bridge the gap between the rich and the poor will eventually be expressed in a system of international taxation to which all countries contribute. The new institution could ultimately serve as a channel for such resources, but need not wait for them before it is established.

6. Major additional multilateral finance is required to support mineral and energy exploration and development in developing countries. Some of this will come from existing institutions, but we believe there is a case for a new facility for this purpose.

7. The commercial banking system should continue to lend to the developing world, and on an adequate scale. Other private financial bodies should also be encouraged to participate. Measures are needed to ensure that middle-income countries receive funds on terms which permit them to manage their indebtedness; and concessional funds should be used to subsidize interest rates so that poorer countries can also take advantage of such loans. The World Bank and other international financial institutions should provide guarantees and play their part in ensuring a continued flow of commercial funds.

Power Sharing

While these specific tasks require major transfers of finance, we believe that the power and decision-making within monetary and financial institutions must also be shared more broadly, to give more responsibility to the developing world. This calls not only for the willingness of member governments to join in a revision of voting structures, but also for a style of management which exhibits closer understanding of and sensitivity to Third World problems, such as we put forward in our new institutional proposal.

A special responsibility falls on the World Bank, which has already done much to adapt itself to a fast-changing world. We are very conscious of its high standards and expertise; but, in order to represent more fully the interests of its clients, we are convinced that it should widen representation of Third World countries in its management and decentralize its operations and operating staff. We believe that the regional and sub-regional banks should play an increasingly important part in development finance, and should be well qualified to maintain closer links with countries in their own continents; therefore they should be adequately funded and should achieve a uniformly high standard of management.

We are aware that the IMF has recently become more sensitive to the wider objectives of nations with balance of payments difficulties, and that it is often consulted at a late stage when drastic measures are required. But we emphasize that the IMF should give practical expression to its desire to (in its own words) "pay due respect to the domestic, social and political objectives of member countries." The repercussions of the rigorous conditions of IMF loans on developing countries can have very serious effects on these objectives, and

we recommend that the IMF should provide for a longer period of adjustment by borrowers. Like the World Bank, the IMF should also pay attention to proper representation of Third World countries in its management and the upper echelons of its staff.

In the United Nations and its agencies it is essential that proliferation, duplication and waste be eliminated. We believe that in particular there is a need for new ways of monitoring and evaluating the performance of world institutions of quite different kinds, in order to make them more accountable to governments and publics. Both industrialized and developing countries have a strong interest in ensuring that the flow of funds, the expertise and the awareness of problems should be as effective as possible. It is important too that all sides have an effective machinery to develop and elaborate their positions in international negotiations.

North-South: A Programme For Survival. The Report of the Independent Commission on International Development Issues [The Brandt Report]. London: Pan Books, 1980.

Towards Common Action: Proposals for Institutional and Legal Change

Gro Harlem Brundtland

GRO HARLEM BRUNDTLAND *(1913–) was formerly the Prime Minister of Norway. She is a physician and democratic socialist who headed the United Nations Commission investigating the political, social, and ecological difficulties associated with sustained global economic growth.*

In the middle of the 20th century, we saw our planet from space for the first time. Historians may eventually find that this vision had a greater impact on thought than did the Copernican revolution of the 16th century, which upset humans' self-image by revealing that the Earth is not the centre of the universe. From space, we see a small and fragile ball dominated not by human activity and edifice but by a pattern of clouds, oceans, greenery, and soils. Humanity's inability to fit its activities into that pattern is changing planetary systems fundamentally. Many such changes are accompanied by life-threatening hazards, from environmental degradation to nuclear destruction. These new realities, from which there is no escape, must be recognized—and managed.

The issues we have raised in this report are inevitably of far-reaching importance to the quality of life on earth—indeed, to life itself. We have tried to show how human survival and well-being could depend on success in elevating sustainable development to a global ethic. In doing so, we have called for such major efforts as greater willingness and co-operation to combat international poverty, to maintain peace and enhance security worldwide, and to manage the global commons. We have called for national and international action in respect of population, food, plant and animal species, energy, industry, and urban settlements. The previous chapters have described the policy directions required.

The onus for action lies with no one group of nations. Developing countries face the challenges of desertification, deforestation, and pollution, and endure most of the poverty associated with environmental degradation. The entire human family of nations would suffer from the disappearance of rain forests in the tropics, the loss of plant and animal species, and changes in rainfall patterns. Industrial nations face the challenges of toxic chemicals, toxic wastes, and acidification. All nations may suffer from the releases by industrialized countries of carbon dioxide and of gases that react with the ozone layer, and from any future war fought with the nuclear arsenals controlled by those nations. All nations will also have a role to play in securing peace, in changing trends, and in righting an international economic system that increases rather than decreases inequality, that increases rather than decreases numbers of poor and hungry.

The time has come to break out of past patterns. Attempts to maintain social and ecological stability through old approaches to development and environmental protection will increase instability. Security must be sought through change. The Commission has noted a number of actions that must be taken to reduce risks to survival and to put future development on paths that are sustainable.

Without such reorientation of attitudes and emphasis, little can be achieved. We have no illusions about "quick-fix" solutions. We have tried to point out some pathways to the future. But there is no substitute for the journey itself, and there is no alternative to the process by which we retain a capacity to respond to the experience it provides. We believe this to hold true in all the areas covered in this report. But the policy changes we have suggested have institutional implications, and it is to these we now turn—emphasizing that they are a complement to, not a substitute for, the wider policy changes for which we call. Nor do they represent definitive solutions, but rather first steps in what will be a continuing process.

In what follows we put forward, in the first place, what are essentially conceptual guidelines for institutions at the national level. We recognize that there are large differences among countries in respect of population size, resources, income level, management capacity, and institutional traditions; only governments themselves can formulate the changes they should make. Moreover, the tools for monitoring and evaluating sustainable development are rudimentary and require further refinement.

We also address, in more specific terms, the question of international institutions. The preceding chapters have major implications for international co-operation and reforms, both economic and legal. The international agencies clearly have an important role in making these changes effective, and we endeavour to set out the institutional implications, especially as regards the United Nations system.

1. The Challenge for Institutional and Legal Change

Shifting the Focus to the Policy Sources

The next few decades are crucial for the future of humanity. Pressures on the planet are now unprecedented and are accelerating at rates and scales new to human experience: a doubling of global population in a few decades, with most of the growth in cities; a five- to tenfold increase in economic activity in less

than half a century; and the resulting pressures for growth and changes in agricultural, energy, and industrial systems. Opportunities for more sustainable forms of growth and development are also growing. New technologies and potentially unlimited access to information offer great promise.

Each area of change represents a formidable challenge in its own right, but the fundamental challenge stems from their systemic character. They lock together environment and development, once thought separate; they lock together "sectors," such as industry and agriculture; and they lock countries together as the effects of national policies and actions spill over national borders. Separate policies and institutions can no longer cope effectively with these interlocked issues. Nor can nations, acting unilaterally.

The integrated and interdependent nature of the new challenges and issues contrasts sharply with the nature of the institutions that exist today. These institutions tend to be independent, fragmented, and working to relatively narrow mandates with closed decision processes. Those responsible for managing natural resources and protecting the environment are institutionally separated from those responsible for managing the economy. The real world of interlocked economic and ecological systems will not change; the policies and institutions concerned must.

This new awareness requires major shifts in the way governments and individuals approach issues of environment, development, and international co-operation. Approaches to environment policy can be broadly characterized in two ways. One, characterized as the "standard agenda," reflects an approach to environmental policy, laws, and institutions that focuses on environmental effects. The second reflects an approach concentrating on the policies that are the sources of those effects.[1] These two approaches represent distinctively different ways of looking both at the issues and at the institutions to manage them.

---

[1] The characteristics and differences of the two approaches are described in our inaugural report, "Mandate for Change: Key Issues, Strategy and Workplan," Geneva, 1985.

The effects-oriented "standard agenda" has tended to predominate as a result of growing concerns about the dramatic decline in environmental quality that the industrialized world suffered during the 1950s and 1960s. New environmental protection and resource management agencies were added on to the existing institutional structures, and given mainly scientific staffs.[1]

These environment agencies have registered some notable successes in improving environmental quality during the past two decades.[2] They have secured significant gains in monitoring and research and in defining and understanding the issues in scientific and technical terms. They have raised public awareness, nationally and internationally. Environmental laws have induced innovation and the development of new control technologies, processes, and products in most industries, reducing the resource content of growth.[3]

However, most of these agencies have been confined by their own mandates to focusing almost exclusively on the effects. Today, the sources of these effects must be tackled. While these existing environmental protection policies and agencies must be maintained and even strengthened, governments now need to take a much broader view of environmental problems and policies.

Central agencies and major sectoral ministries play key roles in national decision making. These agencies have the greatest influence on the form, character, and distribution of the impacts of economic activity on the environmental resource base. It is these agencies through their policies and budgets, that determine whether the environmental resource base is enhanced or degraded and whether the planet will be able to support human and economic growth and change into the next century.

The mandated goals of these agencies include increasing investment, employment, food, energy, and other economic and social goods. Most have no mandate to concern themselves with sustaining the environmental resource capital on which these goals depend. Those with such mandates are usually grouped in separate environment agencies or, sometimes, in minor units within sectoral agencies. In either case, they usually learn of new initiatives in economic and trade policy, or in energy and agricultural policy, or of new tax measures that will have a severe impact on resources, long after the effective decisions have been taken. Even if they were to learn earlier, most lack the authority to ensure that a given policy is implemented.

Environmental protection and sustainable development must be an integral part of the mandates of all agencies of governments, of international organizations, and of major private-sector institutions. These must be made responsible and accountable for ensuring that their policies, programmes, and budgets encourage and support activities that are economically and ecologically sustainable both in the short and longer terms. They must be given a mandate to pursue their traditional goals in such a way that those goals are reinforced by a steady enhancement of the environmental resource base of their own national community and of the small planet we all share.

New Imperatives for International Co-operation

National boundaries have become so porous that traditional distinctions between local, national, and international issues have become blurred. Policies formerly considered to be exclusively matters of "national concern" now have an impact on the ecological bases of other nations' development and survival. Conversely, the growing reach of some nations' policies—economic, trade, monetary, and most sectoral policies—into the "sovereign" territory of other nations limits the affected nations' options in devising national

---

[1] L.G. Uy, "Combating the Notion of Environment as Additionality: A study of the Integration of Environment and Development and a Case for Environmental Development as Investment," Centre for Environmental Studies, University of Tasmania, Hobart, Tasmania, 1985 (to be published).

[2] OECD, *Environment and Economics, Vols I and II*, Background Papers for the International Conference on Environment and Economics (Paris: 1984).

[3] OECD, "The Impact of Environment Policies on Industrial Innovation," in *Environment and Economics, Vol. III, op. cit.*

solutions to their "own" problems. This fast-changing context for national action has introduced new imperatives and new opportunities for international co-operation.

The international legal framework must also be significantly strengthened in support of sustainable development. Although international law related to environment has evolved rapidly since the 1972 Stockholm Conference, major gaps and deficiencies must still be overcome as part of the transition to sustainable development. Much of the evidence and conclusions presented in earlier chapters of this report calls into question not just the desirability but even the feasibility of maintaining an international system that cannot prevent one of several states from damaging the ecological basis for development and even the prospects for survival of any other or even all other states.

However, just at the time when nations need increased international co-operation, the will to co-operate has sharply declined. By the mid-1980s, multilateral institutions were under siege for many, and often contradictory, reasons. The UN system has come under increasing attack for either proposing to do too much or, more frequently, for apparently doing too little. Conflicting national interests have blocked significant institutional reforms and have increased the need for fundamental change.[1] By the mid-1980s, funds for many international organizations had levelled off or declined in both relative and absolute terms.

Bilateral development assistance has declined as a percentage of gross national product (GNP) in many countries, falling even further below the targets proposed in the early 1970s.[2] The benefits and effectiveness of aid have come under serious question, in part because of criticism based on environmental considerations.[3] Yet, sustainable development creates the need for even greater international aid and co-operation.

Nations must now confront a growing number, frequency, and scale of crises. A major reorientation is needed in many policies and institutional arrangements at the international as well as national level. The time has come to break away. Dismal scenarios of mounting destruction of national and global potential for development—indeed, of the Earth's capacity to support life—are not inescapable destiny. One of the most hopeful characteristics of the changes the world is racing through is that invariably they reflect great opportunities for sustainable development, providing that institutional arrangements permit sustainable policy options to be elaborated, considered, and implemented.

II. Proposals for Institutional and Legal Change

The ability to choose policy paths that are sustainable requires that the ecological dimensions of policy be considered at the same time as the economic, trade, energy, agricultural, industrial, and other dimensions—on the same agendas and in the same national and international institutions. That is the chief institutional challenge of the 1990s.

There are significant proposals for institutional and legal change in previous chapters of our report. The Commission's proposals for institutional and legal change at the national, regional, and international levels are embodied in six priority areas:

- getting at the sources,
- dealing with the effects,
- assessing global risks,
- making informed choices,
- providing the legal means, and
- investing in our future.

Together, these priorities represent the main directions for institutional and legal change needed to make the transition to sustainable development. Concerted action is needed under all six.

Gro Harlem Brundtland. *Our Common Future.* New York: Oxford University Press, 1987.

[1] R. Bertrand, "Some Reflections on Reform of the United Nations," Joint Inspection Unit, UN, Geneva, 1985.

[2] V. Fernando, "Development Assistance, Environment and Development," prepared for WCED, Geneva, 1985.

[3] "List of Projects with Possible Environmental Issues," transmitted to Congress by US Agency for International Development, 1987, as included in Public Law 99–591.

We're Killing Our World

Peter H. Raven

PETER H. RAVEN *is Director of the Missouri Botanical Garden.*

I t is with the greatest pleasure that I present this keynote address here to inaugurate the annual meetings of the American Association for the Advancement of Science. By the time I have completed these remarks, I hope you will agree with me that the world that provides our evolutionary and ecological context is in serious trouble, trouble of a kind that demands our urgent attention. By formulating adequate plans for dealing with these largescale problems, we will be laying the foundation for peace and prosperity in the future; by ignoring them, drifting passively while attending to what seem more urgent, personal priorities, we are courting disaster.

Even though we live in a world where far more people are well fed, clothed, and housed today than ever before, we also live in a world in which up to 100,000 people starve to death every day, one in which we consume well over a third of total terrestrial photosynthetic productivity, and one in which our activities are threatening up to a quarter of the other kinds of organisms on earth with extinction in the near future. Since we base our civilization almost completely on our ability to utilize these organisms for out benefit, the loss of so many of them threatens to limit permanently the options that will be available for our children and grandchildren.

Despite these relationships, some of us are apparently so desperate to avoid the need for governmental action of any kind that they attempt to lull us to sleep by pretending that there is no problem, that inaction is best, and that we should simply continue to indulge our selfishness to the fullest extent. To provide such counsel is to offer exceedingly dangerous advice at precisely the wrong time. We scientists, who have the means to know better, must help to inform the public about the facts, and the need for action concerning them.

The global human population, which passed the 5 billion mark for the first time last year, and is growing at an annual rate estimated at 1.7 percent, is a dominant ecological force without precedent. Our numbers have *doubled* since 1950, and will double again in about 40 years if present trends continue. It has recently been calculated that we consume, co-opt, or forego about 40 percent of the total terrestrial photosynthetic productivity, a sure indication of the profound way in which we are affecting the global ecosystem. At the same time, regional climatic problems are becoming increasingly apparent, another sign of widescale danger. How will we respond to these threats, and why should those of us who live in the relative comfort of countries such as the United States even care?

Many of our most serious problems are centered in the tropics, where biological diversity is concentrated and is being lost most rapidly and whole ecosystems are being disrupted. In the tropics, three factors are of special importance: (1) the explosive growth of record human populations; (2) widespread and extreme poverty; and (3) an ignorance of the ways in which to carry out productive agriculture and forestry. Let's look at these three factors in turn.

As recently as 1950, about 45 percent of a global population of some 2.5 billion people lived in countries that lie wholly or partly in the tropics; today, the figure is about 55 percent of a global population that is more than twice as large. If present trends continue, nearly two-thirds of the people in the world will be living in these countries (excluding China) by the year 2020. In actual numbers, the 1.1 billion people who inhabited them 36 years ago will have grown to about 5 billion people in another 34 years: a *quadrupling* of the total in 70 years! Meanwhile, the proportion of people living in industrial countries is falling drastically. For each of us living in countries like the United States in 1950, there were approximately 2 other people living elsewhere; by 2020, there will be 5. Population structure suggests that the global population may stabilize in about a century at a level of perhaps 10 or 11 billion people. As its growth slows down, there will be increased opportunities for raising standards of living—a real reason for preserving as many kinds of organisms as possible and taking some of the steps I shall advocate this evening.

The rapidly growing populations of tropical countries include large numbers of poor people. In 1986, for example, the per capita GNP in the United States was estimated at $14,080, whereas that in neighboring Mexico amounted to $2180; in Honduras, it was $670. Overall, the industrial nations with less than a quarter of the global population, control about 80 percent of the wealth, while the largely tropical developing countries, with 54 percent of the population, control about 15 percent of the wealth. Meanwhile, in both Africa and Latin America, per capita income is steadily declining.

Within tropical countries, about 1 billion of the estimated 2.7 billion people live in absolute poverty; they are unable to count on adequate food, shelter, and clothing from one day to the next. Of these, 300 to 400 million people consumed less than 80 percent of U.N. recommended standards, a diet insufficient to prevent "stunted growth and serious health risks." UNICEF estimates that about 35 million people starve to death every year in the tropics, including more than 14 million children under the age of four. This amounts to nearly 100,000 people, and 40,000 babies, every day. Worse, many millions of additional children exist only in a state of lethargy, their mental capacities often permanently impaired by their lack of access to adequate amounts of food.

In Latin America alone, the 30 million landless rural households, together with those that own less than an acre of land, now represent close to 40 percent of all rural households. The difficulties in improving this situation can be illustrated by Brazil, where President Jose Sarney is attempting to distribute 100 million acres of land to 1.4 million essentially landless families by 1989. These efforts are encountering increasing rural violence; they illustrate how the growing extent of rural landlessness everywhere in the tropics is a serious cause of poverty, malnutrition, and social unrest in many regions.

In addition to large populations and extensive poverty, tropical countries suffer from a lack of information about how to put in place productive agriculture and forestry, and a lack of willingness to apply those facts that are known. As a result, the natural vegetation is often consumed as if it were a non-renewable resource. Many tropical soils are relatively poor, and require careful handling. In the natural ecosystems that develop on such soils, most of the nutrients, except for phosphorus and nitrogen, are held primarily in the vegetation. Cutting and burning the trees releases these nutrients to the soil, fertilizing them and allowing the temporary cultivation of crops; when the excess nutrients are exhausted, usually within a few years, the forests must be given time to recover.

Some traditional systems of cultivation on relatively infertile soils combine trees, which are usually more productive than herbaceous crops, with other plants. *Agro-forestry* systems of this sort will be increasingly important as they are better understood, and as farmers are encouraged to use them by offering them loans for fertilizers, credit for seeds, information about markets, and the like. In addition, relatively fertile soils must be cultivated intensively by the best methods available, with the most suitable crops.

Based on 1981 FAO estimates, about 2.3 million square miles of tropical evergreen forest probably exists in 1987—about half of the original area, now a forest that is roughly three-quarters of the size of the U.S. exclusive of Alaska. In the late 1970s, at least 40,000 square miles of such forest were being cut per year. If that is still the rate of clear-cutting, and if it continues, the forests would last about 60 years—if there were *no* population growth or other increased pressures on the forests from the late 1970s levels.

The decline in tropical forests arises in part

from consumer demand in industrialized countries. We obtain much of our timber there, for example, and logging removes about 20,000 square miles of tropical forest—an area nearly the size of West Virginia—every year. Meanwhile, reforestation is proceeding very slowly in the tropics, with 10 trees being cut for each one that is planted, and, in Africa, 29 being cut for each one planted. The developed-world consumption of tropical hardwoods has risen 15 times since 1950, while in-country consumption has increased only three times. Against this background, the inauguration of the International Tropical Timber Agreement in 1986—an agreement that involves all the major producers and consumers of tropical woods—is a development of high importance. In addition, the organization of the Tropical Forest Action Plan by the World Resource Institute (WRI) is of great importance, both for a stable supply of the commodities involved, and for biological conservation as well. The widespread and simultaneous destruction of temperate forests through acid precipitation and other forms of atmospheric pollution compounds the overall problem that we face in securing wood and pulp supplies for the future.

The clearing of tropical forests for pastures affects an area about half the size of that which is logged. For example, the growing imports of beef from southern Mexico and Central America over the past 25 years have been the major factor in the loss of about half of the forests in these regions, for the sake of keeping the price of a hamburger in the U.S. about a nickel less than it would have been otherwise.

In addition, shifting cultivation and fuelwood gathering together are severely damaging an additional area of tropical, evergreen forest about equal to that which is being clearcut. Only about 200 million people are engaged in these activities worldwide in areas of evergreen, lowland tropical forest. If they were incorporated into the economies of their respective countries, the forests they are cutting would change immediately from a non-renewable to a sustainable resource.

The relentless research for fuelwood is wrecking many tropical forests; about 1.5 billion people—a third of the world population—are cutting firewood faster than it can regrow in the areas where they get it. If plantations for firewood were established on cut over lands, with sufficient economic backing, this trend could be reversed.

Taking both clear-cutting and the kinds of severe disturbance that results from shifting agriculture and firewood gathering together, the current rate of destruction of tropical, evergreen forests may be calculated at roughly 80,000 square miles per year—an area about equal to the size of the state of Kansas. At such a rate, all tropical, evergreen forests would be gone in less than 30 years, even if there were no population growth; this represents roughly the rate of forest destruction that was taking place a decade ago.

Since human populations are in fact growing very rapidly—at the rate of approximately 2.4 percent per year—much of the forest will clearly be gone much sooner, however. Moreover, the actual rates of destruction differ widely from region to region. Three large blocks of lowland, evergreen forest—those in the northern and western Brazilian Amazon, the interior of the Guyanas, and the Zaire Basin of Africa—are larger and less densely populated than the rest, and consequently are being cut more slowly. Their forest might, therefore, last past the middle of the 21st century. The remaining forests, however, will mostly be gone, or at least profoundly altered in nature and composition, much earlier. These include the tropical, lowland forests of Mexico, Central America, and the West Indies, and those of Andean South America, as well as the forests of the southern and eastern Amazon; all similar forests of Africa and Madagascar outside of the Zaire Basin; and all the forests of tropical and subtropical Asia and the Pacific Islands. For the most part, they will have been consumed or severely damaged within the next 15 years or so.

We have been emphasizing lowland, evergreen forests because of their biological richness, and because they are the most extensive tropical forests that have persisted to the present. Dry deciduous forests, and all the other kinds of tropical forests, have mostly been cut over and converted much earlier than tropical, evergreen forests, being better suited to agriculture and cattle grazing. For example, the dry deciduous forests that once occurred along the Pacific Coast of Mexico and Central America covered an area approximately twice the size of Texas 500 years ago. Today, only about 2 percent of this once extensive biome exists in anything resembling its original form. The Guanacaste National Park project in Costa Rica, to which I shall return later, represents an exemplary effort to restore and preserve a significant area of such forest.

The destruction of natural resources in the tropics and sub-tropics is intimately related to the global economy. The global economy is driving the export of cash crops from many regions of the tropics rapidly upward, often resulting in the displacement of poor farmers who are forced to farm less suitable lands and destroy the forests there. This trend has been evident in the Sahel, for example, for which massive exports of peanuts and cotton are sent to Europe, and in Thailand, which exports huge quantities of cassava.

The international debt is greatly affecting relationships between developing and industrial countries in the 1980s. In 1970, the external debt of Third World countries was about $72 billion; today, it is approximately $1 trillion. The existence of this debt clearly encourages many Third World countries to overexploit their natural resources without the creation of stable, productive alternatives: logging restrictions are eased, poor farmers are displaced to regions that will not support them on the long term, the production of foods that the people can eat (remember that on the average, a fifth of them are malnourished) is decreased in favor of the production of export crops. The associated austerity measures can throw large numbers of people out of work, thus increasing the extent of poverty in the nations involved.

Recently, a New York investment banker was quoted in *The New York Times* as saying: "Somehow the conventional wisdom of 200 million sullen South Americans sweating away in the hot sun for the next decade to earn the interest on their debt so Citicorp can raise its dividend twice a year does not square with my image of political reality." Still more succinctly, Willy Brandt termed the effects of the debt, "A blood transfusion from the sick to the healthy." The existence of the debt is making it increasingly difficult for Third World

countries to accept our exports; they must instead export competitively, and to us, to attempt to repay the debt itself. In this light, strenuous efforts to repay the debt, somewhat paradoxically, appears to be weakening, instead of strengthening, our own economy.

The runaway destruction of the natural resources of the tropics is also fueling massive immigration into the industrialized nations of the temperate zone. For example, the U.S. Immigration and Naturalization Service apprehended 1.7 million illegal aliens at the Mexican border alone in 1986, and estimates that more than 3 million might have entered successfully. The hunger and poverty that are responsible for such immigration also underlie economic and political instability in the tropics, and frustrate our efforts to achieve our objectives in these areas.

Another major problem concerns the effects of tropical deforestation on global climates. Such deforestation clearly contributes substantially to the amounts of carbon dioxide in the atmosphere, an issue of increasing concern. In addition, widespread deforestation is impairing the capacities of some tropical systems to recycle rainfall inland, as well demonstrated by the Amazon and possibly related to the past 20 years of drought in Africa also. Combined with the erosion and soil deterioration that accompanies deforestation, these problems are serious ones.

Recent findings suggest that the implications of widespread deforestation may be even more extreme. Last December, at the annual meeting of the American Geophysical Union, it was reported that cutting the evergreen forests in South America would precipitate a regional temperature rise of 3 to 5 °C. This would extend the dry season and speed the deterioration of the remaining forests, including reserves, while greatly disrupting agriculture. The effects of such major changes beyond the regions directly impacted can only be guessed at present.

The effects of forest destruction and climatic change have been most severe in sub-Saharan Africa. Here, per capita food production has dropped 20 percent since 1960, and the FAO projects that it will drop another 30 percent over the next 25 years, with population growth greatly exceeding growth in food production. Right now, a majority of people living in the area have too little to eat, and their collective international debt, roughly $200 billion, is equal to 44 percent of gross domestic product or 190 percent of export earnings.

Africa as a whole suffers from overvalued currencies and from historical political situations, such as artificially devalued food prices, that tend to favor urban dwellers over farmers. When Kenya set a higher, more realistic level for the government-controlled price of corn in 1985, for example, production climbed by almost 50 percent the next year. Another negative factor is that most food aid in Africa is made available in the towns, which tends to pull the people out of the countryside, thus causing them to neglect their crops. Development assistance for Africa is falling rapidly, fewer than 5 percent of the couples use modern contraceptive methods, and there are about 1 million more mouths to feed in sub-Saharan Africa every three weeks, a sure prescription for increasing human tragedy.

The most serious, long-term global problem that is resulting from deforestation, however, is the loss of a large portion of the biological diversity on earth within a few decades. Whether this process of extinction is viewed from a scientific, aesthetic, or moral standpoint, or simply as the loss of opportunities that could otherwise have been used for human benefit, it is unquestionably the one problem that will have the most lasting consequences. The extinction rates of the present are a thousand times those of the past tens of millions of years. Despite this, it is all too easy to say, "Goodbye, California condor—but so what?" There has been an unfortunate tendency for some of the media to jump on this bandwagon: it is more stimulating to give the minority (and incorrect) view that extinction presents no problem, or that everything is fine, than it is to document the extent of the problems facing us—besides, it is comforting, and more fun!

In fact, the loss of biological diversity is important to us for many reasons. For example, three species of plants—rice, wheat, and corn—supply over half of all human energy requirements; only about 150 kinds of food plants are used extensively; and only about

5000 have ever been used. Many of these come to us from the tropics. It is estimated, however, that there may be tens of thousands of additional kinds of plants that could provide human food if their properties were fully explored and they were brought into cultivation. There are many uses for plants other than food, too; for example, oral contraceptives for many years were produced from Mexican yams; muscle relaxants used in surgery worldwide come from an Amazonian vine, used traditionally to poison darts; the cure for Hodgkin's disease comes from the rosy periwinkle, a native of Madagascar; and the gene pool of corn has recently been enriched by the finding, on a small area in the mountains of Mexico, of a perennial wild relative.

Among the undiscovered or poorly known plants are doubtless many possible sources of medicines, oils, waxes, fibres, and other commodities of interest to our modern industrial society. Genetic engineering affords us additional possibilities for the transfer of genes from one kind of organism to another, even though the donor may itself be of no economic interest whatever; indeed, as our techniques become more sophisticated, we shall come to depend even more heavily on biological diversity than we do now.

How fast is extinction proceeding? Although only about 500,000 species of tropical organisms have been named, there are at least 3 million, and perhaps ten times that many, yet to be discovered. Investigating the beetle fauna of the canopy of tropical forests in Panama and Peru, for example, Terry Erwin, of the Smithsonian Institution, has fogged the canopies of the trees with insecticides to obtain comprehensive samples for comparative purposes. Based on these samples, he estimates that the true number of species of insects may approach 30 million, or even more.

If we assume that there are 3 million species of tropical organisms, we can use the distributions of the better-known groups as a guide to how many of the total species occur only in those forests that will probably be destroyed or severely damaged in the next 15 years or so. For plants, the figures would be about 120,000 of the estimated total of about 165,000 tropical species; just under half of the total number of species in the world occur only in forests that are rapidly being destroyed. If the distribution of other groups of organisms is roughly similar to that of plants, then about 2.2 million species, or somewhat less that half of the total, would be restricted to these forests. How many of these species can we reasonably expect to survive?

The formation of parks and reserves in the threatened areas would be an important element in the survival of biological diversity; but such protected areas will survive only if they exist in the context of economies that can support them—particularly ones in which the rural poor are supported. The explicit relationship between conservation and development is outlined well in the *World Conservation Strategy*, issued jointly by the International Union for the Conservation of Nature and Natural Resources, the World Wildlife Fund, and the United Nations Environmental Programme in 1980. The future of such reserves will depend in large measure on the functioning of the global economy.

Granted, however, that fragments of natural vegetation will persist in most areas, what level of survival can we expect? The principal basis for making predictions of this sort lies in the theory of island biogeography. This theory rests on the empirical observation that, in general, for islands and mainlands areas alike, the relationship between species number and area is a logarithmic one, such that a tenfold increase in area is associated with a doubling in the number of species of a given group. The reciprocal relationship, and one that is being verified empirically in a number of experiments throughout the world, is that a reduction of area to a tenth or less of its original extent should place half or more of the kinds of organisms that occurred in the larger area at risk.

The biological basis for this relationship is clear. As areas are reduced in size, the population sizes of the organisms in them are also reduced. When a population is small, the chance of survival of the species is reduced on the basis of chance.

An illustration of the way this process works is provided by the history of bird populations on Barro Colorado Island, an island of about 6 square miles that was formed between 1911 and 1914 by the flooding of the Panama Canal. Set aside as a reserve in 1923, Barro Colorado Island was home at that time to 208 species of breeding birds. It has been protected as a reserve continuously. Over the next 60 years, at least 45 of these birds became extinct, despite the fact that Barro Colorado Island is separated from the source areas on the mainland by a distance of approximately 600 feet, a distance that any of the species of birds involved could cross easily.

Hunting and poaching become more intense when surviving patches of vegetation are small. In addition, inbreeding and the consequent loss of genetic variability puts species increasingly at risk. The borders of the patches are affected by sun, wind, and other factors in ways that damage their integrity. Regional climatic changes, such as those affecting precipitation, can change the climate in the patches, leaving the species vulnerable and with nowhere to migrate.

There are many examples of regional extinction on a massive scale. For example, there were at least 88 species of land birds in the Hawaiian Islands when the Polynesians arrived, 43 when Captain Cook explored the islands, and 28 today—two-thirds of which are endangered. The destruction of the lowland forests and the introduction of exotic species have both contributed to the decimation of the native birds and the plants. The process continues rapidly at the present day, because even as the richest nation on earth, we seem unable to protect our natural heritage adequately. The Hawaiian Islands provide a prime example of the way in which ecosystems are simplified, while pests and weedy species become more widespread throughout the world.

One particularly significant example of an area in which large numbers of species are endangered is Madagascar, an island about twice the size of Arizona that lies about 250 miles off the east coast of Africa. Here grow about 8500 species of plants, some 6500 of which are found nowhere else. Madagascar is also the only place where lemurs, one of the major groups of Primates, survive, and there are many other unique and restricted organisms there. All in all, the island is probably home to about 5 percent of the total globe diversity, probably 80 percent of it found nowhere else.

Unfortunately, less than a tenth of the land

surface of Madagascar is still covered with natural vegetation. The loss of forests in northeastern Madagascar, the main forested area, has been such that in 1949, only about 66 percent of the original forest was left, and by 1984, only 36 percent, as determined by LANDSAT satellite imagery. Where it once was richly forested in many areas, much of Madagascar is now degraded pasture.

Since the forests where at least half 2.2 million species occur will very probably be reduced to less than a tenth of their total extent over the next 15 years or so, we may assume that over a million species will become extinct during this period or soon afterwards. In western Ecuador, for example, a region that was almost completely forested as recently as 1950 is now almost completely deforested. As extensive deforestation of this kind spreads in many other regions, we can expect the rate of extinction to average more than 100 species a day, with the rate increasing from perhaps a few species a day now to several hundred by the early years of the next century. The great majority of these species will not have been collected, and therefore will never be represented in any scientific collection, preserved, or known in any way. No comparable rate of extinction has occurred since the end of the Cretaceous Period, 65 million years ago; and the background level of extinction is perhaps a thousandth of that we are experiencing now.

From any point of view, the situation that has just been described is extremely serious. Scientifically, we are losing the opportunity to understand the nature of much of the diversity of life on earth. Aesthetically, we are losing the chance to appreciate fully the results of the process of evolution over the billions of years since life appeared on our planet. Economically, we are denying to ourselves, our children, and our grandchildren the opportunity to utilize many of the plants, animals, and microorganisms that exist now for their benefit.

A new kind of global thinking will be necessary to manage the world ecosystem properly for the enormous human populations of the future. To demonstrate this fact, simply recall that we are now using directly, foregoing, or converting about 40 percent of global terrestrial productivity, and that these numbers are projected to double in the next 41 years. Stability everywhere is in the interests of all, yet we are doing relatively little to promote it. Sustainable agriculture and forestry systems must be developed in every country, and their development will benefit everyone. When nations are stable and self-sufficient, they can import and export products, repay debts, provide a decent standard of living for their people, improve their governments, and preserve their biological diversity. When they are unstable and dependent, they cannot afford imports and can organize exports only with difficulty, they will default on debts, cannot provide for their people, who then may emigrate in large numbers, will tend to have unsuitable and unstable governments, and will squander their biological diversity for short-term gain.

Peter H. Raven. *Vital Speeches*. 53, No. 15, (May 15, 1987): 472–476. This speech was delivered as the Keynote Address, American Association for the Advancement of Science, Chicago, Illinois, February 14, 1987.

Playing Russian Roulette with World Environment

David Suzuki

DAVID SUZUKI (1936–) *is a geneticist at the*
University of British Columbia. Born in Canada,
he did graduate work at Amherst College and the
University of Chicago. He is a frequent
contributor to journals and is a well-known
populariser of modern science on television and
radio. He is the host of the television series, The
Nature of Things, *and formerly host of the radio*
series, Quirks and Quarks.

In the mid-fifties, while I was returning from
college in the United States for the summer,
I glanced down at the Niagara River as my
train passed over. Below, I could see fishermen
on the banks flailing away at the water and
yanking silver objects from the river as fast as
they could cast. The were catching silver bass
on a massive annual spawning run.

Those spring runs petered out years ago.

Old fishermen on the east and west coasts
of Canada describe an abundance and size of
salmon, cod and lobsters when they were
starting out that younger fishermen have
never seen. It wasn't long ago that we drank
from the Great Lakes with confidence in the
water's purity, and relished fresh fruits and
vegetables without concern about chemical
contamination. Only a few decades ago, the
quality of our water, soil and air was radically
different and there were an abundance and
variety of life that now are found only in the
most remote parts of the country. The planet
has changed almost beyond recognition
within the life-time of Canada's elder citizens.
Their recollections are not simply old folks' romantic musings on the good old days; they
are a living record of the cataclysmic degradation that has taken place around us. In the
past, men took canaries into coal mines as biological indicators of the quality of the air;
today, our elders are the ones who know that
canaries are falling all around us.

Our species boasts the highest ratio of
"brain to brawn" of all life forms, and that
mental power has gifted us with a conscious
strategy for survival. We have invented a notion called the "future," which provided us
with options and enabled us to deliberately
select a future toward which we aimed. Yet
today, with all the amplified brainpower of
computers, communications networks, scientists and engineers, we seem unable to use the
strategy that got our forebears to where we
took over. What has gone wrong?

I believe that we continue to cling to certain
"sacred truths" that blind us to many problems and often cause the ones that we do recognize. Let me list some of those sacred truths.

• We equate "progress" with *growth*—
growth in the economy, income, consumer
goods, material comfort. A need for steady
economic growth is repeated like a cate-
chism by every politician, economist and
businessperson, and has led us to link
profit with the goal of society. But human
beings today are the most ubiquitous and
numerous large mammal in the world, and
it is our unrelenting commitment to
growth that now has us consuming 40 per
cent of the net primary production of energy on the planet. We are only one species
among perhaps 30 million. When our population doubles again within 50 years, will
we then demand 80 per cent? Nothing on
this planet continues indefinitely to grow
steadily.

• The current increases in consumption
and material wealth are a historical aberration, a blip that will come to a stop

within our children's lifetime. The only question is whether we will deliberately bring our demands and consumption under control or allow pestilence, famine or war to do the job.

- We have come to believe in the ability of science to provide us with the knowledge to understand and manage our natural resources. Yet the unique power of science is that its practitioners focus on an isolated part of nature, and thus increase knowledge in fragmented bits and pieces. Modern physicists have learned that it is not possible to put these fragments of knowledge together into a complete picture, because in real life, unlike a jigsaw puzzle, the pieces interact synergistically. Thus, properties emerge from the complex that cannot be anticipated from the known properties of the component parts.

- As a result, there are fundamental reasons why it is not possible to comprehend the behavior of entire ecosystems or even complex components within them. In addition, the degree of our ignorance remains vast. We know very little, for example, about chinook salmon during their four-year stay in the ocean, yet we maintain the illusion that we are managing them scientifically.

- We believe we can manage the effects of new technologies by doing proper cost/benefit analysis to maximize the benefits while minimizing costs. History informs us that every technology, however beneficial, has costs. And invariably the benefits of new technologies are immediate and obvious. That's why we (including me) love technology; it does such wonderful things for us. But the costs of these technologies are almost always hidden, and cannot be anticipated.

- If all technologies exact a price that cannot be foreseen, can we continue to mortgage the future by opting for the immediate benefits of new inventions while postponing the solution to their accompanying costs? Today scientists speak of building machines that can think, tampering with the heredity of babies, manipulating the human mind and releasing genetically engineered organisms into the environment—yet we cannot predict their long-term consequences.

- We believe we can minimize environmental damage from our activity by carrying out environmental assessments. Thus, for example, oil exploration in the high Arctic or off Georges Bank or building a fixed link to Prince Edward Island, depend on the success of an environmental assessment review process (EARP). Of course, there should be such assessments, but in view of how little we know of the constituents of ecosystems and their interactions, fluctuations over time and the tiny window our tests provide, the EARP is far too limited in scope, duration and scale to provide information that is statistically meaningful.

- We cannot assume that once an EARP indicates no hazard, development should have an unconditional green light. Approval should always be provisional, with a continued accumulation of information on which reassessments of that approval are constantly made.

- We believe that in a democracy, we elect people to political office to represent and lead us into the future. Yet most politicians come from two professions, business and law, the two areas whose practitioners have the poorest comprehension of issues scientific and technological.

Today, the most important factor shaping our lives and society is science when applied by industry, medicine and the military. Yet, jurisdictional concerns such as Meech Lake and economic priorities of free trade preoccupy our leaders and subsume the priorities of the planet's ecosystem.

"Conventional wisdom" assumes the truth of the above assumptions. Unless we expose them to the light of critical examination, we will continue to ravage the ecosystem for short-term benefits. We desperately need a new paradigm, a new vision of the human place in nature.

We live in a time when satellites have sent back images of this planet that graphically demonstrate its oneness. I think ecologist Jack Valentyne, who poses as Johnny Biosphere to instruct children about the environment, is on the right track. He reminds us that we all have built into our cells and tissues, atoms and molecules that were once in the bodies of all other people on the planet and of people who lived one or two thousand years ago. Not only that, but we are made of atoms respired by trees and insects and mammals and birds. That's because all life forms share the atmosphere around the world.

Johnny Biosphere tells of an Indian who, on a hot day hundreds of years ago, swam in Lake Superior. Sodium ions from the sweat of his body are still contained in each drink of water that we take from Lake Ontario. And when one realizes that everything we eat for nutrition was itself once living, we realize that we remain inextricably linked to the rest of life on this planet. Seen in this perspective of shar-

ing and connectedness, we have to behave in a radically different way when we dispose of our wastes or apply new technologies that affect other parts of the ecosystem.

Throughout human history, the boast of our species has been that we love our children and hope that they will have a richer, fuller life than we did. Yet now, for the first time, we know with absolute certainty that our children's lives will be immeasurably poorer in bio-diversity and filled with massive problems that we have foisted on them in our shortsighted pursuit of immediate profit and power.

Can we continue to mortgage our children's future so thoughtlessly? Not if we mean it when we say we love them.

David Suzuki. *The Globe and Mail*. April 23, 1988: D-1 and D-2.

Credits

Bertrand Russell, "Political Ideals," *Political Ideals*, George Allen and Unwin, 1963. Sigmund Freud, *Civilization and Its Discontents*, Translated and Edited by James Strachey, by permission of W. W. Norton & Company, Inc. and The Hogarth Press Ltd. Copyright © 1961 by James Strachey. Copyright renewed 1989. Alasdair MacIntyre, "Philosophy and Ideology," from *Against the Self Images of the Age*. © 1971 by Alasdair MacIntyre, University of Notre Dame Press, Notre Dame, IN 46776. Reprinted by permission. M. Patricia Marchak, "Ideology and Social Organization," from *Ideological Perspectives on Canada*, Third Edition, by M. Patricia Marchak. Copyright © McGraw-Hill Ryerson Limited, 1988. Reprinted by permission. Richard W. Miller, "Ideology," from *Analyzing Marx: Morality, Power and History*. Copyright © 1984 by Princeton University Press. Excerpt reprinted with permission of Princeton University Press. C. Wright Mills, "Ideals and Ideologies," *The Marxists*, Penguin Books, 1962. John Dewey, "Renascent Liberalism," Reprinted by permission of Putnam Publishing Group from *Liberalism and Social Action* by John Dewey. Copyright © 1935 by John Dewey, Copyright Renewed © 1973 by The John Dewey Foundation. John Kenneth Galbraith, "What It Means to be a Liberal Today," *The Financial Post*, September 21, 1987. Reprinted with permission. C.B. Macpherson, "The Near Future of Democracy and Human Rights," from *The Real World of Democracy*, Published by CBC Enterprises. Copyright by C.B. Macpherson, 1965. All rights reserved. William M. Sullivan, "The Contemporary Crisis of Liberal Society," *Reconstructing Public Philosophy*, University of California Press. © 1982 The Regents of the University of California. Reprinted by permission. John Rawls, "The Principles of Justice," from *A Theory of Justice*, Harvard University Press. © 1971 by The President and Fellows of Harvard College. Reprinted by permission. J.R. Lucas, "The Theory of Rawls," *On Justice*, Oxford University Press, 1980. Reprinted by permission of Oxford University Press. T.S. Eliot, *The Idea of a Christian Society*. Copyright 1939 by T.S. Eliot, renewed 1967 by Esme Valerie Eliot, reprinted by permission of Harcourt Brace, Jovanovich, Inc. and Faber and Faber Ltd. Eric Voegelin, Reprinted from *The New Science of Politics*, University of Chicago Press. © 1952, 1987 by The University of Chicago. All rights reserved. Robert Nozick, "The State of Nature," From *Anarchy, State, and Utopia*, by Robert Nozick. Copyright © 1974 by Basic Books, Inc. Reprinted by permission of Basic Books, Inc., Publishers. Robert Paul Wolff, "Robert Nozick's Derivation of the Minimal State," *Arizona Law Review 19, No. 7.* Copyright © 1977 by the Arizona Board of Regents. Reprinted by permission. Friedrich Hayek, "The Great Utopia," *The Road to Serfdom*. University of Chicago Press, 1944. Reprinted by permission. T. Boone Pickens, "Free Enterprise Without the Entrepreneur?", *Vital Speeches of the Day*, LI, No. 18, July 1, 1985. Reprinted by permission. Milton Friedman, "Economists and Economic Policy," *Economic Inquiry*. XXIV (1986). Reprinted by permission. Philip Resnick, "The Ideology of Neo-Conservatism," *The New Reality*, New Star Books, 1984. Reprinted by permission. Madsen Pirie, "The Principles and Practice of Privatization," *Vital Speeches of the Day*. LIII, No. 21, August 15, 1987. Reprinted by permission. Ayn Rand, "America's Persecuted Minority: Big Business," *Capitalism: The Unknown Ideal*, New American Library, 1967. Reprinted by permission of the Estate of Ayn Rand. Desmond S. King, *The New Right*, Dorsey Press, 1987. Herbert Marcuse, from *One Dimensional Man*, by Herbert Marcuse. Copyright © 1964 by Herbert Marcuse. Reprinted by permission of Beacon Press. D.F.B. Tucker, "Marx's Response to Hegel," *Marxism and Individualism*, St. Martin's Press, 1980. Reprinted by permission. Harold J. Berman, "Beyond Marx, Beyond Weber," *Law and Revolution*, Harvard University Press, © 1983 by The President and Fellows of Harvard College. Reprinted by permission. Charles Taylor, "The Agony of Economic Man," *Essays on the Left*. Reprinted by permission of the author. Joseph A. Schumpeter, "Crumbling Walls," from *Capitalism, Socialism, and Democracy*, Third Edition. Copyright 1942, 1947 by Joseph A. Schumpeter. Reprinted by permission of Harper & Row, Publishers, Inc. Alec Nove, "Introduction: Socialism—Why?," *The Economics of Feasible Socialism*, George Allen &